Praise for Alger Hiss: Framed

"Joan Brady's highly readable take on Alger Hiss adds valuable, new personal information to his ever-fascinating story. It will be of interest not merely to scholars of the case, but anyone who cares about history and getting it right."

—Victor Navasky, publisher emeritus of *The Nation*, winner of National Book Award for *Naming Names*

"Joan Brady has written an evocative, graceful memoir filled with novel reminiscences of her friendship with Alger Hiss. It is a most unusual book, using memory and a Talmudic examination of legal texts to explore the still contested terrain of the Hiss trials. As such, it is sure to incense those historians and partisans wedded to the national narrative crafted by Whittaker Chambers and Richard Nixon. Insightful and provocative, Brady has reopened the Hiss case to a new generation of readers."

—Kai Bird, winner of the Pulitzer Prize for *The Triumph and Tragedy of J. Robert Oppenheimer*

"Joan Brady's *Alger Hiss: Framed*, a personal story about the Alger Hiss case, written by one of our most talented and accomplished writers, is a wonderfully vivid account that conveys the intensity of some of the darkest days in our post-WWII history. It's also full of revelatory new material about the case that started young Richard Nixon on his road to the White House and convinced Americans that the Reds really were threatening our freedom. It's time to revisit this extraordinary story, which historians have been debating for the last half-century; Brady's fresh and compelling book will introduce a new generation to the trial that transformed America."

—Jon Wiener, professor of History,
University of California, Irvine

"A bracing reminder of what indeed was so hateful, so villainous about Nixon and his political ascent."

—*Spectator*

"[An] extraordinary book . . . part autobiography, part memoir of Hiss, part thriller, and also a reminder of what happens when a society becomes infected by the paranoia that produced the American 'Red Scare' after the First and Second World Wars."

—*New Statesman*

"Brady's book . . . offers a unique perspective. . . . She is an expert storyteller."

—*Guardian*

ALGER HISS: FRAMED

Alger Hiss

Secretary General of the United Nations Organizing Conference
President of the Carnegie Endowment for International Peace
Prisoner 19137 Lewisburg Federal Penitentiary

ALGER HISS: FRAMED

A New Look at the Case That Made Nixon Famous

JOAN BRADY

Arcade Publishing • New York

All rights reserved. No part of this book may be reproduced in any manner without the express written consent of the publisher, except in the case of brief excerpts in critical reviews or articles. All inquiries should be addressed to Skyhorse Publishing, 307 West 36th Street, 11th Floor, New York, NY 10018.

Arcade Publishing books may be purchased in bulk at special discounts for sales promotion, corporate gifts, fund-raising, or educational purposes. Special editions can also be created to specifications. For details, contact the Special Sales Department, Arcade Publishing, 307 West 36th Street, 11th Floor, New York, NY 10018 or info@skyhorsepublishing.com

Arcade Publishing® is a registered trademark of Skyhorse Publishing, Inc.®, a Delaware corporation.

Visit our website at www.arcadepub.com.

10 9 8 7 6 5 4 3 2 1

Library of Congress Cataloging-in-Publication Data is available on file.
Library of Congress Control Number: 2017943951

Cover design by Erin Seaward-Hiatt
Cover photo of Alger Hiss and frontispiece courtesy of the FBI

Print ISBN: 978-1-62872-711-1
Ebook ISBN: 978-1-62872-714-2

Printed in the United States of America

Contents

Introduction

You would expect the President of the Carnegie Endowment for International Peace to win a Nobel Peace Prize, especially when he's the same man who organized the United Nations, served as its Secretary General while he did so, and then carried the UN charter home to the White House on a special army plane. Instead, this very man was tried in a criminal court, found guilty, and sent to prison. It was called the Trial of the Century, and it was a media circus second to none. The year was 1951. The convicted felon's name was Alger Hiss.

I knew Alger for more than thirty years, and I never liked him much. I can't for the life of me figure out why—not even now—but because of that, I didn't bother to learn about his case until I faced prosecution myself, though on hardly a scale approaching his. Still, court cases—the threat of a stretch in prison—do something to a person. Nobody I knew had ever stood in the dock. Except Alger. He was long dead by then, and I started reading about him out of morbid interest in the ordeal of a fellow sufferer. But the more I read, the more outraged I became. Facts had been twisted and distorted to link together chains of events conjured out of nowhere. Witnesses had been intimidated and suborned. Evidence had been created. Evidence had been suppressed. Evidence had been destroyed. This was a vicious, politically motivated frame-up, and it's never been properly exposed. The longest-serving justice of the

United States Supreme Court wrote: "In my view no court at any time could possibly have sustained the conviction."

The Hiss case put Richard Nixon on the road to the White House; he sailed into the Senate while he was still prosecuting Alger, and he went straight from the Senate to the job of vice president under General Eisenhower. A decade later he had the Oval Office to himself. He'd worked hard for his prize. He says in his White House tapes that he had Alger convicted long before the Trial of the Century began. How? "We won the Hiss case in the papers." And so he had. Never before had there been a press campaign like it. Nixon turned the hero of the United Nations into the villain of the Cold War against Communist Russia with headline screamers and an extraordinary jumble of old-fashioned lies. The most jaw-dropping of them involved his proof of the "greatest treason conspiracy" in American history. This was, he said, "microfilm" of "top secret" army documents to be passed to the Soviets. One of his sidekicks plucked it out of a pumpkin, a midnight raid on a vegetable patch that made headlines all across the country. He said the developed film would make a pile three feet high. Three feet high: thousands upon thousands of pages. Photographs of him examining this very microfilm with a magnifying glass—just like Sherlock Holmes—were plastered across front pages everywhere.

What was in this huge, amazing cache? Nobody knew. Nixon wouldn't tell. It was too secret. The Justice Department subpoenaed it. Nixon refused to turn it over; he said the Justice Department was riddled with Communists, that they'd cover up this terrible act for no better reason than to keep the present government in office at the next election. He kept the film top secret for a quarter of a century. An incredible feat. For all those years, he manipulated everybody into believing it was too sensitive to be revealed to anybody.

And what did it turn out to be?

Home camera snapshots of maintenance manuals from a public library.

Literally.

People sometimes call Alger Hiss "America's Dreyfus." The French military command charged army Captain Alfred Dreyfus with passing military secrets to Imperial Germany. Evidence was forged, tainted, planted, suppressed to make a case, and in 1894 they sent him for life to the Devil's Island penal colony. A massive cover-up followed; the press and public opinion swallowed it whole. Dreyfus was a Jew, and antisemitic riots burst out all over France. World opinion was horrified. As Piers Paul Read put it: "How could France, the most civilized country in Europe, experience this eruption of medieval barbarism?"

In Alger's case, anti-communism played the role of that medieval barbarism. Communism was *the* major issue in America back in the middle of the last century; it all stemmed from fears of the Soviet experiment in Utopia that began in 1917: no social classes, no rich people, no poor ones, equal rights for everybody. "I have seen the future and it works," wrote a famous American journalist. The trouble was, it was working only if you averted your eyes from bloodbath and famine. By the time Alger was on trial, the dream was long gone; the terrifying Joseph Stalin had been in power for a couple of decades, and he'd turned a vast land mass into the biggest concentration camp in history. Nobody was allowed out. Nobody was allowed in. Soviet armies gobbled up East European countries one after another and patrolled barbed-wire prison fences that ran for hundreds of miles. Millions of people died trying to escape, and the rest of the world was on high alert.

As always, politicians exploited the vote-getting potential of the threat. Nothing new there. But in America, thought itself became the target. Who might be thinking like a Communist? Who wasn't thinking the American way? How could you tell? How could anybody tell? It wasn't easy. The US Armed Forces Information Services put out newsreels and manuals to help. Watch what people read, what organizations they support. Listen to them. These "secret Communists" use big words and long sentences. They play on your altruism with talk about civil rights, peace, racial discrimination.[1]

Report *any* suspicions to the police. Call up the FBI.

A single anonymous accusation was enough to put somebody on a list of suspected Communists, and there were hundreds of lists. Appearing on one was enough to destroy a reputation, lose a job and any hope of getting another. Friends and colleagues ran for fear of contamination. Here's one ordinary guy who just happened to share a name with another ordinary guy on the suspect list: "This thing . . . has ruined my life, has ruined my livelihood, has ruined me." He'd been told "that I had better get out of the neighborhood. They smeared my windows. Boys threw stones at my apartment. I have lost all my friends. . . . I am through as far as my life is concerned, and everything is through with me."

It wasn't just ordinary people, either. Nobody was exempt. Victims included such American royalty as Charlie Chaplin and Orson Welles.

One presidential candidate told New Yorkers, "The tragedy of our day is the climate of fear in which we live. . . . Too often sinister threats to the Bill of Rights, to freedom of the mind, are concealed under the patriotic cloak of anti-communism." After a few years of this, Eleanor Roosevelt, widow of President Franklin D. Roosevelt—famous for the ringing declaration, "The only thing we have to fear is fear itself"— spoke for many Americans when she said, "I am tired of being afraid."

Parallels with terrorism are hard to escape. Bin Laden and the Islamic State are as real as Stalin and the purges. The accompanying political exploitation—its focus firmly on home-grown converts—is all too real too. We've reached the point where the immediate reaction to anybody with a vaguely Middle Eastern name is fear. The UK.gov and London Metropolitan Police sites give advice just as the US Army did. You're to listen, watch, "trust your instincts," and report to the police.[2] Ring up MI5. Has your neighbor started attending a mosque? Does he invite Muslims to his house? Maybe he just acts funny. Doesn't matter. Report him. You'll remain anonymous, and your telephone call will put him on a "No Fly List."

It's the old familiar pattern. An enemy appears on the horizon. The politicians, the military, the media whip an amorphous force into an all-powerful evil that becomes the focus for people's hatreds and the excuse for their failures. There's solidarity in terror. We're the multitude. If we're to win, we have to think as one. You're either for us or against us. Opportunists like Nixon move in to exploit the situation. That's when casualties like Alger and Dreyfus happen.

Both were injustices on a monumental scale. Dreyfus's has been corrected; he was eventually exonerated. Now it's Alger's turn.

PART ONE

Alger Hiss comes to dinner

1

1960

One Friday afternoon Dexter asked me if I'd like to go out to dinner tomorrow with the greatest spy in American history: Alger Hiss. Public Enemy Number One.

"Alger Hiss!" I cried. "*The* Alger Hiss?"

"The very one. How about the des Artistes?"

Our apartment was on Manhattan's Upper West Side just off the Hudson River. Early summer and already very hot. Manhattan was boiling. A sweaty taxi drive to a restaurant off Central Park. A sweaty ride back. The staff at the Café des Artistes were friendly, helpful, welcoming. At least they were with their ordinary customers like Dexter and me. But how would they react to Alger Hiss of all people? I'm scared of confrontations. I'd remembered the name because my civics book in the ninth grade had said that he was the most dangerous traitor in the history of the United States. He was America's Judas Iscariot, and the glee in Dexter's voice told me that his reputation hadn't changed all that much.

"Why don't I make us something here?" I said. But then I'm scared of people as well as confrontations. And Alger Hiss just had to be one of the scariest people around.

When the doorbell rang on Saturday evening, Dexter said, "You answer it."

"No."

"Come on." "No!"

"He's not going to bite you."

I still remember unlocking the door. I still remember opening it. Usually I'm bad at faces. I didn't even recognize my own sister when I hadn't seen her for a few years. But I recognized this criminal at once from my schoolbook. He'd been decidedly handsome in that picture— boyish, clean-featured, wide-spread eyes, high cheekbones—even though the photographer had caught him in a police van being carted off to jail. He was handcuffed. He wore a dangerous-looking 1940s hat that shaded one eye. The youthful good looks somehow made him more sinister than ever, and the name! Alger *Hiss*! How could anybody with a name like that be anything other than a villain?

There'd been a mere ten years between the photo in my schoolbook and this hot Manhattan evening; the once-boyish Alger Hiss who stood in the hallway had been recast as a mediaeval flagellant, tall and gaunt, all bone and shadows.

He wore a dark suit, tie, white shirt that was a little loose around his neck.

I couldn't think of a single word to say.

"You must be Joanie," he said.

I nodded.

"I'm Alger. This is Isabel."

I nodded.

"Do you think perhaps we might come in?"

I was twenty years old. Dexter was fifty-two. When his wife had died a year and a half before, I'd offered myself up on a plate; I'd been sharing his apartment for several months, and by now I knew I wanted him more than I wanted to dance. I intended to marry the man; I intended to live with him for the rest of my life. Not that I was telling anybody about it. Ballet was the first thing I'd been good at. I really was good at it too, newly apprenticed to the New York City Ballet company itself, just waiting for my contract to come through.

Fortunately nobody in the company cared about the oddities of my private life.

Dexter was Dexter Masters, old family friend, director of an organization called Consumers Union that to this day puts out a magazine called *Consumer Reports*. The way I saw it, Consumers Union was the dullest creation on earth. Testing shoes and soap and underwear. What was a man like Dexter doing with junk like that? I excused him because I knew he needed the money; he'd got into debt finishing a novel. That was more like it. Writing novels and getting into debt suited him. He looked every inch a novelist in a Hollywood blockbuster. Joseph Cotten maybe. He was often mistaken for Cotten.

So. A dinner to produce for a novelist who looked like a movie star and his new friend, the famous spy.

When I'd forced myself into Dexter's life, I couldn't cook at all. I'd bought a book by a man called James Beard because page one opened with a recipe for how to boil water, and that's where I'd had to start. Since then, my repertoire had become serviceable if limited. Herbed shrimp, beef Bourguignon, crème brûlée: that just might live up to Dexter's elegant Riverside Drive apartment.

Dexter lived in one of those glorious old apartments with oak panelling and marble fireplaces. Strange things sat side by side, a Chinese monkey, a stone baby's head, an ancient pewter hookah, all mixed in with New Yorker covers by his dead wife. I resented the pictures—if not quite as much as I thought I should—but I had no idea how he managed to get this mishmash to add up to something rich and deep-textured. Always changing too. He'd bought some napkins at a junk shop for this evening's occasion, very pretty napkins even if many-times laundered, a floral print, hemmed by hand. This sounds like a meaningless detail, but these napkins play an important role—if a tiny one—in the way I've come to think of Alger Hiss and what happened to him.

Criminals have always fascinated me. I'm your usual moviegoer and thriller-reader: the romance of guys who choose their own moral code or have no moral code. That's probably why I'd remembered the name

Alger Hiss. Stories about him did appear regularly in the papers, but I
didn't read newspapers.

Too boring. I think if anybody had asked, I'd have said he was as
dead as America's other great traitor, Benedict Arnold. But then I'd
have said they'd hanged Benedict Arnold, when in fact he fathered
eight children and died warm in his own bed. Which is to say that part
of the reason I was so tongue-tied seeing Alger Hiss at the door was
sheer disappointment.

This was no villain out of a fantasy. Here was a Boy Scout who'd had
a tough life. Virtue shone from every pore. It was very dispiriting. He'd
never cross a street against a traffic light. The idea of him doing something treasonable seemed absurd.

But then I'm a lousy judge of character. Always have been.

Another part of what turned me mute was pure Greek tragedy: how
could somebody like this have got himself into the mess he did?

The high ceilings in those old apartments were designed to keep rooms
cool even in a New York summer, and we had the windows open. But it
was hot. Dexter offered to take Alger's jacket. He declined.

I was abruptly irritated. I didn't even know why. I mean, really, if a
man doesn't mind sweltering in his jacket, it's his own damned business.
Alger had spent years in prison wearing a convict's fatigues; probably
his jacket had meanings for him that people like me can only guess at.
Not long before this, the movie *Twelve Angry Men* had come out with
a character who'd done the same thing in a very hot jury room. One
of the other jurors—the rest of them were dripping—was as irritable
about it as I was and asked something like, "What's the matter with
you? Don't you sweat?" The guy in the movie didn't.

Alger didn't seem to either. Which annoyed me all over again.

Dexter went off to make martinis, leaving me to entertain Alger
and the woman who'd come with him. Her name was Isabel Johnson.
Dexter had told me that she'd been a *Vogue* model, photographed by

Edward Steichen and Alfred Stieglitz, and that she'd slept with practically every famous left-wing intellectual in America. I figured this archtraitor was just one more notch on her rifle. I still think so. She'd even married a couple of these guys. Not Alger, though. At least not yet. She was a dreamy, preoccupied woman, early fifties, willowy, fine-featured, draped over a chair with graceful professionalism that was part coy and part disdainful. To a harsh young eye like mine, the skin was shot and the hair was dyed.

She left the small talk to Alger and me.

I wasn't very good at situations like these although I'd been in them quite a number of times since my conquest of Dexter. Most of his friends were sophisticated New Yorkers, unfazed by the irregular relationship, if not agreeably titillated by it. But they were old enough to be my parents, and most of them treated me as they did one another's grown-up children, that slightly too-enthusiastic interest in somebody who bored them out of their skulls.

After the customary complaints about weather and New York traffic, Alger introduced ballet as Dexter's friends often did.

Yes, I was a dancer.

Yes, ballet was very demanding physically.

No, the pay wasn't good.

With the ones I hadn't met before, I'd usually go on to say that my father—once an eminent economist at the University of California at Berkeley—used to pontificate at me, "The rewards are not commensurate with the effort entailed." Usually they laughed. Alger did too.

By this time Dexter would be back with drinks, and conversation would take off in some other direction. Which was fine with me. But tonight's conversation wasn't usual. While Dexter poured out martinis for everybody, Alger kept his attention on me. He was telling me how hugely he admired Balanchine's musicality, that he'd seen the New York City Ballet's *Concerto Barocco* not long ago and been awed by it.

Lots of people—I'm one of them—think that George Balanchine is the greatest choreographer the world has ever known. But back then, he wasn't famous outside the ballet world. Dexter had never heard of

him before I started talking about him, and Dexter was a highly liter-
ate man. Nor had his friends. Most of them didn't think much of ballet
at the best of times. Like my parents, they were interested in books,
politics, newspapers, magazines. Theater and concerts, yes. Baseball, yes.
Tennis too. Lots of things. But not ballet.

On top of that, *Concerto Barocco* just happened to be my favorite
ballet.

Alger was leaning forward in his chair as he talked. Economical gestures and a gravity of movement rather like a fencer in the presence of
a famous sword, nothing phoney, though, none of Isabel's professionalism. Tense. Intense too. His interest in what I said seemed unfeigned,
deeply personal, but completely without sexual overtones. For all practi-
cal purposes, this man had been the first Secretary General of the United
Nations. He'd held lots of other elegant titles too. People had assumed he
was on his way to being Secretary of State. And I slowly became aware
that he was talking to me exactly as he must have talked to President
Roosevelt and Prime Minister Churchill. Maybe to the King of England for all I knew. I wasn't just the most powerful person in the room;
what I said was itself something of import, something to be assessed and
weighed, not for the sake of flattery but for the sake of its intrinsic worth.

Unsettling. Disconcerting. Very disconcerting. I escaped as soon as
I could.

In the kitchen, I worried that the beef wasn't yet cooked, turned up
the gas under it, and looked away to check the shrimp, only to smell
cloth burning. Pot holder on fire. I dowsed it, heart racing. At least
they'd be smoking out in the living room; they wouldn't smell it. Everybody smoked in those days. Everybody except me, that is. Not because
I was a dancer, only because my sister Judy had started smoking when
she was no more than twelve, and I'd thought a little girl looked silly
playing at Marlene Dietrich gestures with a cigarette. At least I smelled
the beef before I heard it. Burning around the edges. I added water and
prayed.

Back in the living room, conversation seemed to be going on well—
Isabel now contributing—but I'd hardly sat down when I was abruptly

unsure how high I'd set the gas under that beef. I got up to check. Alger got up too.

"Oh, Joanie, please sit with us for a moment," he said.

I sat down at once, again unsettled, disconcerted. Dexter's other friends politely ignored the cook's comings and goings. Or offered help. Dexter gave me an amused glance of reassurance and turned to offer Isabel another cigarette. She took it and waited for him to light it, very much at home with those Marlene Dietrich gestures that had made Judy look silly.

He offered the pack to Alger.

Alger shook his head. "Thank you, no."

"You don't smoke?" Dexter asked.

Alger shook his head again. "I gave up in prison."

I was stunned. It had never occurred to me that he'd be open about any part of what had happened to him, much less that part. And yet that was a part I really wanted to hear about: what goes on there, how real criminals manage metal bars every day and guards and ritual humiliation, not just guys in books. "Why?" I blurted out.

He said that he'd been a pack-a-day smoker but that Lewisburg Federal Penitentiary, where he'd served his sentence, allowed only one pack per prisoner per week. His family sent his quota regularly. Most prisoners didn't have families who helped out, so he shared his with the men on his wing. Dividing one pack among sixty men meant only half a cigarette each, and sometimes there were disputes.

"It was easier to give up altogether," he said.

He told this story as though he were describing a change in habit such as a Christian diplomat might make in a Muslim country. He seemed amused at his inability to find a more suitable solution, but there was no trace of anger, shame, resentment. Nor was there any sense of contempt for, censure of or superiority to his fellow inmates or the prison's rules or the people who enforced them.

I didn't know what I was watching now any more than I understood why I found the man both annoying and disconcerting. Strength of character? Simple stoicism? A martyrdom consistent with the flagellant's appearance? Why no anger or bitterness? Why no contempt or censure?

Where was evidence of what I would feel in his situation?

Dexter told me that when Alger got out of prison, he had no money and no job prospects. Working for a manufacturer of women's hair-clips came first. Then he met a man who owned a printing plant and had just bought an old-fashioned stationery store called Davison-Bluth on the west side of Manhattan. Alger became a salesman for fifty dollars a week against monthly commissions. People who might have refused to see a representative from so insignificant an operation were sometimes intrigued enough to listen when he announced, "This is Alger Hiss."

"I thought maybe he could handle the paper for the *Reports,*" Dexter said, as intrigued as others had been when he heard the salesman's name. But the circulation of Consumer Reports was somewhere near a half-million, and Davison-Bluth was too small to supply a print run that large. So Dexter asked him to dinner instead.

Those pretty, secondhand napkins that Dexter bought: when we sat down at the table, Alger carefully set his aside and put a Kleenex tissue from his pocket into his lap instead. He wasn't ostentatious about it, but he wasn't furtive either. I assumed that I'd missed something, that the napkin I'd given him was stained or torn.

"I'll get you another," I said.

He stopped me, saying that the napkin itself was fine—perfect—but that it always bothered him to use napkins when somebody had spent time washing and ironing them. Besides, a Kleenex did the job just as well. He said this with a touch of humor; it appeared to be concern for Dexter's maid—or for me—and very fetching in its way, and yet . . .

Dammit all, that *really* annoyed me. Far more than the jacket.

It made me feel that I'd somehow lost a moral high ground I'd never tried to claim.

But he was politeness itself when it came to the beef, which hadn't benefited from burning around the edges. We were happily past that—onto the crème brûlée—when the discussion turned to his case. He explained that the charges brought against him gave him his first experience as a defendant in a trial and that he hadn't realized in all the years he'd worked as a lawyer that the defendant was just another onlooker. What matters is the "gladiatorial contest"—his phrase—between the two opposing attorneys. Nothing else.

He was as calm and nonjudgemental about all this as he had been when he talked about giving up cigarettes.

When I was small, my mother told me about a nun in a convent who was admired by all the other nuns for her serenity. One young novice, filled with her own demons and unsure of her vocation, sought out the calm nun, begged for her secret. The calm nun drew up her habit and revealed an open, suppurating ulcer on her thigh. The story still gives me the creeps. But it was at least a theory as to how Alger managed to live, one I accepted for a very long time. The reality—I'm certain of it—was far simpler, but there's nothing in the world harder to grasp than simplicity. For the time being, though, the nun had to serve as an explanation for what looked to me like a surreal detachment in a person describing the battle that had ripped apart everything that was meaningful to him right in front of his very eyes.

"How can anybody call that *fair*?" Isabel demanded. It was the first time that evening she'd seemed really engaged.

"'Fair' isn't what courts are about," Alger said.

"How can you say that?" She was as annoyed as I'd been. "Look what they did to you. They convicted an innocent man. Trials are supposed to find the truth. Courts are supposed to be about justice."

Alger shook his head. "Courts are about law, Isabel. Not justice. Sometimes the jury does deliver justice. This time they didn't come to the right conclusion."

———— ∞ ————

Dexter was a much better judge of character than I am. "Was Alger really a spy?" I asked after they'd left.

"I don't know," he said. He didn't seem to care one way or the other. "I never could decide. Still can't."

2

1948

On Monday morning, 2nd August 1948, Alger Hiss took the train from Vermont into New York City. Every year, the Hisses spent the summer in the village of Peacham; Alger's wife Priscilla and his small son Tony were staying on a few weeks longer. New York always boils in August, and August 1948 was special: one of the most miserable heat waves in American history was getting underway.

The offices of the Carnegie Endowment for International Peace were probably air-conditioned; it was not uncommon even that long ago, and the Endowment is a fiercely prestigious think tank. Alger was its president. There had been only two presidents before him, and both were Nobel Peace laureates. He worked at his office for the rest of the day, then went home to his apartment on Eighth Street and University Place in Greenwich Village, where it would have been hot as hell. That evening a reporter called and told him that a man by the name of Whittaker Chambers was about to testify in front of a congressional committee that Alger Hiss was a Communist.

Did Alger wish to comment?

He did not.

Accusations like this came with the job; there had been rumors around for years, not just about Alger, but about lots of people, important people like him and droves of unimportant ones. For the unimportant and the not-so-important, the consequences could be dire—everybody knew that—but he'd never taken the rumors about himself seriously before, did not intend to this time.

The next day, shortly after twelve thirty, his office phone began ringing: reporters and press agencies. This person Chambers had upped the charges[1]: Alger was the leader of an underground Communist cell right in the State Department. Alger told them all that the charges were untrue and as far as he knew, he'd never even seen the man making them.

He had not expected this upping of the charges. He had not expected nationwide publicity, either, and he was angry. He'd heard the name Whittaker Chambers before. In one of the FBI's investigations into State Department officials, agents had asked him if it meant anything to him. It hadn't then, and it didn't now. Strangers crawling out of the woodwork to make accusations without even a hint of due process: there was "a matter of principle" at stake.[2] It was about time somebody stood up and said so. He consulted friends over lunch. One of his party was John Foster Dulles, Chairman of the Endowment; he urged Alger to "think back" to the bad old days of the Depression when terrible conditions outraged so many Americans and led them to associate with "all kinds of people."[3] Another friend said the Committee was only generating headlines for the election to come. Why hand them more?

Everybody at lunch agreed. No sensible person appears willingly before the House Un-American Activities Committee, much less demands an audience.

Ignore it. Just give it time to go away.

The House Un-American Activities Committee—HUAC for short—was an arm of the House of Representatives with a Congressional budget and a Congressional mandate: investigate subversion among private citizens, government employees, and organizations with Communist ties.

The committee that stood in 1948 grew out of a series of similar committees dating back to 1918 and fear of the Soviet Union, faraway birthplace of Lenin, Stalin, and the rule of the proletariat. The meaning of subversion did shift from time to time over the thirty years that followed. The Committee's work included an investigation into a hoax of a fascist plot to march on Washington and take over the White House; the compilation of the "Yellow Report," arguing that it was not at all un-American to confine the "yellow peril" of Japanese Americans in concentration camps during World War II; and a decision not to look into the Ku Klux Klan because, as one of several white supremacist members said, "The KKK is an old American institution," a comment that's moved into the nation's folklore.

But for the Committee—and the country at large—"un-American" and "subversive" came to mean "Communist." In the first eleven days of its existence, it claimed that 2,850 government employees were Communists and that Communists controlled 438 daily newspapers, 640 trade unions and consumers' groups. HUAC's Chief Investigator,

Robert Stripling, wrote that communism was a conspiracy with a simple goal: "The destruction of life as we know it and of the liberties we won at such heavy cost."[1] That's fearsome enough, but he went further. "The aim and object of communism are always the same—complete control over the human mind and body, asleep and awake, in sickness and in health, from birth to death."[2] If you lived under communism, "you would be liquidated on the slightest suspicion of doing ANYTHING contrary to orders."[3] The capital letters are Stripling's, not mine.

With a vision as terrifying as this, it's hard to keep in mind that the Communist Party of the United States was not only a legal political association but had been one for nearly two decades. It operated out of registered headquarters in New York City. It paid its taxes, ran candidates in local, state, and federal elections, including presidential elections; it operated several publishing companies and published books, pamphlets, journals, and daily newspapers that appeared in bookshops and on public newsstands. There'd never been any court proceedings showing—or even alleging—a connection between Communist ideas and acts of espionage or treason. *Never*. Belonging to the Party was as legal as the Party itself.

But the public face of communism was the least of the Committee's concerns. During the Great Depression of a decade before, many people had turned to communism as a solution to the problems of the poor, the downtrodden, the disenfranchised. HUAC claimed that this very altruism lay at the heart of "the Red plot against America," and the average American was too innocent to understand it[4]; it thrived throughout the country in these post-war years as an underground movement with its aims unchanged and its indoctrination disguised as idealism. The Committee drew up lists of "Communist front organizations." Suspicion fell on groups that lobbied for changes in the law and groups that offered help, education, or friendship to Americans in need or to people in other countries—groups active in racial equality, welfare, prison reform, unions, the education of working people, international peace, international cooperation. HUAC subpoenaed members of these groups, their friends, relatives, colleagues, supporters. "The real center of power in communism is within the professional classes," Stripling wrote. Then he enumerated them: "teachers, preachers, actors, writers, union officials, doctors, lawyers, editors, businessmen, even millionaires."[5]

Many of the subpoenaed were Jews—in tune with an antisemitic America back then—and people who had Jewish or "Negro" friends and colleagues. The world's most famous physicist, Albert Einstein, was a Jew; the Committee accused him of being a "foreign-born agitator" who sought "to further the spread of communism throughout the world."[6] The Boy Scouts and the Campfire Girls were on lists of suspect organizations; both encouraged black children to join, segregated troops to be sure, but the threat was there. They feared that ten-year-old child star and all-American sweetheart Shirley Temple was a Communist dupe,[7] that Elizabethan playwright Christopher Marlowe spoke like a Red, and that ancient Greek playwright "Mr. Euripides" preached class warfare.[8]

Somewhere in their investigations came the exchange:

"But, Mr. Chairman, I'm an *anti*-Communist."

"I don't care what *kind* of Communist you are."

One of the arguments that Alger's lunchtime advisers put to him was that nobody took the Committee seriously, and reports like these certainly explain why. But while sophisticated people mocked, the mocking had a nervous edge. HUAC was very powerful. Its members were elected representatives of Congress, and the Committee acted like a court with all a court's powers. What caused the real nervousness, though, is that HUAC didn't have any of a court's boundaries. Their Annual Report stated: "Rules of evidence including cross-examination are not applicable."[9]

"Rules of evidence" are not just protocol. They originated centuries ago as protection against a criminal charge being brought without proof that a crime had been committed. They're behind what sometimes looks like no more than legal pedantry: *when* questions can be asked, *what kinds* can be asked, *how* they have to be phrased, *who* can ask them. Exemption meant that HUAC—both Committee members and staff—could ask whatever they pleased whenever they pleased:

leading questions, irrelevant questions, questions based on rumor or hearsay or merely whim. They could comment however they wanted to on whatever they wanted to, no matter how inaccurate or damaging. All of it went into the record.

As the chairman of the committee told one witness, "The rights you have are the rights given you by this committee. We will determine what right you have got and what right you have not got before this committee."

HUAC also made full use of its exemption from the rules of evidence when it issued subpoenas; no actual evidence was necessary. They subpoenaed people because somebody said they were Communists or knew Communists or affiliated with Communists. Ten years ago you had a friend called So-and-So. Fifteen years ago you attended such-and-such a meeting or signed such-and-such a petition. Sometimes a listing was all it took to confirm guilt, and lists of suspects were everywhere. People lost jobs because of it. Friends shunned them for fear of suffering the same fate. Poverty and despair often followed. Sometimes prison as well, occasionally suicide.

Soon after HUAC became a permanent Congressional committee, the same Mississippi congressman who'd exempted the KKK from investigation—his name was John Rankin—turned the Committee's attention to Hollywood: "the greatest hotbed of subversives in the United States" as he put it.[10] Who built Hollywood? The Jews. Louis B. Mayer, Warner Brothers, Sam Goldwyn. HUAC couldn't attack Jews outright, but they could finger a lot of them if they investigated the movie people who were "destroying—as best and as subtly as they could—the public's confidence in its leaders, laws, and institutions."[11]

The Hollywood hearings began with testimony from "friendly" witnesses, people who'd volunteered to testify; their reward was a guarantee of immunity against being accused themselves. The studio heads who volunteered—the great Walt Disney was one of them—made their aversion to communism very clear. So did a parade of actors. Ronald Reagan said Communists were "disruptive."[12] Gary Cooper didn't really know what communism was but "from what I've heard, I don't like it."[13]

Actor Robert Taylor objected when people said things that sounded "pink."[14] Ginger Rogers's mother complained bitterly that her famous daughter had been forced to say, "Share and share alike. That's democracy." Not democracy at all, Mrs Rogers testified. This was "definitely Communist propaganda."

Then came the naming of names. What Communists do you know? Which people do you *think* are Communists? Or *might* be Communists? "Friendly" witnesses named lots of names. That was part of the deal. These names—many writers among them—received subpoenas. A subpoena made a witness "unfriendly," a person to be prosecuted rather than questioned. And once subpoenaed, there was no choice; failure to appear was contempt of Congress and a probable prison sentence.

Without a court's rules of evidence to protect them, witnesses who refused to name names had only one legal remedy: the Fifth Amendment to the Constitution. The idea behind the Fifth is even older than the evidence rules. It dates back to the Magna Carta and protection from confessions extracted by torture. The version in the US Constitution reads:

> No person shall be compelled . . .
> to be a witness against himself.

But there is a snag. Taking the Fifth does imply that a person has committed a crime: "I refuse to answer on the grounds that it may incriminate me." In the public's mind, HUAC had turned this ancient right into an admission of guilt: "Fifth Amendment Communists."[15] They were just as likely to lose their jobs—and never find another—as if they had confessed.

HUAC witnesses could bring a lawyer with them, although having one implied guilt, and the lawyer could give advice on how to answer questions. But since cross-examination wasn't permitted, no lawyer could interrupt anything the Committee asked about or commented on. Nor could they question any person who brought or implied a charge against a client, however outrageous the charge or the implication. A group of witnesses might honestly swear that they did not know

Communists, and they'd still be in danger. A new witness might gain immunity by swearing that members of the group—any one of them or all of them—*did* know Communists. Now the charges were perjury and another potential prison sentence. People were so scared that many were willing to become "friendly" witnesses—to swear to anything—in return for immunity themselves.

Hollywood's "unfriendly" witnesses decided to fight. They created their own committee, and many in the industry joined them—Humphrey Bogart, Lauren Bacall, John Huston. These were big names, and it was naming the names that bothered them most. The way they saw it, the Communist Party was a legal association and membership in it was legal; therefore, no Congressional committee could legally compel them to imply they'd committed a crime when they refused to give names of friends and colleagues who *might* belong to the Party or sympathize with it.

They called themselves the Committee of the First Amendment. The relevant part of this amendment reads:

> Congress shall make no law . . .
> abridging the freedom of speech.

———— ⨯⨯⨯ ————

The Hollywood defense was that the First Amendment covered the freedom to remain silent as well as to speak.

Eleven writers and directors—all men—appeared before HUAC to argue the point. Bertolt Brecht was one of them, and at the time one of the most famous writers in the world; *The Threepenny Opera* was already a classic. You can still see some of his testimony and hear the rest of it in ancient recordings.[16] It's not impressive. Despite his commitment to the First Amendment, he cooperates at once in a heavy German accent: he'd never been a Communist, had no idea if he knew any Communists, had never talked to anybody he thought might be a Communist. He left for Germany as soon as he got off the stand.

That left ten. One by one, these ten tried to read statements into the record. One by one HUAC shut them down. One by one they invoked their Constitutional right to silence and one by one were cited for contempt of Congress. Even while they were still testifying, fifty Hollywood executives met in secret and announced that the ten were suspended without pay and that hereafter their studios would hire nobody with suspected Communist affiliations.

On November 24, 1947, Nixon himself, the junior Congressman from California, persuaded the House of Representatives that the Committee had the right to ask its questions and witnesses did not have the right to refuse to answer.[17]

The ten writers—they became known as the Hollywood Ten— landed in prison.

They had committed no crime; all they had tried to do was defend themselves, their families, and their colleagues against vague accusations of subversive thoughts brought by unnamed accusers.

Here is Alger's "matter of principle" at its most dramatic.

4

1948

After lunch—despite his friends' unanimous advice—Alger wrote a telegram to HUAC, demanding the opportunity to meet his accuser and deny the charges under oath.

He told them he had Endowment business in Washington and proposed that he testify that morning. HUAC had never taken on a "friendly" witness of his stature before; he was pushing them into dangerous territory, and he had no doubt that he "would be able to show them promptly that they had been misled."[1] From what he knew of them and of himself, he could thrash the lot of them into a public apology with one hand tied behind his back. A public collapse in front of somebody like him just might spell an end to the Committee's reign of terror.

It probably never occurred to him that they might harm him.

That's one of the things about legal cases, though. You can't anticipate what they're going to toss in your face—it's one reason they make such good thrillers—and an element inserted itself into Alger's case that nobody could have anticipated. The makeup of the Committee was constantly changing. Alger's response to HUAC provoked the special interest of one of its newer members, an obscure young representative from California, first elected to Congress only the year before.

His name was Richard Milhous Nixon.

5

Alger was born in 1904, and the Hiss family was society in Balti-more, Maryland. They had a horse and carriage. There were cooks, chauffeurs, chambermaids as well as nannies and private schools for the children. But when he was two and a half years old, something went badly wrong; the only hope for the family finances was a cotton mill down south in Charlotte, North Carolina. Alger's mother flatly refused to go. The Sunday morning after she had said so, Alger's father shouted downstairs that she was to call the doctor.

Then he slit his throat from ear to ear with one of those old-fash-ioned straight-edge razors.

The horse and carriage had to go. No electricity in the house, no heat except for the kitchen stove—the kids fetching coal for it from the basement. But they kept a servant. The Hisses just might have been connected to the princely family of Hesse-Darmstadt; a tight budget can't take away the sense of entitlement that comes with a name like that, and such people have servants. Mrs. Hiss went right on prepar-ing her children for their place in Baltimore society. After school every weekday, Aunt Lila read out loud: Coleridge, Scott, Dickens, Shake-speare, the King James Bible, some light stuff too, Edward Lear's limer-icks and *Alice's Adventures*. There was tennis and horse riding. Saturdays were for music lessons, art classes, German conversation. Sundays were for Sunday school and church; this was a religious family—grace and family prayers too—an Episcopalian family, the faith of the American elite.

There were five Hiss children, a happy, chattery, close-knit clan despite the family tragedy. Alger was the playful, mischievous one, just like a hero in one of those old-fashioned books for boys. He scared his younger brother Donald with bears under the bed and made him giggle in church by pretending to stick hatpins in ladies' rumps. He was lazy at school and lousy at lessons, skiving off to lie in the sun, practice smoking, play pool. His only distinction was an athletics medal won only because he was so short—they called him "runt"—that the coach could pit him against younger kids.

This clearly would not do. The values of the Hesse-Darmstadts dated back to chivalry: fear God, never lie, fight injustice, protect the weak. When Alger was sixteen, his mother sent him to a prep school called Powder Point Academy, "where everything is bent toward developing self-mastery."[1] In two terms the runt turned into a gangly basketball player of six foot one, arms and legs all over the place but as good-looking as he was tall, deep-set eyes—very blue—dark hair, those high cheekbones, an elegant face, sharply defined, regular features. The Academy did serious work inside his head too; at the end of his time there, the yearbook said, "Alger is the epitome of success."[2] Johns Hopkins University followed. He took the place by storm, fanciest fraternity, president of the student council, member of Phi Beta Kappa and practically every other social and intellectual honor available to an undergraduate. He was voted the "most popular" in his class.[3]

After that came Harvard Law School, where he shone so brilliantly that his illustrious tutor, Supreme Court Justice Felix Frankfurter, recommended him for the job of law clerk to the even more illustrious Supreme Court Justice Oliver Wendell Holmes. Holmes was a popular figure, a Civil War veteran with a magnificent handlebar moustache, the most widely cited judge in US history then as now, famous for the phrase "clear and present danger" and for his courage as "The Great Dissenter." Alger spent a year with him, "a celestial time" in his life,[4] as he told his son long afterward. He read out loud to the great man, learned the secret of writing Supreme Court decisions. It's like pissing, Holmes told him. "You apply pressure, a very vague pressure, and out it comes."[5]

That's where he learned the deepest secret of his profession, the one he'd used to explain the basics of his case over crème brûlée at Dexter's apartment. "This is a court of law, young man, not a court of justice."

One of the conditions of working with Holmes was not to marry, but Alger married anyway. The woman was Priscilla Fansler Hobson, known as "Prossy": heavy eyebrows and a strong jaw offset by gentle eyes, a widow's peak, and a lissom, graceful body made for sex. He'd been in love with her for years, but she'd married somebody else, had a child, divorced, not become available again until now.

Holmes promptly forgave the transgression and allowed them a whole weekend for a honeymoon.

The year with Holmes coincided with the 1929 stock market crash that brought on the Great Depression. Banks started collapsing so fast it makes our own shaky system look positively sturdy. Queues like the ones that stretched outside their doors at the beginning of our recent crunch, stretched outside thousands of banks all over the US. Reserves hemorrhaged at the rate of $15 million a day. The value of money lurched so erratically that global currency exchanges substituted a question mark for the dollar sign.

Nobody could keep track of unemployment, either. Was it one person in six who wanted a job and couldn't get one? One in five? One in four? Nobody knew. There were no welfare programs to help—no unemployment benefit, no housing benefit, no health benefits—and no solution to hunger but breadlines, begging, soup kitchens, stealing, rioting, hobo jungles. With no money for food, mountains of it rotted. Farmers couldn't earn a living; they rioted. Crime rates soared. No solution to cold, either. Whole families huddled together in tar-paper shacks in ghettoes in every city, only to be moved on from plot to plot like the homeless of today. An aimless, hopeless, fearful time.

Businesses were collapsing right and left too, which meant that the need for lawyers was absolute; nobody came with better credentials than

Alger Hiss. He went from Holmes to the most prestigious law firm in Boston, and he shone there as he had everywhere else. The Depression didn't really touch him—except to bring in clients. The most important part of his life was Priscilla. He wanted her happy, and she wasn't happy in Boston. She yearned for the excitements of New York City; in 1932 he transferred to a Wall Street firm.

As he wrote of himself later, "a not too uncharitable characterization" of his life up to this point "could well be the Progress of a Prig."[6] In Manhattan, richest of cities, he saw his first breadlines. He saw his first soup kitchens. He saw shantytowns in parks and vacant lots. He saw beggars on the streets. He watched the misery grow day by day, and he saw how shallow his upbringing had made him. He took on pro bono work in the hopes of using what he knew to help—only to realize how few remedies the law offered people in such a state.

The law needed changing, and Franklin Delano Roosevelt—running for President of the United States—proposed to do just that. Roosevelt was a snazzy Harvard graduate like Alger, but a seriously rich one, the only disabled person ever to come anywhere near the Oval Office. He was as spoiled as they come and almost too charming, but there was a profound optimism in him; they sang "Happy Days Are Here Again" at his rallies. He offered people a New Deal, and he captured American hearts; a third of the electorate switched parties to vote for him, the first Democrat in eighty years to win such a sweeping victory. It was in his inaugural address that he delivered that most famous line: "The only thing we have to fear is fear itself."

Roosevelt had a wonderful brain, and his New Deal was a stroke of genius. As soon as he was in office, he had Congress enacting legislation with dozens of alphabet agencies covering every aspect of economic redevelopment. NRA: the National Recovery Administration. WPA: the Works Progress Administration. FDIC: the Federal Deposit Insurance Corporation. The New Deal's extraordinary achievement is that it managed to string a tightrope between big business and the armies of young idealists, who saw communism as the only way to distribute wealth in a country where so many people were going hungry.

Maybe tightropes are dangerous, but they're exciting. Alger's old teacher Felix Frankfurter urged him to join. He was already euphoric over Roosevelt's victory. He already saw that the New Deal was a crusade worthy of the chivalric code he'd grown up with, and this was a national emergency. He went to Washington in 1933 as assistant general counsel to the Agricultural Adjustment Administration, the alphabet agency AAA, set up to curb the power of the agricultural conglomerates and create a legal structure to support the individual farmers whose crops he had seen rotting in the streets. A big job, a job with serious authority, a "heady experience."[7] Alger himself helped draft legislation to give underprivileged Americans the legal remedies that New York had taught him they didn't have.

He also became counsel for the Special Committee on Investigation of the Munitions Industry, chaired by Senator Gerald Nye: war-profiteering, the scandal of American businesses arming Hitler's war machine. He did both these jobs with such ingenuity, enthusiasm, and success that the Department of State came next, fulfillment of a childhood dream, assistant to the Assistant Secretary of Economic Affairs. World War II broke out. He rose to Special Assistant to the Director of the Office of Far Eastern Affairs, then to Special Assistant to the Director of the Office of Special Political Affairs, then to Assistant to the Assistant Secretary of State, then to Executive Secretary of the Dumbarton Oaks Conference.

That's where the idea of the United Nations was born.

The Yalta Conference came in February of 1945, right near the end of the war. Yalta just has to be one of the most important conferences in modern history. The "Big Three" were all there in person: Roosevelt, Churchill, and Stalin. The agenda was to coordinate strategy to defeat Hitler and Japan, decide how to divide up postwar Europe and how to punish the Nazis. Alger helped draft the treaty signed there, and he attended the conference itself as one of Roosevelt's personal assistants. Photographs at the vast round table in one of the special "Big Three" meeting rooms show him right behind Roosevelt, three seats away from Churchill, straight across from Stalin.

They say that if you mount the wild elephant, you go where the wild elephant goes. Every one of those three was a wild elephant, and they all wanted to go in different directions. Roosevelt didn't want Churchill to invade Japan—he'd demand more colonies when the war was over—but he did want to arrange invasion dates with Stalin. Roosevelt and Churchill wanted to ensure that Stalin didn't make a separate peace with Germany and didn't learn details of the atomic bomb that the US was developing. Stalin's position was so strong he could demand almost anything he wanted from either of them; for the most part, he got it too. The atmosphere was so tense that when Anthony Eden, a mere member of the British delegation back then, went to take a pee and found Stalin in the line behind him, he sprayed the walls.

After Yalta, the peace-to-come preoccupied everybody. How to make it international? How to keep it? Alger was Secretary General of the San Francisco United Nations Conference on International Organization, which set up the United Nations itself. After the war ended, he was Director of the Office of Special Political Affairs: the search for ways to avoid World War III. He left the State Department to become President of the Carnegie Endowment for International Peace; now the search was for a workable system of international law.

The Endowment was founded in 1910 by the robber baron and philanthropist Andrew Carnegie, whose Carnegie Hall is the pinnacle of any musician's career. Nobel Prizes for its two previous presidents had made the Endowment itself world famous. Its chairman John Foster Dulles was soon to be Secretary of State for President Dwight D. Eisenhower. Eisenhower himself was a board member. So was the founder of IBM. So was David Rockefeller, scion of the great Standard Oil family.

Such giddy heights belong in fairy tales. Where could such a man as Alger Hiss not go? No wonder everybody assumed that something as grand as Secretary of State had to come next. Instead came two years of headlines like these from the *New York Times*:

AUGUST 4, 1948

RED 'UNDERGROUND'
IN FEDERAL POSTS ALLEGED BY EDITOR
Ex-Communist Names Alger Hiss

DECEMBER 16, 1948
ALGER HISS INDICTED IN SPY CASE

JANUARY 22, 1950
MR. HISS FOUND GUILTY

JANUARY 26, 1950
HISS IS SENTENCED TO FIVE-YEAR TERM[8]

PART TWO

HUAC in hot pursuit

6

1948

Whittaker Chambers was the HUAC informant whose name Alger had recognized from an FBI file. His testimony was that Alger had been the leader of a Communist cell inside the State Department; he said that he and Alger had been close friends, that he'd tried to get Alger to quit the Party and that Alger had wept at the thought.

He didn't know much about Alger's present job, got the Endowment's title wrong, didn't know what city it was in. A Committee staff member checked Alger's dossier: New York. Which is odd. Official lists of Reds ran to hundreds of thousands, and they have Alger's dossier right on hand? How did they know Chambers was going to name him? Come to think of it, how did a newspaper know the day before?

Rankin—the Congressman who exempted the Ku Klux Klan from investigation—grumbled that Alger had got the position only because state law prohibited asking him whether he was a Communist or not. "Of course, he can get into an institution of that kind in New York, but he couldn't do it in Mississippi."

Karl Earl Mundt, Congressman from South Dakota, threw in his bit: "Certainly there is no hope for world peace under the leadership of men like Alger Hiss."[1]

HUAC added some thirty names to their list during that hearing, quite a net to spread in a few hours. Only three were foolish enough to reply. The first two were a Mr. and Mrs. Gold of Pittsburgh. The

Committee read their telegram into the record: a Miss Bentley's charges against them were "shocking and utterly untrue. The woman is entirely unknown to us, and in all fairness we urgently request the earliest opportunity to testify publicly and under oath to the utter falsity of her charges."[2]

The Committee decided to let the Golds—relative nobodies—defend themselves "as soon as we can arrange the hearing."

Then came Alger's cable: "My attention has been called by representatives of the press to statements made about me before your committee this morning by one Whittaker Chambers. I do not know Mr. Chambers and insofar as I am aware have never laid eyes on him."[3] Alger did not say, as the Golds did of Miss Bentley, that Chambers was "utterly unknown to him," a detail that will become absurdly important all too soon. But like the Golds, he said, "There is no basis for the statements made about me to your committee," and he'd "appreciate the opportunity" to deny them "formally and under oath."

The Chairman's comment: "The Committee will hear Alger Hiss in public testimony tomorrow."

This committee knows a PR opportunity when it sees one.

Black and white film clips of the 1940s are so dark even in full daylight that they threaten claustrophobia and nightmare. Film noir is exactly the right term. There are many old newsreels of the Congressional Caucus Room in the old House Office building in Washington, DC, where Alger presented himself. The room no longer exists, but it must have been huge, ceiling too high to be seen in the clips, barely a sense of walls.

Cinema newsreels of sessions were very popular, and in the film clips, the space is packed, crammed. I'd have expected an attentive audience, but hardly anybody seems to be paying attention. People write, read, some chat, smoke, lots of milling about. The witness is the only place for the eye to rest. The press swarm around him—usually *him*, though occasionally her—like ants at a drop of honey. Flashbulbs explode. Huge double-reel cameras on tall legs and banks of floodlights all aim at him.

The Hollywood people probably took such razzmatazz in their stride, and Alger was an old hand at Congressional hearings. But he'd never seen anything like this.[1] HUAC Chief Investigator Robert E. Stripling said that this August morning "drew perhaps the biggest turnout of reporters and spectators in the history of our inquiries."[2]

Here's another odd thing. It slips by unnoticed on a first reading, even a second or a third. All this is going on less than twenty-four hours after HUAC read Alger's telegram into evidence. Good PR to choose the celebrity, but a response as big as this? Clearly HUAC knew it was going to happen; otherwise, they'd have chosen a smaller room. Getting the press was easy—telephones and wire services—but enough spectators to pack the place? The Hollywood hearings were in the news for weeks beforehand. How did so many people find out about this one so quickly? How did they know there was going to be enough press there to make a real occasion of it? How did so many people arrange to be away from work on a Thursday morning? And at such short notice?

———✺———

There's a raised dais at one end of the room, a fluted, columned wall behind it—funeral drapery at the windows—and a long table atop it, angled forward across both ends. Ten men sit at this table, five Congressmen from the House of Representatives and five members of HUAC's staff. The heat wave that greeted Alger in New York covers the whole of the East Coast; the Caucus Room isn't air-conditioned, and these guys are all wearing suits and ties; no jackets off either, no ties loosened, not a rolled-up sleeve in sight.

The audience would know their faces from the Hollywood hearings. Today's chairman, Karl Earl Mundt is balding, long upper lip, elfin mouth beneath it: a sheep face. He's the one who fears for world peace "under the leadership of men like Alger Hiss"[3]; he's a schoolteacher—psychology and economics—and a white supremacist but not a man without humor. Or a sense of theater. A sweltering audience can hardly be said to need warming up, but that's just what Mundt is about to do.

He calls first on John Rankin from Mississippi, lover of the KKK—stern, gaunt face, wavy gray hair—and Rankin starts in on Roosevelt's first vice president, Henry Wallace, the Progressive Party's candidate for president in the next election. The public needs to know how come Communists "who were plotting the overthrow of the Government, were placed in key positions in his Department at a time when our young men were fighting and dying on every battle front in the world for the protection of this country."[4]

But why talk about Wallace today? He's no part of this. Unless you consider that he was Alger's boss a while back, and lots of the people who see newsreels will know it.

Next come Russian spies in the government in 1943 arranging for the makings of a nuclear bomb to be flown to Russia from "a small obscure airfield in the United States."[5] John McDowell of Pennsylvania—tall, long face, an ex-journalist and editor—explains: "We know that a factory was flown entirely to Russia."[6] A whole atomic bomb factory?[7] In 1943? When nobody knew a bomb would explode?

It just so happens that Alger was chief counsel to the Nye Committee, the Senate committee investigating the munitions industry.

McDowell goes on to "the widespread ramifications of this intense espionage ring" that the Committee has discovered was "deep in the State Department."[8]

Which is where Alger had been working for well over a decade before he went to the Carnegie Endowment.

Now that they've tied him into three separate areas of sabotage—all in the first ten minutes of the hearing—an Illinois Congressman called Fred E. Busby takes the stand: a Clark Gable moustache and finger-waves in his hair, an army man and insurance broker—he does look like an insurance broker—who served four terms as a Republican Congressman but kept losing in between them. He's up for reelection in 1948. This turns out to be important. The Committee is almost all Republicans, and every single member is up for election. All of them are on the campaign trail. And today they have newsreel cameras trained on them, a packed audience, and a New Deal Democrat in the pillory.

Busby starts naming names of suspected Communists in government. The list is as meaningless in the twenty-first century as the Bible's begats: "Tom Tippett, E. J. Lever, Nathan Gregory Silvermaster, Carl Aldo Marzani . . ."[9]

Rep. Busby is very boring. After the begats, he reads out page after page of Civil Service Commission regulations for hiring government employees and finds them painfully inadequate. There are no guidelines for investigating what person reads, believes, does with his spare time, "whether the applicant associates with Negroes or has had Negroes to his home."[10] Busby says failure to probe into areas like this saddled the government with a man everybody knew was "an organizer for the Communist Party on New York City's East Side"[11] and another "whose wife has been a known Communist out in the open for many years,"[12] He also says—more or less out of the blue—that the brigades who "went to fight in Spain were definitely 100 percent Communist outfits."[13]

Democrats have been in power for twenty years. It looked as though they were going to stay there forever when the much-beloved Franklin Roosevelt died in office shortly after starting his fourth term. His much-less-loved vice president Harry Truman succeeded him, and this gives the Republicans a real shot at the White House. Communist subversion among Democrats is their most powerful weapon; they began developing it almost as soon as Roosevelt introduced the New Deal and the idea that society should help people who couldn't help themselves. The Republican Busby says there's been a cover-up. "Truman does not want the truth to come out because it would be embarrassing to the present administration."[14] People like Alger Hiss—he does state the name—were part of the New Deal's Agricultural Adjustment Administration at a time when that department "could rightfully be termed the spawning ground of all Communists in government."[15]

A lot of energy and ingenuity has gone into setting this scene for the morning's star turn: gathering the press, rustling up a crowd for the occasion, spelling out the three separate areas of spying Alger could be tied to. And Busby's role? Chairman Mundt thanks him kindly for showing "how these Communists and espionage agents have been able to weasel their way into Government, escape detection, and secure promotion after they have been there."

Then he says, "Call the next witness, Mr. Stripling."

Stripling shouts, "Mr. Alger Hiss."[16]

Robert Stripling looked like a Mafia enforcer, dark circles around his eyes, the whites showing under the irises. He was Chief Investigator for the Committee, and he fitted right in. A decade before, he was assistant to the publicist for the German American Bund—a powerful US Nazi organization founded in 1933—helping organize parades to protest that the "New Deal" was the "Jew Deal" and Franklin D. Roosevelt was really a Jew called Frank D. Rosenfeld.[1]

In fact Americans saluted Nazi-style before Nazis did. A man called Francis Bellamy wrote the Pledge of Allegiance in 1892 and proposed an outstretched arm as the salute for it. Footage from the 1930s shows members of the Bund, swastikas on outstretched arms, pledging themselves to the Stars and Stripes. Hand-on-heart came in only when somebody noticed the awkward similarity.

Back in the 1948 Caucus Room, sheep-faced Mundt peers from the height of the dais at the man he's already condemned as a danger to world peace.

"Are you Mr. Alger Hiss?"

"Yes, I am."

"Please stand and be sworn." Alger stands. "Do you solemnly swear the testimony you are about to give will be the truth, the whole truth, and nothing but the truth, so help you God?"

"I do."

"Be seated."[2] Both Mundt and Stripling had those pulpy faces that dissolve into pudding as they age. Pulpy bodies too. Not Alger. Here was the guy from my civics book, at ease, in control, a person wholly worthy of the media attention. Since he's a "friendly" witness, he's allowed to make a statement. He speaks without notes, which really annoys Stripling.[3] "I am not and never have been a member of the Communist Party. I am not and never have been a member of any Communist-front organization. To the best of my knowledge, none of my friends is a Communist."[4]

And so forth.

When lines intersect and speed off in different directions, they can get so far away from each other so quickly that it's impossible to see what the angles between them could have been at the crossing. In Alger's case there are only two lines that matter—literally only two—and by the time his trials roll around, it's way too late. But here in this Caucus Room the angle between them is readily visible. The first line emerged from Alger's telegram to HUAC: "I do not know Mr. Chambers and[5], insofar as I am aware, have never laid eyes on him."[6] A lawyer's caution rather than an outright denial like the Golds' about their accuser, Miss Bentley, but as sore a point with him as with them. "I was angered," he wrote later, "that the Committee had allowed this unknown man to attack me publicly before giving me the opportunity to challenge him."[7]

He elaborates in his opening statement: "To the best of my knowledge, I never heard of Whittaker Chambers until in 1947, when two representatives of the Federal Bureau of Investigation asked me if I knew him." He told the agents he didn't. "So far as I know," he goes on, "I have never laid eyes on him."

He adds, "I should like to have the opportunity to do so."

Before the hearing started, HUAC gave Alger a copy of Chambers's testimony; it didn't reveal much about the man himself. Nor did the newspapers. Chambers was a highly paid senior editor at *Time* magazine, born in Philadelphia, educated in public schools, a year and a half at Columbia University, had known Alger—and six other suspects—some time between 1924 and 1937.

Mundt asks Alger if he knew—when the Carnegie job came up—that Chambers had already told his tales to Assistant Secretary of State Adolf Berle.

Alger's anger is there on the page: "I did not."

"You had not heard that?"

"I did not."[8]

Mundt presses again, "The Committee finds it very puzzling that Chambers whom you say you have never seen—"

"As far as I know, I have never seen him," Alger interrupts. This is the lawyer again, somebody who understands rules of evidence and senses something amiss in the line of questioning. "Is he here today?"[9]

"Not to my knowledge."

"I hoped he would be."[10] And again a little later, "I wish I could've seen Mr. Chambers before he testified."[11]

Stripling takes over. "You say you have never seen Mr. Chambers?"

"The name means absolutely nothing to me, Mr. Stripling."[12]

Stripling shows him a press photograph. "Have you ever known an individual who resembles this picture?"

The Sixth Amendment to the US Constitutions contains what's called the "Confrontation Clause." It guarantees the accused's right to see the accuser. In a courtroom, Chambers would be sitting with the prosecution, visible to everybody; but HUAC was exempt from the Sixth Amendment as well as all of a court's rules of evidence. In Committee hearings, the accused gets grilled, harangued, threatened, charged with Communist affiliations, speeches, books, plays, thoughts. The accuser? He can play so minor a role that he's not even mentioned; nobody even has to know who brought the charges.

This carries uncomfortable echoes of sixteenth century witch trials, but if I exchange "communism" for "terrorism," I can begin to see what's going on here. Suppose Chambers had lived as a terrorist in a remote suburb and claimed that he'd studied suicide bombing with Alger, that they'd been close friends and conspirators, that Alger had cried at the thought of parting from him and jihad: at once Alger would be on a "No Fly List," friends, family, affiliations investigated.

He could all too easily end up spirited off in the night to Guantanamo Bay or some other secret service holding facility, where no legal process could help.

Not that the comparison explains the crowd, the huge Caucus Room, the army of press. And why would they want Alger to identify his accuser from a photograph? Especially when he could be here in person so easily?

Alger studies the press picture, a "candid-camera angle from under the chin."[13] "I would much rather see the individual," he says. "I would not want to take oath that I've never seen that man. I've looked at all the pictures I was able to get hold of him in, I think, yesterday's paper. If this is a picture of Mr. Chambers, he is not particularly unusual looking. He looks like a lot of people. I might even mistake him for the chairman of this Committee."

The audience laughs. No pictures of Chambers make him pretty, and humorous Mundt says, "I hope you're wrong in that."[14] Stripling mentions that Chambers "is much heavier than he was at the time."[15] Which makes identification from a photograph all the harder to understand.

"You realize that this man"—Mundt starts in again—"whose picture you just looked at, under sworn testimony before this Committee, where all the laws of perjury apply, testified that he called at your home, conferred at great length, saw your wife pick up the telephone and call somebody whom he said must have been a Communist, plead with you to divert yourself from Communist activities, and left you with tears in your eyes saying, 'I simply cannot make the sacrifice.'"

"I do know he said that," a thoroughly irritated Alger snaps, not noticing that Mundt just made up this quote, that all Chambers had said was that Alger's "reasons were simply the Party line." Alger goes on angrily. "I also know I am testifying under the same laws to the direct contrary."[16]

In those days, men didn't cry. They just didn't. In all the years I knew Alger, I saw him trapped in emotion only twice; both times the provocation was severe. There was icy anger—definitely that—not a hint of tears.

Stripling reads from Tuesday's testimony.

MR. STRIPLING: When you left the Communist Party in 1937, did you approach [any fellow Communists]?

MR. CHAMBERS: I went to Hisses' home in the evening . . .[17]

What's good about this recap is that a reader can actually see the second of the two diverging lines as it crosses the first. It's the year 1937, and it needs watching. During last Tuesday's hearing, Stripling asked Chambers, "How long did you remain a member of the Communist Party?"

Chambers answered, "Until 1937." Then he said, "In 1937, I repudiated Marxist doctrines and Lenin's tactics."

A little later, Rankin wanted confirmation. "When did you cease to be a Communist because of your convictions?"

"1937."

The year 1937 as the end of Chambers's Communist life came up half a dozen times that Tuesday, and by then he'd spent a decade of confessions to the FBI insisting on it. The year was important to him. He signed affidavits confirming it; he'd repeated it to Assistant Secretary of State Berle. It's repeated twice today.

It sounds as meaningless as those flowered napkins, but here's the crossing of those two divergent lines that make up the case against Alger Hiss: his failing to recognize Chambers and the year 1937. That's all there is at the heart of the trial of the century.

———— ⌘ ————

The trouble with reading testimony is that it's dialogue without directions, and transcripts of Congressional hearings have to be the driest dialogue in the universe. You can't tell how people look or what their voices sound like or what gestures they make. You have to read sections again and again to see what's actually going on. Even dramatic climaxes sink beneath the tedium of a court stenographer's text.

Like the one that's about to happen.

HUAC was all about naming names. Stripling asks Alger for a resumé of his Federal employment.

Alger begins with Justice Holmes, although he doesn't say the name. He also says that after private practice he went to Washington at the request of "government officials."[18]

Rankin demands the name of the Justice. Alger tells him. Even with a specially invited audience, there'd have been a few intakes of breath.

That's when Richard Milhous Nixon enters the scene. Alger had barely noticed him: "He was simply a pale nonentity placed inconspicuously on the hearing room dais among the well-known bullies on the Committee who played major roles."[19] But it's still a famous face, and not a pale one, either. Heavy black brows, scoop nose, ineradicable five-o'clock shadow. A surprisingly good-looking man back then, though. One observer described him as "the darkly handsome Nixon."[20] He demands the names of the "government officials" who'd requested Alger to come to Washington.

Fortunately, Alger's autobiography supplies some stage directions. "I recall his tone as unfriendly. I did indeed have a low opinion of the Committee and probably showed it, but at that time I had no reason for selective contempt for Nixon." Harvard schools its lawyers in "sharp, incisive, even sarcastic" questioning[21]; Alger makes no attempt to placate him.

"Is it necessary?" he asks. "There are so many witnesses that use names rather loosely."

Another witness to the proceedings said Nixon turned crimson.[22] "You made the statement."

"The statement is correct."

"I don't question its correctness, but I think it would make your case much stronger if you would indicate what Government officials."

"Regardless of whether it would make my case stronger, Mr. Nixon . . ."[23]

Junior Congressmen don't tell top government mandarins what would make their case stronger. And how come there's talk of a "case" at all? What *case*? Alger is a witness voluntarily answering the Committee's questions. This is an inquiry, not a prosecution, despite Nixon's all-too-obvious aggression.

And suddenly it's over. Nixon just steps back, turns the hearing over to the others. They press Alger to name some more names; they ask him if he knows a couple of dozen of them, many mentioned by Busby earlier. A few he recognizes. Some he doesn't. In most cases he responds coldly, "Not to the best of my knowledge."

The hearing grinds to a halt.

Alger's all-too-obvious contempt for this affair hasn't softened during the entire morning; and yet when the name-naming is finished, the Committee isn't the least bit annoyed.

Mundt says to him, "The Chair wishes to express the appreciation of the Committee for your very cooperative attitude, for your forthright statements, and for the fact that you were first among those whose names were mentioned by various witnesses to communicate with us asking for an opportunity to deny the charges."[24] No mention of the Golds from Pittsburg, who'd beat him to it.

Rankin chips in. "And another thing. I want to congratulate the witness that he didn't refuse to answer the questions on the ground that it might incriminate him, and he didn't bring a lawyer here to tell him what to say."

The press jump out of their seats and run toward Alger, hands outstretched. Chairman Mundt gets down from the Committee's dais to shake Alger's hand himself, even though, according to Nixon, he has "to fight his way through crowds to do it".

Nixon sums it up. "Hiss won the day completely. It would not be an exaggeration to say that probably 90 percent of the reporters and most of the Committee members were convinced that a terrible mistake had been made."[25]

9

1960

Back when I was only twenty years old, everybody close to me wanted me to stop dancing. Dexter was just bored by it. My mother hated it: jealousy for the most part. She'd wanted to go on the stage herself, failed to make the grade. She'd never liked me much anyhow, and the further I got into a professional career, the harder she fought to tear me away. As for friendships, ballet leaves little time for them outside it, and it's too competitive for them inside; if a talented dancer above you on the ladder leaves, your chances jump up a rung. There are tripwires everywhere.

And I was developing Candide-like questions. I wanted to know what it all meant. I wanted to know why people believed in God. Mainly—don't laugh—I wanted to know what truth was. When I was in high school, my biology teacher once said of me in despair, "Oh, painfully honest Joan." I'd puzzled over that for years, certain that truth had to consist of a definitive version of things. If so, how could I find a way to see it? If not, what could the idea mean? The harder I thought, the hazier the whole thing became.

In the autumn, I gave up ballet and entered Columbia University to study philosophy. But I certainly didn't give up Dexter. And he wanted to befriend Alger Hiss.

He asked Alger and Isabel to dinner several times more. There was no way I could bring myself to like Isabel; she wasn't only coy, she was manipulative. Alger? His calm was unfathomable. I couldn't understand it at all. The intensity of his attention when he listened made me wary; when my mother concentrated on me like that, I knew I was in for it. Dexter was intrigued, though, and anything that intrigued him intrigued me. He did have a naughty streak; I'm sure friendship with so notorious a figure was fun for him, but he and Alger had much in common too. Both were born into that upper-class sense of ease and place in the world. Alger was as informed and enthusiastic about things that interested Dexter as he'd been about Balanchine's *Concerto Barocco*. They shared an optimism that came with Roosevelt and the 1930s, a lightness of spirit, a belief in the possibilities of the future, an excitement in the morning about the day that lay ahead of them. Such enthusiasms seemed magical to my doom-laden 1950s pessimism, where everything fell under the shadow of an atomic Armageddon.

The evenings did become easier for me, helped on by an improvement in my kitchen technique. But no invitations came back.

Dexter said he assumed that Alger would have to be certain an invitation from him wouldn't embarrass any of us. In those days socially ambitious New Yorkers held what were called "Monkey Parties"; they'd invite their friends to view a celebrity somehow bagged—sometimes paid—for an evening. I remember one with Sir Huw Wheldon, then MD of BBC TV; I was the only person present who didn't know who he was. There was another with some fiercely eminent American architect. Nobody expected to be invited back by guests like these, although they'd have jumped at the chance. The seamier side of life also offered up "monkeys." Once a famous Madam was on show. That kind of thing made Alger Hiss a prize monkey.

Nobody wanted people like these to ask them back. That was probably the least of it, though. Alger was married, and not yet to Isabel; they were living together in her apartment. As Dexter told me, Alger's friends knew they must not write to him at her address, not even care of her address; all correspondence with him had to be addressed to her personally or to another address. He kept a room somewhere else— I never did see it—that served partly as a mail drop and partly as a smokescreen to keep their relationship out of harm's way. Dangers were everywhere. There were reporters and scandal sheets eager for stories of adultery, philandering, moral turpitude. Cops watched him constantly. They harassed him. One arrested him just for playing ball with his son Tony in Washington Park: "There was no grass to be preserved at the place we had chosen, we were well away from the walkways, and there were no signs prohibiting tossing a ball, but I ended up paying a fine in Magistrate's Court."[1] He was very lucky they didn't rough him up at the station. That's what the man in the street wanted. Dexter said people would run through traffic to shout, shake their fists, take a poke. They saw Alger as the devil incarnate, the destroyer of the American way of life, the soul-stealer who would condemn their children to Soviet servitude. Death threats were constant. People wanted him fried. They wanted him lynched. They wanted anybody connected to him strapped down or strung up right alongside him.

And the thing about Alger is that he'd be damned if he was going to creep away and hide; he was going to walk the streets like anybody else. "As I had done nothing to flee from, I felt that public prejudice should be confronted and faced down."[2] How many people would dare do that? The bravery of it is breathtaking. So is the rashness. Even so, he had to be very, very careful for Isabel's sake—if not for his own. New people in his life had to realize that just befriending him could put them in danger.

Dexter didn't care about that, and he was a man of great personal charm. He was persistent too. One night Alger and Isabel took us to a village restaurant called The Cookery run by one of Alger's supporters, a guy called Barney Josephson, short, bald, spectacled. I didn't know enough to be impressed; Josephson had run Café Society, the first racially integrated nightclub in New York, where Billie Holiday premiered "Strange Fruit." Slowly, gradually, a friendship did develop; maybe not all that close a friendship, not yet, but it was there. We saw each other two, maybe three times a year.

I turned out to be lousy at philosophy. That was clear almost from the beginning. Columbia's staff included some of America's foremost philosophers, and I had one of them for my introductory course. His name was Sidney Morgenbesser; his task was to give beginners like me a glimpse into the excitement of "doing" philosophy. I liked the sound of that; "doing" philosophy was real insider jargon. Exactly what I wanted. I listened hard. I took copious notes. The trouble was, most of the time I had no idea what the man was talking about.

The main question on the exam went something like this: I have a mother. I have an arm. I have a watch. Explain.

Explain? Explain *what?* I like grammar. I do, and if this were some investigation into the various inflections of "to have," I could blather along for a while. But why would I want to? What did grammar have to do with the big questions? Where was the search for truth in this?

My blathering must have been okay because I got a good grade. After Morgenbesser, though, I steered clear of anything that hinted at the actual *doing* of philosophy. But if I'd learned nothing else during that class, I'd learned how to dismiss things I considered beneath me with the withering term "trivial," the only hitch being that it seemed to include what I'd come to Columbia to find out about. What the hell. I kept my mouth shut, sneered with the best of them, and concentrated on history of philosophy, philosophy of science, existentialism, logic.

By the time I graduated in 1965, Dexter and I were married; I was pregnant, and he was getting ready to leave Consumers Union. When our son Toby was born, our apartment in New York was suddenly too small. We looked at bigger ones. Too expensive. We looked for houses in Westchester, just north of Manhattan. The cost was possible—if a stretch—but living in suburbia was such a depressing idea. We decided to spend a few months in England first. The decision made no financial sense, but then finances were never Dexter's strong point. People like him assume that if they need money, it will appear. What's maddening is that it usually does. There was enough for this trip. After that? Who knows? We booked passage on a Norwegian freighter called the *Black Swan* bound for Belgium.

We ordered our passports.

That's when we hit a snag. My passport arrived ten days after I applied for it. His didn't. He knew why at once. I doubt he'd ever have told me about the FBI's interest in him otherwise. Not that he was protecting me. Or even concerned about what I thought. He just hadn't been interested enough in it to mention it. I think he viewed it much as he viewed money, as something that wasn't going to bother him much and would get taken care of one way or another if it did.

The government was interested in Dexter Masters for three reasons, all of them connected to the change in mood that took place in the US between the time of Alger's rise in the government and his downfall.

The first reason was Consumers Union. Dexter was one of its founders—along with both my parents—as well as its director. Despite what I thought of it, I knew that in its young days it had been fiery and radical. There'd been angry demonstrations. Cops. Nights in jail. Information was the real commodity. Consumer products can kill and maim as well as rob the pocket. Trouble was, an informed public cuts into a company's profit margin. Not popular with big business.

Back then, in the early 1930s—when Alger was barely thirty and Dexter was still in his twenties—the Great Depression was at its worst. Germany was in far better shape. My economist father spent a long time there researching a book on German fascism; he loved the country, but the Nazi wedlock between commerce and the military: that scared him. So did the plan for a rewrite of all history, philosophy, and science to "purify" it. So did the plan to purify the Aryan race: "No person of Jewish blood can think German."[3] Nasty to be sure, but it offered a seductive if isolationist hope: *we* will prevail over *them*. "Either the world will turn fascist"—I remember him saying it—"or fascism will be destroyed."

A lot of Americans figured fascism looked pretty good. Germany's economy was booming.

Balanced against it was communism, and the Soviet Union was better off too. US output halved and halved while Russian output doubled and doubled. Nobody knew about gulags or purges or famines then. The upside was what caught the attention of the young and optimistic, equality for all, welfare benefits for the needy, control over corporations and banks. Like Nazism, it offered hope, a more altruistic version this time: we will work together and make things better for all of us.

A choice between the two ideologies doesn't sound easy.

That's when the charismatic Franklin Delano Roosevelt brought out his tightrope. It's called industrial democracy, and no US government before or since has attempted anything so radical. It retained capitalism in that ownership of property stayed in private hands, but the working man and working woman were to become part of the decision-making process; if they couldn't work, the government was there to help. The bankers didn't like it. The big industrialists didn't like it. Use public money to benefit the public? Scandalous! Roosevelt made many enemies, but those New Deal alphabet agencies built dams, bridges, roads, theaters. Maybe it would take a war to revitalize the economy; meanwhile, Roosevelt offered people his own spin on the magic ingredient, hope: "Yes, we can!" Pure Obama.

Then came World War II and Roosevelt's death near the end of it; the hope died with him. Then came the aimlessness that follows a war. Then came the fear of communism that gave this aimless population a substitute for what they had lost with Roosevelt's death: something to unite against, a "them" to frighten us at night, just like the Nazis. Consumers Union got caught up in that along with hundreds of other organizations.

The second reason for Dexter's FBI file was a book he'd co-edited in 1946 with physicist Katherine Way called *One World or None*. The atom bomb terrified everybody. We were doomed. A nuclear holocaust was inevitable. International control? Forget it. No country with a bomb would agree to anything like that, and pretty soon everybody would have a bomb. Dexter and Kate worked with fifteen of the biggest names in science, looking for answers. The *Washington Post* summed up the result: "For the sake of the planet read *One World or None* . . . Don't take our word for it. Take Einstein's."

The book became an international bestseller. It won the prestigious Peabody Award. The government wasn't happy. Share information? With Russians?

The third reason for Dexter's file was a novel that grew out of *One World or None*. We were all so scared of nuclear holocaust that we weren't even considering the possibility of a Chernobyl. He was. His book *The Accident* was a study of the very first nuclear accident. A routine experiment in the laboratory city of Los Alamos, where the first atom bombs were designed and built—the war over, scientists getting ready to go home—and something went badly wrong. Nobody knows just what, but the young physicist in charge died of radiation poisoning a few days later. The story fascinated Dexter. Why had it happened at all? The physicist had done the experiment many times before, why a slip now? Guilt over the horror he'd helped create? If not, then what?

The novel got rave reviews. It too became an international bestseller, and David Selznick, producer of *Gone With the Wind*, bought a movie option on it; it was to be his comeback after fifteen years without a feature film. He hired Dexter to write the screenplay; they went into production. But *The Accident* questioned the reason for dropping the bombs, and it questioned the US Army's role in the project that built them. News came through that the State Department was refusing an export licence for the movie. Without it, not even the name Selznick could raise enough cash to support the project.

What it boils down to is that the US government banned the book.

From time to time there were telephone calls from FBI agents with questions about this person and that one. Some Dexter knew. Some he didn't. His phone was tapped, his tax returns routinely audited, his mail pawed over before delivery. Government questionnaires accompanied such things as a sample magazine from Poland or a letter from publishers in the Soviet Union, where *The Accident* was a best seller.

Getting his passport took attorneys and wrangling as well as a direct appeal to the State Department. But in the end it came, just as he knew it would.

In May, the three of us—little Toby bundled in a blanket—boarded the *Black Swan*. We were just going to have a leisurely look around. That changed when we found a derelict house on a hilltop in Surrey with views across the North Downs. A friend packed our furniture in New York and shipped it over. Almost as soon as the house was ready to live in, another friend—a fan of *The Accident* and an editor at the publishers, Little, Brown—offered Dexter a $25,000 contract for any novel he chose to write.

Now we could justify staying out of Westchester. Live in England for a few years, write the new novel, go home with the manuscript in hand, see it through publication. Once royalties, foreign sales, movie options started coming in, we could start looking for one of those big apartments in Manhattan.

10

1948

Nixon wrote that while crowds swamped Alger with congratulations, reporters swamped the Committee much less agreeably. A *Washington Post* reporter broke through to ask, "How is the Committee going to dig itself out of this hole?" A Chicago *Daily News* reporter shouted that the Committee "stands convicted, guilty of calumny in putting Chambers on the stand without first checking the truth of his testimony."[1] Another reporter caught hold of Stripling—who liked to be called Strip—and said, "Strip, you fellows have really put your foot in it this time."[2]

What with all the turmoil in the Caucus Room and Committee members being besieged by reporters, Nixon says he managed to slip off for a quiet lunch at a restaurant called Horse, where he heard Truman accuse the Committee of a "red herring" cooked up by a Republican Congress to avoid facing such things as price controls, inflation, welfare legislation. A quiet lunch? Why not something sent in and get straight down to the postmortem? The political stakes could hardly be higher with the big election coming up. Every member of the Committee knew that unless they could make a case against Alger, their careers could disappear right along with HUAC. The need for immediate action was absolute.

How could Nixon just slip out for a quiet lunch?

These were supposed to be hearings about espionage; "Hearings Regarding Communist Espionage in the United States Government" was their official title. Despite media excitements, Chambers hadn't said a word about espionage. His accusations had fallen very short of that: Alger was a member of the Communist Party and part of an "elite group, an outstanding group"—that was destined to become of great "service to the Communist Party."[3] He had volunteered to testify this morning for the express purpose of denying these charges. His telegram to the Committee read, "There is no basis for the statements made about me to your committee."[4] He wanted to make his denial "formally and under oath." He did try too. "I deny unqualifiedly various statements about me which were made before this committee by one Whittaker Chambers the day before yesterday."[5] They were "complete fabrications"[6] and "completely unfounded."[7]

Yet nobody in this morning's hearing paid the slightest attention to his denials. Or to the charges against him. No member of the Committee hinted at a question like "What about this 'elite group'?" or "What kind of 'service to the Communist Party'?" Chambers indicated a still-active Party role for Alger too. Right in front of the cameras, Mundt had upped the charges to espionage: "transmitting secrets to the Russian Government."[8]

Nobody had questioned Alger—or Mundt—about any of that either.

Only two members of HUAC gave versions of the executive session that started when Nixon got back from lunch: Stripling, ex-PR of the Nazi German-American Bund, and Nixon himself. Both reported that at the start of it, an unnamed member of the Committee cried, "We're ruined!"[9] Stripling wrote in his bestseller *The Red Plot Against America* that "you could have cut the gloom with a knife." Various of them made suggestions. One was that the only way "to get off the hook" would be "to turn the whole file over to Department of Justice and hold no more hearings in the case." A member from Louisiana called Felix Hébert moaned, "Let's wash our hands of the whole mess."

Not Stripling or Nixon. They agree that they alone kept the Committee from collapsing under the pressure. Both sensed something suspicious about Alger. Stripling wrote that when Alger was sworn in, he "elaborated dramatically" on the normal "I do." "Hiss said"—according to Stripling—"'So help me God . . . So help me God.'"[10]

"You cannot be a Communist and believe in God,"[11] Stripling wrote in *The Red Plot*, explaining that theatrics over the Almighty reveal a Communist's devious and deviant nature. But I've already quoted the full official record of the swearing in. Mundt said, "Do you solemnly swear the testimony you are about to give will be the truth, the whole truth, and nothing but the truth, so help you God?"[12]

And Alger said, "I do."

He sat down without a further word. Not a theatric in sight. Why doesn't anybody say something? These guys heard the testimony only a couple of hours earlier. Could they have forgotten so quickly?

Stripling went on to tell them that Alger seemed to him "curiously reluctant when representative Nixon asked him for the names of the people who'd urged him to come to Washington to work." "*Curiously reluctant*"? Many, many names were tossed around "loosely"—to use Alger's word—in these hearings, and the consequences for the people named could be terrible. All these guys knew that. They had hammered hard at many others—most notably the Hollywood Ten—who were willing to go to prison rather than rat on their friends.

But that's only the start.

Nixon insists in his first book, *Six Crises*, that he'd never heard of Alger Hiss before Chambers's testimony[13], and he told the House of Representatives that nobody at HUAC had met Chambers before that first hearing.[14] How could he get away with that? The public record is packed with evidence that he and HUAC knew all about both Chambers and Alger.

Alger was a famous man back then; it's absurd for Nixon to claim he'd never heard of him. As to Chambers, according to the FBI, HUAC's previous chairman Martin Dies assumed that he was the chief KGB agent in the United States[15]; Dies wrote in a regular column in a magazine called *American Opinion*, that Chambers "had come to my office several times"[16] during World War II. At least six members of the present Committee had been members back then. Dies also wrote that after the war Chambers had begun "contacting my very able chief investigator and secretary, Robert Stripling."[17] Strip held the same job this very day. A mere few months before this executive session HUAC staffers had conducted a series of talks with Chambers at his office at *Time*; they collected a written statement from him naming Alger as a communist. Chambers testified to it later in court.

Nixon himself confirmed it in HUAC's Interim Report: "Testimony regarding communist activities within the government . . . was given before the committee by . . . Whittaker Chambers . . . Disclos[ing] the existence of compact, conspiratorial rings consisting of Communists within the government. These rings . . . transmitted documents and information."[18] Not that there's any record of talk of conspiracy, nor anything about documents changing hands except when Chambers explicitly denies it.

On the Monday before this Executive session, HUAC had announced that the following day's "witness on the subject of Russian espionage in Washington"[19] would be Whittaker Chambers. Tuesday saw the *New York Times* story raising the charges against Alger to "leader of a Communist cell inside the State Department and a hearing opened with Stripling saying, "Mr. Chambers, you are here before the committee in response to a subpoena . . ."

Easy to see how and why Alger's dossier lay in front of Nixon when Chambers first took the stand. But this morning Mundt had talked about those secrets transmitted to the Russians even though he had to know the idea of espionage was nuts. The FBI was the official agency for looking into the matter, and their records on Alger were long and detailed.[20] They'd investigated him numerous times under the Hatch Act—routine for all members of the State Department—and Public Law #135 required them to report to Congress if they suspected a subversive in government. They'd never reported Alger. In early 1947 they'd investigated him under Truman's Executive Order 9835, sometimes known as the "Loyalty Order." They'd investigated yet again in early 1948 on the grounds that as the President of the Carnegie Endowment he might *become* "disloyal."[21] And it isn't as though the army of agents hadn't tried hard enough. They'd bugged Alger's telephones, both office and home. They'd opened his mail. They'd shadowed him. They'd investigated everybody he came in contact with, copied his desk calendar, verified his appointments, including doctors and dentists. They'd tracked family holidays, his children's schools and teachers, dinner parties given and attended. They'd even snooped on his son Tony's babysitters and his stepson Timmy's psychotherapist.

Chambers had also accused Alger of conspiracy; if there was any evidence of that, HUAC could get him under the Smith Act, a piece of legislation specifically aimed at curbing the Communist Party. Up to twenty years in jail.

This afternoon, nobody mentioned any of this. Nobody suggested sending a team of committee researchers to comb through the FBI files on Alger—see if the Bureau had missed anything. Nobody so much as asked how far back the files went. But then several staff members were former FBI agents; the Committee itself had received the appropriation—$100,000—"to be used exclusively by the FBI" to investigate anybody subversive in government. They already knew that investigations under the Hatch Act had turned up nothing and that Secretary of State G. Howland Shaw had informed J. Edgar Hoover himself of precisely that. They already knew that what they were working with today was rumor and hearsay. And they also knew that the FBI's source for it was the same as J. B. Matthews's. Same as Ray Murphy's. Same as Father Cronin's. Same as their own investigative team's.

One Whittaker Chambers.

Nixon does talk about Alger as a plain old Communist—not a conspirator or a spy—but only to dismiss the idea. He says he told the Committee "it would be virtually impossible to prove that Hiss was or was not a Communist—for that would simply be his word against Chambers." But over the years Chambers had given the FBI something well in excess of two hundred names; surely one of them must have known Alger as a Communist too. And then the Communist Party was a legal association. Don't all legal associations have membership rosters? Wouldn't the FBI have access to the Communist Party's? Especially with the Smith Act in force? What about informers? Hadn't the FBI infiltrated the Communist Party? Nobody so much as asked the questions. Nixon told his committee that "we should be able to establish by corroborative testimony whether or not the two men knew each other. If Hiss were lying about not knowing Chambers, then he might also be lying about whether he was or was not a Communist."[22]

If he was lying, he was "therefore guilty of perjury."

⌾

My cousin Eleanor Barrett, retired Deputy District Attorney for Los Angeles County, explains his reasoning:

> Often people are convicted of a related charge because it is much easier to prove: income tax evasion for drug dealing, conspiracy for murder, perjury for some other crime.[23]

Tax evasion is what the FBI used to put Al Capone in Alcatraz. They used it again to put Nixon's mentor Mickey Cohen in the same place. Nixon saw just such an opportunity here: there was a statute that just might metamorphose his total lack of evidence into something very exciting.

Espionage was where that excitement lay in all HUAC's cases; it was their job description: *Hearings Regarding Communist Espionage in the United States.* The trouble is, they'd never come close to pinning it on anybody, and for some time there'd been Congressional rumors of cuts in the Committee's budget and rumors of abolishing the Committee altogether after November's election. There were grumbles in the press about their methods. Espionage has a three-year statute of limitations; it had long since run out for Alger. Sounds like a lucky break for him, doesn't it? It wasn't. Not remotely so.

For Nixon, this was the statute that would nail Alger to the wall.

Espionage is *hard* to prove. Nixon would have needed at least two witnesses to the same overt act—to something that was criminal in intent—with evidence that proved the intent was to injure the state, and even though Chambers had named two hundred people as Communists, Nixon had only the one witness against Alger: Chambers himself. There'd have to be evidence of classified documents destined for the Soviet Union. He'd have to have some important, sensitive material to show for it. He had neither. The FBI was useless. It could produce *nothing* that showed Alger as other than a squeaky-clean Boy Scout.

The statute of limitations changed everything. Because of it Nixon didn't have to bother with any of the messy details, and he could seem outraged that the law stood in his way. All perjury calls for is the one witness, and here was Chambers right on hand and on record. Furthermore, that wondrous statute of limitations kept him safe from charges of espionage himself even though he'd confessed in public to years of it. Nor did perjury need the documentation that the FBI had failed to get on Alger. It didn't need classified documents. It just needed something—almost anything—that might indicate a liar beneath the polished Hiss exterior. Proof was an unnecessary detail.

Most important of all, that statute would get Nixon a head start on his reelection campaign as the hero of the Red Peril—and beat back both Congressional grumbles and media rumors while he did it. But it was a hell of a gamble. Alger was an important man with powerful friends. Nixon was an obscure, first-term Congressman. On the other hand, being a newbie meant he had little to lose; if HUAC went down, it would take the other members with it, but so far his role had been so minor that nobody would remember he'd been part of it.

He also had lots to gain. There is a famous quote by Robespierre:

> Bring me the greatest patriot in France. Get him to write six lines on any subject, and I'll find something in them to hang him.

Nixon was as smart as Robespierre, and all he'd needed was the single sentence that Alger had written in his telegram to the Committee: "I do not know Mr. Chambers and insofar as I am aware have never laid eyes on him." To lesser minds—like mine—there doesn't seem to be anything here to make anything out of, much less a hanging. How he must have dazzled the others, how awed they must have been to watch a modern-day Robespierre extract the first strands of the hangman's rope from that single sentence.

Describing that afternoon session, Nixon wrote that he had been poring over the transcript—when? at the Horse? while he ate his lunch and listened to the news?—and that Alger "had been careful never to state categorically that he did not know Whittaker Chambers. He had always qualified his answer by saying that he did not know a man 'by the name of Whittaker Chambers.'" I reread the testimony. I scanned it. Alger never used the phrase. Not once. The transcript shows him very, very clear that he knew the *name* Whittaker Chambers. As he said, the FBI mentioned it to him when they questioned him. A *person* with that name? No. But he couldn't swear he'd never seen the guy in the photographs they'd shown him. He said so more than once.

Certainly seems like a gossamer thread for a hangman's rope.

But this is Nixon, and he had a trick up his sleeve. He knew that Chambers had not used the name Whittaker Chambers in 1937. HUAC's head of research was Ben Mandel, an ex-Communist. Back when Mandel was an active Communist, he was the very man to issue Chambers with "a red party book" listing his party number and "stamped with the party's rubber seal" (a hammer and sickle).[24] He'd been working for HUAC since 1939,[25] and he had told Nixon that Chambers had been using the name "Carl";[26] Nixon says so himself in *Six Crises*.

So we're back with this morning's enigma: if there is a known confusion between Carl and Chambers, why wasn't Chambers here in person this morning? Just as mystifying, nobody suggests getting him and Alger together now. The evidence of choreography grows stronger and stronger. This morning's hearing gave Nixon a chance to take Alger's measure. He had seen Harvard arrogance and upper-class overconfidence. He'd also seen somebody whose memory wasn't quite as good as he thought it was and whose temper made him rash, somebody who had said, "I carefully read the entire transcript of Mr. Chambers's testimony"—and yet was too angry to catch Mundt's piece of made-up dialogue.[27]

Nixon saw somebody throwing down a gauntlet in a game he did not even know existed, much less how to play.

But probably taking the man's measure was no more than second-ary. Probably the main purpose this morning was to showcase for the American public that this dangerous Communist could fool even a committee dedicated to uncovering Reds like him. That was scene one. This executive session is scene two: we watch lightbulbs clicking on above Nixon and Stripling.

And seeing all this as a scripted performance reveals the reason Chambers was not present this morning. If the two men had come face-to-face, the whole thing would have been cleared up in front of a huge audience of witnesses; however uncertain the identity at first, a little exploration would have clarified it.

Nixon was a decade younger than Alger. His mother was a Quaker from a prosperous family, who'd married into the working classes.[1] His childhood was all in the American tradition, weekends and hours after school in his father's grocery store and gas station. Not that bad a life really, but money was always short, and three of the five Nixon brothers died of those strange illnesses that children don't get anymore. Richard was the smart one. He was seriously smart too, very much Alger's equal in raw brainpower. He won the Harvard Club of California's award for "best all-round student," and there was talk of scholarships to both Harvard and Yale.[2] Nixon yearned for all that, for the East Coast and the upper-class life it offered, but a new baby meant his family needed his labor; he ended up at Whittier College.

It takes a good generation or two to escape the American class system, and Richard Nixon was trapped. His carriage, gait, facial expressions, hand gestures, and especially his use of words and phrasing: they all gave him away. Not even Whittier's elite organization, the Franklin Club, would admit him. Nobody doubted his intelligence, though, and he still dreamed of the East and transmogrification. His chance finally came when Duke University School of Law gave him a full scholarship, a taste of the upper crust, an inside view of how the Alger Hisses of the world functioned. He hadn't met Alger Hiss yet, but he knew the type. Everybody does. The Alger Hisses rule the globe. They radiate power and entitlement, and Nixon was determined to become one of them. He had to work like a dog, but he became president of the Duke Bar Association, was inducted into honor society after honor society, graduated third in his class. This sounds like exactly the kind of student the most prestigious law firms want, and he applied to join the best.

The best wanted nothing to do with him. "Shifty-eyed" was one written assessment.[3] He was what he was, and despite Duke, it still defined him.

But his luck was set to change. As Napoleon said of choosing generals—it could just as easily apply to any other profession—"the most important quality to look for is luck."

Nixon's first great stroke of luck came *because* of those Alger Hisses. As a Quaker and a government employee, he was exempt from the draft, but a war was on and a despising social elite made the military an enticing option. He joined the Navy. That's where the poker bug bit, and poker gave him a route into the big time.

He'd heard good things about the game. He'd done some acting with the Whittier Community Players, been pretty good at it too, noted for his gift at bursting into tears on stage and on cue; he was just plain good-looking back then, broody, pugnacious but vulnerable, curly black hair with a tress tumbling over the brow. His major part was as a prosecuting attorney in Ayn Rand's *Night of January 16th*,[4] where his closing speech ended with: "Simple virtue is more powerful than arrogance. Let your verdict tell us that none shall raise his head too high in defiance of our common standards." His English teacher was his drama coach, Albert Upton, and he's the one who said, "A man who can't hold a hand in a first-class poker game is not fit to be president."[5]

Nixon was still a Quaker, and gambling was taboo. On the other hand, so was military service. Now that he had already joined the Navy, what was there to lose? Nixon never did see any action—not his fault—and bored servicemen occupy their time with poker to this very day. He learned the game from a man called Stewart, who said of him, "He became tops. He never raised unless he was convinced he held the best hand."[6] But big-time poker is about bluffing your opponent into *thinking* you hold the best hand, and Nixon plainly outclassed that first teacher. One of his later playing companions, a lieutenant called Udall, said, "I once watched him bluff a lieutenant commander out of $1,200 with a pair of deuces."[7]

Nixon earned a small fortune in the Navy. There is disagreement about just how much he had in his pockets when he went back home to Whittier; guesses put it at anywhere between $3,000 and $10,000—a lot of money in 1946.

⤜⤛

Nixon also owed his second great stroke of luck to those Alger Hisses, although this time it looks like he had the upper hand. He started out the year 1945 as one of thousands of World War II veterans without a job waiting at home. By the end of summer, he was the Republican Party's candidate for the United States House of Representatives. Most biographers pass over this metamorphosis as though it were an ordinary event, although one does label it a "mystery."[8] Picking through what's known, I've found a possible explanation.

In January of 1945, Lieutenant Commander Nixon was transferred to the Navy's Bureau of Aeronautics to help wind up wartime contracts. Stories differ about just what these were. Maybe to do with "aircraft firms such as Bell and Glen Martin"?[9] That's not going to get him anywhere. The Nazi oil cartel, Kontinentale Ol A. G.?[10] Anthony Summers, in his heavily researched biography of Nixon, *The Arrogance of Power*, borrows a theory from a former Army intelligence officer and prosecutor with the Justice Department investigating Nazis; this prosecutor says British and American agents confirmed that Kontinentale's lawyers were Sullivan and Cromwell of Wall Street, one of the most famous law firms in the world.

It's a reasonable claim. For many years before World War II, Sullivan and Cromwell were enthusiastic supporters of the Nazis, even opening letters to German clients with "Seig Heil." They managed many contracts between US corporations and Nazi cartels that resulted in massive profits for American and German investors.[11] "Nazi Clients" takes up a whole chapter in *A Law Unto Itself*, a history of the firm by journalists for *The Economist* and the *Financial Times* in London. These deals were so widely known even at the time that American columnist Drew Pearson listed some of them in his nationwide syndicated column, the *Washington Merry-go-round*.[12]

The lawyer who had vouched for Kontinentale personally was one Allen Dulles, soon to become Director of the CIA.[13] Sullivan & Cromwell also handled the infamous I. G. Farben, which went on to create and manufacture Zyklon-B, the lethal gas used in the gas chambers. The lawyer who represented Farben—as well as many other German corporations including the steel magnate Krupp—in their agreements with American-based multinationals was a senior partner, John Foster Dulles, Allen Dulles's brother, future Secretary of State.[14] "Without Dulles," wrote the authors of *A Law Unto Itself*, "Germany would have lacked the negotiating strength" to make such deals. As former *New York Times* reporter Stephen Kinzer notes in his book *The Brothers*, John Foster tightened America's ties to Germany after Hitler came to power; the firm "thrived on its cartels and collusion with the new Nazi regime."[15]

War broke out. Sullivan and Cromwell kept up its business with its German clients all the way through. The authors of *A Law Unto Itself* cover many details of the firm's dealings from the files of the Economic Warfare Unit of the Justice Department; they title their chapter "The Dulles War Machine." John Foster continued to represent I. G. Farben, helping them with rubber patents that "almost created a crippling shortage of rubber in the United States." He handled agreements with Bosch that "gave the Nazis a stranglehold on American engine production."[16] But his "most significant wartime activity hindered America's manufacture of diesel-fuel injection motors."[17] Motors like that were vital in war; there was no known substitute for them.

In 1945, this same Dulles was Chairman of the Carnegie Endowment for International Peace. Soon to be Alger's boss.

And Sullivan and Cromwell were the biggest and most prestigious of the Eastern firms the young Nixon had applied to; they were the very ones who'd pronounced him "shifty-eyed" before they tossed him out the door. Biographer Summers's Justice Department prosecutor says Nixon took his information about Nazi collaboration to Allen Dulles. Dulles told him "to keep quiet about what he had seen, and in return arranged to finance the young man's first congressional campaign against Jerry Voorhis."[18]

It's a good story, but Nixon didn't really need money. He had his poker winnings, more than enough for a Congressional campaign in those days—at least a straightforward one. What he needed was political contacts, which he surely didn't have. How is an unknown to enter national politics without them? And in a matter of a few months at that?

In August 1945, the Committee of One Hundred Men in California—representatives of the state's big money, banks, oilmen—placed an advertisement in twenty-six newspapers:

> WANTED—Congressman candidate with no previous political experience to defeat a man who has represented the district in the House for ten years. Any young man, resident of district, preferably a veteran, fair education, no political strings or obligations.[19]

As soon as it appeared, one Herman Perry, Vice President of the Bank of America in California, founding branch of the largest banking institution in the country, talked to Nixon on the phone and asked only two questions, "Arc you a Republican and are you available?"[20]

There is no way a man at the top of the Republican machine in California is going to offer so spectacular an opportunity to an unknown clodhopper like Nixon without pressure from someone higher in the pecking order than he is: someone like Allen Dulles or his brother John Foster.

⟨∞⟩

Nixon's third great stroke of luck was the state he had been born in and his home town's location in it.

Whittier just happened to be in the Twelfth District of Los Angeles, and the Twelfth District was mobster Mickey Cohen's turf. Cohen was a Hollywood thug, tough and brutal, Tommy guns and bleached-blonde molls, such a flamboyant figure that he became a regular feature under his own name in such A-list movies as *LA Confidential*. The story is that a man called Murray Chotiner, Cohen's lawyer and PR man, spotted Nixon at the One Hundred Men's candidate selection board dinner and fixed up a meeting at a restaurant where even the name comes out of A-list mobster films: Goodfellow's Grotto.

> A little fish house where politicians met and where they pull the screens across the booths for these kinds of talks.[21]

At least that's the way Nixon's biographer Anthony Summers tells it, and it's another good story that ought to be the truth. Cohen himself says the Grotto was a coffee shop, and what he told Nixon was, "We got some ideas, we may put some things in motion."[22] Cohen didn't like Nixon, agreed with the "shifty-eyed" assessment, had a "bad feeling" about him, said he looked like "a three-card Monte dealer" or a "rough hustler of some kind."[23] But Cohen controlled the district's gambling rackets, and Nixon was a poker player who knew how to win. They bargained. Nixon wanted more than Cohen was offering. "I jewed him down to $5,000," said Cohen and tossed in office space to house the "Nixon for Congress" headquarters.[24]

Murray Chotiner was more important than Cohen's money, and Chotiner looked like somebody out of *LA Confidential* or *Goodfellas* too: monogrammed white-on-white dress shirts and silk ties, jewelled stickpins, clock-face cufflinks. He had no middle name, introduced himself as Murray M. Chotiner—the monograms read "MMC"—because a middle name had a classy sound.

It was under Chotiner's direction that Nixon acquired the nickname "Tricky Dick." His opponent was Jerry Voorhis, a five-term incumbent, a liberal Democrat, a Roosevelt man, and a loyal supporter of the New Deal. He'd been in office for a decade. He was well-liked and respected.[25] Washington newsmen conducted a poll and rated him highest in integrity of all 435 members of the House of Representatives as well as its hardest-working member. He was unbeatable. He knew it, and he was as certain as Alger that Nixon presented no threat.

There were many innovations in Nixon's campaign, some crude, some ingenious, all of them adding up to a scary new presence on the political scene.

First there's free labor. The Bank of America, the biggest bank in the country, began in California; it had many hundreds of outlets there. Its vice president, Herman Perry was the very man who'd pulled Nixon into this race. Perry made volunteer work for the Nixon campaign a job condition for bank employees.

Second, there's money. Vast amounts of it. Cash flowing in from the Committee of One Hundred Men built up to a Nixon pot of something like $40,000, and that's not counting Cohen and poker winnings.[26] Postwar America was going through tough times. There were nationwide shortages; the display window of the "Nixon for Congress" headquarters was full of things like toasters and pressure cookers that people hadn't seen for sale in years. A sign informed passersby that if they answered the telephone with "Vote for Nixon," they'd get one. How did Nixon get hold of such stuff? Nobody knows. Nobody knows who set up the agreement with the big California papers, either—or at what price—for so much front-page space per week "not for ads but for planted news stories and pictures."[27] One of these stories—it appeared in the *Los Angeles Times*—reported that Nixon's total campaign expenses were $370 compared with $1,000 for Voorhis.

Nixon pressed even the family shopping basket into his battle. When butchers and grocers ran short of supplies, they put up posters in their windows: "No meat today. See your Congressman."

What gave all this cohesion and force was the Red baiting. This is where Nixon's leaking got its start. He leaked that Voorhis had entered "six pro-Soviet votes"[28] in Congress. It wasn't true. The country was plagued with strikes as well as shortages; everybody not in a union blamed the unions. Nixon's leaks tied Voorhis to the pro-labor, Communist, and socialist sympathies of Vito Marcantonio, a left-wing representative from New York City. More leaks tied him to the political action committee of the CIO, the Congress of Industrial Organizations, and offered this as proof of collaboration with Communist-controlled labor unions.

Here's an ad from the *Pomona Progress-Bulletin*:

> A vote for Nixon is a vote against
> Communistic principles
> and the CIO's gigantic slush fund![29]

In the first Nixon/Voorhis debate, Voorhis charged Nixon with misleading advertising just like this. Nixon leaped to his feet, whipped a paper out of his pocket, waved it over his head at the audience, and announced that he held in his hand a document that proved the "Red CIO" was backing Voorhis.

What was this document?

Nobody ever got the chance to see.

A massive telephone campaign targeted potential voters. Sometimes the caller—a woman—would identify herself as a Minutewoman or a Liberty Belle: "Did you know Jerry Voorhis had Communistic sympathies? As a patriotic citizen, I thought you should know." There were variations: "This is a friend of yours, but I can't tell you my name. I just want to tell you Jerry Voorhis is a Communist." Again, none of it even remotely true. Voorhis was a vocal anti-Communist; he was actually a member of HUAC. "I know Jerry Voorhis wasn't a Communist,"[30] Nixon said on his tapes,[31] "I suppose there was scarcely ever a man with higher ideals . . . But I had to win. That's the thing you don't understand. The important thing is to win."[32]

And win he did: by a landslide.

———— ⌘ ————

Nixon's final great stroke of luck was Alger Hiss himself. And he didn't even have to work for that one. Alger demanded it.

Here's *Time* magazine in May 1945, in an article written under the aegis of none other than senior editor Whittaker Chambers: "In a class by himself was young, handsome Alger Hiss, the US state department career man functioning as international secretary general. Relaxed and alert amid innumerable annoyances, Hiss was master of the incredibly complicated conference machinery. Wheels turned. The charter of a world organization was taking shape."[33]

Not long afterward, he appeared as *Life* magazine's "Picture of the Week," stepping out of a special army plane, carrying the UN charter itself.[34]

Alistair Cooke of the BBC pronounced him an American gentleman, a subject for Henry James: "a product of New World courtesy, with a gentle certitude of behavior, a ready warmth, a brighter and naïver grace than the more trenchant, fatigued, or worldlier English prototypes."[35]

How could the boy from Whittier *not* hate such a one? As Stripling put it in an interview with Nixon's biographer, Anthony Summers, "Nixon had his hat set for Hiss . . . It was a personal thing. He was no more concerned about whether Hiss was [a Communist] than a billy goat."[36]

The list of Communists that Rep Busby read out in Alger's hearing? The one that was even more boring than he was? "Tom Tippett, E. J. Lever . . ." That's the thing about working on books. They're like legal cases. You can't anticipate what they're going to throw at you. Just as my eyes were glazing over, I'd hit "Mildred Edie Brady, Robert A. Brady—"

Hey, wait a minute here. That's my mother and father.

What in hell were they doing in that hearing room? I had to think hard to come up with any ideas at all.

My economist father, professor at the University of California in Berkeley, wrote a book called *The Spirit and Structure of German Fascism*.[1] It warned of Hitler's Germany several years before World War II broke out. This foresight was not welcome. It made him a "premature antifascist," a suspected Communist; in HUAC's view only Communists were worried about Hitler back then because only Russia was worried about him. HUAC subpoenaed my father to testify, which meant he was an "unfriendly witness." He lost his job as a consultant in the New Deal's Office of Price Administration.

My mother was a journalist who wrote for *Consumer Reports*, published then as now by Consumers Union; that's the same association Dexter became director of, and it was one of the first that HUAC listed as a "Communist front organization." Because of her, Herman Perry, the very man who'd put his bank behind Nixon's run for Congress, was a familiar name in my house. Bank of America had been heavily involved in financing the illegal rearmament of Hitler's Germany. She'd interviewed Perry; she'd written articles about the bank's dirty practices. Only Communists attacked big banking.

A request for my parents' FBI files under the Freedom of Information Act resulted in a second shock to the system. Here's what they had to say about my father's file:

> The records which may be responsive to your request . . . Were destroyed June 1, 1990 and June 27, 1990.[2]

Destroyed? On two separate days decades ago? What could have happened? Lost in a move from one warehouse to another? Some office error?

There was no explanation.

And then came a letter about my mother's file:

> The records which may be responsive to your request . . . Were destroyed on November 24, 1964, January 26, 1965, February 5, 1990 and January 7, 1978.[3]

There's no escaping it. FBI agents finger through files again and again, shredding one chunk, then another. Why would they do that? Is it even legal?

A follow-up letter from the National Archives only confused things: the files of my mother's that the FBI had destroyed, did in fact exist but contained "national security classified material" stored away in something called "Record Group 65." A review was necessary. The Archives would conduct it. Once complete, my mother's case would "be inserted in our Simple Case processing queue (less than 1000 pages of material) for NARA review for other sensitivities."[4]

My mother has been dead for half a century. How could she be a threat to national security? What "other sensitivities" could possibly be involved? Much less call for *two* reviews?

All I had to go on was the mention of Record Group 65. According to the Archives website, this group has to do with looking into collaboration with the Nazis. Her articles about the Bank of America? But who cares all these years later?

13

1948

Alger's public triumph must have had a nervous edge for him despite his contempt for HUAC. He had gone prepared to answer charges, and nobody showed any interest in them. He had tried to introduce them several times himself, and still nobody wanted to hear.

> Yesterday upon the stair
> I met a man who wasn't there.

Everybody knew this song back then; it spent eleven weeks on the Hit Parade at the start of the war. The absent Chambers was just like that, center stage and yet unseen. Alger wrote that "Chambers' identity pre-occupied me." There was a vague familiarity to the face, but Alger was a bad case of a "name" person[1]: if somebody stuck a face with the wrong name, he couldn't sort out the mixed signals. This was somebody he *had* to see. Some other aspect—the voice, its cadences, the carriage—might well break through the confusion and trigger his memory. Which certainly raises a question. Alger knew Chambers was a senior editor at *Time*. So why didn't he just charge over to the *Time* offices and demand a face-to-face?

The entire case would have ended there and then.

A US Navy medical corps psychoanalyst called Meyer Zeligs asked him why not. "I discussed it by telephone with my lawyer, William

Marbury," Alger said, "who saw no particular *dis*advantage."[2] Nor could Zeligs. It seems the most obvious next step.

But Alger also consulted his boss, John Foster Dulles, Chairman of the Carnegie Endowment. "Dulles was strongly opposed to it as improper" because HUAC had assumed jurisdiction of the matter.[3] "Improper?" That would stop Alger in his tracks. He believed in the rule of law. He believed there was a right way and a wrong way to do things. Dulles knew him well. They'd been at Yalta together, drafted the United Nations Charter together; Dulles had proposed Alger's selection as president of the Carnegie Endowment.

Why would Alger suspect a man like that of plotting behind his back? And with Nixon of all people? And yet there were secret meetings in the Dulles suite at the Hotel Roosevelt. John W. Davis, ex-ambassador to the UK, one-time presidential candidate, and member of the Carnegie board: "Unknown to Hiss, Nixon was encouraged in his resolve to pursue the matter by Dulles and his brother Allen."[4]

The Dulles brothers' wartime collaboration with German cartels had not stopped with the end of the war.[5] It continued—as massively profitable as ever—right into the peace that followed. What could be better cover for it than a chase after Communists in the high echelons of government? And chasing after Communists was certainly the wave of the future for Nixon.

In *Six Crises*, there's no mention of recesses to meet Dulles. Not yet. There's no mention of media interviews about Alger either, even though Nixon's plan, as he revealed it decades later in his Presidential tapes, had little to do with the niceties of perjury. He was going to "convict the sonofabitch in the press."[6] How was he to achieve this aim? "I had to leak stuff all over the place."[7] That very afternoon, while the Committee was bewailing the terrible state the hearing left them in, newspapers were preparing evening editions. Nixon was on the verge of cracking open "the whole spy case."[8] Even the *New York Times* reported "a Committee spokesman" as saying so.[9] The United Press sent out a similar dispatch for the next morning.

There is a "strict security blackout" on the Committee's actions; despite it, there's a "mystery witness" who will corroborate Chambers.[10] Amazing. A volunteer appears to make a statement publicly denying charges, testifies so impressively that the Committee fears for its own survival, and he's hardly left the Caucus Room before newspapers have him down as a suspect spy with mystery witnesses against him.

Nixon doesn't mention travel plans in *Six Crises,* either, but the next day's *New York Times* reported that "a special committee, its members unidentified, left Washington tonight for an undisclosed destination."[11]

Before I started in on this book, I knew nothing about the man credited with bringing Alger down, but anybody who brings down a powerful man has to be interesting. It's hard to imagine a winner more unlike the loser in this battle; Whittaker Chambers was fat, squat, pulpy, a crumpled toad of a man in a dishevelled suit, an anguished bisexual when not being straight was worse than being the Communist he readily admitted to being. It was a fiercely prejudiced and unforgiving time. A repentant Communist was entitled to billing as a prodigal son. A bisexual was filth. A few years on and the two would become equal sinners; the infamous Senator McCarthy would declare, "If you want to be against McCarthy, boys, you've got to be either a Communist or a cocksucker."

There's an intensity to Chambers in the photographs, a difficult face—something of a grumpy pout—but a depth in the eyes, a vulnerable softness around them, and a complexity in the way the brows knit between them. No beauty, yet he catches the attention. And he certainly livens the script.

He says in his autobiography *Witness* that he was born on April Fools Day 1901, a Paul Bunyan of a baby, gargantuan, fourteen inches across the shoulders. But no baby that large could survive. He says there was a fierce snowstorm raging outside. But meteorological records show spring warmth and no precipitation. There was a need for this fabulist's imagination in his childhood. His mother told him that his father didn't want him. The father was never at home, drunk when he was. The mother kept an axe underneath her bed to ward off intruders. The grandmother screamed all night. Maybe Alzheimer's. Maybe terminal syphilis, very common in those days. He and his brother made suicide pacts, and the brother ended up with his head in a gas oven. Chambers was bullied at school, called "Stinky" and "Mr. Chambers Pot." He was very bright, though; when it came to graduation from high school, he was given the honor of foretelling the future of class members. He loved to shock, and he did not disappoint; he said one girl was going to turn into a whore.

He ran away from home right after graduation, worked as a laborer in Baltimore and lived in New Orleans in a house with a real whore called "One-Eyed Annie." Or so he says. Then came a week at Williams College that ended with letters to his roommate about traffic with the devil.[1] He entered Columbia University and shocked people there too: kicked out for producing "A Play for Puppets"—Jesus Christ as a queen. Blasphemy was the charge. His style is ornate and occasionally lapses into gush that doesn't work, but he has that fabulist's imagination and an extraordinary eye for detail. The eminent poet Mark Van Doren, teaching at Columbia at the time, pronounced the play "brilliant."[2] Others thought Chambers would be the literary genius of the age. Columbia pushed him out even so, and there's a tidy irony in that the president of the university was Alger's predecessor at the Carnegie Endowment.

Chambers blames Columbia radicals alone for his communist convictions; he says he went straight from the campus to join the Party. But then he also says that he took a summer trip to Europe, saw war-torn Germany and because of it, plunged into communist literature as soon as he got home; his reading alone persuaded him to join the Party. There is nothing to indicate either story is true. Records show only that he spent more than three years after leaving Columbia—and after getting home from Europe—tending a desk in the newspaper department of the New York Public Library and publishing poems about the beauty of the countryside and the anguish of a misunderstood young man. He bragged to other librarians that he was storing illegal Communist material in his locker. The cops broke into it and found only a box full of books stolen from various libraries, including Columbia's. End of job.

Only then does any record of Communist activity begin.

Chambers wrote that he was the "indispensable man" at the *Daily Worker,* the "acting editor . . .who daily set forth a political line." Sadly, the records of the US Communist Party show that he was only the "Workers Correspondent." He did better with the *New Masses,* this time as a member of the editorial board, as a reporter and as the candidate for a job to write a book about the "'daily life' of a young Communist" in a way that only the "skilful handling of imaginative literature can achieve."[3]

He was also translating for commercial publishers. One of his earliest jobs was the famous children's book *Bambi. Bambi?* What child hasn't seen the Disney film? Baby deer lost in the forest without its mother. And here's the man who introduced the story to an English-speaking audience and to Walt Disney himself. Translators are badly treated—there probably weren't any royalties—but with *Bambi* behind him, Chambers was in huge demand.

Meantime, his poetry took off in a new direction: "As your sap drains out into me . . ." and "The leaves so pensile, so tremulously hung . . .Unable to strain farther into one another." He didn't limit his man-chasing to words, either. Meyer Zeligs, the shrink who asked Alger why he hadn't confronted Chambers, interviewed Chambers's friends and acquaintances—Chambers himself sensibly refused to talk to the guy—and quotes one poor soul who put Chambers up for the night. The man reported:

> In the middle of the night I suddenly awoke in the midst of having an orgasm. When I saw him labouring at my penis still in his mouth, I pushed him aside while moving myself way from him. My shock was so great that . . . the only words I could manage to speak were, "You get out of here."[4]

That's rape, isn't it? He lay in wait for this man, trapped him, exploited him in his sleep.

That's what a predator does, isn't it? He didn't confine his predation to men, either. There were women too, quite a number of them.

When he confessed his misdeeds to the FBI—which he did in surprising detail—it was the abortions that upset them most.

But being a communist was his primary occupation in life. As he tells the story, he wasn't just a Communist, he was a real, live spy of the le Carré variety. There was none of the society flitting of England's famous quintet, the Cambridge Five, all rich boys with the best possible educations behind them. Nor the intellectual circles of accused atomic spies Klaus Fuchs, Alan Nunn May, and Julius Rosenberg. Chambers's was life in the film noir shadows of thrillerdom, handlers, code names, secret meetings, secrets on microfilm. His life was constantly in danger.

During a two-year relationship with a woman called Ida Dales, he used to sit with a shotgun across his knees all night, telling her that he "expected the worst."[5] What? From whom? The eminent critic Lionel Trilling, a fellow student at Columbia, based a character in his book *The Middle of the Journey* on him; this character was always in danger and "always reminding everyone that he was a secret Communist agent."[6] The writer Matthew Josephson, famous for his book *The Robber Barons*, knew Chambers at the same time and reported that "literally dozens of people in Greenwich Village and Connecticut, in 1933, knew all about his espionage activities."[7] He made himself out to be "a desperate sort of secret agent,[8] carried a big revolver with him and told everyone that the US secret service agents were forever trailing him from place to place.

Tying down any of this is an exercise in that wonderful expression, "nailing jelly to the wall." Despite HUAC making heavy duty of the phrase "a man by the name of Whittaker Chambers," he was born Jay Vivian Chambers and didn't become Whittaker Chambers until he entered Columbia University. And Whittaker was only one of a list of aliases: Lloyd Cantwell, David Chambers, David Whittaker, Charles Whittaker, Arthur Dwyer, Hugh Jones, Harold Phillips, John Kelly, John Land, John Grass, Malvern Hill, Julian Fetchner. Sometimes he called himself Adams. Just Adams. No first name. Sometimes he was Bob, who had no last name or Carl, who had no last name either. Except when he was Carl Carlson. He was David Breen for two years via thrillerdom's traditional route of searching out a dead child who'd be about his age, picking up the birth certificate, and applying for the passport.[9] The point? To set up a Communist apparatus in London. Somehow nothing happened. He became Jay Lea Chambers briefly and almost by accident. He was living in Baltimore under variations of the name Jay Chambers and happened to find a Jay Lea Chambers in the telephone book. Poor Jay Lea Chambers. He and his wife were dunned with statements from Baltimore and Washington department stores for purchases made by another Jay Chambers.[10] Not just scrounging now but moving on to credit theft as well as identity theft.

Scrounging was a way of life with him, not that he needed money. His own income probably was pretty meager after he left the *Worker* and the *New Masses*. He says the Communist Party paid him to spy. There were translations and erotic poetry, which probably didn't bring in much. But his wife had a regular job. So did his mother, and she gave him whatever he asked for whenever he asked for it. Over the years, he inherited at least $10,000 as his relatives died off—a lot of money back then. Even so, he was forever telling people about how poor he was, forever borrowing, rarely paying back. He loved play-acting the poverty-stricken man of the people. Not always an American man of the people either. He'd been abroad only once, but he readily assumed foreign accents and foreign mannerisms as well as varying names. Some people thought he was German. Some Polish.

Then in 1937—that crucial year in the Hiss case—he renounced communism. As he said himself in his August 3, 1948 HUAC hearing, "In 1937, I repudiated Marxist doctrines and Lenin's tactics."

He was terrified of the consequences. And he certainly should have been; this was during the period of Stalin's Great Purge and political suspects were being executed by the thousands. Any communist who'd taken any part—however small—in Soviet espionage, opting out and heading for the FBI had to be on a hit list. If Chambers wanted to live, he had to go very deep into hiding and he had to do it at once.

And yet he didn't. Not remotely. He would have been painfully easy for the most amateur of sleuths to find. He was living at 2216 Mt Royal

Terrace, Baltimore, landlord a Dr. Eleanor Pancost, and he was listed at that address in the Baltimore telephone book under the name he was born with, Jay V. Chambers.[11] He'd been working at a regular day job with the Research Project of the Works Progress Administration in Washington again under that name; the index he'd been working on did finish in early 1938, but he remained officially on the WPA's employment books, "furloughed," awaiting a position for which he was "deemed qualified."[12]

He also took a serious risk of getting caught by the cops. The Jay Lea Chambers whose identity he stole from the Baltimore telephone book turned out to be an economist and a senior administrator for the Treasury Department. His personal dossier went missing from the State Department files[13]. Whittaker's wife Esther made out a credit application for the Baltimore Credit Bureau as the wife of Jay Lea Chambers, "senior administrative officer, Treasury Department." That's why the administrator and his wife were billed by Baltimore and Washington department stores for purchases they hadn't made.

As if that wasn't enough exposure, he went looking for writing work under the name Whittaker Chambers, the name he'd come to favor, the name he'd registered at Columbia with, and the name he'd used when he joined the Communist Party. His search took him to his old teacher Mark van Doren, a late-night visit with tales of Soviet agents out to kill him;[14] he wanted recommendations to literary editors. Nor was Van Doren the only one he approached. A Columbia classmate got him a job with an English publisher who worried that his "violently anti-Communist views"[15] showed hysteria and persecution mania, while the author of the book he translated seemed convinced that he was "hiding from the Russian secret service."[16]

❧❧

In early 1939, articles appeared in *The Saturday Evening Post* about the big, controversial literary event of the day: the memoirs of Walter Krivitsky, Russian spy. Chambers composed a story about his own life as a spy, signed it "Carl," which he explained in the manuscript was his KGB codename; he asked another Columbia classmate, journalist Herbert Solow, for advice on how to market the work. Solow had two suggestions: a man terrified of assassination would seem pretty unwise to sign his confessions with his codename, and the best person to consult about publishing was Isaac Don Levine, Krivitsky's editor and a rabid anti-Communist.[17]

Levine said he couldn't publish the manuscript as it stood. Nobody could. It was full of shadowy conspiracies and shadowy conspirators, but this had to be journalism; it needed hard facts and real people. It needed names.

Levine offered to help him "develop" it.

In the fall the two of them took the story to Assistant Secretary of State Adolf Berle. There were names in it now, no spies, but quite a number of State Department officials, one of them being Alger Hiss. The hard facts weren't exactly hard; they were hearsay at best, and only about people who were supposed to have formed a reading group of communist sympathizers. Even so it was a shocking accusation, very much the equivalent of accusing State Department officials today of belonging to a group of terrorist sympathizers. But as soon as Berle asked questions, the story began to crumble; Berle dismissed Chambers as a "crackpot".

That same year Chambers caught the break he'd always wanted; he became a staff writer on *Time*. Not that he changed his name or took himself out of the telephone directory. Nor was he any less noisily anti-Communist than he'd been with the British publisher. But he could act on his convictions. He cut dispatches to remove any favorable references to Russia. This was a serious problem for the magazine because Russia was America's crucial ally at the time; *Time* moved him to the book review department. Nothing could have been better for him. There for the first time in his life he began to gain the respect of people he respected.

What he calls "the tranquil years" crept in.[18]

He did not give up his project with Levine, though. Over the next decade—Levine always ready with counsel—the two of them worked together on it. The US secret service agents who had been trailing him throughout his Greenwich Village years were replaced by Soviet hitmen. The list of secret Reds changed constantly, sometimes shorter but usually longer, and gradually the unsalable story about a reading group of communist sympathizers developed into a secret cell being groomed to influence policy, then to committed communists with no involvement in espionage, then to a network of hardened spies deep in the government and intent on destroying the American way of life.

He made many statements to the FBI, fifteen or twenty of them, but Bureau agents struggled to find some connection they could use—*anything*—between Chambers, the Soviets, and the names. Their liaison, special assistant to the US Attorney General Thomas Donegan, was an experienced interrogator; he'd headed the FBI's "Comintern Apparatus Squad" investigating Communist activities. His conclusion? Chambers had a "loose memory"[19] that was "definite" when it came to "unimportant things" but failed him in "situations that a man of his education and background should readily recollect." Donegan's attempts to "patch" it weren't at all successful.[20]

The US Attorney's Office also tried to dig something they could use out of his stories. Their luck was no better. The Justice Department tried. Still no luck.

Meanwhile, Chambers worked hard at *Time* and rose on the masthead. He became a senior editor. He became a figure to reckon with. The future was delivering its promise.

Then came Nixon.

15

1948

Early Saturday morning, the "unidentified" members of HUAC flew out of Washington for their "undisclosed destination."[1] The Associated Press: "Mystery Witness May Crack Soviet Spy Case." Chairman Mundt "declined to say who the person is or where he is located." The only detail is that he is to be "Quizzed in Locked Room."

The destination turned out to be the Federal Building in Foley Square, New York City. The unidentified men would have landed at La Guardia and taken cabs into the city, right down to the Lower East Side. The Federal Building was one of those massive American buildings of state: Corinthian columns in Minnesota granite with Plato, Aristotle, Demosthenes, and Moses looking down on all who enter. Georgian interiors were the rage when the building went up, richly carved oak panels, fluted pilasters, leather chairs.

The mystery witness was to appear in such a room this morning before the Honorable Richard M. Nixon, who presides behind a long table. Two other Committee members flank him. So do five members of staff. The stenographer doesn't rate a mention, but she's there too. This is to be an executive session. No public. No press.

Nixon received Alger's wire on Tuesday. That left him only a day and a half to choreograph Thursday's hearing and rehearse his company; after that, a mere twenty-four hours to arrange today in New York. Energy and brilliance, yes, but think of the money! The Justice Department was already complaining that HUAC was over budget without results, and in any case, no Junior Congressman could authorize a jaunt like this all on his own and at such very short notice.

Who did? Nobody knows. And who does this mystery witness turn out to be? Whittaker Chambers. Ordinary mortals were summoned to Washington to testify. This special Congressional subcommittee of Nixon's—three United States Representatives and half a dozen staff—has flown all the way to New York to see him in one of the city's grandest buildings. Not that it was wildly convenient for him; he did work at *Time* in New York, but he lived much nearer to Washington. On the other hand, what wonderful PR that "undisclosed destination" made, especially topped off with "spy case" and the "mystery witness" whose "identity was a closely guarded secret" and whose "revelations were so startling that the entire subcommittee had to be flown" to question him.[2]

The revelations-to-come certainly whet a reader's appetite, but Saturday's testimony isn't any easier to read than Alger's on Thursday. One thing is clear at once, though; the Committee isn't acting as it did with him in front of it. The questioning then was prosecutorial—especially Nixon's—and implied all manner of accusations. This time? Everybody is polite, even deferential. Nixon does not waste a minute, though. "Mr. Hiss in his testimony was asked on several occasions," he says to Chambers, "whether or not he had ever known or knew a man by the name of Whittaker Chambers. In each instance he categorically said 'No.'"[3]

Now just a minute here. Alger never said anything like that. His doubt—his desire to clear it up—dominated his testimony. Nixon's account of the post-hearing meeting turned straightforward caution into evasion: Alger "careful never to state categorically" not knowing Chambers. Today, evasion has turned into categorical denial. And that phrase "a man by the name of" is popping up again.

"My relationship with Alger Hiss quickly transcended our formal relationship," Chambers says. "We became close friends."[4] He says he visited Alger's house regularly and many times, stayed there as a guest, made it a "kind of informal headquarters."[5] Nixon's interest picks up.

Chambers must know a great deal about how the Hisses lived back then. Let's have some detail. What about their furniture?

"The only thing I recall was a small leather cigarette box, leather-covered cigarette box with a gold tooling on it."[6]

What about their china? Chambers can't remember.[7] Silverware? Glasses? Pictures on the wall? Books in the shelves? Chambers can't remember. Nixon is endlessly patient, probing here, probing there, and Chambers does hit home with a bird Alger once saw, a black maid, a cocker spaniel. A reader senses acquaintanceship between the two men, nothing deeper, and it gets shallower as the questions go on. Did the Hisses have a piano? Chambers says not, but they did. What about alcohol? They didn't drink. But they did, and by the time I knew Alger, his expertise with wines was terrifying. Their taste in food?

"They cared nothing about food."[8] But Isabel was a good cook, and Alger plainly enjoyed food, knew good restaurants too. Religion? "He was forbidden to go to church."[9] But Alger was a lifelong Episcopalian, a regular churchgoer; his stepson Timmy Hobson sang in the choir. He describes Alger as "a man of great simplicity and a great gentleness and sweetness of character."[10]

The picture is growing into your ideal Communist with no interest in bourgeois fripperies, and yet I guess Chambers senses he is not giving Nixon the right answers because he starts chipping away at the "sweetness of character." His stepson Timmy's father "was paying for his son's education," but Alger and Priscilla "were diverting a large part of that money to the Communist Party." They had "shifted him from one school to another because there was a saving and they could contribute it to the Party."

There had been a shift in schools—Chambers got that right too—but to a more expensive one rather than a less expensive one, and Alger shouldered the difference. Those vast and detailed FBI reports told all about it. Not that anybody lets on. They just don't seem interested.

Timmy was "puny", "nervous", "effeminate"[11]; and as for Alger, "he had rather long, delicate fingers,"[12] and "his walk, if you watch him from behind, there is a slight mince" that "anybody could observe."[13]

And we all know what that means. Pictures show Timmy as a hearty, solid-looking boy. As for Alger, dancers like me notice the way people walk. No trace of a mince in him. All these Committee members had watched him too; they knew the mince was wrong. And of course if there'd been the slightest doubt of Alger's sexuality, those same FBI reports would have revealed all. Those reports also picked apart solid-looking Timmy's uncertain sex life. Nobody here seems interested in any of that.

Ben Mandel—HUAC's Director of Research, the man who issued Chambers with his Communist Party card—says he saw a photograph of Alger with "his hand cupped to his ear."[14]

"He is deaf in one ear," Chambers says promptly. Deaf? Alger? Certainly not. His hearing was exceptionally good. Chambers adds that he was "about five feet eight or nine." He was tall, over six feet, and these guys had watched the press in the Caucus Room swarm around him with congratulations: no mistaking a tall man in a crowd like that.

Time for a change of subject. Nixon asks how Chambers knew that Alger was a member of the Party.

"I was told by Mr. Peters."[15]

"Do you have any other evidence, any factual evidence, to bear out your claim that Mr. Hiss was a member of the Communist Party?"

"Nothing beyond the fact that he submitted himself for the two or three years that I knew him as a dedicated and disciplined Communist."

"Did you obtain his Party dues from him?"

"Yes, I did." At last we're getting somewhere. The Communist Party was a legal political party; its membership roster would be a matter of public record. There were secret members, though. Everybody knew that. Al Capone, jailed for tax evasion rather than big-league crime, was the answer there. A tax audit could reveal all kinds of subversive doings, just as Capone's had revealed all kinds of mob doings; and it would trap Alger Hiss as neatly as it had Capone.

Nixon wants to know how long Chambers went on collecting Alger's dues.

"Two or three years, as long as I knew him."

"And once a month over a period of two years, approximately, he gave you an envelope which contained the dues?"

"That is right."

"What did he say?"

"That was one point it wasn't necessary to say anything. At first he said, 'Here are my dues.'" Chambers adds that he collected the money "individually"[16] and that Alger was "rather pious about paying his dues promptly."[17]

What's bizarre for the reader of this testimony is that there's no excitement in the room. Here's the possibility of solid, undeniable evidence of perjury. Why aren't Committee members scrambling over each other with questions? Why isn't Nixon? And yet he just drops the subject. Nobody else says a word about it. Very mysterious. Then I remembered Attorney General Donegan's frustrations with Chambers as a witness and went back to Tuesday's testimony, the start of all this.

Nixon had asked about dues then too. Did Chambers collect them from Alger?

"No, I did not."[18] A direct contradiction in less than a week. Nixon could hardly miss that. Not that it seems to bother him. He doesn't even mention it. Nor does any other Committee member. There's another thing too. How come Nixon asked Chambers about "an envelope which contained dues"? No envelopes at all on Tuesday. No chitchat about payment, either. How could there be? On Monday Chambers said it was a guy called Collins who did the dues collection,[19] then gave Chambers a bagful of money. There's no way around it: Nixon and Chambers have been schmoozing. Somehow they managed to fit a rewrite into Nixon's frenetic few days.

Also on Tuesday, Chambers testified that Party dues "came to ten percent of whatever the individual's salary was."[20]

Alger's bank statements taken over a period of years could nail him without even bothering with the Communist Party's records of dues. A comparison of regular withdrawals against expenses is the kind of detail that trapped Al Capone. Even more mysterious: nobody on the Committee suggested the possibility on Tuesday and nobody cares about it now.

But poor Chambers. What "factual evidence" can Nixon want from him if not what he's been giving? And what about this Committee? Chambers is dead wrong on the only details they can verify for themselves. Nixon tries another tack, asks Chambers if he had "made an affidavit concerning Mr. Alger Hiss?"[21]

"I made a signed statement," Chambers says. "I should think it was about 1945. Before that, I had reported these facts at least two years before to the FBI and nine years ago to Mr. Berle and mentioned Hiss's name."

Berle? Assistant Secretary of State Adolf Berle? A big-name witness for the prosecution? Nixon pounces. "Nine years ago? Are you certain that you did mention Hiss's name to Berle?"

"I certainly mentioned Hiss's name to Berle, I was there with Berle because—" Chambers breaks off. "May we go off the record?"

This is about as irregular as it's possible to get. A witness under oath testifying on a matter of "national importance" asking to go off the record? What should happen is a stern scolding and a curt refusal.

Not a single member of the Committee seems in the slightest bit bothered. Not one of them so much as asks a question or makes a comment.

Nixon just says, "Off the record." And the transcript echoes him: "Discussion off the record."

⤫⤫⤫

If you can be sure of one thing, it's that everybody in this business is sloppy. Nobody—not even Alger's staunchest defenders—seems to have caught the sleight of hand that's about to appear. The Committee has raced through all this detail, crammed it into about twenty-five minutes. Right at the start of it came this exchange:

MR. NIXON: At what period did you know Mr. Hiss? What time?
MR. CHAMBERS: I knew Mr. Hiss roughly between the years 1935 to 1937.[22]

Here it is again: my crucial year of 1937.

Today's hearing ran for nearly three hours, and yet the testimony is only twelve pages long. Maybe half an hour in total. What this means is that more than two hours of testimony are missing from all official records. Nobody outside that room ever had a chance to know what went on, and everybody inside it is dead.[23]

When the transcript starts again, the very first entry is a question from Nixon: "Have you seen Hiss since 1938?"

This is no less than revelation. It screams, "Something of serious importance went on during those missing hours." There's a profound change in atmosphere to accompany it. The Committee members are satisfied. They're comfortable. So is Chambers. The hearing closes almost at once. Whatever happened during that long recess, it justified these guys flying all the way to New York. The only clue is that until this very moment, Chambers' break with Marx, Lenin and Alger has been 1937. Through a decade of confessions, right up through the start of this hearing the year has been 1937. Always 1937.

As for 1938:

For a year I lived in hiding, sleeping by day and watching through the night with gun or revolver within easy reach. That was what underground communism could do to one man in the peaceful United States in the year 1938.[24]

So how come a couple of hours off the record has turned 1937 into 1938? And *why*?

We have just had two and a half hours of Nixon's missing material, and we are about to enter nine days of the same. Nine *days*!

Since there is not a single official record of what went on to pull together a case against Alger, I might as well let Nixon tell what he's willing to tell. Which is probably more revealing than he had in mind; but then, as he tells it in *Six Crises*, it's embedded in patriotic thoughts and noble intentions. Stripped of all that, here it is.

He went to see Chambers, "alone and informally," out at Chambers's farm in Maryland.

Two days later he went again, this time taking along newspaperman Bert Andrews, Washington bureau chief for the *New York Herald Tribune*, known as a man who'd do anything for a story.[1] Nixon spent a lot of time at the *Trib*'s Washington offices. One day when he left, Andrews said to his protégé Robert Donovan, "Bob, I can make that fellow President of the United States."

A couple of days after that, Nixon went once again with Stripling in tow.

Meantime, he was sharing out Chambers's testimony. Legally, that testimony was secret: "to be kept between these four walls"[2] as the Chairman put it. Nixon turned it over to his *Herald Tribune* friend Bert Andrews. Then he showed it to Andrew Stern, another journalist.

Then came William P. Rogers, Chief Counsel for the Senate in the Senate Internal Security Subcommittee.

Then Congressman Charles J. Kersten, Republican of Wisconsin, who'd introduced Nixon to Father Cronin, the Red-bashing cleric, only a couple of years before.[3]

Then—and only then—does Nixon admit to talking to the Dulles brothers; he met them in a suite in the Hotel Roosevelt. Both read Chambers's twenty-five minutes of abortive testimony. Here's what Nixon quotes Alger's boss, John Foster Dulles, as saying: "In view of the facts Chambers has testified to, you'd be derelict in your duty as a Congressman if you did not see the case through to a conclusion."[4]

Six Crises doesn't give the remotest hint that anything partisan was going on. He doesn't mention that the Hotel Roosevelt happened to be the Republican Party's campaign headquarters or that the Dulles brothers were top Republican strategists and personal advisors to Thomas Dewey himself, the Republican candidate in the presidential campaign that would really hit its stride next month. An August 1948 issue of the magazine *US News and World Report* reveals what was really going on here: Dewey was "enthusiastic about the quality of political paydirt uncovered in the congressional spy hunt."

Nixon's leaking took on epic proportions. Forget the hearings. Forget testimony. He turns his private conversations with Chambers—and his visits to Chambers's farm—into exciting tales of plot and counterplot. He didn't just elaborate. He invented. Who was to stop him? Nobody was keeping records. Screamer headlines appeared across the country. Nixon and his subcommittee were "digging into all phases of the controversy between Hiss and Chambers."[5] Chambers in his role as the "mystery witness" remained a mystery, while Chambers as himself was answering questions because the "case rests on the integrity of his testimony" and the Committee were "unable to find a flaw in his story."[6] But it was not Chambers's photograph that appeared with headlines like "Mystery Witness Talks in Russian Spy Hunt."[7] It was Alger's because he was "the accused." Four of the people Chambers named received subpoenas and made their own headlines: "Key Witness Heard in Spy Ring Hunt."[8]

Newspapers in Washington and New York reported that Nixon had "visited Chambers at his farm in Maryland,[9] trying to determine who was 'lying on the critical issues,'"[10] struggling to crack "the spy case."[11]

Those were such hysterical times, such black and white times. Are you washed in the blood of the lamb? They were times so like our own. Terrorist? Communist? What's the difference? If you're a "close friend" of a terrorist—if he knows you owned a cocker spaniel and once saw a special bird—then you're all too likely a terrorist yourself. If a terrorist in the State Department, then a spy in the heart of government.

⁂

And Alger? As soon as stories started to appear, he was "baffled by what to do next. I continued to believe that the whole business was some kind of fantasy." Day by day the newspapers were turning Dr. Jekyll into Mr. Hyde: "Alger Hiss, the loyal American above reproach" was becoming "Alger Hiss, the liar who denies knowing his Communist comrade 'under any name and in any circumstances.'"

Alger considered hiring a private eye to find out about Chambers and sue for slander and libel. He consulted friends, especially John Foster Dulles, who advised him in the strongest terms to do nothing at all. Private eyes: unsuitable. Libel and slander suits: impossible because hearings are privileged.

At home, the Hiss family struggled to remember people they'd known more than a decade ago. Memory is so variable. Very few people can remember acquaintances after so long, and Alger had hardly anything to go on. "A stranger had unaccountably said that I had been a member with him of a secret Communist group, that he eventually had come to my house to ask me to break with the Communist Party, and that I had cried separating from him, and that he was very fond of me."[12] And "Chambers in his secret testimony of August 7 had said that he'd stayed in my house and driven my car."[13]

How was he to know that Chambers wasn't using the name "Chambers" in 1937? Nixon didn't leak that bit. How were all the millions of other newspaper readers to know? How were they to know that Chambers himself was the mystery witness? That the FBI, the US Attorney's Office, and the Justice Department had all tried hard to find substance in his stories? That every attempt had failed despite years of effort?

Nixon didn't leak any of that.

On the thirteenth of August—a Friday the thirteenth that really justifies the old wives' tales—a telegram arrived asking Alger to meet the Committee in Washington on Monday. On Sunday the Associated Press reported, "A dramatic face-to-face meeting tomorrow of Alger Hiss, the accused, and Whittaker Chambers, the accuser, may make or break the Congressional spy probe."[14]

One week before, Alger Hiss had been the hero of the United Nations and the president of the most prestigious think tank in America, a man likely to be on his way to the job of Secretary of State. He'd decided to act on a matter of principle that nobody else of his stature had had the courage to act on. Sure, arrogance was there, and in full, lush bloom. Humble people don't get very far in national politics. The Dulles brothers were so sure of their invulnerability that they maintained those German contracts throughout the war and right on into peacetime. So did the Rockefellers; Hoover himself warned Secretary of the Treasury Henry Morgenthau that the Rockefellers' Standard Oil of New Jersey was receiving money by order of the Reichsbank.[15] The Bushes weren't any better. Their Union Bank was seized in 1942 under the Trading with the Enemy Act, revelations that came about in 2004 just as George W. was running for his second term; the family's involvement with Germany's Thyssen industries continued as steadily through the war and on into peacetime as the Dulleses' contracts.[16]

But challenge HUAC for its infringement of rights under the Constitution? Not one of them dared. A single week of screamer headlines, and the man who did dare was "the accused" in a "spy probe." Resignation from the Carnegie Endowment was only a question of timing. Alger's public life was over. He was ruined.

On Monday morning Alger boarded the train to Washington with two companions, a legal friend and a colleague who knew about such things as private investigations. They took copies of newspapers reporting Chambers's "secret" testimony and Nixon's visits to his farm.

The hearing was to begin right after lunch in the same building as his public hearing, but this was to be an executive session, a "secret" session. Chambers knew all about "secret" sessions from his first HUAC hearing, the one that the *New York Times* had announced—the one that provoked Alger to volunteer for this mess. Outside, "photographers scrambled, crouched for angle shots, focused, flashed, thrust burnt-out flash bulbs into their pockets." There were pleas of, "Just one more!" "Just one more!" "Just one more!" Beyond the doors to the Committee's hearing room: a long, narrow, bare space. "Across the front, and around one corner, ran a raised platform and desk, at which sat the Committee and its staff." He sat below them in a "durable wooden" chair, designed to cause whoever sits in it "the maximum discomfort."[1]

That would be where Alger sat.

This hearing saw the return of the Committee's formal Chair, not Mundt but J. Parnell Thomas, the one who sent the Hollywood Ten to jail. Most likely he missed Alger's earlier hearing because just the day before it, he'd started making headlines himself: he'd been padding Congressional payrolls with names of people whose only job was to turn their salaries over to him. He was soon to end up in Danbury Correctional Institution, serving his time with a couple of the Hollywood writers he sent there; one of them was Lester Cole, an ex-husband of Isabel's. Cole describes Thomas in his book, *Hollywod Red*: "no more than five feet tall and about as wide," so tiny that at the hearings he had to sit on two telephone books and a cushion to keep his "bald, round, red-faced head and scalp" far enough above the desk to see what was going on.[2]

Nixon, McDowell, and the Louisiana member called Felix Edward Hébert flank him at that raised table. So do six members of staff. Ten inquisitors. That's quite a panel to face, and Alger faces it alone. "As at the first hearing," he writes, "I saw no occasion for having counsel with me."[3]

The arrogance is maddening, and this time it's more dangerous than before. He needed one of his witnesses if nothing else. This is to be the "dramatic face-to-face." The climax. This was why he'd come to Washington. Absurd to think of it as any kind of consolation for the destruction of his long career, but at least—and at last—he'd know who his accuser was. He'd have some idea how his ruin had come about.

But Chambers is not in the room.

"Mr. Stripling, call the first witness," says Thomas. Which is odd since there's only the one outsider in the room.

"Alger Hiss."

No "mister" this time: we're alone here, and the gloves are off. Nixon starts in. "Do you recall having known an individual between the years 1934 and 1937 whose name was Carl?"[4]

1937? Maybe a slip of the tongue? Didn't he and Chambers and the Committee just agree on 1938 even though Chambers has been laying claim to 1937 for a decade?

"Your testimony is then," Nixon went on, "that you knew no person by the name of Carl between 1934 and 1937?"[5]

Two repeats of 1937 in less than a minute of testimony, right at the start of the hearing: not a slip of the tongue then. Nixon repeated it nine times before the hearing was over, several times calling 1934 to 1937 "the period in question."[6]

So the Committee has agreed to a revised set of dates with Chambers, and they aren't letting Alger in on it.

That's the marvel of these transcripts. However tedious they seem on a first reading—a second too—you can put them side by side and actually watch Nixon as he distorts the testimony. The original change in year was odd; keeping it secret from Alger turns an oddity into an active threat. So does the gloves-off harshness of Nixon's tone, also clear from the transcripts.[7] The line of questioning, though—that's familiar. As before, nobody's interested in communism or subversion.

More photographs of Chambers to identify, four of them this time. Alger repeats again and again that he's not prepared to identify his accuser from photographs.[7] Then comes, do you know So-and-So? Did you meet Such-and-Such a decade ago? Or this man? Or that one? How many rooms in your house? Where did you vacation? How many children do you have? How old are they? What are their names? Where is the eldest now? Do you have a sister? Older? Younger? Where does she live? Did you have servants during the "period in question"? What were their names? Where did they live? What about pets? Vets? Pets' names? Vet's name? Kennels?

At last Alger protests, "I honestly have the feeling that the details of my personal life can be used to my disadvantage by Chambers." Then he adds, "I have seen newspaper accounts, Mr. Nixon, that you spent the weekend—whether correct or not I do not know—at Mr. Chambers's farm in New Jersey."

"That is quite incorrect," says Nixon.

"It is *incorrect*?"

"Yes, sir. I can say, as you did a moment ago, that I have never spent the night with Mr. Chambers."[8]

Well, what do you expect? This is Nixon. Chambers's farm is in Maryland, not New Jersey; Nixon spent days there but never a night, and a weekend implies a night. On the other hand, Alger hasn't said anything about nights with Chambers either. I assume he doesn't call Nixon on it simply because he can't quite believe what he's hearing. The diplomat, expert in subtle negotiation, hasn't come geared for a mugging with barefaced lies.

Nixon ploughs right ahead. "There is a very serious implication in your statement, and that is that the Committee's purpose in questioning you today is to get information with which we can coach Mr. Chambers so that he can more or less build a web around you."

Alger is baffled. "Mr. Nixon, I meant no such implication." He's been thinking of those leaks, not conspiracy.

"You can be very sure when I say this testimony is going to be in executive session, it will be. The same assurance was given to Mr. Chambers."[9]

And yet he's leaked Chambers's executive session all over the media, and he *knows* Alger knows it. Alger has to up his game, and his next question looks like a diplomat's way of calling a liar a liar. He asks, "May I say one thing for the record?"

"Certainly," says Nixon. "I have written a name on this pad in front of me of a person whom I knew in 1933 and 1934 who not only spent some time in my house but sublet my apartment. If I hadn't seen the morning papers with an account of statements that he knew the inside of my house, I don't think I would even have thought of his name."[10] No leaks, eh? So how did the press hear about that?

"And where were you living at that time?" asks Nixon, not even swatting the accusation out of his way.

"He was not named Carl and not Whittaker Chambers."

"Where were you living at that time?"

"Again, Mr. Nixon, if I give the details of where I was, it is going to be very easy if this information gets out for someone to say then ex post facto, 'I saw Hiss in such and such a house.' Actually, all he has to do is look it up in the telephone directory and find where it is."

This changes the tone a little, and Chairman Thomas doesn't like it. "Questions will be asked and the Committee will expect to get very detailed answers to the questions."

Nixon ignores them both. "Your testimony is that this man you knew in 1933 and 1934 was in one of the houses you lived in?"

"I can testify to the best of my recollection," Alger starts. "If this committee feels, in spite of what I have said—"

"Never mind feelings," Thomas interrupts. "You let Mr. Nixon ask the questions and you go ahead and answer it."[11]

Felix Hébert chips in with, "Either you or Mr. Chambers is lying. And whichever one of you is lying is the greatest actor that America has ever produced. Up to a few moments ago you have been very open, very cooperative. Now, you have hedged."[12]

A crucial move in a legal brawl is to grab the moral high ground: not fair but easy to turn into a winning position. Alger goes for it. "It is difficult for me to control myself that you can sit there, Mr. Hébert, and say to me casually that you have heard that man and you have heard me, and you just have no basis for judging which one is telling the truth."

"The fact that Mr. Chambers is a self-confessed traitor," Hébert says, "and I admit he is: the fact that he is a self-confessed former member of the Communist Party, which I admit he is, has no bearing at all on whether the facts that he told—or, rather, the alleged facts that he told—"

"Has no bearing on his credibility?" Alger bursts out.[13]

"You show me a good police force, and I will show you the stool pigeon who turned them in. Show me a police force with a poor record, and I will show you a police force without a stool pigeon. Some of the greatest saints in history were pretty bad before they were saints. Are you going to take away their sainthood because of their previous lives? Are you not going to believe them after they have reformed?"[14]

I'm assuming an outraged pause. The moral high ground is as useless as Alger's diplomatic maneuvers. "You have made your position clear," Alger says. "What assurance have I that some member of this Committee wouldn't say to the press that Hiss confessed knowing Chambers?"[15]

He gets no such assurance. None. Instead we're back to the details. Can Priscilla corroborate this? Can she corroborate that? Alger is uncertain. There's talk of a lie detector test. Alger says he thinks polygraphs are bogus science, but he agrees to take the matter under advisement. So Nixon says Priscilla will have to appear before the Committee tomorrow.

Alger explains that she's in Vermont with little Tony. Never mind, there'll be a recess so he can telephone her and make arrangements.

When Alger returns, Nixon relents, says he'll spare Priscilla the trip, interview her in New York at her own convenience.

There are various theories as to why Alger does what he does next. One is that his nerve collapses at this evidence of a small kindness. I don't believe it. He's fully aware he's being played. Another theory is that it's down to the notepad with the name on it. Nixon wants to see it and figures bullying followed by a threat to Priscilla will be enough to make Alger forget all about it. Coming back into the room, Alger has no choice but to spill the name. I don't believe that either. There's nothing in the testimony to indicate it, and Alger is a man who held his nerve with Stalin, Churchill, and Roosevelt when Anthony Eden was scared enough to piss the walls.

What I think is that the name is the opening shot in a new strategy.

"The name of the man I brought in—and he may have no relation to this whole nightmare—is a man named George Crosley."

—————— ∞∞∞ ——————

"I met him when I was working for the Nye committee," Alger goes on. "He was a writer."[16]

Alger's job included acting as Press Officer, taking questions and giving interviews to writers and journalists. Crosley was a freelancer, working on spec on a series of articles about Washington, not making much money but not worried about it. He interviewed Alger about his Munitions Committee work and entertained him with tales of high adventure in foreign lands and in road gangs laying down tracks for streetcars in Washington, DC He wanted to spend the summer in Washington to finish the articles but had no place to live. Alger and Priscilla were in between leases, moving into a house but still paying rent for the last few months on an apartment. A sublet seemed to solve everybody's problems. When Crosley's furniture was delayed, he, his wife, and baby stayed in the Hisses' house for a few days.

Crosley had no way to get around, either. Alger gave him the use of an old car. There were some small loans too.

"I can't remember when it was I finally decided it wasn't any use expecting to collect from him," Alger tells the Committee, "that I had been a sucker and he was a sort of deadbeat; not a bad character, but I think he just was using me for a soft touch."[17]

"You had hard words when he left?" Nixon asks.

"Yes, in the sense that I said, 'Let's not talk any more about your ever paying back. I don't think you ever intend to, and I would rather forget all of this, and I think you have simply welshed from the beginning.'"[18]

"Would you say this would be sufficient motive to do what Whittaker Chambers has done?"

The idea *is* hard to swallow. Maybe no good deed goes unpunished, but ten *years* of attacking the do-gooder? "No," Alger says. "That is why I say I can't believe it was the same man. I can't imagine a normal man holding a grudge because somebody had stopped being a sucker."[19]

Nixon wanted to know everything about this Crosley. Hair? Height? Weight? What was his wife like? What was Crosley's middle initial? Was it L? "How about his teeth?"

Why would he ask about teeth and middle initial and not eye color or facial hair or scars or freckles? Americans' teeth have been well-tended for generations, and pictures of Chambers in 1948 show the standard set.

"Very bad teeth," Alger says. "That is one of the things I particularly want to see Chambers about. This man had very bad teeth."[20] Alger wrote that the front teeth "were decayed and one of them was split, the forward half having come away, leaving a gleaming steel stump against the darkened rear of the broken tooth."[21] Lionel Trilling, a fellow student of Chambers's at Columbia, called his mouth "a devastation of empty sockets and blackened stumps" that "never failed to shock."[22] The questions do give a hint at some of the conversation during Nixon's secret sessions with Chambers: there's no written record before this—not anywhere—about teeth or a middle initial.

Somewhere in here the reader realizes that Alger's new strategy is working. He's answering questions fully, without hesitation, not fretting about HUAC leaks. His answers dovetail. No detail contradicts another. The ease of delivery is as convincing as the story. No audience will think this man is lying, and every member of the Committee seems to know it. No more scolding, accusing, badgering. Even Nixon is backing off, no longer the bully, more a man considering his options and not liking what he sees. He lets Stripling take over the questioning.

"You are an intelligent person," Stripling begins, "and not naïve enough that you wouldn't know a Communist if you saw one."

This is just stupid, and Stripling doesn't stop there: "I have seen your name for years in Government files as a person suspected of Communist activity. Now, there has to be some basis for the thing. Why would Charles Kramer refuse to say whether he knew you on the ground of self-incrimination? Why would Henry Collins answer that way? Why would all these people say that?"

Alger doesn't bother to hide his contempt. "Are you finished?"

"Yes."

"Do you think those are relevant questions to this inquiry?"[23] Stripling makes a tortured little speech to which Alger replies, "Mr. Stripling, that had about fifteen questions in it. One question that I think I distinctly understood was that you asked me to testify as to why certain witnesses refused to answer certain questions. I do not see how I could possibly be expected to be able to testify on that. I haven't any idea."

"Skip that one."

"You also asked me why my name appeared in various government files." Alger repeats what he told them in his public hearing about the rumors he reported to the FBI in 1947. "I can say that I have never had the slightest indication from my superiors that they gave any credence to what you appear to be giving credence to."

"Don't misunderstand me"—it's such a pleasure to see Stripling running scared—"I didn't say I gave credence to that. I said I had seen—" He breaks off. "I would just as soon have this off the record, if you like."

Alger says, "It can stay on."

Stripling has had enough, "Off the record."

And yet Chambers is the one who called the recess in his hearing, and he stayed with the Committee throughout it. Alger is happy to have everything on the record and gets tossed out of the room while his inquisitors go into a huddle.

When they call him back, Thomas grabs the initiative. "Mr. Hiss, the Committee has unanimously decided to hold a public hearing on Wednesday, August 25, at 10:30 a.m. in the Caucus Room on the third floor of the old House Office Building, at which time you and Whittaker Chambers will be the witnesses and you will be asked questions in order to determine which one is telling the truth, and you will have an opportunity to confront one another."[24]

"I will be very glad of the chance to confront Mr. Chambers," Alger says.

This is clearly not the answer the Committee has expected because at once Nixon dumps the public-hearing part of the unanimous decision. "Would you prefer to have it done informally?"

"My desire is to see the man face-to-face."

"Where does it serve your best purpose? You just want to see the guy?" Nixon is all adither. He can see Alger trouncing them in front of the cameras just as he's doing today, bare-handed and alone against the lot of them. "We are honestly trying to get the right way," says Nixon. "If you have a public session, it is a show. Say it will be a meeting on the twenty-fifth in this room."

"This is a kind of unprecedented proposition," Stripling chips in, "and if you say it is going to be a public session, you know it will be ballyhooed into a circus. From everybody's standpoint, I think it would be better—"

"May I speak?" Alger interrupts. "I want to be clear that I am not asking for an executive session as opposed to public. As far as consideration to me after what has been done to my feelings and my reputation, I think it would be like sinking the Swiss Navy. No public show could embarrass me now. I am asking to see this man." He adds, "I think I prefer a public session."

"Just say that it will be arranged at that time, that no decision has been made as to the type of hearing."

Alger lets it go and asks about press coverage of the present hearing.

"Every person in this room with the exception of yourself," says Thomas, "has stood up and raised his right hand and taken an oath that he will not divulge one single word of testimony given here this afternoon, questions asked, so I am going to ask you to take the same oath."

That scares Nixon too. If Alger is sworn to secrecy, who will the Committee pin the leaks on? "No," says Nixon. "That is up to him."

And suddenly his dithering stops. Quite eerie really: an abrupt calm. The cadence gives it away: no more choppy sentences. "There is one thing I think should be done in this case," Nixon says, "and I see no reason why it shouldn't be done. I think Mr. Hiss should be given a copy of the testimony for his own use." At the opening of this hearing, the Chairman made no bones about it: Alger couldn't have a copy until the testimony was made public.

Then I see it. I've just witnessed a genius in a Eureka moment.

The hearing ends with Chairman Thomas saying to Alger, "Thank you for coming, and we will see you August 25."

People like Alger—people who have it all—do tend to bring out the worst in the rest of us. But putting up Chambers, letting him use a car, loaning him money: why would a guy like Alger do that?

It's hard to get a grip on anybody's personality—I certainly never got what you'd call a grip on Alger's—but surely the women a man loves tell a lot about him. I saw Isabel as evidence of the Achilles heel that delivered him into Chambers's clutches. I know Priscilla only from books, but I'd say she reveals hints of that Achilles heel too.

Priscilla comes across as reserved, conventional, somewhat rigid, and somewhat stuffy, deeply private, a person perfectly suited to the man who described himself as a prig when he married her. Then came the terrible media barrage, the notoriety, the trial of the century, the shame of a husband in prison: a Biblical fall from grace that almost matches Alger's. Not even money to soften the fall. Their savings had gone on the case, every penny from friends and relatives too. When Alger went to prison, a Doubleday bookstore gave her a job, hid her away in a basement where customers couldn't be put off by the sight of her, and paid her a salary so meager that she and Tony were dependent on handouts from her family and Alger's.

Even so, she remained loyal; she wrote as often and visited as often as the prison allowed her. But prison changes people.

The man she welcomed at the prison gates before the trip back to New York City was no longer the man she'd married. On his very first night home—forty-four months without a woman—the bed broke.

Priggish Priscilla was mortified.

Once-priggish Alger burst out laughing.

She was mortified all over again. And how to make sense of this changed man's priorities? She seems to have been one of those demanding people, often feeling left out, jealous of his friends, in need of his protection in a room full of them, and in need of frequent sieges of sympathy, understanding, the most attentive comforting. He'd always put her first in his life. When they'd been young and she'd yearned for New York, he'd dropped his brilliant career in Boston for no other reason than to make her happy. What she wanted of him now was what most people would want: escape. Change their names, find a life far away where nobody knew them and nobody cared. What a shock it must have been to realize that this ex-convict had no intention of going anywhere no matter what she wanted. He was going to stay right where he was and write a book to demonstrate that his trials had been a farce. She hated everything about the idea, and he knew it. "Here I was," he wrote, "intent on revisiting her worst times of nightmare, with publication of the book sure to keep the nightmare alive."[1]

There've been few media frenzies to match the Hiss case. Publishers in the US and UK were certain of a best seller. They were wrong. The book is a lawyer's brief, detailed on points of law, devoid of passion. Reviews were what's politely referred to as "mixed." Sales were poor. As Alger put it—as irritating a stiff upper lip as any Englishman ever sported—"I could not hope to better my lot from royalties."[2]

But he had to better his lot somehow. The government had stripped him of his licence to practice law. Universities didn't want to risk so notorious a convict on their staff in any capacity, academic or administrative. Nor did schools. Or publishing houses or executive committees of businesses. Surely the time had come to escape, make a life somewhere else. But no. How could Alger leave? He was preparing an appeal for a new trial, and he was going to win. He knew it. His "self-confidence remained boundless."[3] But the family had to eat in the meantime; he set out to find a job, any kind of job, he didn't care what, $100 a week would be enough. How to understand that a top government mandarin no longer cared what kind of work he did? Tensions in the household escalated. First Priscilla banned him from the bedroom. Then she threw him out altogether.

Then came Isabel. He wanted a divorce so he could marry her. Priscilla refused. Her doorbell plate read "Mrs. Alger Hiss" until she died. Alger guessed that "she's always known, as I did, that this nightmare would get straightened out—and she would then be Mrs. Alger Hiss with status again."[4] The male entitlement in that comment is thoroughly annoying, and Priscilla was smarter in such matters than he was. She'd have to have known the status was gone forever. Denying him the freedom to marry Isabel—and keeping a doorbell plate as constant reminder of her power to do so—looks much more like revenge. Make the bastard suffer for what he's done to me.

The shrink Zeligs wrote of Alger's "deeply embedded altruism and desire to be of service"[5]; he saw the role of caretaker as central to Alger's personality. Certainly Alger was a do-gooder. He could have made himself very rich in private practice; instead, he used his talents to help bring America out of the Depression and keep it out, bring it out of a war and keep it out, create an institution to bring nations together, build a framework of international laws in an attempt at a lasting peace.

It's always your virtues that catch you out; they're Achilles heels, every one of them. Before prison, Alger had bent himself out of shape to make Priscilla happy. Which is to say she exploited his altruism and his desire to be of service. She exploited the caretaker.

So did Chambers.

Isabel fits right into the pattern. Nobody could have doubted that she craved the limelight and that she revelled in the excitement and the notoriety that so terrified Priscilla. Not that Alger was by any means the first famous HUAC victim she'd latched on to: a "martyrfucker" was what an acquaintance of his said of her. None of Priscilla's priggishness here. But she was certainly ready to exploit the caretaker in him. She also shared Chambers's side-line in humiliation; whenever I think of her, I think of Chambers attacking that earlier good Samaritan in his sleep.

Mainly though, I remember Isabel as somebody who knew not just how to exploit Alger's altruism but how to manipulate it.

And that's exactly like Chambers.

I went through letters, looking for something to back up this impression of her. Dexter kept every letter he received—as well as copies of most that he sent—but he died a long time ago, and I'm crap with files. Even so, I still have quite a few from Alger and Isabel. There's an undated one from her after a visit to us. I'd made a picnic for them to eat on the train, and when they got back to London, she wrote that the train had had a buffet car "which we didn't need thanks to Joanie's elegant repast." This sounds just as it should, but Alger adds a postscript. "As I didn't want to deprive Isabel of the Joanie repast, I fared forth to the Buffet Carriage and enjoyed a canned salmon and pale tomato sandwich on well-soaked white bread. Ugh. But the tinned lager (Harp?) was potable and I brought back another tin for Isabel."

I always packed too much food. What could she have done with it? There was more than enough for two. But I can imagine the scene. She tantalizes him with a prawn, waggling it at him, coquettish, coy. "Open wide, there's a good boy." He opens his mouth, and she snatches the prawn back. "No. You can't have it. I'm going to eat it all. Isn't it cute of me to be so greedy?" Food as cock teasing. In later years, he went blind; she kept up the food denial then—it was a matter of serious concern to his friends—and insisted that he sleep on a camp cot in the living room while she kept the bedroom and the double bed to herself.

One time when Alger and Isabel were out of New York, we spent a couple of weeks in her apartment. She lived on Eighteenth Street just off Third Avenue, a tenement-like, ugly building with a tenement-like, ugly lobby and a rattling metal elevator that clanked slowly up to the third floor. We followed twists and turns in a dimly lit, dreary corridor that finally got us to her door: exactly the slumming it that Chambers's ideal Communist would choose to demonstrate his solidarity with the proletariat. But open that door! Inside was pure bourgeois indulgence, a belt-tightened capitalist with a gentleman's taste.

The main room was large, light, airy. Bookshelves lined the near end. Then came a highly polished mahogany dining table and beyond it, a relaxed living room area ending in a wall of windows. A letter from Alger and Isabel lay on the dining table. Her contribution is gone, but his postscript starts, "Isabel has, I'm sure, covered the serious and basic factors of living here. This is to help with the less weighty matters. Please help yourself to the wines." Wine took up a considerable area of the bookshelves: hock to go with fish, clarets that "might need aging," Beaujolais "for general daily red wine use."[6]

The bedroom wasn't nearly so pleasant, small, dark, cramped. At night we could hear people screaming and crying in the distance, a typical New York sound in poorer areas of the city where the slums aren't far away. The closets were locked. Chests of drawers took up more floor space than the bed, and Isabel's litany of house rules—including which drawers we could use, which we couldn't—was so confusing that we lived out of suitcases.

I'd forgotten all that until I ran across another letter of Alger's. He begins by saying he and Isabel had every intention of making a yearly visit to us, and regretting that he wasn't going to be able to make the next one. His job at Davison-Bluth didn't pay much, but he was as well-off as any other successful salesman for a small firm; and Isabel was comfortable enough to own a cottage on Long Island. Trips to England were carefully budgeted, much looked-forward-to holidays; but this year he was working on a project about the New Deal, and it was taking a lot more out of him than he'd expected.

And the date on the letter! It's September 28, 1968, the US presidential election just over a month away: Richard Nixon vs. Hubert Humphrey. In April, Martin Luther King assassinated. Race riots across the country. Demonstrations against the Vietnam War erupting on practically every American campus.

In June, at the Ambassador Hotel in Los Angeles, Sirhan Sirhan killed Robert Kennedy, the Democrats' rising star.

"All the odds," Alger wrote, "clearly favor a Nixon victory."[7]

There's that iron self-control again. How could Nixon's triumph be more total? And yet there's no hint of personal pain, just a worried citizen's dissection of what such a victory might bring down on America: the HUAC era "was a time of intellectual aberration and deep psychological fear. Nixon would bring worse by giving the hardened Right Wingers a sense of coming into their own." Even so, this strange, prescient man ends by saying that he is "not without optimism in the long run."[8] A little over a month after the letter arrived, Richard Milhous Nixon was on his way to the White House.

A note at the bottom of the second page of the letter read: "I am coming in May or June and so I'll see you then, love Isabel."[9]

We picked her up at the station in Farnham, southwest of London, a few miles from our house, and she came bearing gifts, all prettily wrapped, one for Dexter, one for Toby, one for me. I opened my package.

A pair of underpants and plainly not new.

"I found them under the bed after you left last year," she said. It was only then—my mouth agawp—that the damn things even seemed familiar: Marks & Spencer, bikini-style with pastel flowers. "Don't worry," she said with that languorous smile of hers, "I washed them."

Four-year-old Toby saved the day. He decided that she was a child, if a rather oversized one, and took her out to his sandbox to play. I remember seeing them together through the window. She sat cross-legged in the sand, very upright in an elegant beige suit. An hour later over lunch, she told us they'd been building a castle when he said to her, "Won't your mummy be angry?"

"Why?"

"You're getting your pretty dress all mussy."

"Will your mummy be angry?"

"Oh, she doesn't care."

Even I disliked Isabel a little less—for an hour or so anyway—and Dexter wrote to Alger all about it. Alger responded promptly.

> Isabel brought back a glowing account of her day with you and Joanie and Toby. She was particularly pleased that Toby seemed to have accepted her as a large child. Toby is very perceptive for part of Isabel's charm is a continuing child-like innocence of attitude and playfulness, neither of which she displays openly.[10]

One final story.

I spent a weekend with Alger and Isabel at their summer cottage. Dexter's cousin Andrea—black-haired, very pretty, an actor on her way up—came with me. Isabel detested her on sight. Instructions came thick and fast. Where to put suitcases. How to wash out the bath. Where to dry swimming suits. And a real odd one. We weren't to have breakfast with her and Alger; we were to wait until they'd left, then make our own. We did as we were told; I knew better than to cook anything, but Andrea heated up a bun. Isabel came after us, tearing her hair. Andrea had ruined her oven. Ruined it! Just look at the state of it! She brought out a box of Brillo pads and set us to work.

That noon—we were having a drink before lunch—Alger said he was so pleased we'd slept, only sorry that he'd missed us at breakfast. Before we had a chance to answer, Isabel said, "Oh, Alger, you must forgive them at once." She rushed on to explain that we'd been so dead to the world we hadn't even noticed cooking smells; then we'd offered to clean the oven as an apology. "It was so funny. There they were on their knees, Joanie all in black looking like she was on her way to a cocktail party."

The wretched woman was smiling as she came out with this, head tilted to one side, winsome, languorous, victorious, her message clear: if we contradicted her, Alger would think we were ganging up on her, that we were trying to wheedle out of our bad manners by throwing mud at her.

———— ∞∞∞ ————

Alger thought people were good at heart. He really did. Worse, he assumed it. "My great moral dread," he told his son Tony, "is that I might be exploiting people morally, psychologically, or financially."[11] And Tony wrote, "despite an alpha double plus intellect," his father "continued to navigate through life with one sense missing. He couldn't, or couldn't let himself, sense when someone, either inadvertently or deliberately might harm him."[12] What lay behind the missing sense? "I just couldn't believe that anyone wouldn't love me," Alger said.[13]

Add this to a caretaker who believes in a right way and a wrong way that dates from the code of chivalry, and you have a combination ripe for the manipulators of the world. This is half the reason he was blind to Chambers for so long. The other half is Chambers's very oddness. Strange people fascinated Alger in the way zoo animals and circus clowns fascinate children. People with accents or different-colored skins, people with curious backgrounds and stories to tell. Some people thought Chambers was Polish. Some thought he was Russian. Some, German. And he wasn't just a good storyteller, he was spellbinding.

As Alger told the Committee, Chambers made himself out to be a cross between writers Jim Tully, vagabond and professional fighter, and Jack London, famous for stories of high adventure and social injustice. Chambers told tales of exotic excitements in foreign countries; he "had been everywhere," Alger said. He told of down-and-outs at home too. "I remember he told me he had personally participated in laying down the tracks of the streetcars in Washington, DC."[14] And then Chambers had a mouth full of blackened stumps; he dressed like a beggar. Alger felt great pity for the poor of the world like that. A friend of his tells of walking down Fifth Avenue with him when a homeless guy said, "Do you have any change?" Alger handed over every nickel he had and asked, "Is that enough?"[15]

Even so, it couldn't have taken Alger long to realize there was something genuinely unpleasant about Chambers. The "uncanny valley" is what scientists call a shiver of distaste about another person. They say it's impossible to justify because it doesn't come from the reasoning part of the brain; it's a "dissonance in the system that helps us feel empathy."[16] But Alger had an intensely logical mind. Until he could justify his aversion to Chambers, until he could demonstrate to himself that the man was not honorable, he couldn't act on it.

And yet Alger's generosity wasn't entirely honorable either. New England arrogance is legendary—self-righteous, effete, insolent—Harvard epitomized it and Alger epitomized Harvard. But his desire to do good was as literal as his logical mind. It touched his sense of superiority with a fairy-tale, childlike dreaminess that gave him a charm all his own: all those stories he'd been brought up on, Knights of the Round Table, St. George and the dragon, code of chivalry, love God, honor the maiden, protect the weak, give to the unfortunate. Doing good was his duty as a member of the upper classes: that Harvard education and the ancient name of Hesse-Darmstadt. Why stoop to people like Chambers?

Noblesse oblige.

Alger would not have liked Canadian author John Ralston Saul's setting for the phrase:

"Indeed you can usually tell when the concepts of democracy and citizenship are weakening. There is an increase in the role of charity and in the worship of volunteerism. These represent the élite citizen's imitation of *noblesse oblige*; that is, of pretending to be aristocrats or oligarchs, as opposed to being citizens."[17]

19

1948

That executive session of Alger's was a triumph. It's the kind of thing most people achieve only in daydreams. Especially when their lives lie in ruins around them. Even Alger admitted to a win: "I again had the sense of having accomplished something."[1]

On the train back to New York, he read about Harry Dexter White's HUAC appearance on Friday. White was an economist, a formidable figure, one of those guys with his face on *Time* magazine's cover: architect of the International Monetary Fund and the World Bank, as well as a long-term friend of Alger's. Chambers had been pointing fingers at him too. His appearance—like Alger's first—was a "public grilling"[2] in the huge Caucus Room with klieg lights and flashbulbs. Like Alger again, he had a good part of the audience with him. That irritated Chairman Thomas. "You are the guests of the Committee," he scolded. "The Chair would appreciate it if you would not applaud."[3]

White mentioned playing ping-pong, and Thomas interrupted. "Just a minute, right there. One thing I cannot reconcile, Mr. White, you send me a note and you say that: 'I am recovering from a severe heart attack. I would appreciate it if the Chairman would give me five or ten minutes rest after each hour.' For a person who had a severe heart condition, you can certainly play a lot of sports."[4]

White said he that hadn't intended the note—or his illness—to be made public, that he had indeed played many sports before his heart attack, and this was only ping-pong. The audience burst into applause again.

"I would say you had an athlete's heart,"[5] Thomas grumbled. Tuesday morning's newspapers announced that White was dead: a second heart attack only hours after that grumble. The Committee was proud of its record in such things. The head of the South American desk of the State Department fell out of a window and died only days after HUAC had publicly damned him as a Red; Mundt bragged at a midnight press conference that proving Reds in government was easy, just count them "as they jump out of the windows."[6]

News of White's death got buried beneath HUAC banner headlines in Tuesday morning's papers.

HISS ADMITS ACQUAINTANCE[7]
WITH CHAMBERS

LIE DETECTOR TEST FOR ALGER HISS[8]

The United Press story ran:

> The Committee had been unable to reach a decision on who was telling the truth: Hiss or his accuser, Whittaker Chambers.[9]

And the Hearst papers:

> Alger Hiss, who first denied knowing Chambers and now admits that he lived with him briefly, refused today to submit to a lie detector test.[10]

So much for oaths of secrecy—to say nothing of accuracy.

About midmorning, Alger got a call from Donald Appell of the Committee staff; Rep. McDowell of the Committee itself was to be in New York late that afternoon and hoped to be able to see him for ten or fifteen minutes. Alger asked why. Appell didn't know. Alger said he'd be in his midtown office at the Carnegie Endowment all afternoon; they could meet there.

McDowell didn't telephone until the Carnegie offices were closing for the day; he invited Alger to the Commodore Hotel instead.

Then he added that Nixon and "one other" were with him. The Commodore was built in the 1920s as part of Terminal City, which certainly sounds like an evil portent but comes about only because it was part of the complex built around Grand Central Terminal. A Donald Trump facelift in the 1970s turned the hotel into just any building, but postcards from the 1940s award it "the most beautiful lobby in the world." Also the biggest. It once housed an entire circus—had a real waterfall in it too.

Instead of a drink with McDowell in that splendor, Alger was directed to Suite 1400. He knocked on the door. The suite was full of activity, men rearranging furniture into "an improvised hearing room."[11]

So here's Nixon's Eureka moment of yesterday. Here's what has to have sprung into his head when that abrupt calm came over him and freed him to make a concession—to let Alger have a transcript of the hearing—even though he'd started out unshakeably against it. It's an old-fashioned cowboy ambush, timed for rush hour when Alger wouldn't be able to get hold of a clutch of lawyers or a group of supporters. Appell, who made the morning telephone call, sits right there; McDowell, who "invited" Alger to the Commodore for ten or fifteen minutes with "Nixon and one other," is settling down behind the dining table as chairman of a panel with Nixon and eight others. What a gamble, though. Alger was suspicious enough this time to bring a Carnegie colleague with him, George Dollard, one of the friends who'd urged him to have nothing to do with HUAC. Suppose the two of them just walked out and slammed the door behind them? But Nixon is the poker player who won $1,200 from a superior officer with only two deuces; he knows his man. Alger's arrogance is no barrier. Nixon has learned to handle it. It's the trap itself; it's perpetrated by the men Alger sees as no less than White's murderers. These are the very same men who'd taken only days to destroy his own reputation and a life devoted to public service. And now they set a trap for him? Injustice burns. Outrage makes the smartest people blind, reckless, stupid. Nobody knows that better than Nixon, and he knows that anger makes Alger rash. Now he has fury. All he needs is a match to ignite it.

Hotels liked to call themselves "palatial" in those days: deep carpets, satin drapery, cornices and moldings, panelling and mirrors, handsome prints on the walls. The Committee clusters in team formation at one end of the room with that dining table and a sofa. Nixon sends Alger and Dollard to the other end of the room, a makeshift dock facing the ten-inquisitor panel, their backs to the bedroom door.

McDowell opens. "The record will show that this is a subcommittee of the Committee on Un-American Activities sitting now in the city of New York in the Hotel Commodore." He names the people present. "Mr. Hiss, will you please take the oath?"[12]

And Alger does. He lashes out at yesterday's leaks, especially one that appeared in the *Herald Tribune*.

"In that connection, Mr. Hiss," says Nixon—there's no hint of yesterday's dithering—"I might suggest that in order to satisfy your own mind as to how that information may have gotten into the press that you get in touch with Mr. Carl Levin, the correspondent for the *New York Herald Tribune*, who wrote the story."[13] Levin worked under Bert Andrews, Nixon's inside man on the paper.

But this is not why Nixon has gathered us here. "Mr. Russell," he says, "will you bring Mr. Chambers in?" "Short, plump, perspiring, and very pale": that's what Alger sees.[14] No call for noblesse oblige here. It is Chambers who ranks in this hierarchy. Nixon directs him into Committee territory, surrounds him with the Praetorian guard of HUAC.

"Mr. Hiss," Nixon says, "the man standing here is Mr. Whittaker Chambers. I ask you now if you have ever known that man before."[15]

"May I ask him to speak?" There's no eye contact; the guy just stares at the ceiling.[16] Alger turns to Nixon, "Will you ask him to say something?"

"Mr. Chambers, will you tell us your name and your business."[17]

"My name is Whittaker Chambers." The mouth is nearly shut; the sound comes out "tight", "high-pitched", "strangled."[18] Yesterday Alger told the Committee that Crosley spoke "with a low and rather dramatic roundness."[19] I wanted to hear it myself, found it on YouTube.[20] Any actor would prize a voice like that—intensity, conviction, emotionally charged pauses and hesitations, range, resonance.

"Could you open your mouth wider?"[21]

"My name is Whittaker Chambers."

"I said, would you open your mouth?" Not easy to see devastated teeth in a shut mouth. "You know what I am referring to, Mr. Nixon." He turns back to Chambers: "Will you go on talking?"

"I am senior editor of *Time* magazine." Voice as weird as before.

"Are you George Crosley?"

"Not to my knowledge. You are Alger Hiss, I believe."

"I certainly am."

"That was my recollection."

A bafflement. Alger, the "name" person, doesn't know how to make a pattern from what he sees and what he's hearing. Months later, Chambers admitted that he might have been George Crosley back then. A year and a half more, and he confirmed it.[22]

"Some repartee is going on between these two people," Nixon says. "I think Mr. Chambers should be sworn."

"I think that's a good idea," says Alger, Harvard sarcasm in full flow.

"Mr. Hiss," says Nixon, "when I say something like that, I want no interruptions from you."

"Mr. Nixon, in view of what happened yesterday, I think there is no occasion for you to use that tone of voice in speaking to me."

Chambers is sworn, and Alger tries to pick up where he'd left off. "I would like to ask of Mr. Chambers if I may—"

"I will ask the questions at this time," interrupts Nixon.

"I feel very strongly that he is Crosley"—Alger addresses the Committee in general—"but he looks very different in girth and in other appearances—hair, forehead, and so on, especially the jowls. The voice sounds a little less resonant than the voice that I recall. The teeth look to me as though either they have been improved upon or that there has been considerable dental work done."[23]

Out comes the explanation that the work on Chambers had been really something. I can't follow all of it, but it sounds as though a whole new mouth has replaced the blackened stumps and sockets. Also, he's a blimp. He'd put on something like forty pounds. He'd been skinny, bony. Wore a moustache. No moustache now. Receding hairline. A pulpy face that's aged badly and sags despite the fat. Even so, Alger tells Stripling, "If this man had said he was George Crosley, I would have had no difficulty in identification. He denied it right here. I asked if I could ask some further questions in identification. I was denied—"

"I think you should be permitted—"

"—that right. I am not, therefore, able to take an oath that this man is George Crosley."

Stripling and McDowell urge that Alger be allowed to ask questions.

"Do I have Mr. Nixon's permission?" When Nixon accedes, Alger says to Chambers, "Did you ever go under the name of George Crosley?"[24]

"Not to my knowledge." Exactly what he said before. "Did you ever sublet an apartment on Twenty-ninth Street from me?"

"No, I did not."

"You did not?"

"No."

Alger rephrases the question. "Did you ever spend any time with your wife and child in an apartment on Twenty-ninth Street in Washington when I was not there because I and my family were living on P Street?"

"I most certainly did."

"Would you tell me how you reconcile your negative answers with this affirmative answer?"

"Very easily, Alger. I was a Communist and you were a Communist."

There it is, prettily rephrased from Edgar Allan Poe's *Annabel Lee*: "I was a child and she was a child in a kingdom by the sea." Not a poem anybody would expect to encounter here. "Would you be responsive and continue with your answer?"

"I do not think it is needed," says Chambers. The line from Poe even has Chambers's trademark erotic undertone. The next line: "We loved with a love that was more than love, I and my Annabel Lee." I assume that by now the voice has dropped its strangled, tight sound and moved back to the low and rather dramatic roundness, because Alger says, "That is the answer."[25]

Nixon had an epiphany in the previous hearing. Here's the beginning of one for Alger. If Crosley, the Communist, thought Alger was one too, it explained why he'd never bothered to pay rent or repay small loans. If Chambers lived in the Hiss apartment, he was Crosley, denial or no denial. A Communist would change his name. An ex-Communist turned anti-Communist would attack people he thought had been Communists. Alger wrote later that he felt "a vast sense of relief" that at last he knew his tormenter.[26]

The relief exploded into rage. "To come here and discover that the ass under the lion's skin is Crosley—" He breaks off. "I don't know why your committee didn't pursue this careful method of interrogation at an earlier date before all the publicity."

"Well, now, Mr. Hiss," says McDowell, "you positively identify—"

"If he had lost both eyes and taken his nose off, I would be sure."

McDowell turns to Chambers. "Mr. Chambers, is this the man, Alger Hiss, who was also a member of the Communist Party at whose home you stayed? You make the identification positive?"

"Positive identification."

Alger gets up. It says so in the transcript. He was tall, athletic, in good condition. He takes a step toward Chambers. "I would like to invite Mr. Whittaker Chambers to make those same statements out of the presence of this Committee without their being privileged for suit for libel. I challenge you to do it, and I hope you will do it damned quickly."[27]

The threat is real. Staff member Russell jumps up, grabbing at Alger's arm. In Nixon's description, Alger "recoiled as if he had been pricked with a hot needle."

"I am not going to touch him," Alger says. "You are touching *me*."

"Please sit down, Mr. Hiss," Russell pleads.

"I will sit down when the chairman asks me."

Russell tries again. "I want no disturbance." "I don't—"

"Sit down, please," McDowell interrupts.

"You know who started this," Alger fires back.[28]

McDowell calls a short recess, and after it, Chairman Thomas—soon to be an inmate at Danbury Correctional Institution—arrives to take over the hearing. Nixon delivers a summation of the testimony so far.

> Mr. Hiss maintains that Mr. Chambers was the man known as George Crosley to him. He rented his home, took over a lease, an informal affair, nothing signed, if I recall. Mr. Hiss insists that he paid no rent, he gave him a rug as part payment on the house, and Mr. Hiss included in this transaction the gift of a 6- or 7-year-old car, a cheap car, a Ford.[29]

Within a very short time, Alger's life will be buried in hundreds of household details—leases, rugs, cars are the least of it—all of them so tangled up in dates, cross-references, and concocted stories of spies and Russians that to this very day, more than half a century later, the sheer confusion keeps people from getting close enough to see what's actually there. It's an old magic trick. Fool the senses. Distract the eye. And just as with magic tricks, what's really going on is painfully simple: all Nixon has to work with is the year that Alger assumes is 1937—yet to appear in full form—and Alger's not knowing Chambers. That's it. That's all there is to it.

The midden of inconsequential details, the half-remembered junk data that clutter every life—and mile upon mile of FBI files—is key to Nixon's strategy. Over the next hour, he dumps everything he can think of onto it. How long was the lease for the apartment? Weeks? Months? Did it include July? October? What kind of transfer document was there for the Ford? Did Alger eat meals with Chambers? Walk with him? Drink with him? Give him any furniture? Loan him any books? Give him any books?

How about those Party dues?

There they are again, the single, easily provable charge. The Committee hammers away at it, repeating it half a dozen times. Alger gets angrier with every repetition but fails to grasp its significance. Nixon seems to miss it too.

Meantime, Stripling has his own drum to beat. "You are fully aware," he says to Alger, "that the public was led to believe that you had never seen, heard, or laid eyes upon an individual who is this individual, and now you do know him . . . You led the public and press to believe you didn't know such a person."[30]

This is the very distortion that Nixon has been feeding the press day after day. "Will you show me where that is?" Alger says. "Reading from your statement . . ." Stripling pauses, then begins again. "I've started in on it, but here is one sentence. 'So far as I know, I have never laid eyes on him, and I should like to have the opportunity to do so.'"

"That is correct," says Alger. "I did not say that I have 'never seen' this man. I said, 'So far as I know, I have never seen Whittaker Chambers.'"

"'Never laid eyes on him.'"

"I wouldn't have been able to identify him for certain today without his own assistance."

A little later Alger asks, "You are still looking for the statement you said was in there?" And a little later still, "Have you found the testimony, Mr. Stripling, you were referring to?"

"I have several references here, Mr. Hiss, but as you stated, it is purely in my opinion based upon these."

It's a real tribute to Nixon's genius that Stripling, his right-hand man, can't bring himself to believe he won't find what he's looking for, even though yesterday's testimony demonstrated to him that it didn't exist.

Thomas calls for another private powwow, sending Alger and Dollard off to the bedroom. When they return, he announces, "The Committee has decided to bring about a meeting of the full Committee in public session Wednesday, August 25, at 10:30 in the Caucus Room of the old House Office Building. I instruct the chief investigator to serve a subpoena on both Mr. Hiss and Mr. Chambers to appear on that date."

So Alger is to lose his status as a "friendly" witness even though yesterday ended with all parties in full agreement to the meeting, and yesterday's Associated Press story gave the venue as "probably in secret."

Again it's the expense that defies explanation. It wasn't unusual then—and isn't now—for people in New York to hire a suite for the day: brides for their weddings, Hollywood filming a New York scene, clubs for meetings and parties, especially if hookers are involved. But it was—and still is—very expensive. Who authorized it for ten members of a subcommittee? It's not just a suite for a day either. Ten men going from Washington to New York—nobody says whether by train or plane—it's meals for ten, rooms for ten. All these guys are staying here tonight. And how does the Junior Congressman swing the snazzy suite for himself? We know Nixon stayed there that night because the hearing ended with him telling Alger that Priscilla would have to testify tomorrow; Alger was to call Nixon at the suite as soon as he'd made arrangements.

Alger did try; the line was engaged hour after hour. He called Dulles instead and told him that he was now at war with the Committee. The next morning HUAC's leaks flooded America. The United Press Service reported Stripling. "Alger Hiss not only knew ex-Communist Whittaker Chambers but lived with him for a short while in the middle 1930s."[31]

The Associated Press got the big cheese himself. "'The impression given to the public,' Representative Nixon said, 'was that he (Hiss) had never known this man at all. This identification today is a direct contrast with that impression.'"[32]

20

1970

When Dexter finished his novel, we sold the house in Hindhead. With the money the novel would bring in, we could forget the terrors of suburbia. Dexter loved looking for apartments, and seeking out a big one in Manhattan was really going to be fun.

By the time we docked in New York, Nixon had been the thirty-seventh President of the United States for a year and a half. The famous Watergate scandal that brought him down was in the future, but nobody would have claimed America was a happy place. The Vietnam War dragged on. Protests against it continued, as widespread and violent as before. So did civil rights protests. Riot police, the National Guard, rifles, tear gas, batons, arrests, injuries, even deaths were common front-page news. There was anger and tension on campuses and in the streets. There was a lot of fear.

Before we had a chance to find out what friends thought of all this, Dexter got a telephone call from his cousin Niels Gron, who'd promised us his house in Maine while we saw Dexter's new novel through publication. It was a very mysterious telephone call. Niels said he was flying over to New York that very night because he had something he had to discuss with Dexter. No, he could not explain further than that. It was too sensitive to be discussed over the telephone.

Everything about Niels spilled out over the edges, his waistline, his enthusiasms, the money he spent, the houses he owned, the women he pursued, even his eccentric left-wing politics. He'd been a chess and piano prodigy, who'd spent a year seeing America with a piano in the back of a van; he'd stop in some small town, checkmate everybody willing to play for money, then open his van and hold a concert for more money if he could get it.

That was before he got fat, when he still had the family beauty. He'd needed it. Neither talent turned out to be good enough. Even so, he harbored ambitions, first as a pianist, then as a conductor. In order to fulfil them, he worked on his real gift: conning people. He hit the big time with Nina, Countess of Seafield, the richest peeress in Britain. She owned half a million acres of Scotland, and she adored him. They became engaged; when the engagement was several years old, he married a young French woman. His engagement to Nina continued right on. He and his French wife had three daughters. The engagement to Nina didn't falter. Nina paid for lessons with Nadia Boulanger, famous composer and conductor, then bought the old Boyd Neel Orchestra, changed its name to the Philomusica of London and gave it to him so he could build a career. Her money bought the house he lived in with his French family. It bought him half a dozen other properties in Paris—including a sound studio and a nightclub called *Le Temps Perdu*—several properties in London, a dozen acres off the Brittany coast, and the huge property in Maine so he could be a neighbor to Pierre Monteux, the legendary conductor of the London Symphony Orchestra.

When Monteux died, the Maine property became redundant. Niels had put it in his French wife's name—tax dodges surrounded all his properties—and she turned out to be tougher than he thought. He wanted to sell it; she refused. So while they bickered, he'd said Dexter and Toby and I could have it to ourselves.

He arrived in New York the evening after his telephone call, dumped his expensive leather suitcases in the hallway, complained about the way I was cooking the prawns and about the impenetrable American habit of storing bacon fat in coffee jars. Then he brought out a bottle of twenty-five-year old Glenlivet, poured us all a drink, and got down to business.

He'd called us from a converted water mill near Tours in Southern France, where he'd been discussing the state of the world with Alexander Calder, famous sculptor, originator of the mobile and his French wife's godfather. They had the answer to the world's ills: Richard Nixon.

Dexter had strong feelings about Tricky Dick; Niels had even stronger ones. What I understood from the conversation was that Nixon's predecessor Lyndon Johnson had been well on the way to a treaty that would have ended the Vietnam War. But Nixon had pitched his election campaign on a Law & Order ticket—Red-bashing was losing its zing—and if the war stopped, the protests stopped. If the protests stopped, Nixon would lose. He'd leaked to the South Vietnamese that Johnson was selling them out.[1] They boycotted the treaty talks. The peace initiative failed. The war continued. So did the protests. Never mind that this was treason. Nixon was the man who had to win. That's just what he did.

Niels went on to say that Dexter's friend Alger Hiss bore a great deal of the blame for all this. As he put it, "Without Alger Hiss, that fucker never would have got anywhere. Hiss got him in. It's his personal responsibility to get him out."

Well, yes, Dexter said, but surely Niels couldn't have flown all the way across the Atlantic to talk about Alger's role in American politics.

Niels set down his drink. "We've decided to assassinate Nixon," he said.

⸙

Dexter burst out laughing—clearly not what Niels had expected. Niels was a con man, not a conspirator. Even so, he explained, affronted, that both he and the great Calder assumed that Dexter and his friend Alger Hiss would want to help. It took a while to convince Dexter that Niels really had got on an airplane and flown all the way across an ocean to talk about this. Hilarity dissolved into exasperation. No, he did not want to be part of it. And he knew perfectly well Alger wouldn't want to be part of it either.

Niels pressed on. How could Dexter possibly know what Alger's reaction might be?

Dexter's impatience hardened. Even so, he did what he could to explain Alger's integrity, but integrity wasn't a concept that came easily to Niels. He'd told us once that he was "a whore who sold to the highest bidder." Such unvarnished self-assessment was part of Niels's charm, but even I could see that this was a charm that Alger wasn't going to understand any better than Niels could understand why Alger wouldn't want to assassinate the guy who'd risen to power by fitting him up.

Dexter asked Niels how they were planning to do this deed. Niels said he'd rather hoped Dexter and Alger might have some suggestions, but he and Calder had thought probably introducing poison gas into the air conditioning system would be best.

By this time, Dexter was seriously irritated: hadn't it occurred to Niels that that this might kill an awful lot of people and not get anywhere near Nixon?

Well, no, it hadn't, but still—

Dexter had had enough. "Niels," he interrupted, "this is the stupidest idea I've ever heard. Just shut up about it."

Niels shrugged, refilled his whiskey, said, okay, Dexter was probably right. He'd give up the plot, but he'd like to meet Alger anyhow. To that, Dexter said no. Just no. Flat no. Niels started haggling, and he was a good haggler. We weren't going to find anywhere as beautiful as his Maine property, not at this short notice. Not for the whole winter.

"Is that a threat?" Dexter asked.

Niels backed down at once. Having people in the property lowered the insurance premiums and deterred thieves; he kept a number of very valuable items there. "Can't you at least introduce me to Alger Hiss in exchange?"

Why?

"I really want to meet the guy. I admire him. He has guts."

Dexter was a pretty good haggler himself. Niels had offered the house for nothing if we'd cover heating and electricity. But if he was this eager to meet Alger, what about fuel? Sure, Niels said, he'd even toss in the car. Dexter hesitated, then said he'd arrange a meeting provided Niels agreed to pay for a superb dinner with a superb wine, and Alger would know if either was less than the best. The venue had to be public. There had to be lots of other people present. Niels agreed to everything.

Dexter's final condition was that Niels swear he'd say not a single word to Alger about his idiotic plot.

Niels swore. But even I knew it would come up.

I wish I could remember which restaurant it was or who the other guests were. There must have been about a dozen of us all together. Niels was at one end of a long table with Alger; I was halfway down one side, Dexter at the other end near Isabel. Champagne came first. Quite a lot of it. Then caviar. We'd barely started the main course—I didn't notice any sudden drop in the conversation—when Alger got up, walked past me to Isabel, whispered in her ear. She got up and they both went to the front desk.

When they'd been standing there a few minutes, I followed. "Is something the matter?"

Alger turned to face me. The medieval flagellant was gone. So was the iron self-control. This was a man in a rage. "I'm leaving," he said.

I asked if he wasn't well, or if Isabel wasn't well, and I assured him that he needn't pay the bill if that was what he was waiting for. Niels would cover it.

Alger could barely control his voice, and he was as furious at me as he was at whatever nonsense Niels had managed to blurt out. "I will not owe that man anything," he said.

"Not even a dinner?"

That only brought on a spasm of anger like the one Chambers had provoked. "No."

"But, Alger, this is a hideously expensive place, and Niels . . ." Alger was looking at me as though I were the most contemptible form of life he'd ever run across. The maitre d' handed him the bill. There was shock on his face at the amount, but he paid up, told Isabel to get the coats while he flagged a taxi; he walked out of the restaurant without a backward glance.

Isabel was her usual dreamy self, not remotely concerned as she collected the coats. "Oh, Joanie, don't look so worried," she said.

"I'm afraid I made Alger very angry with me, and I don't even know why."

She smiled and patted my cheek. "He'll get over it. He always does."

21

The FBI letters informing me that they'd destroyed my parents' files ended by saying I could appeal the "decision." I couldn't see what there was to appeal, but I did it anyway. They confirmed the destruction. The National Archives confirmed their position too: my mother's file existed, despite what the FBI said, but it was still classified.[1] All I had to cling to was Record Group 65. Here's how the Archives describe it:

> The files . . .include information on how U.S. corporations profited from operations instigated by and supportive of the Third Reich.[2]

This begins to make a pattern. There's the theory about Nixon using illegal contracts with Nazis to blackmail his way into Congress. The Dulles brothers managed profits of US corporations locked into Nazi corporations and the Nazi military. My father, who'd warned of exactly that, disappeared into the FBI's shredder while my mother's anti-fascist attacks on such as Bank of America got her actually hidden away in Record Group 65.

As for Alger, he was working for the Nye Committee back in the 1930s. He was part of investigations that showed United Aircraft selling commercial airplane engines to Germany for use in Luftwaffe fighter planes,[3] Nazi troops "nearly all armed with American guns,"[4] the Union Banking Corporation in a cartel agreement with the German I. G. Farben, soon to be gas-maker for Holocaust gas chambers.[5]

Then the war broke out. That's when war profiteering like this became treason, trading with the enemy. Big-time crime.

22

1948

Alger had just a week to prepare for the HUAC circus on August 25th. Odd to have to find proof of details of your life over a decade ago: tax records thrown away, house moves, job changes, and circles of friends and colleagues with them.

He needed to show that George Crosley wasn't a figment of his imagination. He needed documentation of his cars and his apartment leases. His many friends were willing and eager to help, but there was so little time, not much money, not one of them experienced in detective work. They did manage to track down one record—the title transfer of the old Ford—only to find the FBI had already impounded it. Alger, being Alger, ignored this warning signal and decided such details were "unimportant"[1]; he'd rely on his memory as before but be careful not to let the Committee tie him down to specifics.

Most of his time went on preparing a statement. As for Nixon, he was spending eighteen to twenty hours a day on those "unimportant" details. He had lots of help. The FBI had all those years of coverage to start with—details of daily life—and FBI Director J. Edgar Hoover had started leaking directly to Nixon as soon as he got into Congress.[2] One FBI agent said, talking of HUAC's Chairman, "Let's put it this way. He had access to see information that was in the files Mr. Hoover had. This was a personal relationship"[3]; the courtesy extended to Nixon. Then there was HUAC's own investigative team and the FBI's active help in the field. That's not all. Professor Stephen Salant of the University of Michigan tracks the helpful hand of the US Army's Counter Intelligence Corps as well. Scores of agents and investigators combed records for car sales, rentals, schools; everything they found, they impounded.[4] As a close friend of Nixon's said, the information "was handed to him."[5]

Father Cronin went into more detail. He had an FBI source called Ed Hummer who called him "every day" and told him what was going on, "and I told Dick. He knew just where to look for things." Cronin summed it up: "Nixon was playing with a stacked deck in the Hiss case."[6]

While all this was going on, the Committee subpoenaed as many of Alger's colleagues and acquaintances as they could; they subpoenaed his brother, Donald. All but Donald took the Fifth to escape dragging friends, family, colleagues into the mess with them. All at once they became Fifth Amendment Communists who'd implicated themselves rather than admit to knowing Alger Hiss.

As for Donald, "I deny them categorically," he said about Chambers's charges[7]. "If I am lying," he added, "I should go to jail."[8]

HUAC forgot him.

But every day the press had a revelation.

The *New York Times*: "Representative Nixon" told the reporter by telephone that Chambers had described "furniture, paintings on the walls, and other objects of the Hiss home."[9]

And yet two weeks ago, the only item he could remember was a cigarette box.

International News Service: "Nixon predicted that, after "the tardy identification, Chambers, confessed Red courier, will reiterate that any money he received from Hiss was in payment of Communist Party dues."[10] But he said he'd never collected Alger's dues. No, he'd collected them every month for years. They came to 10 percent of Alger's wages. Which would show up on his bank statements. No, they came in irregular cash payments of $5 or £10. Which wouldn't show on his bank statements. But they'd show up on Party records.

Nobody suggests looking.

Associated Press: "Representative Nixon, Republican of California, said today that Alger Hiss and Whittaker Chambers were introduced to each other by J.V. Peters, alleged 'brain' of the entire Communist underground."[11]

Anybody ask Peters himself? If anybody did, there's no record of it. He kept a low profile, and not long after, he was allowed to leave the country—nobody knows why—and secrete himself in deepest Hungary, out of everybody's reach.

The Hearst papers: Nixon said Chambers "had not changed perceptibly" in a dozen years. What happened to the fifty pounds? The jowls? The devastation of a mouth? The shaved-off moustache? "Nixon's one-man subcommittee" reporting from "a closed-door session" told reporters that "Alger Hiss was linked to the Communist movement as late as 1944 or 1945, according to Louis Budenz, former editor of the Communist *Daily Worker*."[12] The testimony itself didn't become public until many months later; all Budenz said was that he'd heard the standard rumors that Chambers had started.

Weren't the odds high that this time Alger would at last come to his senses and take the Fifth? Less than a month since he'd demanded the right to appear, and his public life was history; but if he took the Fifth as so many of his friends had before him, he could go back to private practice. HUAC couldn't charge him with anything beyond contempt of Congress, and they couldn't even do that if he took the Fifth.

What good is Father Cronin's stacked deck if Alger won't play? Even so, here's the unbelievably gutsy Nixon gambling that the game will go on.

23

"Ballyhooed into a circus."[1] That's what Stripling threatened for the 25th August, and a portion of Nixon's long hours had gone into a barrage of advertising for the show. Maybe Alger's first hearing drew "the biggest turnout of reporters and spectators in the history of our inquiries"—as Stripling put it—but this one really does belong to the world of circuses.

Not only that, it marks a technological dawn: the very first hearing to go out on the new medium of television. An audience of five hundred packs the huge Caucus Room in the old House Office. Over them crawl journalists and broadcasters with flash cameras, newsreel cameras, television cameras; the stage is lit up with those blinding spotlights used in filmmaking. The central role? That's where Alistair Cooke, covering the story for the Manchester Guardian, described our star as "the darkly handsome Nixon." They say there's fear, hope, and paranoia battling inside a gambler as a game begins, and this is certainly the biggest gamble of Nixon's career.

And what about the heat! Cooke wrote that the day was "infernal."[2] The heat wave that began in early August is at its height. Alger shares headlines with it. "Sweltering", "blistering",[3] "sun rays like hammer blows."[4] People were dying. Literally. No air-conditioning in the Caucus Room; klieg lights and the tightly packed crowd turn it into a giant sweat machine from a weight-loss gym.

J. Parnell Thomas, seated atop his telephone books, opens the proceedings with talk of "the operation within the Government of the Communist apparatus."[5] He repeats Chambers's charge: "Mr. Alger Hiss was a member of this group, which had as its purpose Communist infiltration of the American Government, with espionage as one of its eventual objectives."[6] He ends his summation with a ringing cry that gets this sweaty audience on the edge of its seats: "As a result of this hearing, certainly one of these witnesses will be tried for perjury."[7]

"Mr. Stripling, the first witness."

"Mr. Alger Hiss."[8]

Alger asks to read his statement. Denied. He rephrases his request. "Not at this point," says Thomas. "Go ahead, Mr. Stripling."

"Mr. Hiss, would you kindly stand up, please?" says Stripling. "Mr. Chambers, will you stand up? Mr. Hiss, have you ever seen this individual?"[9]

I found a grainy press agency photo: tall, elegant Alger standing opposite fat, sloppy Chambers; Stripling in a white suit pointing at Chambers like the Ghost of Christmas Future, all wearing jackets and ties above a headline about that blistering heat.[10] Alger must have paused because Thomas tells Stripling to repeat the question.

"Have you ever seen this individual who is standing?"

"I have."

"Do you know him?"

"I identify him, Mr. Stripling."

"As who?"

"As George Crosley."

Everybody in this Caucus Room has gobbled down Nixon's by-the-name-of mantra with morning cornflakes.

"When did you know him as George Crosley?" Stripling asks.

"According to my best recollection—and I would like to repeat what I have said to the Committee before, that I have not had the opportunity to consult records of the time—I first knew him sometime in the winter of 1934 or 1935."

"When did you last see Mr. Crosley, as you have identified him?"

"Prefacing my answer with the same remarks I have just made, I would think sometime in 1935."

Stripling turns to Chambers. "Mr. Chambers, do you know the individual who is now standing at the witness stand?

"I do."

"Who is he?"

"Mr. Alger Hiss."

"And when did you last see Mr. Hiss?"

"About 1938."

Here's the year of 1938 making its first public appearance. Alger pays no attention. Only 1937 was on show in his Washington hearing. No year at all appeared in the ambush. But with 1938 firmly implanted in the record, Nixon proceeds to Alger knowing Chambers. The evidence? Newspaper reports. Their source? His own press releases. He reads them out one after another, a magnificently clever ploy. The *New York Daily News*: "I don't recall a man by the name of Chambers ever coming to my house."[11] The *Cleveland Plain Dealer*: "Hiss went on the stand today and denied the charges completely. He said he didn't even know his accuser." The *Associated Press*, the *Christian Scientist Monitor*, the *Washington Evening Star*, the *Chicago Daily News*.

Nixon quotes them all, quoting himself as he misquotes Alger.[12] Mundt sums up this recital: "The impression is that you categorically deny knowing this man."[13]

Alger says, "The evidence before this—"

"Never mind the evidence," Thomas interrupts.[14] There are the photographs again too, this time of the young Chambers as well as the old Chambers. Hébert tells Alger he has shown them "to innumerable people. Without hesitancy every individual remarked about the striking similarity between the two men. And yet you sit here today as a lone individual who hedges and resorts to technicalities that you can't tell."[15]

Nothing about forty pounds, missing moustaches, rotting teeth. Or who the identifying horde might have been. How is the audience to know? Nixon leaked none of these details. Alger has a lawyer with him this time, John F. Davis. His area of expertise? The Security & Exchange

Commission. If Alger won't plead the Fifth, he badly needs a top-flight criminal lawyer. Not only is Davis the wrong man for the job, he promptly makes an ass of himself. His aides were the ones who'd found out about HUAC impounding records, a police-state seizure of evidence that could well swing the Caucus Room behind Alger. But Davis bungles it into a niggle over just exactly which aide told him about it.

Mundt grabs at the niggle with both hands. "I would just like to register a protest at this continuous evasion on the part of these witnesses. I am getting tired of flying halfway across the country to get evasive answers. If the gentleman doesn't know who told him, let him say, 'I don't know.' If he knows, let him say 'I do know.'"[16]

And with that Nixon launches into the "unimportant details."

The title to this car Alger turned over to Chambers: did he sign the paperwork? Does he *deny* that he did? The Committee has subpoenaed three officials of the company. They have proof of where it was sold. They have the name of the man it was sold to. How much was the car worth? $25? $35? What about its Blue Book price? You didn't check? Why not? Here's the car's certificate of sale. Why doesn't it indicate any exchange of money?

"Just checking through the record," Nixon says, "eighteen occasions in which you were asked the specific question as to whether you had given him the car, sold him the car, threw it in, given him the title, and as to whether it was part of the apartment deal, and in each case you said yes, and at that time you did not qualify your answers with 'to the best of my recollection.'"[17]

Alger said, "I gave Crosley, to the best of my recollection—"

"Well, now, just a moment on that point," Nixon interrupts, "I do not want to interrupt you on that 'to the best of my recollection,' but you certainly can testify 'yes' or 'no' as to whether you gave Crosley a car. How many cars have you given away in your life, Mr. Hiss?"[18]

The Caucus Room bursts into laughter; brilliant Nixon has turned Alger's lawyerly caution into a joke.

"I wish you would make a statement and stand by it," Mundt complains. "Once you say, 'I sold him an automobile, period.' Now, you come here and say, 'I gave him the use of the car,' and then you say, 'I cannot tell whether or not after he had the car he gave it back to me or not.'"[19]

Chambers and Alger agree that all this happened in 1934, fourteen years ago now. Fourteen years is a long time.

Davis tries to object. "Mr. Chairman, I suggest—"

"Never mind. You keep quiet,"Thomas interrupts.[20] Davis tries again. "No, no. You be quiet for moment."[21]

Nixon starts in again. When did Alger sublet his apartment to Chambers? Summer of 1934? Spring of 1934? July? August? Nixon had a statement from the apartment manager that shows that the lease ended on 28 June, 1935. He had the records of the Potomac Electric Company showing they'd turned off the electricity on the same day. So it couldn't even have been 1934, could it? What about that bird Alger saw in Arlington? Nobody could find out about it from Who's Who, could they? What about the rug? What about Timmy's school transfers? And more and more.

"On every point on which we have been able to verify," Mundt says, "or on which we have had verifiable evidence before us, the testimony of Mr. Chambers has stood up. It stands unchallenged."[22]

At last it is possible to see why Nixon is embedding this confusion of household detail into Chambers's stories of espionage. It's a technique he learned from Murray Chotiner, and he used it to shaft the incumbent Jerry Voorhis and get himself into Congress. You accuse the other guy of something vague, a minor fact tied into a damning fiction, no proof is necessary. While he is explaining, accuse him of something else. While he's fielding two explanations, accuse him of a third something. A few more stabs, and the sheer weight of accusation begins to turn your opponent into a suspect in a line-up. To this very day, it's the sheer size and complexity of Nixon's construction that makes people see a fantastically convoluted spy story when all that's there is a simple setup.

Mundt complains that Alger has "used the phrase 'to the best of my recollection' over seventy-five times before this committee."[23] Mundt's wife has warned him not to be taken in by such "suavity."[24] Alger's "testimony seems clouded by a strangely deficient memory," and "it is very hard to know very much about this evasive type of testimony."[25] Hébert says Alger is "a very agile young man"[26] and "a very clever young man."[27] In America—at least back then—the word clever wasn't a compliment. It meant sly, crafty, artful.

Like Isabel. Or Chambers.

Then the audience hears about "Lee Pressman, Nathan Witt, John Abt, Henry Collins, Donald Hiss, Harold Ware, Charles Kramer, and Victor Perlo." They all took the Fifth rather than admit to knowing Alger. Donald is clubbed with the others despite denying the charges with real vehemence, not taking the Fifth at all, which leaves the impression that Alger's own brother won't admit to knowing him.

Then comes Mundt's summation, rehearsed in last week's executive session. "Either you or Mr. Chambers is the damnedest liar that ever came on the American scene," and "whichever of you is lying is the greatest actor we have ever seen in this country."[28] As for which man, Mundt has no doubts. "I have had some occasion to check the activities of Alger Hiss while he was in the State Department. There is reason to believe that he organized within the Department one of the Communist cells."[29]

By the time Thomas lets Alger get to the statement that he has spent the week perfecting, it's past going-home time. The audience is hot, tired, bored, and Alger is no more a Perry Mason than Davis is. What comes across is a list of important people who believe him to be upright and honest.

Nixon needs only one card to make this day perfect for him, and Alger hands it right over. He challenges Chambers "to make the statements about me with respect to communism in public that he has made under privilege to this committee."[30]

———— ∞∞∞ ————

It's past seven in the evening when Chambers takes the stand, and he's just so refreshing.

He hints at a Communist underground of secrets and shadows, right out of the movies. He talks of "risks" to himself and his family, fears of "assassination" and "ambush."[31] The threat of Soviet assassins means he can't so much as indicate where he lives; Alger's comrades would come after him and his children. He answers questions readily, easily. If he doesn't know, he says so. When he can't remember dates, places, times—which is often—he says he can't, and nobody accuses him of a "strangely deficient memory." Nobody hectors. Nobody badgers.

More than that. The Committee carries out the canonization they'd proposed for him in Alger's executive session. "You admitted frankly that you knew what you were doing," Hébert says to Chambers, "and then had a change of mind, and decided to be loyal to your country, and do what you could to make amends. With your knowledge and your education of history and religion, isn't it a fact that there are many saints in Heaven today who were not always saints?"

"I believe so," says Chambers.

"We would not take their sainthood away from them after they have become saints and repented."

Chambers does protest modestly that he isn't a saint, which ought to sound absurd but somehow doesn't.[32] He's even able to build on the idea: "We are caught in a tragedy of history. Mr. Hiss represents the concealed enemy against which we are all fighting, and I am fighting. I have testified against him with remorse and pity, but in a moment of history in which this nation now stands, so help me God, I could not do otherwise."[33]

The blatant theft of Luther's "Here I stand, I can do no other" would embarrass most people. Not Chambers. The words were powerful when Luther said them, and they're powerful in this Caucus Room. They resonate in the transcripts. Beside him everyone else sounds pedestrian. But put aside the sound, and he's hard for a reader to keep track of. Things change so fast that even Nixon gets lost.

That emotional scene when Alger was supposed to have shed tears at the thought of leaving the Party and losing his friend Carl: crucial to the public perception of the case. The last time Chambers told this story, he'd gone to the Hisses' home in 1937 "at considerable risk" and found Priscilla there; she'd tried to make a telephone call, which he assumed "was to other Communists," who would come at once and bundle him off to a dark alley and execution. She hung up as soon as he approached. Alger came in a little later, and the weeping scene took place.

"At that last meeting in 1938," Chambers begins—getting in the year—"I went to Mr. Hiss—he was then living on Dent Place—and I had supper with him there, and with his wife."[34]

Supper? Where'd that come from? "Well, now," says Nixon, "will you describe for the Committee how you happened to go to his apartment? I mean, how you happened to go to his house? Did you go to the door, do you recall, or what was the occasion?" None of these questions makes much sense; the man has already said he'd gone for supper, and he's hardly going to climb in a window.[35]

Chambers answers, "I went to the door, I suppose, about seven o'clock at night, perhaps. I was afraid of an ambush, but when I got there, only a maid was at home."

Nixon can't get his head around it fast enough. "What is that?" he asks. Where did this maid come from? Wasn't it Priscilla who let him in? Has he been invited to this "supper"? Is it formal?

Chambers isn't the slightest bit perturbed. "Only a maid was at home."

"What did you do?"

"I waited nearby, and very shortly Mrs. Hiss drove up, and we went into the house together, and—"

"Well, how did you get Mrs. Hiss?" the addled Nixon interrupts. This question doesn't make sense either, but you have to sympathize with him. A car? What's Priscilla doing in a *car*? "Do you remember that?" he asks even more senselessly.

"Not particularly." Chambers is as unfazed as ever. "I do not recall."

And yet three weeks ago, he recalled precisely, and there was no car or supper or maid.

"You met her at that time?" Nixon still hasn't managed to show he's following the story, and his confusion is beginning to confuse Chambers.

"What is that?" Chambers asks.

"You say you met Mrs. Hiss as she drove up."

"She drove up and stepped out of the car."

"I see," says Nixon, who clearly doesn't see at all.

"And we went in together." What about that important, secretive telephone call, probably to Communists? Priscilla's betrayal? Nixon decides—wisely—not to go there. "And you discussed breaking away from the party at that time with Mr. Hiss?"

"Yes. I did."

What's striking—aside from Nixon's confusion—is Chambers's absolute certainty. He was certain when he first told the story. He's certain now. But what's even more striking is that not a single member of this investigating committee, all of whom heard the previous version, intervenes to comment on or question the exciting changes in it.

Mundt asks Chambers if he thinks that when Communists "come before this committee, as they so frequently do, and deny under oath that they are Communists, they can do that without difficulty and with comparative impunity, even though they are, in fact, Communists? Is that right?"

Chambers is happy to agree.

"From your knowledge of the Communist operations in Washington in Government," Mundt goes on, "would it be your belief that Communist cells are still functioning in Government now or that they have terminated them at the conclusion of the war?"

"It is unquestionable that they are still functioning in Government, and will continue to function until they are rooted out."

You can practically see Mundt's heart jump for joy: "It would be your firm conviction that they are here, and will stay here until they are ferreted out by hearings like this, or by the FBI, or by grand jury proceedings, or some other legal methods?"

"Certainly," says Chambers.[36]

Nixon opened with prosecution, closed with prosecution, and squeezed Alger's defense into a boring statement: enough to nail anybody. And yet reports of HUAC's success were "mixed."

**Spy Probers Hunt 1929 Jalopy
Attempt to Determine Who Lied**[1]

**Committee Fails to Trap Hiss
in Seven Hours of Grilling**[2]

So much for J. Parnell Thomas's ringing cry that either Alger or Chambers would surely be indicted for perjury as a result of the hearing.

A *Washington Post* writer—the *Post*'s archives don't give his name—knew what HUAC had been trying to do: "if it could show Hiss to be inaccurate in any detail, it would follow that his denial of the charges made by Mr. Chambers would not merit credence." A technique well-known to prosecutors in criminal trials, but here? The Committee's attitude to Alger, "grilling him mercilessly" contrasted badly with a reference to Chambers as "our witness" and the lack of attack on his testimony. Alger "was obliged to testify on short notice, on the basis of mere recollection" about "minutiae" from years ago, and HUAC paid no attention to the "overriding substantive issue": "The American people want to know whether Mr. Hiss was part of a Communist apparatus, not whether he can remember what he did thirteen years ago with a $25 Ford automobile."[3]

The writer concluded that the Committee "is simply not equal to the task."

Even the weather was behaving badly for Nixon. In Ohio, "Death Toll Climbs to Five,"[4] and in New York, "Two Hundred Deaths Blamed on Heat."[5] Headlines like these squeezed him off front pages across the eastern half of the country.

Two days after the hearing, Chambers appeared on a radio program called "Meet The Press." Tom Reynolds of the *Chicago Sun Times* brought up that "substantive issue" about Alger. "Did he do anything wrong? Did he commit any overt act? Had he been disloyal to his country?"

"I am simply saying that he was a member of the Party," Chambers answered. He "certainly wasn't doing anything directly for the Russians."[6]

At once, the Committee issued an interim report, saying that Chambers had disclosed "the existence of compact, conspiratorial rings consisting of Communists within the government. These rings . . .transmitted documents and information." Alger's testimony had been "badly shaken" and "the verifiable portions of Chambers's testimony have stood up strongly." It went further. "Mr. Chambers had been a forthright and emphatic witness, while Mr. Hiss had been evasive. Mr. Hiss had prefaced one hundred ninety-eight statements with 'to the best of my knowledge.'"[7]

One hundred ninety-eight statements! Every book I have that touches on the subject repeats the figure as though it were absolute truth. I did a search. My computer count of various versions of "to the best of my knowledge" or "recollection" makes a total of sixty-four, or about once every eight or nine minutes. Not bad for a guy on the stand steadily for closer to eight hours than seven, knowing that if he's "inaccurate in any detail," he might find himself indicted for the perjury charge that Chairman Thomas was hoping for.

But figures like that fire the imagination. Exact figures sound so, well, exact. An outrageous price will con most people if it looks like it's figured to the penny. Then of course, there's that marvellous secrecy of committee hearings. To be sure, there'd been lots of witnesses present at the event itself—and millions watching on TV—but only HUAC had a copy of the testimony to check.

Nixon issued a press release to back up the report. He claimed "a definite, provable link—not simply on the basis of Chambers's testimony or on hearsay—but a provable link" between Alger and known spies that he could "document through official records."[8] Again Nixon could rely on the privilege of secrecy. Nobody but he and HUAC had seen the "evidence." Nobody but he and HUAC could see it.

Here's what it turned out to be.

An informer called Elizabeth Bentley—she's the one who pointed fingers at Mr. and Mrs. Gold of Pittsburgh—named a government economist called Irving Kaplan in one of her lists of spies. Alger worked for the Department of State from 1936 to 1938, when it shared a vast and hideous building—Mark Twain called it "the ugliest building in America"—with the Departments of War and the Navy. From the end of 1937 into the beginning of 1938—the two crucial years again—Chambers was in that building compiling an index for WPA, the New Deal agency that Kaplan worked for.

That's it. That's Nixon's "provable link." No mention whatever of Alger. Nobody bothered Kaplan, no prosecution, not so much as a subpoena.

Nor were privilege and press manipulation Nixon's only weapons. He wrote to his ally John Foster Dulles, saying of Alger that, "There is no longer any doubt in my mind that he was trying to keep the Committee from learning the truth in regard to his relationship with Chambers."[9] Dulles and Alger had been close, and they'd both been called Reds. Dulles mentioned the smears against the two of them when he proposed Alger as President of the Endowment; he'd assured the board, from his own "personal knowledge," of Alger's "complete loyalty to our American institutions."[10]

Dulles had done his best to dissuade his old friend from the foolishness of appearing before HUAC; but there was that presidential election at stake, and the Republicans had lost the White House four times in a row to the much-loved Roosevelt. He'd died in office, leaving behind his vice presidential successor, the unpopular Harry Truman. The Republican Party had a real chance here; they weren't going to let it slip, and within days they'd be launching their campaign into its final and most intense phase. Alistair Cooke noted their eagerness to show that the "Roosevelt administration had been criminally 'soft' towards communists, if it was not actually riddled with them,"[11] and that Russian power was "a waking plot initiated long ago in the reign of the New Deal."[12] As the the *New York Times* put it, "A cornerstone of the Republican campaign strategy was the oft-repeated charge that the Roosevelt and Truman Administrations had been dyed pink by Moscow."[13]

When Alger demanded that HUAC hear him despite all the good advice, Dulles cut him loose; a man who tends post-Holocaust contracts with I. G. Farben is unlikely to be sentimental, especially when he expects to be the next Secretary of State. He circulated Nixon's letter to the board. He also circulated memos distancing himself from Alger, saying he hadn't known the man well.

Nixon was running for his second Congressional term in the election to come, and his fireworks lit up the whole Republican campaign.

SENSATIONAL SPY DISCLOSURE FORECAST
Alger Hiss further enmeshed in the Communist web[14]

INQUIRY TO EXPOSE THIRD SPY COMBINE
Hiss Chambers Hearings To Continue[15]

Nor was Nixon going to let the promise of that libel suit lapse. the *New York Daily News* complained, "Well, Alger, where's that suit?"[16]

As for Chambers, he writes in *Witness* about his state of mind after those August hearings. "Deeply emotional people" like him and his wife, he says, found "the enveloping silence" almost impossible to bear.[17] He himself was "the spirit of a man on the rack of necessity. The nerve was torn . . . Only someone who has been alone against the world will know what that means."[18] The arch spy Alger, who could reveal God-knows-what-all about spy networks all over the world was the only person it would make sense for the Soviets to kill; even so, Chambers, who's been no part of anything for a decade, fears the Communists intended "to remove me as the one dangerous witness against the conspiracy."[19] He sees Soviet agents in every car that passes. He sees them prowling at the edges of his property. He sees them in any stranger who appears in the neighborhood and any passerby who asks a question. He warns his children's schools to make sure that no spies spirit them off during playtime.

But none of this fear and trembling quite fits the record. Recently released HUAC reports confirm that FBI agents were spending many hours at the Chambers farm with him. In *Six Crises* Nixon confirms that he too paid many private visits after the hearings as well as during them. Chambers forgets the FBI in *Witness* but confesses—although only in the small print of a footnote—that "throughout the most trying phases of the Case, Nixon and his family were at our farm, encouraging me and comforting my family." Nixon became so familiar a figure at Chambers's farm that the little Chamberses started calling him "Nixie."[20]

As for Alger, despite the media barrage, despite Dulles's obvious change of heart—and by now the rest of the Carnegie board's—he had no intention whatever of sinking to Nixon's level. There was a right way and a wrong way of doing things; the papers buried his lawyerly rebuttals on back pages while Nixon hogged the headlines. And then, at the end of September, precisely a month after Chambers's radio appearance, he handed Nixon what Nixon's heart desired:

HISS BRINGS SUIT AGAINST CHAMBERS
Hiss sues Chambers for slander
The damages were set at $50,000.[21]

Chambers issued a press statement: "I welcome Alger Hiss's daring suit.[22] I do not minimize the ferocity or ingenuity of the forces that are working through him."

This constituted an additional libel. Alger raised the damages to $75,000.

⸺ ⌘ ⸺

All the opinion polls—all polls of every kind—showed that the Republican strategy was working exactly as planned and that Democratic President Harry Truman was on the way out. For months the pundits had been saying that: nominating him doomed the Democrats to certain defeat. Not that Nixon was a man to leave anything to chance.

"The full story of Communist espionage will not be told until we get a Republican President," he told the press, "who is not afraid of skeletons in the closet." HUAC issued a twenty thousand page report naming eleven Americans as Communist spies who'd stolen atom bomb secrets and delivered them to Russia. Nobody was ever charged. The FBI caught quite a few bomb-secret stealers; HUAC never even identified one. But the publicity was enormous. Nixon campaigned for the removal of the Fifth Amendment altogether in such cases. He campaigned for the removal of double jeopardy.

He spoke all over the West Coast; the archives show him popping up at breakfast meetings and Chambers of Commerce speaking about "Communists in High Places."[23] Ads ran in newspapers for days announcing his speeches:

**HEAR THE TRUTH
TOO HOT TO PUBLISH!
CONGRESSMAN RICHARD NIXON
AMERICA'S GREATEST ENEMY
OF COMMUNISM!**[24]

He openly accused the Truman administration of a Communist cover-up. He claimed that they'd "prevented J. Edgar Hoover, director of the Federal Bureau of Investigation, from testifying before Congress on espionage matters" because they "are afraid of the political consequence."[25]

The Justice Department was not moved. Its press release said that Congressman Nixon had "one eye on publicity and the other on election results."[26]

The grand jury wasn't impressed either. It questioned Chambers at length; he told them that he had "information" and "certain contacts" with "various people" who were "in touch with other people" who were Communists. But he was so vague. The special assistant to the US Attorney General—the man who'd found Chambers a "difficult witness" some years before—tried again for the jury. "Could you give one name of anybody, who, in your opinion, was positively guilty of espionage against the United States? Yes or no."

Chambers took twenty-four hours to reply. "I assume that espionage means in this case," he said then, "the turning over of secret or confidential documents."

"Or information—oral information."

"Or oral information. I do not believe I know such a name."[27]

Which would have been really bad for Nixon, but again privilege came into play: grand jury testimony is secret too. On the very day the jury was getting negatives out of Chambers, newspapers all over the country were quoting Nixon quoting him on Communist spy rings in the State Department[28]: "One of the undergrounds was headed by Alger Hiss."[29]

Nixon had so routed his opposition that he ran for his seat in the House unopposed.

But the Republican candidate for the White House, Thomas Dewey, didn't fare so well, after probably the most famous upset in US electoral history. There are wonderful photographs of the exultant, newly elected Democratic President, Harry Truman, holding up the *Chicago Daily Tribune*, clearly printed the night before:

DEWEY DEFEATS TRUMAN[30]

Nobody expected the House Un-American Activities Committee to survive this wholly unexpected victory. In an address delivered to the American Association for the Advancement of Science and broadcast throughout the country, Truman had rebuked HUAC for creating an "un-American" atmosphere. "It is the climate of a totalitarian country" in which even prominent thinkers are "expected to change" their ideas "to match changes in the police state's propaganda line." The point of his quip about Alger's case—that it was a "red herring"— was that the Red Scare's purpose was to distract attention from the country's postwar economic woes. Clearly millions of people agreed with him about the economy if not about Alger; the Democrats secured the House of Representatives as well as the White House, and the Committee itself was dwindling because of it. To be sure, sheep-faced Mundt, who'd feared for world peace "under the leadership of men like Alger Hiss," was going on to the Senate, where the perks are better and the status higher, but it meant he was gone. Committee members Vail and McDowell were just plain voted out. And as for fat little J. Parnell Thomas, who'd inveighed against "Fifth Amendment Communists" and scolded Alger with "never mind the evidence," he took the Fifth against corruption charges—fraud and kickbacks—and was on his way to a stretch in Danbury Correctional Institution.

Press dispatches indicated the Committee was likely to be dissolved in January as soon as Truman was sworn in.

It certainly looked as though the Committee itself and anybody connected with it was on the way out. Nixon says in *Six Crises* that he just shrugged his shoulders mentally with the thought that there wasn't anything he could do about it. He was going to forget about it all and turn his attention to his wife and their long-planned holiday cruise down the coast toward the Panama Canal.

Doesn't sound quite like him, does it?

Suppose Alger was the spy Nixon wanted him to be? A high-level New Dealer like Alger would be a Soviet "prize asset," as they say in spy-speak, and even ordinary spies are special people. It's not your usual personality that betrays for a living, and people who turn against their own countries take a while to become what they become. For the well-educated, university is a common route. When the famous ring of spies known as the Cambridge Five were undergraduates, the Soviet Union filled them with revolutionary zeal: a classless society, no private property, the population as a whole owning the farms, factories, produce. They wrote, debated, gave fiery speeches. *Everybody* knew they thought only the Russians could defeat the Nazis as well as release the stranglehold of the business and banking giants.

Alger was very different. At Johns Hopkins he was convention personified: a clutch of social clubs, editor of the student newspaper, president of the student council, cadet commander in the Reserve Officers Training Corps. His politics fitted right in; he was one of those middle-of-the-road liberals who believed in the Bill of Rights for everybody, including the right to own property, whether a house or a farm or a factory. His friends did include left-wingers, which is to say he was certainly exposed to the ideas, but there's nothing that so much as hints at his taking part in radical activity of any variety. Harvard was no more rebellious.

This would never do. I needed people with first-hand experience of espionage to fill out the picture. I found Svetlana Chervonnaya—what a wonderful name for a spy expert—in *The American Scholar*. The KGB trained her. She was actually in Russian intelligence, and she promptly got Nixon's story into worse trouble. She told me that as soon as recruits like the Cambridge Five went underground, their instructions were to make a public jolt in the opposite direction. She says that the spy Elizabeth Bentley was told, "You must cut yourself off completely from all your old Communist friends," and "you must pose as an ultraconservative, with a slight leaning toward fascism." This "was considered basic stuff."[1]

A political about-face is as visible to friends, relatives, colleagues as a newly shaved head. Nobody noticed any such changes in Alger. He didn't cut off those left wing friendships. His New York pro bono work only made him a more active and more vocal liberal; Roosevelt's election turned him into a real enthusiast. Liberalism was what the New Deal was all about, and Alger was a New Dealer through and through. He began in government in the spring of 1933 with the Agricultural Adjustment Administration, thrilled at the thought that he could supply small farmers with the legal remedies he'd found missing in New York. Svetlana sent me an article by a friend of hers: that spring American Communists were working hard "to prove concretely" that the aim of Roosevelt's farm program was "to assist the bankers, insurance companies, marketing trusts, and the rich farmers at the expense of the workers, and the poor, small ruined middle farmers."[2]

Nobody caught Alger doing anything like that or saying anything to indicate thoughts like that. Nor did anybody note changes to his politics—or his expression of them—at Yalta or Dumbarton Oaks or in San Francisco when he was setting up the United Nations.

Toward the end of his career in government, the Marshall Plan was the big topic, an American aid program designed to help reconstruct war-torn Europe with a $13 billion loan that eventually led to the Common Market. The Soviets hated the idea, wanted no part of it, reacted angrily against it as an imperialist plot to dominate Europe. Alger supported it strongly and publicly. He wrote for *The New York*

Times Magazine: "Our abandonment of Europe would expose 270 million people . . .to absorption in the vast area already dominated by Communist ideology."[3]

With Alger as Nixon's spy, this consistency is going to be a headache.

Alger was President of the Carnegie Endowment for International Peace when the article came out, and he'd risen through increasingly important positions of state to get there, a life of formal dress, exquisite manners, and constant media attention. Which brings up another stumbling block. How can a spy function in company like that?

Svetlana reminded me of Arkady Shevchenko, the Soviet diplomat and UN Under-Secretary General. He approached the CIA for asylum in 1975, knowing he came to them as a prize asset who'd have to trade a period of spying for life in America. His defection was a huge undertaking for the CIA as well as for him. Everything about it was in tune with that elevated company. Nobody looked out of place. His contacts were specialists whose job was to listen to him talk about Soviet policy and political decision-making. Troops of discreet top operatives were on constant watch for signs of Russian secret service activity around him. Despite all this care and concern, the CIA couldn't keep the operation going as long as three years, even with the United Nations based in New York and the CIA on home ground.

The Russians must have been truly extraordinary to manage this for more than a decade with Alger—and deep in enemy territory at that, with the danger of exposure constant and extreme. And planning all the way from Moscow? A nightmare. Nor was their only threat from the CIA. The FBI was everywhere, and surveillance of Alger was targeted according to the accusation Chambers had made: "for the purpose of determining the extent of his activities on behalf of the Soviets and for the additional purpose of identifying espionage agents."[4]

Studying what they found is too daunting a task for me, but Senator Daniel Moynihan headed a Commission on Government Secrecy, and he had a good look. The best the FBI could come up with was that Priscilla Hiss "may have been a member of the League of Women Shoppers,"[5] that both Alger and Priscilla "had attended the Senate Hearings on the question of atomic power," and that "Hiss had closely read the Smyth Report on the bomb."[6]

There's no mention—not one—of the outrageous Chambers bursting into that polite and courtly existence with his mouth of blackened teeth, his baggy clothes, and his bragging that he was a Communist spy in fear of his life with the US secret services shadowing him. Maybe the FBI destroyed chunks of Alger's file, just as they destroyed my parents' files; maybe all traces of Chambers disappeared into that paper shredder. Why would the FBI do such a thing?

But suppose they did. Suppose Alger and Chambers really were partners in espionage despite the monumental obstacles. Which certainly puts both of them in the genius class.

"The best genius in espionage," runs one of Dr. Elsbeth Schragmüller's maxims, "is the one who is never conspicuous."[7] Dr. Schragmüller—also known as Mademoiselle Docteur, Fräulein Doktor, Fair Lady, La Baronne, and Mlle Schwartz—was a pioneer in intelligence who ran a whole spy school in Germany in the 1920s; the manuals she wrote still ruled the world of spying in HUAC's day. Alger the genius didn't seem to pay any more attention to her than Chambers did. He was already a conspicuous figure, used to seeing himself on the front pages, and he goes right on to demand an appearance in front of a Congressional Committee, knowing full well that the media will be crawling all over him as a result. Svetlana echoed Schragmüller: "You keep as low as possible." If you have to speak "take the 5th Amendment." "And better, run to avoid compromise."[8]

Three options. Alger ignored them all.

What about entrapment? Here's former British secret service officer, writing under the name of Vernon Hinchley: "It is impossible to understand why a man of such high intelligence, and in a position where a hint of treachery could—and in fact did—hit the headlines overnight, omitted the most elementary precautions to protect himself."[9] All petty crooks know better than to tell the cops anything but their names; everything else will be used against them. Alger not only demanded his HUAC hearing, he answered every question put to him, even though the Soviet secret services were in total agreement with the petty crooks.

Then he deliberately and publicly tangled with Chambers. "In the Soviets' view," Svetlana wrote, "Chambers was an agent provocateur. You absolutely don't engage an agent provocateur."[10]

Speak of a story with plot holes. The genius spy did everything wrong.

The spymasters were behaving very oddly too. Here's Ladislas Farago—another marvelous name for a spy expert—military historian, coiner of the phrase "psychological warfare," and expert in it for US Navy Intelligence. He says governments "do everything possible behind the scenes to protect" their spies, but an exposed spy is "regarded as expendable."[11] Chambers was always on about Soviets trying to kill him. Shevchenko was terrified of being drugged, bundled away to Moscow, and executed; apparently that's what happened to his wife. Why didn't something like it happen to Alger?

The Russians must have been terrified. Think of our hard-line action over Edward Snowden's revelations. Wikileaks too. Both are more about embarrassment than state security, and yet the hunt is international and the penalties to be doled out very, very harsh. Alger was in a different league altogether; I can only imagine how much top secret Soviet information he could reveal—or be forced to reveal. No matter what movies and thrillers say, nobody stands up under torture for long; he had a wife and two small children too. A prize asset like him could bring down a massive part of the Soviet network in the US, destroy God knows how many operations in progress, put God knows how many agents at risk of capture, imprisonment, death. And think of the secrets they could reveal. Maybe chunks of the European network too.

This is a man who needs killing. And quick. And yet nobody has found hints of so much as a restraining action planned against him, much less anything more violent. Nobody has found any sign of Soviet concern about Alger and HUAC at all. It looks as though the Russians just ignored his plight.[12]

Here's a plot hole you can throw a frying pan through.

27

1948

November 4, the very day after Truman's surprise win, was the first day of Chambers's pre-trial deposition in Alger's libel suit.

The legal system would fall apart without some way of settling in advance. There aren't enough judges, juries, and courthouses to go around; 90 percent of criminal cases end in settlement before trial. The money saved is staggering. Full-blown criminal trials are hugely expensive for the government; for a private citizen caught up in a civil case like this one, they're a quick route to bankruptcy. Just as important, full-blown trials are as much lotteries as hearings are. Judges, juries, witnesses are unknowns. Anything can happen.

Anything can happen at a deposition too. This one took place in the library of the Marbury firm in the Maryland Trust Building, where Alger's lawyers practiced. Chambers arrived, his head filled with thoughts that "William Marbury might be a Communist," his lawyers, Cleveland and McMillan at his side. Here's the setting as he describes it:

> The library was a large room, with windows at the far end and part way down the two long sides. In the middle was a conference table. I took my place at one end of this table. At my right was McMillan, and, next to him, Cleveland. Facing me at the opposite end of the table sat William Marbury.[1]

Chambers wrote that he "felt incredibly alone." He says he sensed "gleeful malevolence" and "blistering condescension" in Alger's lawyers, one with eyes "bugged" in a "stare of pure hatred," another speaking in "a tone of carefully modulated evil." He says the ordeal reminded him of school bullies who'd peed on a lollypop before they handed it to another boy, "only, now, that lollypop was being offered to me."[2]

All this terror and loneliness fit no better here than they did in September with Nixon and the FBI comforting him while he waited for Alger's suit. The lawyers that flanked him came from a firm called Semmes, Bowen & Semmes, a huge, diverse enterprise—one of the most influential in Maryland—with arms in every branch of the law and branches in several cities, including Washington DC. The firm is huge and powerful to this day; its alumni include presidents of the Maryland Bar Association and of various US agencies. Richard Cleveland, sitting on Chambers's left was the son of Grover Cleveland, twenty-second and twenty-fourth President of the United States. And that's not all. Chambers doesn't mention Harold Medina, a third on his team. Medina was a son of one of the most eminent judges in the country; he'd been specially picked for the job by Henry Luce, magazine king of his day, publisher of *Time*, where Chambers was a senior editor.

As for Alger, well, it's pretty clear he assumes he's won already. Which is to say we're back with his Harvard arrogance. He doesn't even show up. His lawyers? Friends. He'd waited for his childhood friend, William Marbury, to come back from Europe. Old boys together: unbeatable. Marbury was a corporate lawyer, pure and simple—tax and antitrust stuff—no experience in libel, espionage, crime courts. He opens the proceedings.

"Mr. Chambers, will you state your full name please?"

"Jay David Whittaker Chambers."[3]

"Jay" doesn't appear as part of his name in his HUAC hearings until the day-long, televised extravaganza, although he was born with it. Not with "David," though. Or with "Whittaker."

The idea is to grill him about his background, find out just how reliable a witness he is, but Marbury's inexperience shows up at once. He hands Chambers a piece of paper and asks him if he said what's on it.

One of Chambers's lawyers interposes, "Don't you want to identify that in some way?" Shouldn't lawyers do that kind of thing automatically? Never mind. This is Chambers's show, and it has the surreal excitement of his fear and loneliness in this room where he's so well protected.

He begins his tale. We watch an underground agent called Arthur take him to Grant's Tomb on Manhattan's Upper West Side to meet a Russian called Herbert, who leads him to another Russian, this one called Ulrich—nobody has a last name—who is the personal embodiment of "the international apparatus"[4] and tells Chambers, "You can be shot by them or you can be shot by us."[5] Ulrich gets into a power struggle with yet another Russian called Herman—or is it Herbert in disguise?—who had "very soft brown eyes and hair clipped off that stuck right up and a deep bass voice."[6] Not wise to battle Ulrich. Herman is beaten to death by two thugs. Or murdered by the American Secret Police. Or recalled to Moscow, directly to Molotov, and murdered there. Then comes Oscar, then Henry, then Charley. In Chambers's autobiography, there's Don, Otto, Carl, and Bob too. Henry lives in an apartment hung with Ethiopian appliqué and tapestry from Abyssinia. So Ethiopia and Abyssinia were one and the same. Who cares? The names are so wonderfully exotic. There are subversive dealings with a bishop—or is it a man called Bishop?—who lives in the turrets of a wooden castle on the Hudson River.

As a result of all this Chambers had "fortnightly" meetings with the acting secretary of the Communist Party, a man called Max Bedacht. Or is it "weekly" meetings?[7] Bedacht said no such meetings happened, not ever, much less on a regular schedule. Chambers said he was out of the Party for a bit, then back in "in fifteen minutes" to edit the *New Masses*.[8] The publisher said, "Impossible." It not only didn't happen, it couldn't have happened.

William A. Reuben was a widely published investigative journalist who spent the last four decades of his life on the Hiss case. *Nobody* knew the case like he did. And the single most important observation he made as a result of his forty years of research was that "The first thing to note about Whittaker Chambers's confessions" of Communist underground work is that "it has never been corroborated, either by documentary evidence or by the word of any other human being."[9] This is yet another truly crucial element of the tale that Nixon's vast midden of detail has completely obscured.

This extraordinary sense of disorder continues even into Chambers's record as a money-earner. He told Nixon and HUAC he'd quit Columbia University in 1924 to become a full-time, paid employee of the Communist Party. "I believe my nominal salary was something like $10 a week," he tells Marbury; it seems "incredible,"[10] but this is what he lived on until he left the Party. A little later he's holding down a $15 a week job as well—for "about a year and a half "[11]—as a clerk in the Newspaper Division of the New York Public Library. Except that in a few pages more, he pares that down to "perhaps six months."[12] And yet he worked in the library from 1923 right up into 1927: three and a half years at a beginning salary of $60 a month, rising to $90.

Marbury asks why he left the job.

He spins his fantasy of cops forcing his locker open and finding not only "Communist handbills" but "evidence that there was a Communist cell working in the library."[13] He doesn't say a word about the armfuls of books he'd stolen from the stacks, but the library's records are clear. There was no Red material in the locker; he'd even defaced those books to hide their provenance, and he was fired because he was a thief.

Then there's money from translations. Marbury has to press to get the information; Chambers admits to a fee of $250 for translating the children's classic *Bambi* from the German. Translators really are badly done by, but the book had an introduction by the great John Galsworthy. Reviewed everywhere. Massive sales. He could get whatever work he wanted.

Marbury asks, "Did you publish any other translations during this period?"

"No," Chambers says, "I don't think that I did."

What about the other fifteen? Later he does admit to a couple of them, but only a couple. He mentions his erotic poems. No money there. What about his wife's income? She worked for the Soviet Trading Company Amtorg.[14] No mention of it. What about the $10,000 from his father and his two grandmothers?[15] A hell of lot of money back then, especially for a committed Communist. No mention of it.

He says of his wife, "We were married in 1930, which will give you one landmark to go by."[16] The landmark fades almost at once into 1931. He can't seem to get straight when he graduated from high school either, when he went abroad, when he returned, how many years he was in the Party, where he and his wife lived and for how long. He says his mother was a housewife who never worked even though she'd spent twenty years as a highly paid investigator for the Welfare Department of the City of New York. He gets his own brother's suicide wrong. His father's death too, both date and cause. Then there are all those aliases, so many that even he starts getting lost in them. He isn't embarrassed at contradictions or inaccuracies or confusions; he just shifts a little this way or that and goes on.

He's been doing it for years. In his first confession to Adolf Berle in 1939, he'd named thirty-eight communists. Confessing to the FBI two years later, he left out twenty-six of those and added twenty-two new ones. Another three years and the list fattened up into fifty-eight names, well over half of them no part of either previous list. The same year he named a mere twenty-odd to Raymond Murphy, the Chief Security Officer of the State Department.

But this deposition is about libel and how well he knows only one of the people he fingered, his close friend, Alger Hiss, and yet he can't quite remember how, where, or when he first met Alger, except that it was with a man called Ware. But he'd sworn before HUAC that he never met Ware. He swore that Alger knew him by the name Carl; now he can't recall which name Alger knew him by, although the name George Crosley "is not beyond possibility."[17] So many details start out concrete then turn to gossamer like this that nobody can keep track of them. One of his biographers documents seven full versions of his involvement with Alger and spies; in the course of them a quiet study group of four ordinary citizens blossoms into a Communist cell of seven hardened spies committed to espionage.[18]

It's a dazzling performance. But how is Nixon going to make anything out of it that will hold up in a court?

It's a point for Alger's lawyers too. Perjury calls for only one witness, but it needs documentation. On the first day of the deposition, Marbury asks that Chambers turn over any documentation he has from Alger. Chambers says, "I never obtained documents from him." On the second day, he implies he has some papers. He talks about Alger showing him "not particularly interesting" State Department documents from around the time of the German invasion of Austria, including "Mr. Messerschmidt's reports from Vienna."

Now wait a minute here. Nazis charging into Austria lit the fuse for World War II. That's what started the whole thing off, and everybody back then knew that Messerschmitt—forget the spelling—was manufacturer of the first jet engine, fighter planes faster and better than anything the Allies had been able to produce. And it's "not particularly interesting"?[19]

As the next day's session starts, Marbury presses the subject. "Have you any such papers with you Mr. Chambers?"

Chambers says, "No, I have not." But one of his lawyers interposes, "Mr. Chambers has advised us that he has not explored all the sources where some conceivable data might be."

He's given twelve days to produce something.

When the time is up, he doesn't appear. He sends his wife instead. She doesn't have any papers either.

Pictures of Esther Chambers are hard to come by. The one I found shows her as high-cheekboned and attractive. But Alistair Cooke, who watched her testify, described her as a "small severe figure", "very dark, thin-lipped", "a frail body and a small voice and a habit of licking her thin lips." He said she fingered her handbag nervously.[20]

It must have been difficult for her to appear like that when Alger's lawyers expected Chambers himself, but it sounds as though she coped pretty well to start with. Unlike her husband, she seems to know the details of her own life, background, education, marriage, birth of children. But when it comes to life with him, the accuracy slips away. She can't remember what kind of work he was doing when they met. Like him, she insists their income was a mere pittance from the Communist Party. But she lets it escape that she employed three maids—and bursts into tears when asked how she and Chambers could afford maids and then stretch the Communists' pittance to a new car, an apartment, a house, and a farm that Alger had taken a fancy to before them.

As for the details of her husband's Communist activities and his relationship to Alger, her account is novel, not covered by any of her husband's various scenarios, often contradicting all of them. When pressed, she says her memory is "vague" about such things. She says that after Chambers left the Party, they went into hiding, saw nobody, never dared go out of the house. But a few minutes later, she's talking about how they took a trip to Florida and how he went to New York during this period to meet his publishers. When she sees the two stories couldn't possibly marry, she bursts into tears again.[21]

The real oddity of all this is that she'd been a strong character before she met him, a staunch and committed "revolutionist," and yet as soon as she'd married him, she became an automaton. She was later to testify at Alger's trials that she agreed with everything her husband did, never asked him what he was doing, gladly accepted work assignments and his every word without question.

One of the lawyers prompted her, "If he told you that starting tomorrow we are going to Ypsilanti and your name was Hogan—"

"We would go to Ypsilanti," she interrupted, "and we would be the Hogans."[22]

The poor woman shows up at the Marbury law office again the next morning, again alone. Alger's lawyers finish with her before lunch. If this case seemed open-and-shut before, it's doubly so now.

After lunch Chambers himself arrives with his team. His lawyers announce, "Mr. Chambers desires to make a statement at this time."

Chambers begins. "In response to your request to produce papers from Mr. Hiss, I made a search and I have certain papers in Mr. Hiss's handwriting and certain other papers."[23]

Chambers said he'd put these papers in an envelope a decade before and hidden the envelope in a dumbwaiter shaft at his wife's sister's house in Brooklyn.

He says in *Witness* that he'd hidden them so long because he is "so constituted that in every question I will range myself upon the side of mercy"; he'd been driven "to spare those whom I had so far shielded" and "not to do injury more than is necessary to Mr. Hiss." But on finding the documents, he sensed the "physical hush that a man feels to whom has happened an act of God."[1] He was David facing Goliath, with his "little sling" aimed at "the Communist conspiracy" in the person of Mr. Hiss himself. [2]

He says the envelope he recovered was "big, plump, and densely covered with clotted cobwebs and the dust of a decade.[3]" He says his nephew pulled it out of the shaft and brought it to him. Like all his tales, it's evocative, colorful—even alliterative this time. The thing is, though, the nephew testified at the trials that he hadn't been present when Chambers extracted anything from the dumbwaiter shaft. He hadn't been around when his uncle opened the manila envelope either. When this first came up, nobody realized that the envelope wasn't "big" enough to become "plump" enough to hold so much for the simple reason that nobody saw it. The documents arrived at the FBI in "manila folders."[4] Chambers hadn't brought any manila folders with him to his deposition. Nobody knew anything about folders of any variety for nearly thirty years. He hadn't brought the envelope with him either. Nor had he brought the bulkier items. They were to appear later amid great drama.

His lawyers showed Marbury the originals. They let him look them over, then took them back, leaving the man with only a set of photostats.

And Marbury just let them get away with it.

What did the man think was going on? A photostat machine was a photocopier's slow, cumbersome ancestor—negative copy first, then positive copy—easy to "amend" with scissors and paste. The firm of Semmes, Bowen & Semmes included specialists in crime and corporate espionage. They knew what they were doing. Marbury? What does an antitrust lawyer know about this kind of thing? He was shocked to see any documents at all.[5] He had no more experience in forgery or fraud than he had in libel. He had no idea what kind of things the guilty can do to protect themselves or what a defendant is entitled to do or must do to escape traps set by the opposition. It didn't occur to him to demand that the originals stay with him until his firm had had time to examine them properly. It didn't even occur to him to insist that the documents be kept in the same order they appeared when Chambers produced them.

Combine Marbury's ignorance with Alger's arrogance, and you have a man on his way to prison.

"In the year 1937," Chambers says to Marbury, "I arranged a meeting between Alger Hiss and Colonel Bykov." This Colonel Bykov has grown into a favorite of Chambers's. He wasn't mentioned in the 1939 interview with Roosevelt's advisor Adolf Berle. In the 1942 and 1945 confessions to the FBI, he was somebody met in passing. During the HUAC hearings, he'd faded off screen entirely again. Today he's served for years as Chambers's superior in the underground; he's an insane tyrant whose tantrums terrify everybody, even Moscow.

The FBI tried hard to trace him. They found no hint that he'd ever so much as existed. "Colonel Bykov raised the question of procuring documents from the State Department, and Mr. Hiss agreed. Following that meeting, Alger Hiss began a fairly consistent flow of such material as we have before us here. The method was for him to bring home documents in his brief case, which Mrs. Hiss usually typed."[6]

A typewriter is slow, labor-intensive, noisy. A camera is quick, easy, silent. As early as the 1920s, cameras were standard spy gear. By the 1930s, 35mm cameras had built-in rangefinders coupled with a lens-focusing mechanism. Families took 35mm cameras on holiday to snap the kids on the beach. Images were sharp and clear, up close or at a distance. Typewritten documents are easily traced to the typewriter, then to the typist. Film documents are anonymous; the source stays hidden.

In those days, a camera also proved the document was accurate. Who *really* trusts a spy? Certainly not the spymaster. The person who betrays for a living really is different; switches of allegiance come with the territory. The former British secret service agent Vernon Hinchley wrote, "Original documents, not copies, would have been handed over and later returned."[7] He goes on to explain the absolutely critical reason why: "The spy's hardest task is not to get information but to persuade his employers that it is accurate."[8]

Here's Svetlana on how difficult the job can be:

> Stalin didn't trust anyone, up to paranoia, incl. his two intelligence services. Both services were aware of this and requested their field operatives to guide their sources to obtain photo copies of the documents, which Stalin would trust as original . . . an authentic doc as it was pilfered from government files. Hence, you see the document's properties—filing numbers, routing and other things.[9]

The only certified spy to appear in Alger's trials didn't know anything about Alger as a spy, and he'd never typed anything. Documents went straight onto 35mm film. Chambers himself told Assistant Secretary of State Berle that "important papers would be microfilmed."[10]

And yet now he's claiming his prize asset's wife not only typed out documents but that he—Chambers—went right up to their house to collect her work. Ronald Seth, British espionage agent, is scornful: Chambers's story runs "absolutely counter to accepted techniques."[11]

Hinchley is more than scornful: "Chambers's story is wildly improbable—a defiance of strict basic rules imposed by the Soviet secret service on its agents."[12] It was Dr. Schragmüller who laid down the rule: "When procuring information, make your informant travel as far as possible from his place of residence."[13]

Chambers also insists he did his pickups from Alger's home on a regular basis, and he went on doing it for years. Since Chambers is Chambers, "regular" has been varying from every day to every few days, to weekly, to every ten days, to fortnightly. Sometimes he volunteers the time too: between four thirty and six o'clock. How long did this go on? Four years. Four years? This bizarre-looking character? Creeping around in respectable neighborhoods just before dawn right at the time milkmen were delivering? The CIA explained to Shevchenko how important it was to avoid a "set pattern or routine."[14] Ladislas Farago explains, "If a courier makes numerous visits at regular intervals to the home of an informant, you invariably attract attention in any country where counterespionage is alert." For this reason "it is a strict rule of Soviet espionage that all meetings in the course of which documents are transferred from one person to another must take place on the street or in a public place."[15]

Svetlana gives details of correct procedure. "If the meetings were to be regular, there would be instructions on their place and time. For instance, at the entrance to a movie house at six p.m. on each second Friday; if the meeting does not take place, the arrangement would be for a meeting at the same place and time on the next Friday."[16] "Usually, as a recognition signal, they'd use two halves of the same thing (like parts of a jello box in the Rosenberg case)[17] . . . . There would be a password arranged with a response. For instance, a courier or an operative would say to a source, 'Have you been in Prague last summer?' With the answer, 'No, last summer I was in Bath.' (In Soviet time, there was a popular anecdote. A man rings the bell of an apartment and asks, 'Do they sell a Slavic wardrobe here?' with the answer, 'No, the spy lives upstairs.'"[18]

But Chambers goes on.

There occasionally came to Mr. Hiss's knowledge certain things, or he saw certain papers which he was not able to bring out of the department for one reason or another . . . notations in his handwriting are notes of such documents.[19]

Handwritten documents? In Alger's own handwriting? Alger's script was very distinctive. These notes weren't even printed out in capitals, which might have disguised them a bit. Typed documents are silly enough, but handwritten documents? Stalin certainly wouldn't accept anything like that as accurate. Besides, countless mystery stories revolve around people trapped by handwritten notes; they date at least as far back as Shakespeare's Twelfth Night. As espionage agent Seth says, Alger "must have been genuinely mad" to turn over anything like that.[20]

People do have a tendency to believe their opponents are stupider than they are, but nobody could think Stalin's spy networks were that stupidly run. The problem is, nobody on Alger's team knew anything about spies. None of them so much as looked at the implausibility of the idea itself. Not one of them raised the point, not at the pre-trial hearing, not even in the trials to come. The Hiss case remains the only case—unique in the history of espionage—that involves spies employing such clumsy and irrationally dangerous methods of passing information.

Of all the books I've read on the case, only the ones written by espionage experts—one of them a thriller writer—mention this extraordinary anomaly.

29

The year 1938? Here's where it comes alive. It's the year on all the documents that Chambers produced. Every single one. The first one is dated January 5, 1938. The last is April 1, 1938.

So *this* is why Chambers went off the record for over two hours during his executive session with Nixon. He had documentation that didn't fit the story he'd been telling for a decade—leaving the Party and last seeing Alger in 1937—and the documents couldn't be changed. But the story? Who would notice just another Chambers shift a little this way or a little that?

Alger looked over the photostats and said that at least three of the handwritten notes looked like his. In 1938, his job was assistant to the Assistant Secretary of State, Francis B. Sayre. The office got some two hundred telegrams a day. Sayre couldn't possibly read them all. Alger did it for him, took notes, briefed Sayre—notes in hand if he needed them—then threw the notes out or clipped them to the material they summarized. Sayre confirmed all this at the trials. Alger didn't remember any of these four notes, but he couldn't see anything in them that would interest the Soviets.

He didn't recognize the typed documents, although he thought many of them would have crossed his desk. But he couldn't see anything in them either that would interest the Soviets.

One thing he was sure of: Chambers shouldn't have had the material. His lawyers turned the originals over to the Justice Department even though they didn't like the idea. The dates scared them. Alger had sworn in his HUAC testimony that he hadn't seen Chambers since 1936 at the latest, and the 1938 date on the documents could be presented as evidence that he'd lied: a first count of perjury. He had also sworn that he'd never given Chambers information to be passed to the Russians; Chambers could claim that the documents were evidence of precisely that: a second count of perjury. Whether the Soviets would be interested or not was beside the point.

But these Harvard lawyers trusted the Department of Justice. Turning the originals over to them was legally and morally the only thing to do. That's how the Hiss team lost their chance to examine the papers themselves until it was way, way too late.

—⚭—

Justice needed time to make the examination that the Hiss team had failed to make; the department ordered a two-week embargo on media coverage of the case.

Keep a secret like that in Washington? As Stripling put it, Chambers had dropped a "bombshell,"[1] and the marvel is that the embargo lasted a full ten days. On the first day of December, the United Press reported that Justice was going to agree with Alger. Nothing in the papers was secret. There was no proof that the material had come from Alger or been destined for the Soviet Union. There was no evidence that any law had been broken. Nor was there enough in any HUAC transcript to indict anybody for perjury or anything else.

This is important. This is the second beating back of Nixon's hopes for a perjury charge against Alger. HUAC failed to bring one after its final hearing despite Chairman Thomas's claim that it "surely" would. After Chambers's deposition, Alger's lawyers had been afraid that the documents might be used to show Alger had seen Chambers and given him documents: that could be turned into perjury. But now the Justice Department has ruled against the charge.

But that very same day, the *Washington Post* reported "a startling development in the libel suit."[2]

Stripling wrote that he was "in a frenzy" to find out what the *Post* meant and that he persuaded Nixon to go to Chambers's farm with him.[3] Nixon says he suggested the two of them go. "A hunch," he says.[4] Out at the farm, Chambers talked of a second "bombshell." Stripling says Nixon wanted it at once. Now. No delay. Nixon says no, no. Nothing like that. He wasn't even interested. It took thirty years for Stripling to embrace Nixon's not-much-interested story. Here's his revision. Nixon and his wife were about to board ship for that ocean cruise, and Nixon said to him, "I'm so goddamned sick and tired of this case, I'm going to Panama. And to hell with it, and you, and the whole damned business." As for Chambers's bombshell, "I don't think he's got a damned thing."[5]

And yet Nixon called Louis Nichols of the FBI to tell him that Chambers had a lot more new material, material the Justice Department had *not* seen, material they had *not* been given a chance to dismiss as they were dismissing the dumbwaiter shaft papers. Nixon told Nichols to keep the information to himself, discuss it only with Hoover; if Justice got wind of it, they'd bury it. Nichols discussed the plan with Hoover. Hoover agreed to it. Nixon also scheduled HUAC hearings, and he scheduled them to begin well before the cruise ship was due back. On top of all this, he issued a subpoena for Chambers and the bombshell. And then he arranged for an amphibious plane to be on standby to pick him up from the *SS Panama* on an emergency basis. Coast Guard logs say so.[6]

On his way out of the House of Representatives, the doorkeeper could see "he was so delighted with something he had to share it."[7] Doorkeepers don't often write memoirs, but this one did. His name was William Miller; in his book *Fishbait*—that's what Congressmen called him—he reported that Nixon was "very elated and keyed up, as if he were dancing on wires." Nixon told him he was "going to get on a steamship." And the excitement? "They are going to send for me. You will understand when I get back."

The Nixons embarked from New York.[8]

———&&&———

As the *SS Panama* was heading down along the east coast toward the canal via Cuba, Chambers was stopping in at the HUAC offices to pick up Nixon's subpoena. Stripling and two members of staff went back to his farm with him to collect the new evidence.

It was ten o'clock by the time they arrived, pitch dark and bitterly cold. The HUAC officers carried midnight lanterns and followed Chambers across icy fields to . . .a pumpkin. A *pumpkin*? In midwinter? After a month of kill-ing frosts? All they should have found was black and shrunken remains. If finding a fresh, live pumpkin isn't miracle enough for you, there's a pattern of squashes—equally spectacular survivors—in the shape of an arrow pointing to this pumpkin. The center of the pumpkin had been carved out and the top plugged back in just like a Halloween jack-o'-lantern.

Inside the pumpkin, wrapped up in waxed paper, were two rolls and three canisters of film.[9]

One of the agents pocketed them all. All top secret affairs of state, and yet the person who first notified Nixon was Bert Andrews of the *Herald Tribune*. "Hiss-Chambers has produced a new bombshell . . . Justice Department partially confirmed by saying, 'It is too hot for com-ment.'"[10] How come Andrews knows all about it? Next came a cable from Stripling. "Case clinched. Information amazing. Heat is on from press and other places. Immediate action appears necessary."[11] Now all the press is in on it? Then another from Andrews: "Hiss's handwriting identified on three documents."[12]

Stripling called a massive press conference. As Chambers tells it in *Witness:* "Before I was out of bed the next morning, a news photogra-pher was trying to decide which pumpkin to take a picture of."[13] He went out at once to help. He explained to reporters that he'd hidden the films like this "so Communists wouldn't find them."[14] But what about their finding *him*? Only a couple months ago, he couldn't tell the Committee his home address for fear of Soviet hitmen, and now he's showing every newspaper in America where he lives. What could have happened in the interim to make him feel so much safer? There's no explanation.

The pumpkin was an immediate sensation. It was colorful. It was eye-catching. It was *fun*. Newsreels showed him reenacting his role, kneeling down, opening the pumpkin, removing film from it.

Nixon? The man had nerves of steel. He went to his meals at the captain's table on the *SS Panama* as though nothing had happened.

———— ⧯ ————

Nixon stayed aboard and let HUAC's Mundt hold a press conference late that Friday night. Mundt announced that the Committee was keeping a twenty-four-hour armed watch on the pumpkin's contents. This pumpkin contained, he said, "microfilmed copies of documents of tremendous importance which were removed from the State Department for the purposes of transmittal to Russian Communist agents."[15]

Investigator Stripling said that when they were developed, they'd make a pile more than three feet high.

This word "microfilm" caught the imagination almost as much as the pumpkin itself. It smacked of wars and armies and serious secrets; it dates all the way back to the Siege of Paris in 1870 when homing pigeons carried microfilmed dispatches from Tours to the besieged capital. Archives use it to this very day because it reduces paper storage space by something like 95 percent. There were two rolls and three canisters of film: that much microfilm could easily make a pile of paper three feet high.

Chambers said both rolls and canisters had been in the manila envelope from the dumbwaiter shaft along with the typewritten and handwritten pages he'd turned over at his November deposition for the libel suit. He hadn't mentioned them then because he was terrified that the Russians and the "Hiss forces" would get them; he'd hidden them on his farm instead.[16] Why in a pumpkin? The Communists wouldn't look for them there, even though he'd taken the idea from a Soviet spy movie called *Transport of Fire*. It says so on his own website. These rolls and canisters of film were bulky. No way they could have fitted in that envelope; he'd have split it trying to force them into it along with all those pages. Not that anybody noticed such a discrepancy. How could they? All the FBI had seen were manila folders of documents. Nobody outside HUAC and the Justice Department knew anything about envelopes—big enough or not big enough—to hold film as well as documents. Nobody beyond them had the faintest idea what either of the two bombshells consisted of. Except Bert Andrews of the *Herald Tribune* of course. And not even the Justice Department knew the secrets he did.

Nixon issued a press release from shipboard. "Will reopen hearings if necessary to prevent Justice Department cover-up."[17] Odd. He arranged these hearings before he left. Anyhow, the *New York Times* reported that members of HUAC were rushing to Washington "to bring into the open the new documentary evidence" and that the Justice Department "meanwhile arranged for presentation of enlargements of the microfilm to a grand jury in New York City on Monday."

It was not until Sunday that Nixon made his entrance. A Coast Guard amphibious seaplane scooped him up from the cruise ship and set him down in Miami, cameras catching every moment. Photographs of the young Congressman eclipsed even the pumpkin, and to a modern eye, he still cuts an impressive figure: lithe, athletic, young, handsome, concerned, important, emerging over the seaplane's wing—for all the world as impressive as Alger Hiss emerging from his jet with the UN Charter in hand. Despite the fact that Nixon had orchestrated all this himself, he told the howling pack of reporters and photographers that the Secretary of Defense had ordered it. He announced to them that the new evidence—not that there'd actually been time for him to see it in this scenario, much less examine it—showed that the Hiss Case "is no longer one man's word against another's." This new evidence, he said, would "prove once and for all that where you have a Communist you have an espionage agent."[18]

On Monday morning, instead of taking the film to the Justice Department, Nixon and Stripling called a press conference, the first in what were to become daily press conferences for the next week and a half.

Stripling told reporters that the filmed documents were all Top Secret State War and Navy Department documents. He and Nixon posed with a stack of paper not just three feet tall, but a good four feet. There they were: Strip stretching out a strip of film while Nixon peered at it through a magnifying glass like Sherlock Holmes himself. A brilliant image. There couldn't have been a more popular hero in

1948. The last of Basil Rathbone's fourteen films had premiered barely two years before, and decades of radio Sherlocks had just introduced the best-loved American version yet, Leigh Lovell, a Londoner living in New York. Newsreels of the day showed Nixon, this living, breathing modern-day Sherlock with his magnifying glass, alongside a fuzzy document with TOP SECRET in huge letters across it.

The *New York Times* reported that the microfilms were evidence that Alger had "slipped Chambers 'restricted' documents for delivery to a Russian agent." Nixon went further. He said they were "conclusive proof of the greatest treason conspiracy in this nation's history . . .proof that cannot be denied."[19]

After the press retired for the day, Nixon met with Justice Department officials. A quarrel developed. Nixon refused to give up the pumpkin's film.

On Tuesday, Nixon's press conference reported on the discussions with Justice; he told journalists that even the drift of the conversation was too sensitive to reveal. Headlines screeched across the country:

SPY NETWORK IN STATE DEPARTMENT UNCOVERED[20]

Chambers Claims He Hid Films From Alger Hiss[21]

SAYS HISS LET OUT WAR SECRETS[22]

At least the *New York Times* had the sense to complain, "The audience received no hint as to the contents of the documents."[23] At Wednesday's press conference, Nixon began a subtle shift of attention away from the documents themselves and toward the failure of the Red-infiltrated government to address the threat they represented; Republican scaremongering had failed to elect a president only by the slimmest of margins. Congressmen must whip up voter excitement every two years, and no head start could be better than this pumpkin. Nixon said he feared that Chambers would be indicted in New York, and that it would all happen before action was taken. "This will thereby probably destroy the only opportunity to indict other individuals involved," he warned, "because the star witness will be an indicted and convicted person."

Thursday showed how accurately Nixon had hit home. The Justice Department attacked his technique of "trial by headline," stating that nobody—but nobody—outside HUAC had seen any of the evidence. How were they to know Andrews of the *Tribune* was in on it too? The Attorney General demanded that Nixon turn over "any and all information and documents which you may have regarding the subject matter."[24] Nixon ignored the demand while Chambers distributed the dumbwaiter shaft papers to journalists.

Friday's press conference announced HUAC's own investigation into the documents.

Saturday, and another Nixon press conference gave the first glimpse of what the pumpkin material itself might contain: "Twelve documents produced by Whittaker Chambers to substantiate his charge that Government Officials passed secret data to him," said the *New York Times*. Three pages were handwritten; a government handwriting expert had "declared conclusively and without qualification that the penmanship was that of Mr. Hiss."[25]

Were these the earlier handwritten notes? The ones Justice had dismissed? A new set maybe? Are there now seven handwritten pages all in all?

"Hiss's guilt," Nixon said, "is unmistakeable."

The US Attorney General sent a formal telegram requesting that Nixon turn over the microfilms. Nixon ignored the request. Not even Sunday went by without a press conference. Nixon devoted this one to setting out the Republican platform for the election to come. "'The Espionage Law is full of holes,' Mr. Nixon said." This is the *New York Times*. "Recent disclosures before the House Committee on Un-American Activities make it vital that proposals to tighten the espionage law should have"—as Rep. Richard Nixon of California put it—"the highest priority in the new congress."[26] Papers headlined with a "Plot to Seize the Government,"[27] and the Associated Press reported "800

Moscow-trained American Communists" being "drilled to overthrow our government."[28]

Monday, the Justice Department issued a subpoena directing Nixon to appear at once before a Federal grand jury investigating espionage, turn over the microfilm, and justify daily press conferences about material that nobody outside HUAC and Bert Andrews had been allowed to see.

This is the moment Nixon had been driving toward.

D oesn't "a Federal grand jury investigating espionage" sound like legal sages, black gowns, and gray hairs? It turns out to be no more than an oversized jury—twenty-three people rather than twelve—all drawn from us hoi polloi like any other jury. The job description is what sets it apart. A grand jury can subpoena witnesses and ask them questions; there's no judge, just the jurors, the prosecutor, and the witnesses. The term can last a full eighteen months. It doesn't even decide guilt; it decides whether or not a crime has been committed and, if so, who's the likely criminal.

Which is to say it's all about prosecution. Nothing about defense. Just like HUAC.

Also, its verdict doesn't need to be unanimous. Only a dozen need agree—only a bare majority—and here before this clutch of perfectly ordinary voters—just like the ones who'd landslided him into office— appeared the media star of the day, fresh from sea plane, pumpkin, and daily, country-wide headlines, clutching a new calfskin briefcase and explaining modestly that he was only "a messenger for the House" and that a grand jury was "an institution as great as Congress." He said to them, "You ladies and gentlemen are faced with probably the conundrum of the age for a grand jury."[1] The flattery was so outrageous that nobody noticed him sidestepping any description of the conundrum beyond it's being a "problem" that Congress had already "solved" by proving that Alger knew Chambers.

Nixon opened his briefcase and took out the two rolls and three canisters of film from the famous pumpkin. The canisters he dismissed—what was in them was "worth nothing whatever"—but the rolls of developed film were a different matter.[2] These rolls, he told the jury, contained material so sensitive that it couldn't "be released even at this time, ten years after the message was written, due to possible injury to the national security." He said the office stamps on it demonstrated that it came from a "locked cabinet" in Alger's boss's office to which only Alger, his boss, and two others had access.

He said the jury should subpoena all these people.

His story of the film put Alger's treason in 1938. Espionage had a three-year statute of limitations; he told the jury that because of this "legal technicality" Alger was all too likely to go "scot-free."

Book after book and article after article comment on how lucky this three-year statute of limitations was for Alger. How can they say that? It was disaster for Alger. For Nixon? It was a dream come true. A formal charge of espionage was entirely out of the question. Espionage does call for at least two witnesses, and the Espionage Act of 1917, in force to this day, describes spy material as information "to be used to the injury of the United States or the advantage of any foreign nation." The Justice Department had ruined the promise of the dumbwaiter shaft papers by declaring them innocuous. Chambers had dropped the wondrous pumpkin into the breach. Nixon could now substitute its contents and imply all manner of things about Alger, and because of the equally wondrous statute of limitations, he didn't have to prove a word of it. Not only that. He could rail against the statute as unconscionable legal protection for the guilty, outraged at being unable to bring the real charge while giving perjury an extraordinary zing.

These are "legal technicalities" that he doesn't even mention, much less explain.

And treason? Nixon has been bandying the word about as though it were interchangeable with espionage. But it isn't. Treason is really bad stuff. It's like murder. There's no statute of limitations. This is another "legal technicality" that he fails to explain.

He tells the jury that if Alger went free, the Department of Justice would bring perjury charges against Chambers, and he would be rendered useless as a witness while the treason would go unpunished.

What he does explain is that there are ways out of the dilemma.

"As most of you are aware," Nixon said, "Mr. Hiss after a good deal of persuasion and faced with certain facts changed his story, and changed it considerably." The conclusion? "He did lie."[3]

Nixon had that jury completely in thrall, so much so that, despite the Justice Department's subpoena, he walked away with the rolls and the canisters in his very own hands. The contents of these canisters remained classified for a quarter of a century. The testimony he just gave? Nobody saw it for more than half a century.

"Without question," he said in the press conference that followed, "there will be an all-out attempt by the Administration to suppress any further public airing of this case. If the Justice Department succeeds in keeping witnesses from the Committee for the next few weeks and a grand jury returns no indictment, it will mean, in effect, that a whitewash of the guilty people is inevitable."[4]

Simple blackmail: either the jury comes through with a perjury charge or gets tarred as Reds and traitors themselves. Just in case they hadn't quite got the message, the next day's press release made it all too clear. The pumpkin's films, Nixon said, were "documentary evidence" that "conclusively established" the link between "Soviet agents" and "officials and employees of our own government."

"Their crime, in effect, is treason."[5]

The following morning, Wednesday, newspapers ran banner headlines across entire front pages:

TOP SECRETS STOLEN FROM ARMY

"Spies got away with American secrets of great military significance,"[6] the stories ran. "Representative Nixon says that our espionage laws are full of holes."

Only hours after the papers hit the streets, the jury indicted Alger Hiss for perjury.

The upside? HUAC's future was safe. Talk of its dissolution stopped at once. As for Nixon, he was the national hero of the war against communism. He was already sailing toward the Senate. Next stop after that: vice president under General Eisenhower.

B ut the treason inside that pumpkin! What could it be?
      More leaks to the press came out every day, and more and more;
the jury must have been on pins and needles to hear testimony from
Alger's boss Assistant Secretary of State Sayre, the man who could
reveal all about the documents seen by only four people in his department, then locked away in a safe because revealing them still threatened
national security. He was the man who could confirm Nixon's "documentary evidence."

The jury had to wait a whole week.

Sayre said to them: "I have seen it suggested in the papers—I think
it was suggested by Mr. Mundt of the Un-American Committee—that
four people only had official access to these documents." He explained
that these secret papers—every single one of them—had been "readily accessible" to everybody and anybody. Not just "accessible" either.
They'd been "mimeographed" and "circulated" in Sayre's department
and beyond: "to each of the departments concerned."[1] The State Department Chief of the Records Division, a man called Walter Anderson,
testified later that papers like these were so un-secret that a messenger
delivered them to a couple of hundred State Department employees in
a shopping trolley. Alger's was one of the offices the trolley stopped at,
but so was the State Department's Communications office, where press
releases were prepared. Such papers were also available to a select group

of non-Government people, authors, historians, researchers, and one-time officials writing their memoirs.

That grand jury had been had.

Nixon had invented practically everything he told them, from the routine in Sayre's office, to the secrets that the rolls of film contained, to the reason for not wanting the Justice Department near his pumpkin: Justice would have seen at once that the Sayre material was about as treasonable as an invitation to an office party, as innocuous as the dumbwaiter shaft papers that they'd dismissed the month before. Furthermore, his testimony was under oath. Alger's perjury was murky at best. Nixon's! Why didn't they indict him? Why didn't Justice take action? Why didn't the press go wild?

The timing was perfect. This was a new grand jury. Federal grand juries are a regular feature of legal life in the US to this day. Twenty-three ordinary citizens are impanelled, and at the end of an eighteen-month term, a new twenty-three take their place. This new grand jury knew nothing of Nixon's testimony; its predecessor had served its last day on the very day it indicted Alger. Since all grand jury testimony is secret, this new lot couldn't compare what Sayre said to what Nixon had said.

They didn't *know* they'd been had. Nobody even had the chance to put the pieces together for fully half a century.

It wasn't just genius with Nixon—and not just genius combined with guts either. This was a brilliant poker player, gambling everything on a bluff that had only the slimmest chance of succeeding. Without the Sayre documents, he'd never have gotten his indictment, and the jury's secrecy made him safe from perjury himself. And his extraordinary bluff had to carry him further still. His newspaper leaks continued to imply all kinds of scariness about the Sayre material, but concentration shifted to the remaining three canisters of film, the ones Nixon had dismissed at the beginning of his speech to the jury as "worth nothing whatever."

It's a shift as magical as 1937's shift into 1938. The "unimportant" films became the ones that threatened national security. Nixon guarded them fiercely. They made headline after headline, and all he'd say about them was that they were top secret State War and Navy Department documents that proved "the greatest treason conspiracy" in America's history.[2] And if anybody needed proof of the traitor's identity, there were the pages that the government expert had declared to be in Alger's penmanship. Never mind that those were from the dumbwaiter shaft. It was all such a muddle, nobody could follow it. Alger's team? They held themselves above the fray, and the evidence of the greatest treason in American history disappeared into government files. Nobody saw it again for decades.

"We won the Hiss case in the papers," Nixon said in his White House tapes.[3] "I had him convicted before he got to the grand jury."[4]

PART THREE

Smoking guns

33

1970

If Dexter hadn't fallen in love with physics, I wouldn't be writing this book now.

He didn't start out in science. From the time he was very little, he wanted to be a writer. Nothing else. Ever. That's what he did until World War II began and he went to the Board of Economic Warfare as an expert on East Africa, about which he knew absolutely nothing. When the army needed somebody to explain new technology to men in the field, they decided teaching a writer some physics was easier than teaching a physicist to write. Dexter was the writer they chose. After the war, he'd collaborated with Kate Way on *One World or None*, caught the physics bug working with scientists such as Einstein and Oppenheimer, and wrote *The Accident* partly as a tribute to them.

He'd tell me about his fascination while we sat around a log fire in Hindhead. Or at least he tried to, and I tried to respond. But one evening he said, "You have no idea what you're talking about, do you?" It was true. I knew so little—I thought it all had to do with strange bits of machinery in white-coated labs—that I didn't even realize I could learn what I needed from books. I plumped for the language of science instead, ordered Teach Yourself Arithmetic and started in on the ground floor.

I also read some of Dexter's books. One was E.T. Bell's *Men of Mathematics*, and there I ran across Evariste Galois, nineteenth century mathematician, who has an important role to play in Alger's story.

It's as romantic a life as any ballet librettist could dream up. The set-ting is Paris, early part of the century, the reign of Louis-Philippe. A rebellious French boy, too brilliant to conform to the rules of the École Polytechnique, gets tossed in prison twice before he's twenty years old for dramatic gestures against a repressive king. When politics doesn't obsess him, mathematics does; he turns algebra on its head, sorting out classic problems that date back to the Greeks. Then he's trapped into a duel over "quelque coquette de bas étage"—"some common girl"—and is left for dead by the side of the road. He spends his last hours madly trying to scribble out his life's work before he dies.

He had not yet reached his twenty-first birthday.

They buried him in a common grave, and nobody realized for another forty years that he'd been one of the greatest mathematicians the world has ever known. There aren't many pictures of him, but the most famous engraving became a French stamp in 1984 with the peculiar denomina-tion 2,10+0,40. It shows a fine-featured, very good-looking boy, large, dark eyes, somewhat almond-shaped, straight nose, tousled hair, that touching vulnerability that some young men have, hind or wildebeest in the savannah where lions are on the prowl.

Nobody seemed to have heard of him. I haunted bookstalls, found only a dreadful fictionalized version of his life by Leopold Infeld, Ein-stein's collaborator. All other references—there weren't many—were in French. I knew no French; I found a teacher, began at the beginning just as I had with math. I have a tendency towards obsession, and this boy really preoccupied me. I studied hard during the winter in the Maine house that cousin Niels loaned us. Snow and pine trees everywhere. Toby off to school in a yellow bus. Dexter on the phone with editors over his novel, now called *The Cloud Chamber*.

In spring, when *The Cloud Chamber* came out, we'd deal with the excite-ments of publication, then start looking for a place to live in Manhattan.

Publication day approached. The publicity department didn't secure interviews. The idea of a launch party fell to one side. So did marketing plans. The book came out. No reviews. Not one. Not even from old friends in the trade. This is every writer's nightmare, and Dexter had never failed before. He'd never even come close, one of those charmed lives of praise and garlands, international best sellers, prizes, even television quiz shows. He brushed off attempts at sympathy, but the buoyancy left him, if so slowly that I barely noticed it. I didn't realize how desperately hurt he was, not even when he started talking about going back to Europe.

We could live in France for a while, and I could work on my Galois project. A couple of weeks at a friend's apartment in Manhattan. A couple of weeks in Illinois with his family, then back to New York, sail to England, cross over to France.

⌘

During the weeks in Manhattan, we spent a long evening with Alger and Isabel. She'd been wholly right about Alger's getting over things; it was as though the fiasco of dinner with Niels and his assassination plot had never happened. I have to admit that I remained wary. There'd been no hint of the traps I'd been guarding against in that intense interest of his. But he still made me uneasy; there's something unnerving about a person who bears no grudges. Even so, I lost no time in getting to Galois.

"You won't have heard of him," I started. "Nobody has, but—"

"Evariste Galois?" Alger interrupted. "Of course I've heard of him."

"You *have?*"

"Not only do I know him, I know where there's a complete collection of his work and everything that's been written about him."

I was all in a dither. Where was this place? Where had the material come from? Who'd done the collecting? Could I see it? Alger said he couldn't answer all my questions, but he could point me in the direction of the collector. He wrote down a name for me.

William Marshall Bullitt of Louisville, Kentucky.

Then he paused, considered, and said something along the lines of, "I'd be happy to introduce you myself, but I don't think that would be a very good idea. Best if you make contact through someone else. Mr. Bullitt is an attorney. I'm certain he'd see you if another attorney approached him on your behalf."

We stayed with Dexter's brother Tom and his wife Mary Jane in Illinois.

Dexter called the firm of Bullitt, Dawson & Tarrant from there. To my horror, I heard him saying to Mr. Bullitt himself that I was a mathematician from Columbia University on a departmental research project into Galois's life and work. Dexter was impishly pleased with himself when he hung up. Old Mr. Bullitt, the one who'd collected the Galois material, was dead. His wife had given his collection to the University of Louisville, and his son—the present Mr. Bullitt—had taken over the law firm and the stewardship of the collection. He'd make the arrangements personally; we could photocopy whatever we wanted.

There was one condition. He wanted this Columbia University mathematician—me—to do him the honor of having lunch with him when we were finished; Dexter was welcome to come along if he wished.[1]

We left Toby with Tom and Mary Jane and borrowed Mary's little red Ford for the trip. She'd attached a posy of brightly-colored plastic flowers to the aerial so she could spot it easily in supermarket parking lots. These posies made me squirm, and I was already very uneasy. How in the name of Christ was I going to carry off being a mathematician on the basis of a Teach Yourself education? Especially with a posy of plastic flowers flying from the aerial? The man was probably an amateur mathematician. He'd laugh at me.

And then, I'd never been south before. Kentucky is in the Ozarks, south and hillbilly both. "Way down in ol' Kentucky" where they hunt "the possum and the coon" and all that. It was only 1970. Not long since segregation. I had visions of a boiling hell out of the film *Easy Rider* where rednecks in pickups shoot outsiders on sight and lynchings are a regular feature of life.

There wasn't a pickup in sight. Lots of horses though. Horses everywhere, grazing behind white fences, exercising in fields, being led by the occasional stable boy. Always a black stable boy. We even passed a dressage school with riders—white riders—in velvet hats jumping over barriers. South? This wasn't south. It was mile after mile of gentle New

England nostalgia right out of Currier & Ives lithographs. The University too: red brick buildings on broad lawns, wide flights of steps, white columns rising to peaked porticos, domed roofs, windowed cupolas. Ekstrom Library was one of the duller buildings, but the head librarian greeted us at the door; she carried a huge jailer's ring of keys, led us to a dark wooden door, unlocked it. Beyond it was a second door like no door I'd ever seen before. It was made of heavy metal mesh—copper, I think—and belonged in Fort Knox with machine-guns on either side of it.

Opening it wasn't easy either. "Nobody gets in here unless they have young Mr. Bullitt's permission," she told us, struggling with her keys. Then she added, "You two are the first visitors this year."

The room beyond was smallish, its walls solidly book-lined. Windows on two sides looked out over university lawns. She told us to come to her when we'd found what we wanted, and she'd organize the photocopying while we had lunch with Mr. Bullitt. "The books are in alphabetical order," she said, leaving us to them.

I went at once to the Gs, couldn't find any Galois, assumed the material had been separated, filed under editors and/or publication. I started at the top shelf on the right hand side of the door. Dexter was idly studying titles, pulling out the occasional volume; I didn't pay much attention until he burst into a laugh. The book in his hands was very old. He showed me the card inside the front cover; it said this was a copy of Isaac Newton's *Principia*, annotated by Newton himself, part of an exhibit at Harvard in 1953. Turn the pages and lines were crossed out here and there, a few added in a sloping, illegible hand with curlicues and blobs of ink from a quill-tip pen.

So *that's* why all the security. A book like that has to be close to priceless, something to be guarded in a glass case at the British Museum or the Bodleian Library. But, no, here it was on an ordinary shelf, filed under N, in a room that hadn't had a visitor all year.

I kept looking for the Galois material, pausing only for further discoveries of Dexter's: a first edition of Galileo's Dialogues printed in Florence in 1632, a first edition of Copernicus printed in Nuremberg in

1543; Einstein on relativity, with an inscription from Einstein himself to William Marshall Bullitt.

Whoever this William Marshall Bullitt was, he clearly wasn't your usual run of Louisville lawyer.

But an hour of careful scanning of shelves failed to turn up any Galois, nothing by him, nothing about him. I'm easily defeated. Not Dexter. If Alger said the material was here, it was here. Maybe not in the library, but somewhere else.

Young Mr. Bullitt was Thomas Bullitt, known as Tommy when he was little. He turned out to be somewhere past forty, not a bad-looking man, beginning to bald, remaining hair a suspicious, shoe-polish brown. He greeted us enthusiastically and listened with concern while we explained that the Galois material was missing. But he wasn't any more worried than Dexter. He said he didn't know much about the collection, but he knew nobody had broken it up when his father died.

In the parking lot, his big, fancy Cadillac stood right beside Mary Jane's little red Ford with the posy of plastic flowers on the aerial. "I was going to take you to lunch at Mother's anyhow," he said. "That's probably where it is." He suggested that he drive me to Mother's and that Dexter follow; that way we could stay on and search for Galois when he went back to his office for his afternoon appointments.

Tommy Bullitt was a mannerly man in a very Southern way, charming, a lot of gestures, amusing to listen to, not much interested in a response. I could have said anything. Or nothing. My mathematical credentials never even came up. "See that?" He pointed to a narrow bridge arching high above Interstate 64. "That's my daddy's bridge." He explained that the family owned all this land and that the state had made a compulsory purchase order to drive the highway through it. But because William Marshall Bullitt was head of one of the founding clans of Louisville—and a famously hard bargainer—the state agreed to foot the bill for a bridge to keep his many, many acres intact.

"Local people didn't like it," Bullitt said. "They still don't like it. They say, 'Where does it come from?' 'Nowhere.' 'Where does it go?' 'Nowhere.' 'Who uses it?' 'Bullitt's sheep.'"

We exited the highway into a shopping mall that he told me with a smile was "Mother's front yard." He'd sold it off himself. She didn't need it. The estate didn't need it. We drove over a stretch of parking lot, between a warehouse-like retail outlet and a sizeable McDonalds. A curve in the road, and abruptly everything changed. We were in *Gone With the Wind* country, a long drive with old trees equally spaced on either side of it; he told me the estate was called Oxmoor after Tristram Shandy's farm. But when we reached the house, it wasn't a match for Tara, a house-house rather than a mansion, with yet more white board fencing across the front garden.

It was much grander inside, spacious, dark wood and high ceilings in the entrance hall. Mother came to greet us, wispy white hair around a white crepe-paper face, a tremulous voice, very, very gracious.

"This is Mr. Dexter Masters, Mother," Bullitt said, "He's a writer. And this, this is Miss Joan Brady. She's a mathematician."

"Oh!" said mother, "This is exciting. A mathematician." But she turned her attention at once to Dexter. She took his arm, gazed up into his face. "Oh, how good of you to come to see me," she went on. "A *writer*! What did you say your name was?" Bullitt took my arm; he and I followed Mother and Dexter into the dining room. It was as grand as the entrance hallway. The four of us sat at one end of a table that would have been more comfortable with twelve around it. The glasses were cut crystal, linen napkins, armadas of knives and forks, all highly polished. A black maid in a black dress with a white frilly apron appeared with a pitcher.

"Iced tea?" Mother said, turning to Dexter. Before he could answer, she went on. "It's *so* kind of you to come and see me. A writer! Isn't that what you said? What did you say your name was?"

The uniformed maid brought lunch on gold-edged plates: McDonalds hamburgers from Mother's front yard. I stared down at mine, not at all sure what to do with it. Pick it up? Cut it into bites with one of the knives at my place? Which one?

Bullitt was explaining that we'd like to take a look at Daddy's books. Mother nodded, smiling. "Of course," she said, turning again to Dexter.

After lunch, Mother retired for a nap, and Bullitt led us into the library. This was a two-storey room, entered through a door in a wall of books, a movie-set salon of an Edwardian aristocrat complete with huge chandelier and vast fireplace. The molded ceiling was so high that the bookcases needed a mahogany ladder—it slid on brass rollers—to reach the highest shelves. Bullitt told us that we'd probably find what we wanted up there; he invited us to dinner at his house that night, then left. Dexter laid claim to the ladder while I started in on the lower shelves. Neither of us found anything distinguished: the collection was homely and rather boring, some popular science, a lot of popular fiction from the 1920s and 1930s.

Just as Dexter was climbing down, Mother appeared barefoot and in a bathing suit with several rows of ruffles at the rear. She greeted us as graciously as before. Our names still escaped her, but she remembered what we were there for and was sad that we hadn't been successful in our search.

"Perhaps Mr. Bullitt kept those books in his desk," she said. She pressed a hidden button, and a panel of books slid open just like in an Agatha Christie story. Beyond it was a sizeable study with a large desk. The shelves were bare. She told us that this was where her husband kept the collection that had gone to the University; perhaps some had been left behind in the desk drawers. She took Dexter's arm as she had before lunch. "I wrote a book once. Would you like to see it?"

I opened a drawer as she was leading him away. "There's a gun in here," I said.

Mother turned back. "That must be Wolfgang's Luger. I'm so glad you found it. He'll be very pleased."

Wolfgang was Mother's swimming instructor. Beneath his Luger was a typescript. The more I think about this now, the odder that typescript seems. On the cover it said, "For my friend William Marshall Bullitt from G. H. Hardy." The title? *A Mathematician's Apology.* This book became an instant classic. It's been world-famous for three-quarters of a century, and G. H. Hardy remains one of England's most prominent mathematicians. I can't find any reference to this manuscript in the Bullitt Collection now; I did look through it though. It seemed to be the original. There were annotations, just as there'd been in Newton's *Principia*, some of them in the handwriting of the dedication, some of them in another hand. C. P. Snow is supposed to have read the original. Perhaps they were his. I put it back gingerly as Dexter and Mother returned.

Dexter had a small volume open in his hand. "This is absolutely charming," he said. He read some out loud while Mother beamed at him.

The book was called *Three Weeks in Russia*, and it is charming.[2] I wasn't really listening—too preoccupied with that Hardy MS—but I bought a copy of it while I was working on this chapter. Mother had written it in 1935 and had it privately printed in 1936. She'd wanted to publish it, but explains in an introduction "the powers that be vetoed the plan, due to the relationship between my husband and our ambassador to the Soviet Union."

She describes parades and dancing and balloons with a childlike delight. More to the point—considering Dexter and I were here in Louisville because of Alger Hiss, pilloried as a spy for the Soviet Union—are passages like these:

"The young Communist is a fine animal; upright, a beautiful carriage, with head erect and shoulders back, alert, and enthusiastic."[3] She describes her train trip to Yalta, where Alger joined Roosevelt, Churchill, Stalin in the famous talks that planned the defeat of Germany and the dividing of the spoils of WWII; the train, she wrote, "zigzagged down through vineyards and forests, passing beautiful palaces on vast estates owned formerly by the nobility. The whole coast was the playground of the rich; now it is the rest and vacation spot of the workers."[4]

This is the kind of writing that could well have put Mother in serious jeopardy. Not a single one of the blacklisted Hollywood entertainers showed such innocent delight over the joys of communism. She ends the book saying she hopes to go back to see how the social experiment develops.

She never did. When Dexter finished reading a short passage, she said to me, "Not what you're looking for?" I shook my head. She agreed that this was all very vexing and then said, "They might be in the family files."

The family files, she told us, were in Wolfgang's quarters, and Wolfgang appeared as though on cue. He was tall, young, dark-haired, dressed all in white except for brown jackboots, exactly the kind of man to carry the Luger I'd found. Mother told us—she didn't consult him—that we were welcome to look through the files in his rooms, which were in an outbuilding.

He led her off in her ruffled bathing suit for her lesson while the black-uniformed maid showed us where we were to go.

Wolfgang's quarters occupied the rambling upper floor of a stable-like structure. The biggest room held a long table of open files. On the wall was a poster—edges foxed, paper discolored—advertising

$100 REWARD FOR RUNAWAY SLAVE

It showed a black man running, a chain around one ankle. The files looked formidable. They were also badly jumbled. Deeds for Oxmoor Farm dating back for more than 150 years gave way abruptly to letters between Mrs Bullitt and young Mr. Bullitt when he was at school in England and those gave way to reams of tax returns. There were multiple carbon copies of boring correspondence on that fine onion-skin paper that professional typists used before computers. The day that had seemed pleasant in the high-ceilinged main house was a steam bath up here. Dexter and I stripped, trying to keep sweat from dribbling onto that delicate paper.

The first material touching on Galois was in a file of old Mr. Bullitt's correspondence. In 1937, he'd written to G. H. Hardy, author of the manuscript beneath Wolfgang's Luger, saying, "I want to make a collection of the great mathematicians. Who are they?" We didn't find the original response, which was probably handwritten and certainly not punctuated as in the American copy that we saw:

July 8 1937
TRINITY COLLEGE
CAMBRIDGE

Dear Mr. Bullitt: Harald Bohr of Copenhagen happened to be staying with me when I got your letter, and we made the following list (it omits people whom we regarded as primarily physicists).
CLASS A. Archimedes, Gauss, Newton
CLASS B. Abel, Cauchy, Euler, Fermat, Galois, Lagrange, Reimann

This was promising. The letter ended:

With all kind regards to Mrs. Bullitt, and many thanks for all your kindness, I am,
Yours very sincerely,
G. H. Hardy

"He got the whole of Class A except Archimedes," Dexter said. We'd seen several Newtons in addition to the annotated *Principia* and several works of Gauss.

Mr. Bullitt was clearly proud of this letter that had started off his quest. There were at least half a dozen copies of it on that fine onionskin paper. Dexter "borrowed" a copy. For years he kept it in his wallet and brought it out at parties to show people.

———— ∞∞ ————

We were still ploughing through correspondence when we hit our first references to Galois himself.

One of old Mr. Bullitt's cousins had been the ambassador to France in the late 1930s, and he'd badgered his aides to get everything by or about Galois at any price. When one aide wrote pitiably that everything he hadn't acquired was in the National Archives, the ambassador ordered him to get it out again. The letters don't tell him how to go about this feat and don't indicate whether or not he succeeded.

But towards the end of our search, a piece of paper fluttered to the floor.

It was smaller than an index card, very old, very fragile, perhaps originally yellow in color, one corner torn off, a large spot partially smearing the ink. It stated in French that it was a burial certificate. The date on it was 2nd June 1832. In the space for the dead person's name was written "Evariste Galois" in a copperplate hand. The same hand had written "en fosse commune"—in a common grave—in the space left for burial arrangements.

"It couldn't be the real one, could it?" I asked. Dexter shrugged. "If I'd got somebody to steal a national hero's burial certificate out of some national archive I'm not sure I'd pin it up on the wall. Kind of hard to explain away."

"Maybe we should take it for safe-keeping," I said.

"Joanie!"

"You started it," I said, thinking of the onion-skin carbon he had in his wallet. But I put the certificate back—and have regretted it ever since.

———— ⊗≫ ————

We had dinner that night with young Mr. Bullitt and his wife in a big house high up over the Ohio River. She'd been an English tennis star and a friend of JFK's, blonde, very pretty, as gracious as her husband. The martinis were plentiful and chilled, and Bullitt suggested we come to his office in the morning on the off chance that we might find the Galois material among his father's books.

We showed up at opening time. In my first thriller—written many years later—I modelled the offices of a murdered Springfield lawyer on Bullitt, Dawson & Tarrant. The Bullitt suite branched off a long, high-ceilinged library lined with Kentucky law books, floor to ceiling. Polished wood tables ran down the middle with green-glass-shaded lamps on them. Windows at one end were tall and arched.

Bullitt took us to his father's office, which was in great disarray. Several desks crowded it, one of them against a bookcase that was empty from about head-height down. Piles of books stood on the desks and the floor. He was getting rid of these, he said; we'd find nothing there. He'd already got rid of many of them—anything that wasn't of interest to the firm—and he hadn't yet found a single one on mathematics. But then his father's collection had never interested him. If any remnants from it were still hanging around they had to be on the top shelves of that half-emptied bookcase. Dexter climbed up on the table, reached for a volume—he'd plainly spotted it almost as soon as we walked into the room—opened it, took in a sharp breath.

"Something rare?" Bullitt asked.

"Maybe priceless," Dexter said. He was reading a card inside. This book, like so many in the University Library, had been exhibited at Harvard in 1953. "It says it's the first edition of Archimedes, printed in Greek in Basel, 1544."

So old Mr. Bullitt had completed G. H. Hardy's A-list after all. It's not a list that anybody today would add to or subtract from; Bullitt of Louisville, Kentucky, had bought the complete first editions of the three greatest mathematicians of all time.

"Toss it down," said his son of the Archimedes. "I'll put it in the safe."

The very next book, a tall slender volume, was the first that concerned Galois.

It turned out to be an archive of the *Gazette des France* for 1830 covering the first of Galois's trials for treason. Inside the front cover was a three-sheet list:

Brief Memorandum of Galois Items Acquired by Mr. Bullitt in Paris in 1937

The memorandum listed some forty items, first editions of books by and about Galois, originals of journals that contained articles by and about him, further volumes of the *Gazette de France* covering his second arrest, arraignment, trial and conviction in 1831 as well as collections of Galois letters.

We set out to find everything. If we were successful, we'd have something on the order of a thousand pages. Young Mr. Bullitt told us to use the photocopier in the Bank of Louisville next door; his firm had an arrangement with them. We told him that we'd never finish before closing time. "Just keep track," he said. "Ten cents a page. Send me a cheque when you get home."

Dexter found only a handful of the Galois items in the top shelves of that bookcase. But while he was up on the desk, I started going through the piles of books on the desks and the floor. Bullitt was even less interested in his father's collection than he let on. I found quite a number amongst those. Even so, no more than half the items on the list were still in that room. Some lucky second-hand bookseller may well have walked off with the rest of them. Or maybe they'd just ended up in a Louisville dumpster.

We also found a couple of items not on the list: original prints of the famous engraving of Galois, the very one used for the French stamp issued in 1984, and many photographed letters from Galois. Mr. Bullitt noted beneath the entry for them on his Memorandum that several of the original letters had not yet been recovered and that "researches are now being made in Paris for them and they will probably be located among some of his relatives."

If he'd had any luck, those irreplaceable letters too had disappeared into the dumpster or into the cache of that lucky second-hand book dealer. Certainly old Mr. Bullitt had been a ruthless man when he was on the trail of one of his mathematicians.

Item 15J of the Memorandum recorded the "Certificate of the burial of Galois' body" on June 2nd, 1832 "en Fosse Commune"

Which meant that the burial certificate we'd found in Wolfgang's quarters really was the original.

⸺◆◆◆⸺

Before young Mr. Bullitt left for the night, he'd looked in on us. "You wouldn't mind saying goodbye to Mother, would you? She wants to show you the magnolias."

Mother was as gracious the second time around as she had been the first; she took Dexter's arm, and they talked about writing as we strolled down a boulevard of evergreen magnolias, huge and old and in full bloom. On the way back to the house, she took us past the swimming pool where Wolfgang had given her a lesson the day before. It wasn't Olympic in size, but it was large and nicely proportioned. Mother pointed out a statue at one end of it.

"That's the first integrated statue in Kentucky," she said. She'd carved it herself. It was surprisingly good too, and maybe the stone was very white, but the two children playing were clearly one black and one white.

"We have letters from three presidents here," she went on, leading us into the library again and still holding Dexter's arm. "Would you like to see them?" They hung together in her own study. The first was from Teddy Roosevelt.

"Dear Bullitt," it said. "The news is bully."

"I don't remember what 'the news' was anymore,' Mother said. The second letter was from Eisenhower, addressed to Mrs Bullitt herself. It was a dull and unmemorable condolence on the death of her husband. The third, though: that was a revelation. It was from Richard Nixon, also addressed to Mrs Bullitt, another long letter of condolence.[5] And the final paragraph!

My notes recorded it: "I will always be very grateful to Mr. Bullitt for his invaluable help in the case of Alger Hiss."

"What could that old bastard have done?" I asked Dexter as we drove back to Springfield.

"No idea," Dexter said. "The name is familiar. I remember the ambassador. But William Marshall Bullitt . . . Maybe . . . No, I just don't remember."

I worked hard on my Galois project when we got back to Europe, even learned enough maths to take an Open University course in Galois Theory, but slowly began to lose interest. No idea why. But who could forget the Bullitts? Dexter and I told the story many times, and yet I was well into this manuscript before I realized the old bastard's "invaluable help" was steering me in the most unexpected of directions.

Since the search for my parents' FBI files criss-crossed with what I was finding out about Alger—and since I'd reached a dead end with them—I tried for Dexter's file. He knew both my parents, worked with both. Maybe his file would give hints of what the FBI didn't want me to know. But Dexter's FBI file turned out to be "unavailable" because "the records are palletized and designated for shipment to the National Archives and Records Administration (NARA)." "Due to logistical limitations, we cannot determine how long these records will be unavailable."[1]

"Palletized"?

The letter suggested trying the National Archives. The Archives half-agreed with the FBI and half-disagreed. The files still existed and were in the process of transfer, but access was entirely the FBI's responsibility.[2]

I appealed both decisions. The records remain palletized to this day.

But the pattern was looking pretty solid. Svetlana said, "Wherever I dig, I stumble upon some German connection or, better, Nazi cartels connection."[3]

In my FBI searches I'd had the help of an investigative journalist called Jeremy Bigwood; I asked him if what she said rang any bells. "It is Big Ben on steroids."[4] He referred me to a *New York Times* article: "A secret history of the United States government's Nazi-hunting operation concludes that American intelligence officials created a 'safe haven' in the United States for Nazis and their collaborators."[5]

Here's Svetlana again, "There is another aspect to safe-haven, which is even more ominous. This is economic safe-haven and, particularly, the close ties between German cartels and some of US monopolies."[6]

The German wedlock between the military and industry is what my father railed against in *The Spirit and Structure of German Fascism*. My mother investigated banks intimately involved with Nazi finance. When the US government banned the film of Dexter's novel, it didn't give any reason; but the book was harsh about the Army's push for "big science", which meant big bomb factories and big profits—that same union of war and profit that made the Nazis so powerful so quickly.

And Alger's work for the Nye Committee exposed the reality of war profiteering that turned Nazi Germany into the monstrosity it became. Here's a headline from the *New York Times* in December of 1934, just as the Committee's work came to the end of its first stage:

VIVID PICTURE OF ARMS TRADE
DISCLOSED IN CAPITAL INQUIRY
Testimony Indicates That Munitions Firms,
Profiting by Wars, Have International Tie-Ups
and Are Assisted by Government

Revelations like that just had to have put Alger on the hit list of some very, very powerful people.

35

1949

Before the Trial of the Century can start, there's a key player to introduce. It's not even human. It's a machine: a typewriter. Never mind the inanity of a spy with typewritten material that no other spy would ever use and Stalin wouldn't accept if they had. The Hiss case is a piece of theater, and it involves a quest like so many good pieces of theater. Kind of a comic book version of Wagner's *The Ring*.

Chambers swore in his deposition that in 1938 Priscilla Hiss had typed the documents from his dumbwaiter shaft, and she'd done it on the Hiss family typewriter. The Hisses did own a typewriter in the 1930s—Priscilla's father gave them one he'd been using for a while—but they got rid of it when they moved house at the end of 1937—before those 1938 documents even existed.[1] Priscilla was a lousy typist; she didn't even know how to change a ribbon. The photostats were clean, professional work. The typewriter she'd discarded was broken. The keys stuck. So did the ribbon she couldn't change. The letters blurred. The roller had to be turned by hand. Nobody could actually *type* on it anymore.[2]

The machine that typed the dumbwaiter-shaft documents produced good, clean copy.

Alger was certain, absolutely certain, that finding Priscilla's old machine would provide proof positive that Chambers's accusations were nonsense.

He and his brother Donald—no experience in sleuthing between them—tossed every spare hour into the search. They racked their brains. The condition of the machine ten years ago made it at best a toy. Could it have gone to the kids of the cleaners who'd worked for them back then? The Catletts? On the other hand, it might have gone to the Salvation Army. Or to a second-hand shop. They weren't even sure what make it was. A Royal? An Underwood?[3]

As they started out on their search, the two brothers thought themselves very lucky to have the help of an ex-OSS agent by the name of Horace Schmahl, an experienced person, somebody who knew how to ferret things out. The OSS was Office of Strategic Services, a World War II agency set up to coordinate spying behind enemy lines, the Central Intelligence Agency's predecessor, known at the time as "America's Gestapo." He'd find the typewriter for them.

Some newspapers reported that Nixon was pushing HUAC investigators hard to find the typewriter too. Other newspapers said the FBI had dozens of agents at work combing Washington and the countryside around for it. Some put the number of agents at as high as two hundred and fifty.[4] Chambers says there wasn't an FBI field office in America not involved.[5] Since this is a fairy tale, it can't come as any real surprise that on December 13, 1948, two days before Alger was indicted—several days before he and his brother started their search—the *New York World-Telegram* reported that HUAC investigators had found the Hiss typewriter "with the assistance of the FBI."[6] The next day, the *Philadelphia Evening Bulletin* reported that the Hisses' ex-OSS agent Schmahl was looking for a Woodstock when the Hisses didn't know the make of the machine they were looking for.[7]

These weren't just random journalistic errors either. John McDowell, the HUAC Congressman who baited the ambush in the Commodore Hotel, wrote to a constituent confirming the report, both the date and the FBI's role in the discovery.[8] Nixon himself confirmed it in *Six Crises*: "On December 13, 1948, FBI agents found the typewriter."[9] The passage disappeared from later editions.

FBI records also indicate that the Hisses' investigator Horace Schmahl found the typewriter around then.[10] Not that he told the Hisses anything about it; they hadn't even hired him yet. Even FBI intelligence chief William Sullivan confirmed the find. "To the best of my knowledge the FBI did have the typewriter before it was found by the Hiss defense," he told Professor Peter Irons in 1975. His only uncertainty was "whether it had been located by the FBI or brought to the Bureau labs by Nixon".[11]

Even HUAC confirmed it. At the end of 1948 the Committee published a 120-page report titled "Soviet Espionage Within the United States Government." It said that Chambers's documents had come from Alger's office and that investigators had "conclusively established where and on what machine these documents were typed."

While the typewriter was safely with the FBI, the public search went on. The first items of importance the Hisses turned up were the "Hiss Standards", documents presented in court as acknowledged examples of material typed on the Hiss typewriter. The Standards included such things as an application form for the University of Maryland that Priscilla had typed and a report to her son Timothy's school. Alger turned them over to the FBI. Of course he did. An FBI expert identified the typewriter from the font—a Woodstock—and the Hisses were only grateful to know the make of the machine they were looking for.

While they were pondering how to begin their search, Alger's brother Donald got a visit from Mike Catlett, the man whose children might have inherited the typewriter as a toy.

"I guess you know what I want to talk to you about," Catlett said.[12]

Donald said no, he didn't know.

"Some people have been around to see me."

"Our people?" Catlett said no.

"They were the FBI." Here beginneth the quest.

Catlett said there'd been two FBI spooks, and they'd wanted the typewriter. He said he knew where it was, and he wasn't about to talk to *them* about it. It was in his closet. He and Donald drove over to pick it up.

But the typewriter wasn't in the closet. Catlett said it had to be at his brother Pat's. They drove there. It wasn't at Pat's either. His wife had used it for a bit, but it was in such bad shape that she gave it to his sister. The sister left it with Dr Easter. Dr Easter was dead. A man called Marlow had cleared out the doctor's house. The Hiss brothers went to see him.

Marlow was cagey. He said he'd have to get some "information" first. They'd have to wait, come back later. When they did, Marlow still didn't have the "information" he needed. He thought "Bill" might. Bill had done the actual moving; a yellow washing machine and the old Woodstock were part payment for his work.

Bill didn't have the typewriter. He sent the Hisses to Ira Lockey, another mover. Lockey's sister-in-law said she remembered the Woodstock—said it had been sitting right there on that table for a long time—but they'd have to talk to Lockey himself about it, and Lockey was a sick man. They'd have to come back another day when he was better. When they did, he said he'd dumped it in a junkyard ages ago.

Donald and Catlett poked around nearby junkyards and found the yellow washing machine and a typewriter, but the typewriter was a Royal, not a Woodstock. They went back to Lockey. They felt he must know something more—he hinted at it—but numerous visits produced nothing. Catlett persisted on his own. He told Donald that one day outside Lockey's house he'd seen the same two FBI men who'd questioned him back at the beginning of the search.

His sister suggested that the typewriter might be in Marlow's old shack, across the street from dead Dr Easter. No luck. Next-door neighbors remembered a junky old machine sitting outside in the tall grass. Donald and Catlett poked around in the grass. Again no luck.

By this time a five full months had gone by, and the trials were looming. Alger and Donald paid one last visit to Lockey. Guess what?

Lockey brought out the typewriter at once. Just like that. A Woodstock #230,099: no rust, no dirt or dead weeds, no faulty parts. It worked as good as new. Another miracle. Nobody so much as questioned it. They'd found the typewriter, and they were triumphant. Jubilant. They broke out the champagne.[13]

Then they turned this Woodstock over as crucial evidence. Of course they did.

PART FOUR

The trial of the century

Flashbulbs popped and reporters mobbed as soon as Alger and Priscilla emerged from their apartment on the first day of the first trial. May 31, 1949. Photographers walked backwards a few paces ahead of them. Journalists scrambled around them, shouting questions all the way to the subway entrance at Astor Place in lower Manhattan. The whole jumble of people squeezed together down the subway stairs, through the turnstiles, into the carriage. More press joined in when they reached the Federal Building in Foley Square, and more as they approached the thirty-storey courthouse.

It's the same building where Nixon and Chambers spent two hours off the record changing 1937 into 1938, and right as Alger's trial was starting, eleven top officials of the Communist Party of the United States were preparing to argue a point: should the Communist Party be outlawed as a criminal conspiracy to overthrow the government by force or violence? Rival picket lines battled each other in the square while Alger and Priscilla and their cloud of paparazzi forced a route through to become a physical focus of the scare that Nixon and HUAC had worked so hard to perfect in the months leading up to this day.

All throughout February, Stripling had made daily headlines with 28 chapters from his soon-to-be-published book, *Red Plot Against America*, one chapter a day, all of them syndicated across the country:

COMMUNIST CONSPIRACY[1]
IN THE UNITED STATES
THE SPY STORY OF THE CENTURY[2]

And Stripling was just one of many. No day had gone by without something scary, much of it stemming from the case of the "evasive" Alger and the "repentant" Chambers.

SPYING AIM OF REDS
DECLARED PROVED[3]
AN INTERNATIONAL CONSPIRACY[4]

COMMUNIST CURBS FORECAST BY NIXON[5]

New York itself had eight major newspapers back then, three national wire services, three national radio networks, four national magazines as well as a greedy young television industry and dozens of specialized feature services. There were the regionals too, hundreds of them from Washington to San Francisco, from Chicago and St Louis to Houston. The rest of the world was almost as fascinated; international press services flew reporters into New York to cover the case full time. On the first day of Alger's trials, there were more news people in court than potential jurors and counsel put together.

The Federal Building's eighteenth century gentility showed off well in the courtroom: oak panels, green leather chairs, carved wooden palisades cutting off the well of the court.[6] One American legal virtue—not anywhere near enough to make up for its vice of trial by newspaper—is the lack of a dock where the accused is displayed like Quasimodo in the pillory. There'd been little enough presumption of innocence in this case so far, but the layout of the room gave the thought a nod. The judge's bench faced the prosecution table; behind that came a table for Alger's counsel and only behind that came the table for Alger and Priscilla. The trial opened with the court clerk bellowing, "Hear ye, hear ye! All persons having business with the United States District Court, Southern

District of New York, draw near, give your attention, and you shall be heard."

Everybody stood for the judge.

According to Alistair Cooke, covering the case for the BBC, Judge Samuel H. Kaufman was a "pink, genial rabbit of a man who almost vanished behind the high bench."[7] He rocked in his chair while the two lead counsels selected the jury.

In the trial of the Communist Party next door, jury selection was running into its ninth week. Counsel in Alger's case did the job in just over two hours. Most of the dismissals were people too terrified of Communists to serve. Or too terrified of being hounded as Communist sympathizers if they became a part of the panel. The remainder were middle- aged, middle-class, all-white: ten men, two women, managers, brokers, an accountant, a secretary and a dressmaker. As Cooke says, by law only saints can serve on a jury, and this one was no exception. Not a member of it was afraid of Communists. All could be as impartial in judging a person whose aim was to destroy their way of life as they could be in judging anybody else. Despite a media hoo-hah that had barely let up for ten months, they had formed not a single prejudice against Alger or Chambers or any other person who might appear for or against either side.

The charges?

First: Alger had lied when he swore he'd never given documents to Chambers for transmission to the Soviet Union. Second: He had lied when he swore he hadn't had anything to do with the man since the first of January 1937.

The opening arguments began.

Thomas Murphy for the prosecution—a huge hulk of a man in a double-breasted suit, walrus moustache, witty, breezy, down to earth— explained that "to convict a person of perjury, the law needs a witness plus corroboration." He said he would "corroborate Chambers's testimony by the typewriting and the handwriting." But his emphasis lay on the man: "If you don't believe Chambers, then we have no case under the Federal perjury rule."[8] He was finished in half an hour.

There's nothing to beat brevity, but he'd handed Alger a gift by turning Chambers into the issue. Alger's lawyer, Lloyd Stryker looked like a bank manager, but a reporter for the *Herald Tribune* described his courtroom manner as "borrowed from both the pulpit and the operatic stage." He launched into Chambers with fire shooting out of both nostrils: "low-down, nefarious, filthy", a "blasphemer", a "Communist, conspirator and thug", a "liar by habit, by training, by preference" a "moral leper" who ought to be greeted in the street with cries of "Unclean! Unclean!"[9] He contrasted this with the extraordinary accomplishments of Alger, "the best in America, the most trustworthy man."[10] As for the papers from the dumbwaiter shaft, he pointed out that Alger himself had insisted they be handed over to the government. "Is this the conduct of a guilty man?"[11]

It's another of those really bad plot holes.

Then there's the typewriter. Stryker joked that the FBI had "turned Washington upside down" looking for it.[12] He bragged that the defense had found it when the FBI failed.

Alger was absolutely certain that a proper court—away from HUAC's madness—would clear away the entire mess. "I welcomed the chance to go to court, the setting in which I felt happiest, and disprove every-thing."[13] He said to a friend, "I simply don't believe that twelve jurors are going to listen to Chambers and me and believe Chambers and not me. I just don't believe it."[14]

What he didn't know is that his battle was not just in this courtroom and in the press, where the leaks continued full steam and as vitri-olic as ever. The real battle was behind the scenes with Nixon. Nixon kept in daily contact with the prosecution; his friend the journalist Victor Lasky—a close friend of Chambers's too—wrote to Prosecutor Murphy, "Dick has a heck of a lot at stake in the outcome."[15] Nixon advised that Alger "be kept under cross at least three days . . .boring the jury . . .[with] great and tedious detail."[16]

It's a two-pronged strategy. First, get any group of people bored, and whatever breaks the tedium is what'll stick in their minds.

The second prong is nastier: destroy sympathy for the accused.

It wasn't all that easy a job. Alger was a man who'd devoted his life to public service, and yet he'd been vilified in the press without the opportunity to tell his side of the story. He was also a very attractive person. "He had a fine articulation of chin and mouth and brow and nose that would defy softening tissue and leave him handsome at eighty," the BBC's Alistair Cooke wrote. "Whatever he did had a rather charming gravity and grace, when he deferred with a dark smile to some lady tapping across the well of the court; when he unfolded his handkerchief and wiped his nose; when he uncrossed his legs, and his head tilted over to the left, as a lever effortlessly helping his left ankle onto his right knee. In any society, a very striking member."[17]

But Alger had no idea what he was getting into. The courts that made him happy were courts that argued contracts, procedures, the laws themselves. He knew nothing about criminal trials, and here he was, the accused in one. He'd never even seen a jury. Forget the United Nations. Forget Yalta. Forget hobnobbing with Roosevelt and Churchill. This courtroom turned the man fascinated by human curiosities into a human curiosity himself. He was a specimen in a public exhibit, "naked"—his word—before a dozen ordinary citizens who were as inquisitive and as unselfconscious when they stared at him as children staring at shrunken heads in the museum.

He was also a man who fought his own battles and protected his people himself. He'd challenged HUAC and fought them all—one man against ten—but here had to sit silent and listen to ugly insinuations, open lies, wild accusations. The prosecutor Murphy bullied Priscilla; he badgered defense witnesses. Alger had no choice but to hold back and let Stryker do the hand- to-hand for him. His optimism did come to his aid from time to time, but only to be shunted aside by the "sense of powerlessness" that increased his outrage as he watched "the theatrical solemnity with which factitious documents became formal exhibits." Outrage usually helps. Alger's turned in on him; he found himself swept by "gusts of anger" that threatened to overwhelm him.[18]

Nor did it take him many weeks to realize he was "facing trial by ordeal in the medieval sense of whether or not I could summon up sufficient physical strength to survive." He meant this in the simplest way. The days were exhausting enough, and at night, there were Priscilla's terrors. She was terrified by what had happened in court today, and terrified by what would happen tomorrow. She was terrified that the FBI was bugging the house, and Alger—who refused to believe the FBI would stoop so low—feared she was slipping into paranoid delusions. She insisted they go on long, long walks at night so they could talk out of snooper-range; during them, she needed intense reassurance and intense comforting. But the harder Alger tried to reassure and comfort, the more agitated she got. When he finally did persuade her back home and into bed, the threatening telephone calls began. He got up in the morning already exhausted to begin another exhausting day; during brief court recesses, he had to lie down on the tables in the room reserved for counsel.

As the trials wore on, he came to see himself as a beast with bandarillos being thrust in its hump. His background and his training told him that he had to suppress all show of pain. "The etiquette of the bull ring did not permit the tormented to show even annoyance." He feared that if he did, the jury would think the prosecutor had scored a point.

Even his belief in the rule of law and in the right and wrong of things—central pillars in his life—began to falter. He began to despair of justice and to sense that the law was no more than "rules for a game of chance."[19]

Nixon was born cannier, and he'd played lawyers on the stage. He knew that trials are theater, that they're about emotion, not about controlling it; he knew that what people would sympathize with was exactly what Alger was hiding from them: the tortures of a wronged and innocent man battling the vast resources of an unjust state. And he knew that "great and tedious detail" was the trick that would keep everybody from seeing it. Alger would fight to remain the Harvard lawyer—sharp, incisive, precise, sarcastic—throughout his testimony, just as he had during the seven hours of the final HUAC hearing, when sarcastic precision had come off as no more than evasion and pedantry. It's exactly what happened.

Nobody in court caught so much as a glimpse of the tormented beast with bandarillos in its hump.

⸻⸺∞⸺⸻

Chambers the prodigal son made a joyous contrast: sad, rumpled, battered-looking, and remorseful in a baggy blue suit. He did everything wrong—and was fascinating.

He'd had to sign a loyalty oath to get a job in the State Department in the winter of 1937–1938.

"You took that oath, did you not?" bellowed Stryker for the defense.

"Yes," said Chambers.

"And it was false from beginning to end, was it not, Mr. Chambers?"

"Of course."

"What?"

"Of course," Chambers repeated.

"And it was perjury, wasn't it?"

"If you like."

"And you did it to deceive and cheat the United States Government?"

"That is correct."

"Yes or no?"

"Perfectly true."[20]

That's what prodigal sons do: come home and 'fess up. They also have exciting tales of adventure to tell: mysterious Colonel Bykovs with Yiddish accents who haggle over state secrets in foreign languages, clandestine meetings, exotic places, fears of assassination, torn emotion, and profound remorse. As always, Chambers spoke with absolute conviction. As always, he didn't so much as blink when what he said proved to be wrong or contradictory or both almost as soon as it was out of his mouth, face as expressionless as a pudding bowl, eyes usually fixed on the ceiling, eyelids fluttering as he began to speak, often speaking too softly to be heard. His wife was the same when she took the stand, except that she constantly licked her lips.[21]

Since Chambers himself was the issue, his and his wife's intimate knowledge of Alger and Priscilla as friends was critical. He was well prepared. He'd spent five months, five days a week, eight hours a day with FBI agents—something like a thousand hours in all—going over testimony. But it was dull stuff, dental appointments, shopping trips, school lunches; and whatever else Chambers was, he wasn't dull.

So there was an Easter Sunday drive with the Hisses to Long Eddy, New York. Chambers remembered it because "at a red light in Norristown we passed a policeman carrying an Easter lily."[22] Who could disprove a drive or an Easter lily? He remembered a New Year's Eve party with the Hisses where there'd been lots of champagne. It was an anniversary party. No, a New Year's Day Party. No, it was New Year's Eve. Esther Chambers knew it was because she remembered her husband drinking port. It was the first day of 1937. Of course it was. No, it was 1938. When Alger's team disproved any kind of party for either year, Chambers said, well, maybe it wasn't New Year's Eve after all, but he was sure they'd drunk champagne because it had made him sick.

Alger's house turned from gray to white with green shutters, then yellow with blue blinds. The living room went pink. A rug from the HUAC hearings changed color too. A forsythia bloomed out of season. A stone porch appeared on a house where there hadn't been one until ten years later. A swallowtail coat popped out of nowhere. Cars that belonged to Alger and Chambers or Alger then Chambers danced so merry a jig that even Stripling confessed they "remained something of a mystery."[23]

Alger had introduced the Chamberses to a woman called Plum Fountain at a restaurant in Georgetown. But if Alger knew them as only "Carl" and "Lisa", how did he introduce them to Plum Fountain? Manners in the 1930s seem absurdly formal now; respectable people didn't introduce their friends by first names or even by full names. They just didn't. American etiquette guru Emily Post laid down the format:

"Mr. Jones, may I present Mrs. Smith." No way was that a convention a State Department official like Alger could flout. Chambers agreed that he must have used a last name. He sifted through the aliases available to him: not Chambers, not Breen, not Dwyer, not Cantwell. He was utterly unable to remember just what it was. Lisa and Carl had inherited a maid called Julia Rankin from the Hisses; Alger had never heard of her (the name does sound suspiciously like HUAC Congressman John Rankin), but at the time, maids simply did not call their employers "Carl" and "Lisa." Chambers couldn't remember how he'd handled that. Nor could he remember what name he'd used in subletting Alger's apartment. Or what names they'd used to register in hotels for overnight trips with the Hisses. But Chambers did remember that on August 10, 1937, the two families drove to New Hampshire and stayed in a tourist home called Bleak House to watch a performance of *She Stoops to Conquer*.

Who wouldn't be wafted away on tales like these? How could a jury not be entranced with "Carl" and "Lisa" and Bleak Houses and policemen carrying Easter lilies? It hardly mattered that Alger's team disproved item after item, dates, places, plays, house colors, coats, out-of-season forsythias. By this time Nixon's mass of "unimportant details" was deeply embedded in Chambers's tale of spying, and Alger was running so hard to show what nonsense it was—to explain the real where-how-why of each item without any help from the FBI's massive records—that he couldn't see the trap he was caught in, much less battle it effectively.

But here's a whole new species of curiosity: there's a once-important item missing from the prosecution's story. Nobody seemed to notice it was gone during Alger's trials. A couple of years later, William Jowitt, Lord High Chancellor under Prime Minister Clement Atlee, studied the Hiss case, published a book about it.[24] To him, "the most extraordinary feature of an extraordinary case" was the question of Alger's dues to the Communist Party.[25]

There were all these versions of Chambers's to contend with: dues as a 10 percent whack out of Alger's salary and dues as an occasional

$5 or $10 donation; dues that Chambers never collected and dues that Chambers alone collected; dues collected every month for years and dues collected only once in all the time he knew Alger. Jowitt searched Chambers's *Witness* for a definitive version. All he found there was that Alger was a dues-paying member of the Party even after he joined the underground. Jowitt wasn't worrying the contradictions. That's just Chambers being Chambers.

The puzzlement was that payment of dues did not come up during the trials. Here was the *only* piece of direct evidence to show that Alger had been a Communist, one that had been a prominent feature of the hearings—and nobody mentions it?

Jowitt was writing several years later and from the other side of the Atlantic. Nobody could expect him to know that in the courtroom right next door to Alger's trial, the Party itself was fighting for its life. Public opinion was wildly in favor of the Communist Party being outlawed. So were the media. So was every government agency in the country. In that trial, the prosecution's most powerful witnesses were its turncoats and its FBI informants. There were plenty of both. One of the turncoats was Louis Budenz, who'd been a Soviet spy and a member of the Party's National Committee. He'd spent literally thousands of hours explaining to Bureau investigators how the Party worked. He'd also exposed lots of secret Communists.

Why didn't the Prosecution in Alger's trial ask *him* about dues collection? Why not about Alger himself? But, no, he'd never do, would he? He was the one HUAC had already interrogated and—despite Nixon's headline-making claim that he could tie Alger to the Reds as late as 1945—all he'd been able to tell them was that he'd heard Chambers's rumors about the 1930s. But there were so many others testifying next door. Morris Childs joined the Party back in 1927, became a member of the underground and turned to the FBI in 1947. His time completely covered Nixon's "period in question" of 1934 to 1937. Why didn't the prosecution ask him? There's his younger brother Jack with a similar history. There's Harvey Matusow, Balmes Hidalgo, Gerald L. K. Smith, William Nowell, Bernice Baldwin. All had been party members who turned themselves into the FBI, and any one of them could have walked across the hall to testify for the government against Alger. HUAC had a fresh turncoat it could volunteer too. Nicholas Dozenberg had spied for Soviet military intelligence for a decade after 1927, another witness like Morris Childs, in just the right place at just the right time to answer questions about Nixon's "period of interest." Right as Alger's trials were in progress, the Committee was collecting affidavits from him. Surely investigators asked him the crucial questions about dues and Alger? But no. They didn't.

As for FBI informants, the Party was riddled with them, had been from its inception; the Church Committee Senate Investigation of the FBI in the 1970s proved it. At one point there were so many of them that Hoover considered amassing them to influence Party conventions. In the courtroom next door, there's Matt Cvetic, known to the Reds as "Cvetic the Rat" because he sold his memoirs to the *Saturday Evening Post* and got a movie made of his life: *I Was a Communist for the FBI*. There's Mary Markward, who rose to become Secretary-Treasurer of the Maryland-District-of-Columbia Communist Party; she actually collected party dues and maintained registration rolls. She'd have been able to find out about every Red in DC from the party's inception. Yet another was Angela Calomiris. She'd spent seven years rising through Communist Party ranks to become Finance Secretary; she had access to the membership list as well as extensive information about everybody on it.[26]

All of these people were testifying only a few steps away. Surely one of them would have had something to say about dues or about Alger. The prosecution even had an inside line on them that nobody else did: Judge Medina, presiding every day over that very trial, was the father of one of Chambers's team. The prosecution didn't call a single one of them. The subject of dues—so easy to confirm with all this expertise—might as well not have existed.

The Hiss defense concentrated on character witnesses. They'd lined up a roll call nobody could equal today if for no other reason than the cost of security arrangements. John W. Davis, presidential candidate in 1924; Supreme Court Justices Frankfurter and Reed, the first Supreme

Court Justices in history to testify at a criminal trial; Governor Adlai Stevenson, soon to be a presidential candidate himself; Assistant Secretary of State Francis Sayre, who was Alger's boss, and many more like them.

Just as the defense was about to begin this parade of worthies, an ancient, red-faced man—thick glasses and a shiny bald head—entered the courtroom with an armful of pamphlets and began distributing them to the press. He was very deaf.

His name?

William Marshall Bullitt, lawyer of Louisville, Kentucky, the self-same Bullitt whose widow Nixon had consoled with special thanks for her husband's "invaluable help" in the Hiss Case.

The pamphlet is slender, only thirty pages long, privately printed. Its title is *A Factual Review of the Whittaker Chambers—Alger Hiss Controversy*. Its author is none other than William Marshall himself, who turns out to have been a trustee of the Carnegie Endowment for International Peace, a board member under Alger's presidency.[27] The Review is an indictment that leads its readers through Nixon's press leaks to the conclusion that Alger was everything Nixon said he was.

> Mr. Chambers's testimony appears as a blunt, straightforward, positive, unqualified statement of facts . . .none of which have been shown to be inaccurate.

While

> Mr. Hiss' testimony . . .has been constantly contradicted and torn to shreds by indisputable third party public and private written records and disinterested oral evidence.[28]

The judge banged his gavel. He scolded the old man. But the old man had the press with their tongues hanging out. A magazine called *Plain Talk* declared Alger "another Benedict Arnold and another Judas Iscariot."[29] The judge scolded the court and the media. He said there were grounds for contempt in the continued smears against Alger in the press. He admonished the jury not to read papers or listen to reports on the case. Who was going to pay attention to a direction like that? Who could pay attention to it?

What plagues me though is that this doddery old fool with an armful of pamphlets just can't be enough to justify Nixon's touching condolence to his widow. Lots of people did much more to further Nixon's crusade; Stripling, the other members of HUAC, Hoover, Father Cronin, the Dulles brothers, Nixon's contacts in the press are just a few of the important ones. But pamphlets do look like a start.

Despite this excitement, the surreal Chambers, and all the famous names, the star of the show was Priscilla's antiquated Woodstock typewriter, the defense's proof that Chambers was a liar and Alger was an innocent man. It sat there, right out in plain view: a pretty thing with white-faced keys and elegant gold lettering, serial no. N230099, vintage late twenties, one of those stage-set pieces like a Model T Ford. But this was no ordinary object. It had already undergone one magical transformation. The broken-down wreck from the Hiss apartment had bounced via toybox, multiple cupboards, and attics in multiple households, to scrapheaps, to open fields in the rain, and then arrived in the courtroom a perfectly functioning machine. The prosecution called an FBI agent to try it out. The whole courtroom heard its keys go clackety clack as they were meant to. A couple of jurors tried it.

An FBI laboratory expert called Ramos Feehan displayed individual "e's" and "g's" on a huge board. He said they matched the "Hiss Standards" to the sixty-five typed pages Chambers had presented to Alger's lawyers in his pre-libel-suit examination. He swore it was so, even though he testified a little later that he couldn't be certain what kind of machine had produced one of the documents. A Royal? An Underwood? No way to tell for sure. He said there'd been only one typist: Priscilla Hiss. He swore that was so as well. The defense didn't contest him for the simple reason that every typewriter expert they approached—and they approached many—was too scared to examine the machine or the documents: excoriation in the press, exile from friends and relatives, the loss of a job and probably a life's career.

Which is to say that even as this all-too-mutable machine sat there right out in full sight, it was undergoing a second transformation: proof of Alger's innocence changed to an "immutable witness" of his guilt. All prosecutors dream of real, live smoking guns. There's "a natural tendency to infer from the mere production of any material object," as a famous jurist called Wigmore put it, "the truth of all that is predicated upon it." This pretty machine was Murphy's smoking gun. In his summation, he told a story of Alger and Priscilla—naughty children caught with their hands in the cookie jar—whispering nervously together for fear that Chambers would tell on them:

"The only thing remaining about to get us in trouble other than his word is the typewriter."[30] So what do they do? If they sold the typewriter, they might be traced. If they brought it over to the bridge going to Roslyn and dropped it into the Potomac, somebody might see them. Guilty knowledge. So they give it to their trusted maid's children, knowing full well that they couldn't type, that it would be put to abuse and gradually disintegrate.

But even *I* can think of a dozen better methods of disposal. And if they wanted it to stay hidden, why did they spend five months combing the countryside to find it? When they did find it, why didn't they get rid of it properly? Why in the name of God did they turn it over at once as evidence?

The jury retired in the afternoon to consider their verdict. Shortly afterward, they requested documents and typewriting specimens. Nothing came out of the jury room during the afternoon. That evening, the judge ordered them locked up in a hotel for the night. After breakfast the next morning, they asked the judge for clarification and retired to the jury room. Lunch came and went; they sent out a note saying they could not reach a verdict.

Kaufman sent them back to try again.

An hour and a half later out came another note. Kaufman sent them back.

Toward evening out came a third note.

Kaufman sent them back. Just before nine, they filed in. A verdict?

"Impossible," said the foreman,

"Well," sighed the judge, "that leaves me no alternative but to discharge the jury." A hung jury and a new trial.[31]

And Alger? Whose confidence had been unshakable? Alistair Cooke said he "sat rigid, with a keen dizzy look about his eyes, like a man steeling himself against the first undeniable symptom of an internal haemorrhage."[32]

37

1961

Alger's last words to the court were, "I am confident that in the future the full facts of how Whittaker Chambers was able to carry out forgery by typewriter will be revealed."[1] It was that typewriter—that smoking gun—that convinced eight out of the twelve jury members that he was guilty as charged.

When Dexter and I visited New York and stayed in Isabel's apartment, it wasn't the first time we'd seen it. Long before we left New York, Dexter had broken the social barrier that kept strangers away from Alger's private life; we'd had dinner several times at home with them. That first time, though: that was memorable. To start with I was taken aback to realize that they lived so close to the Lower East Side. People's cleaners lived down there. If their cleaners were white, that is. Grimy storefronts, security grilles, broken pavements, upended garbage cans. Isabel's tenement-like building fitted right in. So did the rattling elevator and the dimly lit corridor leading to her apartment. But the light and airy elegance of the room beyond that dreary-looking front door! I really did feel a little like Dorothy waking up to Technicolor in the Land of Oz.

I remember that Alger was scarily knowledgeable about the wine and Isabel was a good cook (if not in my opinion as good as I'd become). The atmosphere was a shade formal but not disagreeably so. Nobody got drunk. Nobody raised a voice. Nobody got upset or over-excited, not even the slightest whisper of the tensions that spoiled the evening with Niels. Nobody said anything memorable, but conversation didn't flag. There wasn't so much as a moment of boredom. It seemed as though no obstacles even appeared; but since obstacles always appear, I assume Alger's consummate tact guided us past them.

It was too good to be true, as though the currents that usually show in an evening among friends lay hidden beneath a surface that reflected all of us in the best possible light. As always with Alger, unsettling, disconcerting. And yet that night I got my first glimpse of those bandarillos and the tormented beast beneath them. I also caught a glimpse of how prison's etiquette improves on Harvard's. Both agree on the central principle: never, never, never let them see you bleed. Prison's addition? Don't just sit there and take it even if there's no way to fight it openly. Mock the pain. Laugh at it. Make them see you laughing. That's how to get the better of being a salesman for a Dullsville paper company. That's how to actually enjoy announcing to potential customers for a paper company: "This is Alger Hiss." Just think of these guys looking forward to cocktail parties where they can say, "Guess who wants to sell me rubber bands and paper clips?"

From that night on, I was fond of Alger in ways I couldn't wholly make sense of. And the reason for my insight?

A full-color poster of a Woodstock typewriter dominated the whole space, serial no. N230099, vintage late twenties: the evidence that even the impartial Earl Jowitt, Lord High Chancellor, saw as the most damning. The crowning glory of Nixon's gift for amalgamating reality and fiction.

There was no place in the living area from which you couldn't see it.

38

1949

A hung jury was not what Nixon wanted. As his friend Victor Lasky had said, he'd had "a heck of a stake" in this trial. He had the next election to think about—he was preparing his campaign for the Senate—and he started at once making sure the second trial would deliver. Here are front-page headlines on the very day after the verdict.

KAUFMAN ACCUSED OF HISS CASE BIAS[1]
Capitol Hill Demands Probe Into Hiss Trial;
Judge's "Prejudice" Hit[2]

"Congressman Nixon said"—many papers ran this Associated Press quote—"'I believe a full investigation should immediately be made of Judge Kaufman's fitness to serve on the bench in view of his conduct during this trial.'"[3] He said that when the "full facts of this trial are laid before the nation, the people will be shocked."[4] In a radio interview he attacked the Moscow-tainted Democrats for covering up their dirty linen: "I think the entire Truman administration was extremely anxious that nothing happen to Mr. Hiss."[5]

Several of Nixon's cronies from HUAC echoed him. One of them said Kaufman showed "bias bordering on judicial misconduct."[6] Another called for a "minute examination" of Kaufman's record.[7] A third said, "The matter should be turned over to the Judiciary Committee for impeachment."[8] The barrage went on for weeks.

Attacks on Judge Kaufman were the most dramatic, but they were by no means the extent of the harassment.

The two Supreme Court Justices Frankfurter and Reed, who'd testified for the defense, were setting a "degrading precedent"[9]; they'd "dragged down the high position of the Supreme Court."[10] The four dissenting jurors really got it in the neck; the details of their vote—along with their addresses—appeared in newspaper after newspaper:

For acquittal—Louis Hill, a business secretary; Arthur L. Pawliger, an advertising company employee; James and Mrs. Torian.[11]

Nobody bothered with Mrs. Torian's first name or her profession because she was only a woman, but the car salesman James was a different matter. Hubert Edgar James had served as foreman, and he "was sympathetic to Hiss." An FBI agent said so. The agent's source? "An informant" visiting a patient at a resort in New Jersey "had a conversation with a woman who said she was" James's wife.[12] Just in case an outraged American wanted to take a pot shot at the foreman but wasn't sure what he looked like, full-length pictures of him were part of the coverage. Nixon wanted him prosecuted.[13]

All four dissenters signed affidavits detailing middle-of-the night calls—phone ringing and ringing until they woke and answered, caller hangs up at once, only to ring again a few minutes later. If the caller spoke, it was to say, "Go back to Russia," or to make threats of terrible ends. All four received hate mail. They faced local press accusations of communism and whisper campaigns about "Communist sympathies." Nixon pressed to have them subpoenaed—all four of them—before HUAC.[14]

***

Back in 1945, Roy Day, advertising salesman for the Pomona Progress Bulletin, first spotted Richard Milhous Nixon at the dinner held by the

Republican candidate selection board; Mickey Cohen's lawyer Chotiner had spotted him there too. They'd both been very impressed. Chotiner saw somebody smart and tough as hell who just might win big. Day saw "saleable merchandise."[15]

The merchandise needed a little working over, though. Nixon had worn his Lieutenant Commander's uniform that night. Dump it, said Day: too many veterans hated their superior officers during the war and resent them now. Nixon dumped it, bought an ill-fitting gray suit, dumped that as soon as he could find a navy blue one that fitted him. But his taste in clothes was as bad as it had been when the Eastern establishment turned up its nose at him. Get rid of the loud ties, Day said. Nixon got rid of them. His stumbling, tongue-tied manner with women marked him out too. Look them in the eye, Day told him; smile graciously. Nixon worked on it. He mastered it. Almost, anyhow.

Day is the man who backed him to the hilt with the ads that squashed a powerful Democratic incumbent: "A vote for Nixon is a vote against Communistic principles and [the incumbent's] gigantic slush fund!" And in the summer of 1949, with Alger's trials and the excitement of treason filling the headlines, Day told him, "When your star is up, that's when you have to move."[16] Nixon moved. His star wasn't just up, it was soaring. Here's the *New York Times* headline that ran shortly before Alger's second trial was due to begin:

3-Way G. O. P. Senate Race in California
Forecast as Nixon Announces Candidacy[17]

Nixon was one of those rare people who really was born to lead; where he went, others followed. The pumpkin's revelations proved to Republican after Republican that Red-baiting could win when nothing else had a chance. The Democrats had held the presidency for sixteen years—Roosevelt, Truman, the New Deal—and because of them millions of people around the world "had been delivered into Soviet slavery."[18]

But the greatest peril was right at home. A New England electrical union had three hundred Communists in control. In the Midwest, the hunt was on for a mysterious "Scientist X" who was giving away bomb secrets to the Soviets. In the South, singer Paul Robeson was a "black Stalin," and the Soviets were carting "poor colored boys" off to Russia to teach them bomb-making and turn them into urban terrorists. Key Communists in Washington, driven underground, were infiltrating every level of government. The FBI revealed that there were 12,000 dangerous Communists at large in the US, half of them citizens. Hoover said that when Russia went Red, there was one Communist per 2,277 head of population; the US contamination was much more serious: "one per every 1,814 persons in the country,"[19] exactly 6,977 of them in California, many in the movies.[20] The Congress of American Women was full of hard-core Reds. Teachers all over the country were distributing Communist propaganda in their classrooms.

Alger and his trial-to-come brought all this into sharp focus for the public, and HUAC wasn't going to let them forget it. The publication of Robert Stripling's *The Red Plot Against America*—following its syndication across the country in spring—was poised to coincide with the opening of Alger's second trial in October. HUAC member John Rankin read the dumbwaiter shaft papers into the Congressional Record and gave interviews about "the American boys who were killed, who lost their lives as a result of this treason." If Alger had been caught in time, Rankin said, "we might not have had a Pearl Harbor."[21]

A fair trial in New York? Forget it.

The Sixth Amendment ensures the right to an impartial jury, and high-profile cases like Alger's get moved all the time. His legal team entered a motion for a change of venue from New York to Vermont, where he'd spent summers for the past decade, much longer, all in all, than he'd spent in New York. Vermonters have a reputation for independent thinking; New York hysteria rarely takes them in.

This time Alger was going to win. He knew it. There wasn't a doubt in his mind. Never mind the brilliant Stryker's warning that nobody—nobody—could win this case in any state in the union. Alger knew he could, and he was going to do it his way. He was going to argue the evidence. He was going to concentrate on the detail. He was going to burrow his way into Nixon's confabulation. He didn't approve of Stryker's "florid" courtroom style anyway,[22] booted him out, hired a gentle Bostonian called Claude Cross, a short, stocky Harvard Law School graduate with a "solid background in corporate cases involving complex documents."[23]

The man had no criminal experience. None. He'd never faced a jury, not in New York, not anywhere.

A court delay from October to November did get agreed; Stripling moved his book launch to coincide. But a change of venue? The government prosecutor Murphy opposed it on the grounds that if jurors said they had no prejudice, the law was satisfied. The case went to one Judge Alfred Coxe. Judge Coxe had spent a holiday in Vermont; he'd seen New York newspapers in his hotel. Surely that was proof that Vermont couldn't be any more impartial than New York.

He denied the motion.

39

A Canadian friend said, "Well, Joan, you've known all these dangerous people, you're probably dangerous just for knowing them. Why not try for your own FBI file?" The results took a while but sounded not unfamiliar—to start with. Nobody could find me in their "main file records" and "unfortunately" couldn't find me in their manual indices because those were "being prepared for automation"[1] and were "unavailable for searches."[2] I appealed. The FBI turned me down. They could "neither confirm nor deny the existence or nonexistence of records" that would indicate I was on a watch list.[3] A watch list? Joanie the terrorist? I wrote to the American Civil Liberties Union. It's called a "No Fly listing," and it turns out to be a standard disclaimer. Which means *all* American citizens are terrorist suspects.

That's not very nice.

While I was pondering it, a man from the National Archives called the Washington journalist Jeremy Bigwood to say that they'd found my father's records. They found records they'd destroyed? "Apparently some of your mother's records have also been found in his file, which is about one thousand pages long. It is being put on 'fast' lane, but that will take six months."[4]

Nearly two years passed. The cover was as old and yellowed as Galois's death certificate:

Federal Bureau of Investigation
DO NOT DESTROY
HISTORICAL VALUE
NATIONAL ARCHIVES

It's stamped "SECRET" and "SUBV-CONTROL." More stamps show it being reviewed again and again over the years. There turned out to be only 327 pages and only a few of them on my mother and Record Group 65. "Access Restricted." My father takes up the rest of the file. J. Edgar Hoover himself was involved. So were more than two dozen named agents and literally scores of informers. Confidential Informant T-30 discovered that a "colored servant"[5] slept in the room next to the Bradys and called them by their first names.[6] Confidential Source T-1 tracked an unrelated Robert Brady to a Los Angeles "'flop house' run by a Jap."[7] What's most peculiar is that quite a few informers insist that Brady was not a Communist. One says that he was thrown out of the Soviet Union for criticizing the regime.

Even so, Hoover annotated his file, "Red Tab this case." Then come some real surprises. Hoover writes to San Francisco about "custodial detention." Jail? What for? The file gives no hint. The Department of Justice writes to Hoover with an application: Robert A. Brady is "possibly amenable for service action." Meaning? A letter follows with a "view toward denaturalization and deportation." Is the US really prepared to deport its own citizens? Not that it would be difficult. A forged Canadian birth certificate and a discredited American one would do the job.

One thing that's clear is that the FBI did destroy the bulk of the file; a summary covers well over a decade, but except for a few random sheets, the file covers only 1942. The only clues as to why are reports like these. Confidential Source G said Brady was "violently anti-Nazi."[8] An article quoted him as saying that "Nazi Germany is a capitalist's paradise."[9] Confidential Source T-21 said he believed "a capitalist country would eventually become fascist."[10] It doesn't sound like much, but there were the passionate anti-fascist books he wrote, the equally passionate lectures he gave, the students and audiences who applauded him.

I was getting more than a queasy sense of just how very dangerous ideas like this were.

Svetlana talks about Nazi safe havens in America. Jeremy Bigwood's work ties the US cover-up of this collaboration to the attacks on premature anti-fascists like my parents. "Some of the American purges of the late 1940s and 1950s are directly related to it (in my opinion based on archived material)."[11] I found confirmation in a book called *Nazi Hydra in America*. It echoes Bigwood, states my parents' fate straight out, and fixes it right in the heart of my story.

They fell victim to "the purge of the stringent anti-fascists" that climaxed "with the trials of Alger Hiss."[12]

1949 – 1950

Alger's second trial opened in the same courthouse in New York City that the first had: the Federal Building in Foley Square. All the courtrooms inside were the same—same oak panels, same green leather chairs, same carved wooden palisades—although crossing the hall must have turned them into mirror images. In the courtroom right next door, pre-trial testimony was going on in the Judith Coplon spy case. Coplon had been a political analyst for the Justice Department, and she'd been turning confidential documents over to the Russians for five years when one of the FBI's Confidential Informants spotted her. Thirty agents closed in on her—this was just as Alger's first trial was beginning—right as she was in the act of passing something to a KGB official.

Two Red trials side by side. Again.

So far, so familiar, but there wasn't the excitement this time around. No rival picket lines fighting outside in Foley Square, media coverage down in amount if not in viciousness. This muting continued for years too. Alistair Cooke in his *A Generation on Trial*, based on his BBC coverage of Alger, gave the second trial a quarter of the words he gave the first. Alger himself passed over it in a few pages. It's a puzzlement.

There's a sense of the Lotus Eaters about the courtroom. The judge was seventy-five-year-old Henry Goddard, a Republican appointed to the bench way back in the early 1920s, "a magnificent old American bald eagle"—this is Cooke—"with two white nests of hair sprouting from long ears."[1] But he napped throughout much of the proceedings; his portrait for *Life* magazine shows him with the smug and ample middle of a man who enjoys a glass of port after lunch. He doubled this time-honored joke about judges by allowing ladies of fashion to sit in as privileged guests.

Alice Roosevelt Longworth was President Teddy Roosevelt's daughter, famous for hating her daddy's relative Franklin Delano Roosevelt and everybody connected with him. Each morning, just as the session opened, she appeared in court with her sister-in-law and her daughter-in-law. The three of them trekked into the well of the court itself and across to a special area reserved for just such people, right opposite the jury. They knitted and made sketches. All three nodded when the prosecution scored a point. All three shook their heads at the defense.[2]

Alger referred to them as the *tricoteuses* after the women who knitted beside the guillotine in the French Reign of Terror. They do sound terrifying in their way. He was good at metaphors like that, and I can well imagine the "gusts of anger" beneath that imperturbable exterior at the defense table. During my first evening with him, he'd called trials "gladiatorial contests," and certainly a gladiator is what he needed, a William Garrow, stopper of thief-taking in England, or a Clarence Darrow, who separated science from the church in America. Or the fire and brimstone Stryker. Poor Claude Cross was a gray-faced, gentle, apologetic plodder, pernickety, pedantic, confusing; and he faced Stryker's old opponent, the huge, witty, breezy Murphy. Worse, he was unfamiliar with HUAC's approach. Worse still, he agreed with Murphy—on Alger's instructions—that the real issue was the documents that Stryker had dismissed in a few minutes of his summation.

This makes no sense at all. None. This is where Alger desperately needed a criminal lawyer, somebody like Stryker, somebody who was fully aware that fighting the documents meant proving himself not guilty of espionage in a trial for perjury. Espionage? That's thinking too small. It's treason that's now on the table. Exactly what Nixon wanted. Murphy must have been falling all over himself in delight. The first time around he'd relied on Chambers to swing it alone. Didn't work. Those four dissenting jurors had voted for acquittal because they just couldn't believe him despite the public pressure for a guilty verdict. A switch in tactics should take care of that. The typewriter and the documents—the immutable witnesses—were what mattered, not Chambers, whose testimony was as gossamer and as enchanting as before.

One of the typed exhibits—Number Ten—wasn't done on a Woodstock at all. Nobody seemed to notice that this anomaly invalidated the claim that Priscilla had typed all those pages on the Hiss Woodstock. Chambers didn't care. Alger gave it to him. Well, no, Alger hadn't. A guy called White from the Treasury gave it to him. No, no. Wrong again. Alger *had* given it to him.

Cross said Chambers was crazy. He brought in shrinks to prove it. A Dr. Binger said that "Mr. Chambers is suffering from a condition known as a psychopathic personality," which showed itself in "chronic, persistent, and repetitive lying and a tendency to make false accusations." A symptom of this was that Chambers fixed his eyes on the ceiling when testifying. He cited Chambers's "equivocation" in his testimony as evidence of his "ineluctability."[3]

"*Ineluctability*"? Murphy, man of the people, pounced on the word. That was an Alger word, an egghead word. What is that? He joyously yanked back the old HUAC trick of numbers: was Dr. Binger aware that he himself had looked at the ceiling fifty-nine times in twenty minutes? Fifty-nine? Really? How could he deny it? Was he aware that Alger had equivocated one hundred fifty-eight times? Much more than Chambers? Who'd been counting? When?

But such excitements were thin on the ground, and this trial lasted nine weeks. Nine weeks of documents: a gauntlet of doing your taxes. Even so, I thought I ought to have a look at them. I contacted Svetlana.

Her comment?

In the 60 years since the case NOBODY—repeat NOBODY—has cared to investigate this material evidence as it should've been investigated in the first place.[4]

Nobody? This evidence may be boring, but it launched Nixon's political career, created a panic in an entire country, put Alger in prison, and
paved the way for the notorious Senator Joseph McCarthy who ruined
so many, many people, and nobody's had a good look at it since?

I assumed getting hold of copies of the documents would be the
easy part. I tried the National Archives. There I found *M1491. Photographs: Documents reproduced from the "Pumpkin Papers," and used in U.S.
v. Alger Hiss, 1948-51 (268 images).* Two hundred sixty eight images?
What could they be of? The pages from both pumpkin and dumbwaiter
shaft came to half as many. A couple of eye-watering hours later, the
site yielded up Jeremy Bigwood, Washington journalist and researcher.

The first job he did for me was getting that file. The frames from
the pumpkin were there, all fifty-eight with evidence numbers marked
on them. But that was it. Not two hundred sixty-eight images at all:
only fifty-eight plus a couple of blank frames and a short introduction.
Where were the papers from the dumbwaiter shaft? Jeremy had no
idea. The Archives had nothing more.

Alger's son Tony suggested the Tamiment Library. Their UK arm had
thirty-three reels of Alger Hiss evidence at £95 per reel, and the librarian
was friendly but had no idea even if they contained what I wanted and no
idea how to find out. Tamiment's New York arm was less friendly. First
they had no Hiss-case papers, then just a list of them, then thirty of them.
When it turned out that the list didn't include the material Chambers
had turned over to Alger's lawyers, and the thirty were a random selection
from somebody else's copies—not the court exhibits themselves—
Tamiment wanted nothing more to do with me or my search. The Harvard Law School Library sent Jeremy three hundred pages, but many
were illegible. None was in order, and none had exhibit numbers.

I finally located an historian in Canada who was kind enough to
send on a full set of copies, but what was I to make of what I saw?
Here's how Chambers describes them at his deposition; he has his lawyer William MacMillan speaking:

"I will just read off the first and last words of each in sequence." There
began half an hour of stunning itemization. 'Paris: to the Secretary of

State, Strictly Confidential, Signed Bullitt. Rome: To the Secretary of State, I learn strictest confidence . . ."[5]

This really does sound like serious stuff, doesn't it? But hang on a minute . . . *Bullitt?* What's he doing here?

41

I would never have bothered to check out the name if it hadn't been for that Louisville trip and Nixon's condolence letter to old Mrs. Bullitt. I got out her book on the Soviet Union. Her short foreword went more or less as I remembered it: the "powers that be" didn't want her to publish because of her husband's "relationship to our ambassador to the Soviet Union."[1] I reread the pamphlet that her husband had distributed to the press during Alger's first trial. I'd completely missed the reference to a William C. Bullitt as an example of "disinterested oral evidence":

> Chambers' 1939 statements to the Government of . . .the infiltration of Communists (including Hiss) into important Government positions (1105, 1106) . . .[were] conveyed to William C. Bullitt, then Ambassador to France.[2]

Could it be? The Ambassador to the Soviet Union and the French ambassador were one and the same man? And could this ambassador be the Bullitt cousin whose minions had stolen Galois's burial certificate? Surely not. But it's true. William Christian Bullitt, ambassador, and William Marshall Bullitt, Louisville lawyer—receiver of the stolen burial certificate—were first cousins with just a middle name to differentiate them.

Before William Christian became ambassador to France, he was the United States' very first ambassador to the USSR. In a thriller, there'd have to be a reason for planting an ambassador to the Reds in a trial like Alger's, where being a Red was so crucial an issue, especially when the ambassador is a close relative—and a fond one—of the distributor of a rabidly partisan pamphlet.

William Christian—Bill to his friends and relatives—was famous in his time, seriously famous as an author as well as a diplomat, a real charmer by all accounts too. But he was a rich boy with an unshakeable sense of upper-class entitlement. The historian Kenneth Davis describes him as "a romantic idealist of conspiratorial temper for whom everything was purest white or deepest black . . .inclined to over-commit himself to people and then be bitterly disillusioned when they failed to act according to his preconceptions."[3]

In 1919, when the Soviet Union was a fresh young state, Bill was in his early thirties, married, a successful working journalist as well as top of America's social elite and President Woodrow Wilson's greatest fan. Nobody in government trusted the Soviets, certainly not Wilson; he sent Bill to take a look. Bill just plain fell in love with the social experiment, like so many who got caught in HUAC's net; he pushed Wilson hard to establish diplomatic relations. Wilson wouldn't play, and when spoiled rich kids don't get what they want, they can turn as dirty as Nixon; Wilson became the first in a string of those bitter disillusionments. Bill spread anti-Wilson rumors. He wrote a book making fun of Wilson, and it's a tribute to his charm that he persuaded father of psychoanalysis Sigmund Freud to write an introduction.[4]

Bill wrote a book about the Soviet Union,[5] too, right in the spirit of Mother's little volume if much more sophisticated. He even divorced his wife because of it; he wanted to marry Louise Bryant.

The name Louise Bryant doesn't ring bells any more except to people who are Diane Keaton fans. She was the beautiful widow of John Reed, writer of *Ten Days that Shook the World*, a book about the Russian Revolution that took on rock star status. In the movie *Reds*, Reed is played by Warren Beatty to Keaton's Bryant; after his death she became a celebrated authority on Soviet Russia in her own right as lead reporter for the Hearst papers.

She was pregnant by the time Bill married her in 1923. They moved to Turkey, rented a villa that had belonged to ministers from the Ottoman Empire, held grand parties, lived like pashas. From Turkey, they went to Paris, rented English novelist Elinor Glyn's old house with a ceiling of mirrors in the bedroom. Anne Bullitt was born, and the partying continued with the Duke and Duchess of Windsor in attendance. Bill wrote a novel,[6] slashing the American elite he'd grown up with. It had sex in it—a verboten subject at the time—and it was a hit.

The idyll ended when Bryant became seriously ill. She was always in pain, always exhausted. She started drinking too much. Somehow—nobody knows how—she got caught in what looked like a lesbian affair with a British sculptor called Gwen Le Gallienne.[7] Back then, as Chambers knew all too well, homosexuality represented the depths of depravity. Not that depravity worried Bill all that much; gossips reported a gamut of sexual tastes that included his gay private secretary, Carmel Offie. What really matters is that Bill was flirting with politics again. Adiposis dolorosa—Louise's disease—isn't just debilitating and very painful; it makes beautiful people into ugly ones. The brain is involved too, depression, epilepsy, confusion, dementia. A wife like this was a serious liability. Did he set her up with Le Gallienne? The gossips thought so. The divorce was kept very quiet. Her disgrace wasn't. Bill took Anne back to America and denied her mother access; mother and daughter never saw each other again.

Bryant died alone in poverty in a cheap Paris hotel.

Three years after the divorce, Bill's political career took off with Roosevelt's election in 1932. "I love you," Bill wrote to FDR,[8] and it must have been mutual because despite rumblings in Washington about disloyalty to Wilson, the new President sent Bill back to the USSR. That's how he became America's first ambassador there, and as a vocal pro-Soviet, he was a passionate anti-Nazi. Then something happened. Again nobody knows just what, except that in three months, he made a total about face: now a passionate anti-Soviet and vocal pro-Nazi.

Roosevelt sent him to Paris instead, but by this time he was so rabid a fascist that he pushed hard for a Franco-Nazi rapprochement. His reports became wildly inaccurate. FDR recalled him.

Back home, he hungered after the job of Under Secretary of State. Sumner Welles held it. Welles wasn't only FDR's close friend, he was one of those stringent anti-fascists like Alger. One night when Welles was in his cabin on a sleeper train—so the story went—he called in a string of porters, propositioned them one after another, and they all ran away horrified. None of them was willing to sign an affidavit; Welles denied all of it, and the whole thing stinks of the way the gossips said Bill set up Louise Bryant to get a divorce. Bill spread the news everywhere. Pressure built up on FDR to fire Welles. FDR was a peaceable man; he hated firing people. The pressure increased. Welles had to go. FDR did it in person.

This time there were repercussions. FDR summoned Bill to the Oval Office. As always with Bill, nobody seems to know exactly what happened, but Roosevelt's stenographer said the president "was raving after Bullitt left his office, raving!" "He was sure Saint Peter would let Welles into heaven" whatever his sins, but Bullitt, who'd "destroyed a fellow human being, would go to hell."[9]

The predictable polar shift took place. According to Bill's successor as ambassador to the USSR, he became "savage about Roosevelt."[10] He started spreading rumors about New Dealers, just as he had with Wilson, "this one's a commie, that one's a queer."

But what about Alger in all this?

Louisville cousin Bullitt—in that pamphlet he distributed to the press at the first trial—quoted Bill as "disinterested oral evidence," evidence that emanated from Chambers in 1939, just like HUAC's evidence, the FBI's, and the various others'.

And yet Bill testified later—in an appearance before the Senate's version of HUAC in the early 1950s while Alger was in jail—and told them that in 1939 his source for Alger's treachery was none other than Prime Minister Edouard Daladier of France. Which sounds seriously important. It's real corroboration. Bill said that when he was ambassador, Daladier told him that he'd received French intelligence reports about both Hiss brothers—not just Alger but his younger brother Donald too. Bill said he told FDR all about it; he said FDR just laughed it off.

How come William Marshall didn't use that in his pamphlet? What could be more convincing than a head of state and his intelligence service confirming Alger's treachery a full decade ago? Why put it all down to Chambers? Especially when the prosecution's greatest weakness was the lack of support for his story?

Orville Bullitt, Bill's brother, published a book called *For the President: Personal & Secret*; it's the correspondence between FDR and Bill during Bill's stint as ambassador in Paris. There are scores of exchanges during 1939. Daladier is all over the place—that's as it should be—but no exchange mentions Alger or so much as hints at him.

The book's index doesn't even list an Alger Hiss. Or a Donald Hiss for that matter.

In 1946 Bill published a book called *The Great Globe Itself*,[11] warning of the Soviet "forces of evil"[12] planning war with "overwhelming attacking forces of Communist-driven slaves."[13] He saw the Yalta conference at the end of WWII as no less than Roosevelt's collapse before Stalin; he described it in some detail with his usual vitriol. He attacked several of FDR's aides by name. "A repetitious and bitter book," according to the *New York Times* reviewer Orville Prescott.[14]

Alger was at that conference; he sat right behind Roosevelt. Not a peep about him from Bill. No mention of Daladier either. There's more. The next year, 1947, Bill was testifying before HUAC itself that Soviet parents ate their young. He'd seen the evidence with his own eyes. He told them so, and he named names like the "friendly" witness he was.

Not Alger's.

The year after that, in August of 1948, right as Alger was making his first headlines with his appearances before HUAC, Bill published an article in *Life* magazine called "How We Won the War and Lost the Peace."[15] Again he ripped into his enemies: the "lost peace" was not just Roosevelt's feeble-mindedness but the pro-Communist duplicity of his advisers at the 1945 Yalta Conference. Again Bill named names. Again there's no Alger.

During Alger's trials, Bill was alive and active. Ex-Prime Minister Daladier was alive and active too. Yet Bill sent his ancient cousin into court with a home-printed pamphlet when he himself could have clinched the deal. Why isn't somebody attached to the French Embassy in Paris getting a statement from Daladier right this minute? Even without that French intelligence report, we'd have full-blown treason and a proper hanging.

On the other hand, this is Bill Bullitt we're talking about. And that testimony of his before the Senate didn't come until 1952, when Alger's trials were safely in the past. On April 9, 1952, the same day that news of Bill's testimony appeared, an Associated Press report—beneath a portrait of him—carried an interview with Daladier. The prime minister "did not recall either the name Hiss or a conversation with Mr. Bullitt, then US ambassador to France, about brothers in the State Department."[16]

And so back to Chambers's documents.

Alger fully agreed with his lawyers that that Chambers should turn the dumbwaiter shaft papers over to the Justice Department. The Justice Department agreed with him—nothing secret, of no interest to the Soviets, no law broken by anybody, not even by Chambers. Assistant Secretary of State Sayre, in front of a grand jury, thoroughly debunked Nixon's "proof of the greatest treason in American history."[1] And yet these are the pages that sat in front of the jury as the "immutable witnesses"[2] to Alger's treachery along with the typewriter that he'd looked so hard to find, then turned over too. We're deep in the Queen of Hearts' courtroom:

> "I don't believe there's an atom of meaning in it," said Alice.
> "Off with her head!" the Queen shouted at the top of her voice.

John Chabot Smith, a reporter for the *Herald Tribune*, calls Chambers's papers an "odd assortment."[3] They certainly look that way. Twenty-two typewritten pages make up a nitpickingly detailed—and unbelievably dull—report on economic conditions in Manchuria; it had passed from hand to hand in the US State Department for more than a month. There's a thirteen-page aide memoire in German from October 1937, a sixteen-page comment on it from January 1938—with excerpts, an undated, four-page memorandum on it, a twelve-page aide memoire on

German relations with Brazil from June 1937. What Soviet spymaster could possibly be interested in any of this?

Much of the material had appeared in the *New York Times*,[4] doubtless via press releases from the State Department's Record Division, to which copies of low-level information like it was delivered by shopping trolley. Some of it reports conversations with Russians that the Russians already had.[5] The boring Manchuria report came from a series of articles that ran in the *Japan Advertiser*. Some of those "To the Secretary of State" cables—the ones that so excited Chambers—go into what Smith described as "vague reports about Japanese troop movements in China, lacking enough detail to give a clear picture."[6] Some are just ordinary letters, not marked "Private" or "Confidential." Some are copies from abroad. Some never left Washington. Some pages are organized by place of origin: "Far East", "Europe", "England", "Spain", "Great Britain", "France." Some look like complete documents. Some are summaries. Some are both. Some summaries draw material from the same day, some from weeks or even months apart; some summaries are chronological, some not. Some are verbatim copies of the original, some accurately summarized, some not. Some are just garbled. Some of the originals had never gone to Alger's office at all. Others have his initials on them.

His own initials? No spy is that stupid.

The original State Department copies of all the documents were easy to find, including the ones Alger had made handwritten notes on for his boss. Two look promising. One of the typewritten ones discusses Hitler's takeover in Austria, the opening shot in World War II—probably the cable Chambers referred to in his deposition—and the Soviets would certainly have been interested.

But, but, but . . . the takeover part isn't included in the papers Chambers turned over. One of the handwritten notes is similar; it leaves out the only information the USSR would have wanted: a stunning paragraph that says Japan was certain she could win a war against Russia.

Now the poor guy can't figure out what's spy-worthy and what isn't.

I sent everything I had to Svetlana. "What doesn't let my brain stop," she responded, "is that it's so unlike the high-grade intelligence I used to see in the Soviet files of the period." She checked intelligence reports from the 1930s in Stalin's papers. "The contrast is striking—all reports from 'agent sources' in Berlin, Paris, Poland, and one in the USA—very analytical, many analytical surveys of what looks like diplomatic correspondence, confidential oral reports, etc."[7]

John Chabot Smith of the *Herald Tribune* writes that entering this strange hotchpotch into evidence was "tedious, frustrating, at times ludicrous and often exasperating." It "stupefied" Alistair Cooke.[8] At least the two of them were getting paid to sit and listen. Pity the poor trapped jury. A government witness explored in intricate detail the subtle distinctions between dispatches, reports, aides memoire, letters of transmittal. The prosecution presented three versions of every document, an "action copy", a "code room copy", an "information copy."[9] Murphy read every one of them out loud. Each exhibit had a number and each group of exhibits, another number. The prosecution referred to them sometimes by exhibit numbers, sometimes by date, sometimes by content, sometimes by origin. They displayed pages on a seven-foot-tall billboard but often showed only a summary without date or exhibit number. Nixon's confabulation of fact and fiction is taking second place to an old, old trick sometimes known as an "evidence dump." Legally minded people use it to fiddle their income taxes: multiple-page, single-spaced, heavily cross-referenced letters accompanying their tax returns. A single glance should leave an inspector too cross-eyed to brave the return itself. That's what the prosecution was doing, swamping the jury with a mountain of exhibits so dense, so boring, so complex that nobody could stay awake, much less burrow a way through it. Who can claim intent? Especially when there's so much of it?

What needed hiding in the Hiss case was the simple innocence of the documents themselves. Just what Alice told the Queen of Hearts.

But where did the documents come from in the first place?

Chambers would have had no difficulty getting hold of any of them. None was secret. His WPA job in the State Department wasn't active after early 1938, but he remained on furlough waiting for that job for which he would be "deemed qualified." He'd have had ready access to whatever he fancied. Not that this would have been his only illegal foray into government files. There was the economist in the Baltimore telephone book, the senior administrator for the Treasury Department whose personal dossier went missing—Jay Lea Chambers,[10] the unfortunate who shared Chambers's name—and whose details Whittaker's wife Esther used when she applied to the Baltimore Credit Bureau before she went shopping.

As for the four handwritten notes Chambers handed over during his deposition, nobody doubts that they originated with Alger. Stealing somebody's identity from a government file is a tidy crime if not a nice one, but rummaging around in wastepaper baskets? Chambers really was creepy. Guy Endore, who was at Columbia with him, told the psychoanalyst Dr. Zeligs that it was a regular habit. Chambers liked searching people's wastepaper baskets; he found "pieces of identity" there.[11] Zeligs diagnosed a "psychic scavenger." Friends and colleagues said that Chambers targeted people who obsessed him. Wastepaper was the least of it with the Hiss family. He collected bits of their furniture too: a love seat, a wing chair, a table, a child's rocker, a child's chest. He kept this booty in his basement storeroom along with a much more intimate prize: he'd removed a square of material from a chair that Alger had sat on, folded it neatly, and tucked it away for safe-keeping.

Here's Part One of a scenario.

When Chambers and Nixon started spending time together right after Alger's first appearance at HUAC—back in early August 1948—these handwritten notes were all the documentary material that existed. And what good were they? The dates were early 1938, and Chambers had sworn again and again—under oath and sixteen times over ten years—that he'd had nothing to do with Communists after 1937. He'd sworn to it just before Alger's first hearing. He'd sworn to it in the first few minutes of his executive session with Nixon, the one where he was the "mystery witness" the Committee had flown all the way to New York to interview.

He interrupted that testimony to go off the record. There's two hours and some of unrecorded whispering, and when the record picks up again the date-change has happened. And the handwritten notes he's held on to for all these years: they fit into his story! It's that glorious, perverse, mythic imagination at work. Who's going to notice a change in year, much less care? Chambers told so many lies and created so many fancies that nobody was likely to pay attention to just one more.

But we still need motive.

The prosecution really grappled with the problem, and the best they could manage was pure patriotism. In those hysterical times—and well buried in Nixon's confusion of fact and fancy—it almost worked. It does call for Chambers the saint—something of a stretch at the best of times—and was almost possible then only because the public couldn't see HUAC's testimony, Chambers's many confessions to the FBI, the grand jury testimony, or the Justice Department's dismissal of the evidence. All anybody outside HUAC saw was Nixon's media onslaught. Fear and titillation did the rest.

An alternate motive is "the woman scorned." Chambers was delicately balanced. He was a sexual predator. Who can forget the shocked Good Samaritan who woke to find that devastated mouth wrapped around his penis? A predator like that gives off signals as he closes in. They'd have broken the spell of Alger's noblesse oblige, and a harsh rejection just might explain a long-standing grudge for somebody like Chambers. He wasn't alone. Bill Bullitt's hatred of President Wilson was a lifelong obsession; he published his vicious attack on the president forty years after they'd parted company. The woman scorned could have provoked the name-naming in Chambers's early confessions when he was a down-and-out loser, and Alger was a rising star; it might well have sustained a drive for revenge throughout the entire case.

The life of an informer can be a hard one emotionally, especially for somebody who fingers innocent people. Harvey Matusow, one of the turncoats who'd testified for the government in the Communist Party trial, fingered some he knew were innocent. He gave his reasons as "need, greed, and fear." But it cost him in unexpected ways. "As I reported on a friend, he was no longer my friend; I began to distrust and hate him. I stopped trusting people by knowing myself untrustworthy. I grew to hate people because I had injured them." Tacitus said it first: "It is a part of human nature to hate the man you have hurt."

Even so, I don't think Chambers was a willing participant in Nixon's crusade. He hinted as much in an exchange about the case with William Buckley in 1954. "For you see, after six years, my side still does not really know what this is all about."[12] And there's backing from Clare Booth Luce, rabid anti-Communist wife of rabid anti-Communist Henry Luce, owner of *Time* magazine and Chambers's employer; she was a journalist of serious substance on her own—famous for the phrase, "no good deed goes unpunished"—and the United States' first female ambassador anywhere, Italy in her case. She describes Chambers as "a deeply tortured man who loathed the spotlight, and had no appetite for martyrdom—and indeed none at all for bringing Alger Hiss down."[13]

Chambers's advocates say that in a bid to preempt disaster—nobody so much as suggests whose idea it was—he added an account of his sexual adventures to his many FBI confessions. He wrote out eight pages in longhand. He told the agents that the troubles in his parents' marriage came about because of his father's "homosexualism," that he had inherited the trait but wasn't aware of it in himself—had no personal experience of it—until 1933 or 1934 when he was "more than 30."[14]

The people of Lynbrook, where he grew up, weren't so blind. Mrs. George Morgan, whose kids went to school with him, told one of Alger's investigators that from the very outset Chambers "was termed a sissy by the neighborhood children" and that he "retained his effeminate mannerisms as he grew into manhood."[15] The *New York Post*'s Oliver Pilat talked to Chambers's seventh-grade teacher: "None of the boys had much use for him," she said.[16] His only companion during the eight years he spent at grade school was "a little girl named Vermilia."[17] Things didn't pick up in high school. The FBI questioned every classmate they could find about Chambers's "effeminacy."[18] Their reports are not available, and witnesses were sworn to secrecy, but the agents couldn't have helped finding out what one of them said years later: the general view was that "he had a touch of lavender in him."[19] The June 1919 issue of South Side High School's *The Breeze* features the graduating class and lists his nickname as "Girlie."[20]

When Chambers was twenty years old and first going to Columbia, his companion on the subway ride from Long Island to Manhattan was another freshman, sixteen-year-old Henry Bang. Henry had a younger brother called "Bub," who was eleven or twelve; the three of them often went camping together in the woods around Lynbrook. According to one of Chambers's biographers, several years later Chambers was shocked to hear his friends whispering about his "homosexual relationship" with Bub.[21]

And yet his wife Esther could hardly have had any doubts that what was going on was physical. She was gay herself. When she met Chambers, she was in a lesbian relationship with a writer called Grace Lumpkin; Chambers was in bed with another writer called Michael Intrator. The four moved in together: an odd-couples distribution that started out as Whitaker-and-Michael and Esther-and-Grace, then somehow ended up as Whittaker-and-Esther and Michael-and-Grace. The story was too well known in New York for the FBI to have missed it, and Bureau agents questioning Henry Bang years later simply assumed a sexual relationship between Bub and Chambers.[22]

Chambers's poems from the period are blatant. This is when he was comparing cottonwood saplings to "boy-trees" with

> *The leaves so pensile, so tremulously hung, as they leaned*
> *toward one another;*
> *Unable to strain farther into one another*

While beneath the ground they're

> *Writhing in struggle; heavy, fibrous, underearthen life,*
> *from which the sap mounts filling those trembling leaves.*[23]

And another poem, published in another magazine the same month

As your sap drains out into me in excess Like the sap from the stems of a tree that they lop.[24]

By the time Chambers was thirty, he was attacking the good Samaritan who put him up.

Chunks of Chambers's FBI longhand confession remain blacked-out to this very day,[25] but putting aside his usual confabulation of dates and events, he wrote that his first gay encounter was "a revelation." It "set off a chain reaction"[26] in him that was "almost impossible to control" until 1938. Which would indicate he was a sexual predator throughout his relationship with Alger.

The notoriously homophobic FBI treated the information "in a strictly confidential manner."[27]

Nobody could swallow a tale like this. He didn't have to write it down. How could writing it down preempt anything? It put both him and the prosecution in greater danger. It was proof of the prosecution's withholding evidence from the defense. Besides, it wasn't even remotely necessary. HUAC had already laid the grounds for swatting off any inconvenient rumors. Chambers had had an episode of serious mental instability after his brother died; there'd been what used to be called a nervous breakdown. Alger himself brought up the question in one of the hearings: "Is he a man of sanity?"[28]

"A typical Communist smear"—this is how representative Hébert of the Committee answered that very question—"when a man gets up to testify, and particularly a former Communist, is to say he is insane or an alcoholic or something else is wrong with him."[29]

Like homosexuality: a security risk as well as a leper-like disease. Preachers damned homosexuals to hellfire. Doctors used shock therapy, lobotomies, castration to cure them. If that didn't get them, the law did. Sodomy was a felony in every state in the union.[30] The government certainly wasn't going to expose Chambers. If his sex life got out, their case would collapse.

And it looks as if there could be more to that sex life than mere homosexuality.

A man called Ernie Lazar has been flooding the National Archives with Freedom of Information requests for decades, nearly nine thousand of them; he's collected and archived something like six hundred thousand files. I ran across a stunning one while I was seeking out newspaper reports of Chambers's childhood. A few months after the handwritten FBI confession, the Special Agent in charge of the Washington office is telling the Special Agent in charge of the New York office about a rumor that Chambers himself reported:

"Sometime in 1936 or later, Hiss is supposed to have discovered that Chambers was having homosexual relations with Timothy Hobson—"

Alger's stepson Timmy? But Timmy was only nine years old in 1936. That's even younger than Henry Bang's little brother, Bub.

"—and thereupon Hiss ordered Chambers from the house and forbade him to return."[31]

There's not much support for the allegation in the HUAC testimony. In Chambers's first secret hearing, he'd told Nixon that "Timmy was a puny little boy, also rather nervous . . . He was a slightly effeminate child." It's not so. Pictures of Timmy in the 1930s show a confident, stocky boy, big for his age; in one of them, he's sitting on the grass, feet solidly planted and well apart, elbows on his knees, hands examining a piece of foliage with Tom Sawyer's insouciance.

What's more shocking in the agent's report than the charge itself is that there is no denial from Chambers, nor does the FBI seem surprised by the information or so much as interested in finding out if it's true. The Washington Special Agent's report goes on to say that "Chambers is supposed to have returned to the Hiss home when he knew that Alger and Priscilla Hiss were not there and that on such occasions Chambers had been admitted to the house by Timothy Hobson." *Years* of sexual abuse? This does cause the FBI some concern, but not because of the crime or its duration. They're afraid the defense could claim that if Chambers was abusing Timmy into 1938, he'd have had all the time he needed to type the dumbwaiter-shaft documents on the Hiss typewriter. Follow-up investigations indicate that Timmy could indeed have been home alone and available.

Certainly if homosexuality alone could have destroyed the government's case, the government's cover-up of abuse of an nine-year-old boy that gave Chambers access to that typewriter would have been political disaster for the entire Republican Party. So *why* wasn't there serious concern about it?

And if there's truth to it, why didn't Alger use it in his defense? Nobody can do other than guess at another person's motives, but what the evidence does show is that Alger was adamant about *not* involving Timmy in the case because this sexual element turns out to be complicated. Timmy was tossed out of the Navy for being gay. If Alger had allowed him to testify, the Naval discharge would have come up; Timmy would have become subject to those legal and medical punishments. Given the rigidities of the time, his life would have been ruined—and very publicly. He'd never have had a chance to become the doctor he did become.

Even so he wasn't just willing to make the sacrifice, he *wanted* to make it.

The thing is, he *knew*.

And what he knew had nothing whatever to do with sex. It was far more dangerous to the government's case than that. The man who became Dr. Timothy Hobson was the only witness who knew Chambers had *not* been a family friend at all, much less the "close friend" he claimed to be, and he had *not* made those regular visits to drop off and pick up documents.

As he says: "I was there, and Chambers wasn't."[32]

There's a sort of a double take here. Could he really mean he never once saw Chambers in the Hiss house where all this skulduggery went on? Never saw this filthy, bedraggled man who opened his mouth to reveal a devastation that adults cringed from and would give any child nightmares? That no child *could* forget?

That's exactly what he means.

He does need a bit of evidence, though.

In the first place, it's pretty clear from Chambers's own testimony that he'd never seen the boy: he told Nixon during that New York hearing that Timmy was "puny", "nervous", "effeminate." He couldn't have been further off the mark; pictures of Timmy at the time do show that hearty, solid-looking boy, something of the Tom Sawyer in him, sitting on the grass, knees bent, feet apart, elbows resting on them to examine a piece of leaf or bark, an amused expression on his face.

But much more importantly, during the entire period when Chambers claimed he was in and out to Hiss house on a regular basis, picking up and returning documents, dining and enjoying parties and trips with Alger and Priscilla, young Timmy was living with his parents, and for a good part of that time, he was confined to a bed in the living room, recovering from a very badly broken leg. He couldn't help seeing whatever went on, whether it went on during the day during the night.

He was the *only* eye witness—and he was one people would believe. Even so, Alger overruled him absolutely, too concerned with the risk to Timmy's future, was prepared to go to prison to protect him.

⸙

Whatever Chambers had in mind when he said to Buckley that after all those years his side didn't know what the case was about, just think of the poor man's position as he faced it!

His whimpering and self-pity are an annoyance, but nobody could doubt that he was in real agony. While HUAC and Nixon secured their political futures, he was terrified, on tenterhooks all the time. How could he be otherwise? As Alger said, the prosecution had him "under their thumb."[33] To be sure, he'd secured immunity from charges of perjury. That did leave the possibility that he could stop lying. He could stop playing fanciful games with the mass of trivia that HUAC and the FBI had collected on Alger. He could stop betraying. He could just say, enough is enough. But how could he risk that?

Hoover was an old hand at coercion of witnesses,[34] and there was so much to coerce Chambers with. The dead baby trick he'd used to get a passport was a felony that could get him up to ten years. There was identity theft—the unfortunate who shared a name with him in the Baltimore telephone book—credit fraud, and the theft of the files from government offices that gave him the information to carry it out. But what really mattered was that handwritten confession in the FBI files.

Sodomy could get him twenty years hard labor. Child abuse? Literally unthinkable. That's a life far more terribly ruined than Alger's.

The FBI report and a handwritten confession to illegal sexual adventures sure as hell looks like insurance that Chambers would stay on track throughout the trials and keep his mouth shut when they were finished. Just getting him to write it out by hand shows the power they had over him: either write it or we charge you with any or all of the above—and be fully aware that if there's a peep out of you before you die, we publish.

The alternative? Fame as the man who exposed a spy in the heart of government, fame to be lived as a great American patriot and a deeply revered writer of whatever he wanted to write.

Here's Part Two of my scenario. It starts with the typed pages and brings more people into play.

Taken just as objects, the pages are even odder than what's printed on them. A mere sixty-five show ribbons changed four times, sometimes halfway through the page. Why would anybody do that? Those old ribbons could eke out a couple of hundred pages easily, and new ribbons were literally wet with ink. They made the hands dirty. They smudged. They blurred the letters, got fingerprints on the pages.

The paper itself has oddities. Some of the pages have deteriorated. Some haven't. Pressure marks and staining marks show that the Baltimore batch couldn't have been stored in the same place in the same envelope for ten years—not in Chambers's dumbwaiter shaft or anywhere else.[35] Oddest of all is the type of paper: onionskin, all of it. People used onionskin for carbon copies on those old machines, but nobody typed directly on it. It jammed the platen. It slipped. The letters blurred; they'd have made very poor photographs. No spymaster would accept copies of documents like these, especially given Vernon Hinchley's comment that the spy's hardest task wasn't to get information but to persuade his boss that it was accurate.

So why this onionskin?

A good possibility is just to add to the drama. This whole tale bubbles with theatrics fit for a Christmas pantomime. Assassination plots. Yiddish colonels with only one arm. Spies with only Christian names creeping about in the dark. A dumbwaiter shaft and a pumpkin spewing top secret documents. Especially that pumpkin: a sleight of hand so magnificently farcical that it diverted an entire country's attention from what was happening right in front of their eyes. Chambers knew exactly what he was doing. "The point about the pumpkin," he writes in *Witness,* "was not that it was absurd, but that it worked."[36]

It worked so brilliantly that nobody had to explain how innocent documents could threaten national security. Who could follow the reasoning anyway? At least Nixon had given the grand jury a hint. He'd said to them, "The message involving China, which Mr. Bullitt wrote—"

Bullitt? *Again!*

In court, prosecutor Murphy displayed a part of this message, but only a part, a bare two paragraphs; they went up on the seven-foot billboard. In the first paragraphs, Bullitt is in conversation with French Foreign Minister Yvon Delbos; they're discussing French hopes for reconciliation with Hitler's Germany. Delbos doesn't tell him anything he wouldn't have discussed with the Russian ambassador, but that innocent material was all the court was allowed to see. Everybody assumed that the missing part had been in the pumpkin too. Rumors flew. Was it the secret of the atom bomb? Names of double agents? The code Bullitt used? Was this what Nixon meant about the pumpkin threatening national security right now? More than ten years after the event?

Whatever else it meant, it meant that this man Hiss was still a threat.

And then abruptly, the missing section burst onto front pages all across the country. Here's the *New York Times*:

BULLITT MESSAGE SHOWN
TO HISS JURY;
Cable to Hull, Which Chambers Says
Defendant Gave Him

A secret high-level cablegram from France . . .
the highlight of the documentary exhibits.[37]

The disclosure was sensational. Bullitt reported the Soviet ambassador's warning to Delbos that "if France should begin serious negotiations with Germany, the Soviet Union would come to terms with Germany at once."[38] This was in January 1938, when official Soviet policy was implacable hostility to Germany. An American ambassador aware of a possible secret rapprochement between a friend and an enemy? That was a prize titbit for a spy and without doubt "the highlight of the documentary exhibits." But, but, but . . .

The *Times*'s readers couldn't escape the impression that the "highlight" had been in the pumpkin along with the rest of the cable and that Murphy concealed it only because it was so shocking. The jury couldn't help thinking the same thing. Even so, that "highlight" hadn't been in the pumpkin at all. Where did it come from? That's something of a question, but not from Chambers's vegetable patch. Not even Nixon claimed it had.

Just as important, both sections of the cable had gone to Alger's office; his initials were on the originals of both. Which is to say, if he were the spy, here once again, he'd prepared to pass worthless information on to the Soviets and withhold supremely important information.

It made a real splash in the headlines—and how many people read more than headlines? How many realized that what looked like serious secrets being revealed to enemies of state was a total non-event? Had never happened at all?

But picking up a document like that is very different from rummaging in wastepaper baskets. No way Chambers could have been responsible. Papers like that don't just lie around. Nor are they kept in ordinary files like Jay Lea Chambers's.

Enter Bill Bullitt. Svetlana told me that quite a number of Bill's cables languish in Soviet archives; they're from back when he was ambassador to the USSR, in love with Roosevelt and Russians. Nobody doubts that Bullitt himself is the one who got them there. A Soviet spy called Ludwig Lore told the FBI all about "his dear old friend comrade Bullitt" who was "doing a wonderful job both as ambassador and as a comrade in keeping the 'crowd'"—that's Soviet intelligence in Moscow—"informed on the inside goings on in Washington."[39] Bill did lots of little favors for his comrades. Lore asked Bill for an American passport stamped for travel to Spain. "Nothing easier than that," Bill said. "I do that for dozens of comrades almost every day." The job took five minutes.

Svetlana says the information that Bullitt supplied to the "crowd" gives a sense of what real espionage looks like. She was studying Stalin's "personal archive" where he kept his most important intelligence—with "notations in his own hand"—when she "located Russian translations of two of Bullitt's" cables. They looked nothing like Chambers's papers. They were "microfilm copies from photocopies of documents for Moscow as against typed copies" that no spymaster would accept.[40]

Fifteen years later, Bill was a rabid anti-Communist, wreaking revenge on Roosevelt and anybody in Roosevelt's New Deal.

Like Alger. *Especially* Alger. Jealousy again. Just as he'd coveted Sumner Welles's job as Under Secretary of State, he'd coveted Alger's job as president of the Carnegie Endowment. His cousin William Marshall, pamphleteer, was a trustee of the Endowment and in a position to guarantee the job. He wrote to Bill's brother Orville about his hopes that "Bill might be selected"; he'd "talked many times with Bill about it." It would have been a "splendid opportunity."[41]

Alger stole the plum right out from under their noses. William Marshall must have been as furious as Bill. A Philadelphia Bullitt exposed as unable to swing a vote? One he'd bragged to his cousin he could swing?

—❦—

With all the players on stage for the second half of my scenario—Nixon, Chambers, and the two Bullitt cousins—how did they get together?

Chambers knew Marshall Bullitt. He says so in *Witness*.[42] He claims in italics that they didn't meet until *after* the trial—the italics are his—but who believes Chambers? His emphasis makes the meeting all the more suspect. Why bother to emphasize that? Nobody cares. Besides in 1939, Bullitt had a meeting with Levine—the guy who helped Chambers hone his story—and Levine told him all about it. As for Bill, Chambers says that Daladier told Bill about Alger. Which means he knew Bill too, because *Witness* was published in 1952, and Bill wasn't publicizing the tale about Daladier until he testified to it that very year. But then a rabid anti-Red editor of *Time* like Chambers could hardly help knowing Bill, favored columnist of his boss, the rabidly anti-Red Henry Luce, owner of *Time*.

Nixon? Two guys on Capitol Hill with opinions so closely allied as his and Bill Bullitt's were likely to be fully aware of each other if not the bosom pals they became, and they certainly did become that. The singer/songwriter Ray LaMontagne bought Bill's mansion in Pennsylvania for more than a million dollars; a local called Russell Williams, talking about the purchase, remembered the old days and "Richard Nixon landing there in a helicopter to visit Bullitt."[43]

The source of the papers themselves, though: that remains the mystery of mysteries in the Hiss case. Not even the most energetic anti-Hiss writer can tie him to all of them. But if not him, then who? There are lots of theories. A really rabid anti-Red called Isaac Don Levine, Chambers's bosom pal, kept file cases full of State Department documents. Why not him? Then there's that small army of low-level people—trash collector, cleaner, file clerk—that Chambers could so easily have hired to lift stuff. As to the typing, his wife Esther was a professional typist. So was Pat Nixon. Ben Mandel—the HUAC staff member who gave Chambers his party card—had access to practically anything he wanted, and he'd taught typing in a high school before he became an investigator of Reds.

My theory though is that Bill Bullitt supplied the original material, and an FBI team—or an army team or an OSS team—did the typing.

Nixon quotes Bill in *Six Crises* on why the documents were important. "An ambassador's reports to his government can only be as reliable as his sources. These messages disclose the names of my best sources— representatives of other governments who were providing information to me on a confidential basis. Once their activities became known to others, the source immediately dries up."[44]

And yet not a single vulnerable name appears, and the Justice Department ruled that the information wouldn't be of any interest to the Soviets: nobody even could have been compromised—although I imagine a number of people were compromised in the cables Bullitt himself passed on to Stalin. Why would he let Nixon quote him spouting such nonsense unless they were both in on it?

The pages themselves make the possibility even stronger. There's the testimony from Walter Anderson, chief of the State Department's Record Division—he was on the stand for several days of unbelievably boring testimony—explaining that low-level information like this, delivered to hundreds State Department officials in a shopping trolley, was also available to qualified people not in the government. Ex-officials at work on memoirs for example. People just like Bill.

And Bill was probably the only person around who would have been interested enough in that long, dull economic report on Manchuria to keep a copy. In *The Great Globe Itself*, he devotes a considerable number of pages to just that. Group this cache by country, and they look very much like research. China, Japan, Germany, Czechoslovakia, France: Bullitt's book covers them all. For Nixon's purpose, any handful of such papers would serve if their dates fit with Alger's handwritten notes.

The one really important cable, though, the one that made such a splash in the *New York Times*, the "highlight of the documentary exhibits," the one no cleaner or trash collector or file clerk could have lifted: who'd written it? Bullitt. Who might have a copy of the entire cable on file? Bullitt. And then it looks to me as though all the ambassadorial cables from the pumpkin—as against the ones from the dumbwaiter shaft—were typed out on a European machine: the letter "e" comes out as "ε." These aren't transcriptions either. They're carbon copies, identical to the originals. How come nobody showed any interest in finding *that* typewriter? Who on the US side of the Atlantic could have supplied documents from a European typewriter but the guy whose office decrypted them in Europe?

Nixon underestimated Alger's integrity, just as Dexter's cousin Niels did. The dumbwaiter shaft papers were useful only if mystery and intrigue surrounded them; it probably never occurred to him that Alger would insist they go at once to the Department of Justice. When he did, Nixon knew that Justice would do just what it did do. He had to improvise, and the pumpkin has all the feel of a rush job. Rolls of film with a few more of Bill's originals and a clutch of completely unimportant papers, but how to catch the headlines in discovering them? Chambers's website says that he got the idea from a Russian spy movie, *Transport of Fire*.

Just so. Then there's the onionskin paper of the dumbwaiter shaft material. Aside from the drama it introduced, there's the date of its manufacture. William Marshall's files in Louisville, Kentucky—the ones Dexter and I scoured for material on Evariste Galois—were almost all onionskin carbons, and most of what we saw dated before 1938. I still have the copy of G. H. Hardy's letter to William Marshall.

> Dear Mr. Bullitt: Harald Bohr of Copenhagen happened to be staying with me when I got your letter . . .

That's the one Dexter carried in his wallet to show at parties. It's very tattered now, but it's the same kind of paper that was used for Chambers's documents; there were lots of spare sheets in the Bullitt files. The Bullitts were pack rats. They kept *everything*.

With Bill as the source of the papers, another oddity of Chambers's material finds an explanation. Most ambassadors in the cache are represented by only one cable, a couple by two, old Joe Kennedy by three. Bullitt contributed nine, one of them in a series of four, making a *dozen* cables in all. He was very vain. He'd have been unable to resist the temptation to show his importance in the conduct of international affairs.

Pumpkin Papers? Not to me. I call them the Bullitt Papers. And with William Marshall Bullitt working as the liaison for all this, there's at last a full explanation of Nixon's heart-felt gratitude in his condolence to Mrs. Bullitt.

43

1950

"**I** knew that we had demonstrated the failure of the documents . . .to buttress Chambers's flimsy and inconsistent fantasies."[1] That's what Alger said about the second trial. They're the saddest words in the entire case.

How could he think the evidence in court had any relevance to *anything*? The scariest sci-fi movies are the ones with unseen aliens; there's just this sense of an evil beyond the mind's capacity to imagine it. Nixon had splashed himself all over the front pages, peering through his magnifying glass at microfilm that proved the "the greatest treason conspiracy" in American history, film that would print out to make a three-foot-high pile of "top secrets stolen from the army." The jury had been allowed to see only the merest fraction of the pile, maybe an inch and a half. The conclusion was obvious. Out of all those thousands of pages, only those few were safe enough to show in public even a decade after they'd been destined for the Russians.

In his summation at the end of the trial, prosecutor Murphy waved a hand at the pages, seen and unseen. "Each of these documents," he told the jurors, "the typewritten documents, and the handwritten documents, each has the same message. And what is that message? 'Alger Hiss, you were the traitor.'"[2]

The jury retired.

"That's a hanging charge," a friend of Alger's said to him.[3] But prosecution summations always sound terrible. Alger was buoyant. So was

Priscilla. So were the others who accompanied them to lunch at a restaurant called André's. Their lawyers posed for a victory photograph. An ex-*New York Times* journalist sent them a message saying the press opinion was "'acquittal in fifteen minutes.'"[4]

The fifteen minutes were long over by the time the defense got back from André's. The Hisses and the lawyers played word games during the afternoon. A summons back to court had their hopes soaring, but the jury wanted only further instructions and more information. The evening went the same way. Nerves began to fray. Prosecutor Murphy dropped his face on his arms and said, "The dumb sons of bitches. If there's another hung jury, I'm through with this case." For Alger, this "discouraged growl added to my belief that instead the jury would acquit me."[5]

The jury spent the night locked in a hotel. No news in the morning. No lunch at André's today, only sandwiches and coleslaw from a delicatessen, the mood now "quiet and restrained."[6] But beneath the restraint "the momentousness of the outcome became enormous." Alger worried about the forewoman, a hard-faced matron who'd seemed hostile throughout. But his optimism was as strong as ever; he was sure the others were with him. "They had to be."[7]

Midafternoon, the jury filed in. The judge woke up to ask, "Madam Forewoman, have you and the members of the jury agreed on a verdict?"

"I have."

"And how say you—"

"Guilty on the first count," Hard-face interrupted, "and guilty on the second."

"Guilty on both counts?"

"Yes."[8]

———— ∞ ————

Indicted on the basis of documents the grand jury hadn't had a chance to examine and convicted on the basis of undeveloped film so secret that the trial jury could only guess at its content. And of course the oh-so-solid typewriter that Alger had looked so hard to find.

"Three years at Lewisburg is a good corrective to three years at Harvard."[1] That's what Alger said to his son Tony. It's got to be the understatement of understatements in a life that belonged to overstatement.

Alger's first stop on the way to Lewisburg was ten days at New York's West Street center, where he was photographed, fingerprinted, clothes exchanged for jailhouse drabs. He gives no detail. The wife of a Federal prisoner describes the ordeal: "No one can be prepared for the dehumanizing that it does to you," she writes. "It's particularly devastating for 'regular' people who suddenly find out that they are considered garbage just like a child molester. Your medical conditions don't matter, your kids waiting for you at school don't matter, your pets outside in a blizzard don't matter—hey, you are garbage."[2]

It is this that shocks people who've spent no more than a few hours in jail; it shocks them far more than the loss of freedom, and the West Street building was the crudest of warehouses for men en route to bigger prisons. Alger was locked into a "cage" in a "zoo"—literally—bars across the top as well as on all sides.[3] Total lack of privacy. Where do you hide? How do you wash? How do you pee? Take a shit? Naked light bulbs burned all night long—a recognized torture technique now—and he desperately needed sleep after so many months of unrelenting tension and the terrible blow of that verdict. It wasn't just the light either.

Like all jails, this was a place of chaos, misery, relentless noise, tense and fierce battle lines between guards and prisoners. The only moments of relief came in the visiting room, where a pane of glass separated him from Priscilla and talk was only through a "speaking tube."[4]

Then came the eight-hour trip to Lewisburg. Alger should have gone to Danbury, a gentler place and closer to home; most Federal prisoners are sent closest to home, and Danbury is where they sent HUAC fraudster Thomas. But what an outcry there'd have been if America's greatest traitor had gone there. At least they didn't send him to Atlanta; Atlanta Penitentiary was maximum security—such as Lewisburg is today—where inmates serve out long, long sentences for hard crimes or multiple offences. He doesn't mention restraints on the bus that took him and twenty other prisoners from jail to prison; prisoner transport usually involves a belly chain, hands cuffed to it at waist level.

Towards the end of the ride, the countryside is peaceful, hilly, wooded. The private road to the prison grounds is lovely, very like the road to Mother Bullitt's mansion in Louisville, Kentucky: mown grass, rows of trees evenly spaced for a quarter of a mile. The prison hasn't changed much since Alger first saw it: walls thirty feet high with hexagonal turrets, as pretty as a castle in a story book. Inside the walls, the prison itself is a huge single building in brick, clearly an institution but—stripped of rifles and razor wire—not at all clearly a prison. It was built in 1932, the most modern prison in the world at the time, and yet the design was Italian Renaissance. There are Gothic arches, ornamental corbels, geometric bas relief patterns; the architect was a reformer who believed that beauty would inspire convicts and staff to be "wise" and "tolerant."[5]

Offload the prisoners from the bus. Shuffle them inside, chains clanking, and everything changes. Inside, the West Street center "processing" began all over again. Alger Hiss, President of the Carnegie Endowment for International Peace, emerged as prisoner 19137.

But Alger was a scholar. When he knew he was going to prison, he'd consulted a man who'd served as an assistant director of the Federal Bureau of Prisons. His advice seems penetrating even now. On top of the staff's general contempt for prisoners, they'd be as hostile to him personally as the rest of America. So would most of the prisoners. Forget the small number of white-collar offenders, businessmen caught for evading taxes; they'd be frightened and bewildered. The people to ally with—and there's real poetic justice in the recommendation—were the Mafiosi, the "Italian Americans," as Alger respectfully calls them. They dominated the prison and set its code of conduct. They were smart. They were loyal to one another, a cohesive group. They knew trumped-up charges when they saw them, and they'd have to be impressed with exactly what Nixon himself admired in Alger: "I got to say for Hiss. He never ratted on anybody else. Never. He never ratted."[6]

Alger spent his first month in a six-foot by eight-foot isolation cell with an open toilet, a metal bed, a high window that couldn't be opened. All freshmen prisoners spent about a month there. These days, the cells are used for punishment only. The reason for a month of isolation? New prisoners had diseases; other inmates needed protection from them. No cigarettes. Nothing from the commissary. The reason for this? It takes time to set up inmate accounts. Isolation was total. Even conversation between cells was forbidden.

Alger spent the time reading. It must have made the ordeal somewhat easier for him than for the uneducated. Time in prison is an agony all its own. Prisoners and writers about prison struggle to capture it. They all say that seconds last for minutes, minutes for hours, hours for days. There's something in it that resembles a child's aching boredom at adults' conversation, something of an insomniac's early-morning hours; but both of these are going to end, and the prisoner's day is going to be exactly the same tomorrow.

After this period was up, prisoner 19137 was sent to live in a huge dormitory, beds all around three walls and a double row down the center, a washroom at one end: open showers, toilets without seats, a common urinal. Alger wasn't a young man in prison terms, but he looked much younger than he was; he was slender, long fingers, soft hands, and his highly educated manner made him seem girlish in the company of guys used to the streets. That and the inmates' hostility made him sexual meat—not that he mentions any of this—but it's something his informant had to have filled him in on. Another reason to ally with the Mafiosi: they were family men, men's men, no fags allowed. Alger had started forging his first links to them right back at the West Street center; he'd used the extraordinary tact that put presidents and prime ministers at their ease to make friends with a man he refers to only as "Danny F." Danny himself was headed for a long stretch in maximum security Atlanta, but his brother-in-law "Mike M."—again, Alger gives no more of a name than that—was in Lewisburg. Alger lost no time. At his very first meal in the general population mess hall, he asked if anyone at his table knew the man.

The introduction from Danny F. to Mike M. made his safety a Mafioso matter.

Alger's stepson Timothy Hobson said that when Alger went into prison he had "no sense of evil"; and his belief that people were good at heart certainly helped Nixon to bring him down, but it also allowed him to see genuine virtues in his Italian American friends. They were polite. They were decorous. They took serious matters seriously. They admired his learning, and he admired their stoicism and their wisdom. They saw prison as an occupational hazard. Alger wasn't all that dissimilar. He'd declared war on HUAC, and he saw himself as a prisoner of war. Even the Lewisburg staff noticed it; they reported that, "He seems to be taking his incarceration in the form of an enforced vacation rather than a penitentiary sentence."[7]

One day, in the first year of his sentence, he got word that "Mr. Frank" would like to meet him for a private talk. Back then, everybody knew about Frank Costello. His organization was the "Rolls Royce of organized crime"; he himself was "the prime minister of the underworld," model for Vito Corleone, Marlon Brando's role in *The Godfather*. Next to these guys, Nixon's mentor Mickey Cohen was an office boy. The grapevine had it that "nobody in New York City could be made a judge without Costello's consent." But the Senate's Special Committee on Organized Crime in Interstate Commerce had been in Washington. Costello's right hand man, Willie Moretti, had spilled a few inconvenient details; Moretti went to his maker in a movie land shoot-out in Duke's Restaurant in Cliffside Park, New Jersey.

The Senate committee put Costello in Lewisburg.

Alger's meeting with Mr. Frank was arranged in the yard during recreation period. Alger went to it accompanied by two of his Italian-American friends. Costello approached with two of his. Introductions were formal. The four intermediaries removed themselves. Costello and Alger walked around the track alone. They sat on a bench to talk. Mr. Frank turned over his brief, the statement presenting his side of the case. Alger read through it carefully while he waited.

Costello had appeared before the Senate committee and refused to answer six or seven questions. Then, on the advice of counsel, he'd answered all but one. The charge against him was contempt of the United States Senate for that one refusal. This right to refuse had been upheld in court; even so, he was convicted of contempt and sentenced to prison.

When Alger finished reading the brief, he explained—his account of it is full of lawyerly phrasings in the passive voice—that "the law, as I'd been taught it, was on Costello's side."[8] His conviction was a miscarriage of justice.

Costello thanked him formally, and as in high-level negotiations all over the world, a few minutes of informal conversation followed. Costello commiserated with Alger that they were both victims of injustice. They turned to politics. I do love a real villain. They're so honest, so surprising. Their machismo is so confident. Mr. Frank said that Eleanor Roosevelt was his favorite political figure. What lower grade of tough guy would have said something like that? And it was a genuine bond between the two men. Alger admired her greatly too. He told Mr. Frank that all the young New Dealers like him "regarded her as President Roosevelt's conscience."[9] He'd met her a few times, escorted her to a state occasion, enjoyed her sharp wit and her political finesse.

The meeting with Costello ended as formally as it had begun, the two parties withdrawing in opposite directions across the yard. After Alger's release he sent word to Mrs. Roosevelt of Costello's admiration and—so very like him—was "surprised to learn that instead of lightly accepting the compliment, she had expressed annoyance."[10]

There was little the Mafiosi could do about the more minor insults of prison staff who singled him out much as he'd been warned they would. A handwritten note refers to him as "The modern Benedict Arnold,"[11] just as many of the newspapers had during his trials. Trousers allotted to him routinely had one leg shorter. When other prisoners' shoes were replaced, his were not. But Alger's Italian American friends repaid Mr. Frank's debt to him in true gangland tradition. Not long after Alger became a fellow inmate, Julius and Ethel Rosenberg were electrocuted as Soviet spies. And not long after Alger's talk with Mr. Frank, two young Mafiosi, low in the hierarchy, entered the prison; they got assigned to the early-morning job of cleaning the kitchen. The guard overseeing them said that the Rosenbergs were dead, why should Hiss "continue on"?[12] The young men were fully aware that they were being instructed to kill Alger; an economist sent to Lewisburg for denying he was a Red got clobbered to death with a brick in a sock. A difficult position to be in; the guard could make their lives very disagreeable if Alger lived. The two consulted Mike M. Mike assured them that Alger was "one of them" and told Alger to stay close to the group for a few days.

Not long afterward, news of the guard's suicide came through.

It's part of Alger's charm—and the extraordinary brand of innocence that allowed him to get caught in a trap like this in the first place—that it never occurred to him the death might be payment for legal services rendered. He assumes the man was "emotionally unstable."

There was a very great deal Alger could have done to be of use to Lewisburg; they rarely had such highly qualified inmates. Another note in his file comments on his "calmness and self-assurance" and goes on to say, "He undoubtedly should be able to function at a high-level institutional assignment although the range of possible assignments may be limited by external pressures."[13] One of the better aspects of prison in those days—abandoned now—was the emphasis on education as rehabilitation. Alger would have made an excellent teacher, endlessly patient, sympathetic, as rapt by his pupils' troubles as he'd been by FDR's or Churchill's. He wasn't allowed near the Education Department; he might instil Communistic ideals. He'd have liked to work as an orderly in the prison hospital, but he knew that if he did, other prisoners would think he had access to drugs; he'd either have to refuse or supply them and risk getting caught.

He did teach a man to read, and he was proud of it. He wrote letters for another. Men lined up in the yard to consult him about their cases, and he did what he could to advise every one of them. But for three years and eight months, he worked as an assistant to the officer in charge of issuing nonedible supplies. Supervision was constant. That's what prison is all about. It's enforced childhood, and it brought out the rebellious child in Alger—hints of the playful, mischievous child too—a side he'd kept hidden for decades, even from his family. He thumbed his nose at authority by refusing to shave. He wrote fantasy stories in his letters to little Tony and illustrated them with silly drawings. Prison food is "shit on a shingle"; the Organizing Secretary General of the United Nations, expert in security, stole steaks from the kitchen stores and hid them under his shirt for late-night feasts with friends: beef cooked sometimes in the shower, sometimes on a smuggled electric hot plate, once on a heat lamp from a doctor's prescription. Not exactly chivalry. His rashness worried and amused his fellow inmates, but they admired his bravery.

And like most prisoners who adapt, he raged beneath that calm self-assurance: the depersonalization, daily humiliations, restrictions, loss of freedom, the burning injustice of it all.

And the years of wasted time? Here's a surprise; those he did not even regret, much less rage against. He meant every word he said to Tony about prison and Harvard; he meant it literally too. His trials had turned his world upside down, "topsy-turvy," as he put it. Harvard had taught him to believe in the rule of law; his approach throughout his entire case, from start to finish, had been "circumspect, honorable, above-board."

He'd been convicted anyhow, and he'd been convicted by means of fraud and trickery right in a United States Federal courtroom. He needed a way to come to terms with what had happened to him. He needed a second education.[14]

That's just what he got. He listened. He watched. Other prisoners demonstrated to him how worlds get turned upside down, what the difference is between law and justice—exactly the lesson Oliver Wendell Holmes had tried and failed to teach him—and why there isn't always a right way and a wrong way.[15] Because of them, the aristocrat's democratic principles and noblesse oblige developed into a citizen's understanding of how fellow citizens live, think, and suffer.

Also how badly, easily, guiltlessly they hurt one another. Alger's stepson Timmy said, "Jail is where Alger became a human being."[16]

Alger made friends in Lewisburg. Lots of them. That wonderfully intent listening was part of it. So was the freely given legal advice and the bravery of stealing steaks. But the real reason was that strange blindness of his, the belief that people are good at heart, that they mean no harm: these guys realized that he saw good in them, and it was a once-in-a-lifetime experience for many. When he walked out through the prison yard for the last time—just after Thanksgiving of 1954—they jammed the windows. They waved. They cheered and applauded.

A few of those friends remained friends for the rest of his life, and they must have helped keep the experience alive in his mind. When people were clamoring for Nixon himself to be sent to prison, Alger said, "Never! Don't ever send anybody to jail. It's a terrible place."

Not even Nixon?

"No! Jail doesn't do anybody any good."[17]

Years later, he said, "In my sleep I always dreamed of freedom . . . Today I dream of prison."[18]

45

1971

While Dexter and I were still living in Hindhead, he'd bought an old Riley, a 1952 model that looked as though it should have Al Capone at the wheel. We'd taken it to America with us, driven all over the country in it, and brought it back to England on the QEII. We landed in Dover and headed toward France. The idea was to eat wonderful food, drink lots of wine, and well, live in a country where nobody knew what a terrible failure his novel had been. My French wasn't brilliant—little more than serviceable tourist—but Dexter's was lousy. He wouldn't try. The whole idea of struggling to buy a loaf of bread in French embarrassed him, and I could feel him getting more and more tense as we neared the coast and Plymouth; we planned to cross the Channel from there to Roscoff on the Brittany coast.

Totnes was the last turnoff from the highway before the docks. Without a word, he veered onto the slip road and headed west toward the town. We spent the night at the Seven Stars Hotel in the Plains, and the next day we began looking at houses. What the hell, we could eat and drink well in England too. The Hermitage on South Street had a little of the quality of a New York townhouse, long and narrow, walled garden, nice old features, garage closing it off from the street. We bought it. England was cheap back then. The moment we had possession, we went to work with sledgehammers and opened up five tiny rooms to make a large open area that included living room, dining room, and kitchen, all rolled into one.

In the autumn of our first year in the Hermitage, Dexter's cousin Marcia came to visit with her husband. Dexter was very fond of her; he said she looked like Anna Karenina, a honey blonde, regular features, full mouth, large eyes, tall. I liked her too—except for Freud. Marcia wasn't just a Freudian; she was one of the faithful, a fundamentalist. She and I had gone to lunch in New York once, just the two of us, and over her ravioli, she'd said to me, "You know, Joanie, *I* have it."

"What?"

"Penis envy."

In those days everybody had an opinion about Freud and psychoanalysis and what women wanted: Freud said it was a penis. "Handy on a picnic?" I suggested.

"I'm not joking."

"You wish you were a man?" She shook her head again.

"I just want a *penis*." Meanwhile, she married eminent philosophers. The first was a Harvard professor whose specialty was the General Theory of Value. I don't have any idea what that is, despite my years at Columbia. I think there was a second one. Then came Donald Davidson, the one she brought to Totnes. I'd never heard of him. Even so, the evening in Totnes started well. Conversation was easy until we strayed onto the subject of truth. Since I didn't know who Donald was, I didn't realize that he was really important on the subject.

I told him that I'd decided the fashionable view was close to right: there was no truth. The only certainty is my version of events. Not yours. Not Plato's. Not Einstein's. Mine. Even so, I wasn't happy with it. Here was this concept that people had been worrying for millennia. It had to mean something more than that. All I'd learned from philosophers at Columbia was to dismiss it as "trivial." I told him so. I also told him I'd just read that the great physicist Richard Feynman thought philosophy was a "dippy subject." I quite liked that.

Donald's face got red. "You want to know what truth is?"

"Sure," I said. "You got an answer?"

"Is it raining?"

"I don't know."

"Well, if I say it's raining, and you go outside and find that it is **in** fact raining, that's truth."

I was a little taken aback. "Yeah?"

"Yeah."

"If that's all it is, I'm not interested."

Donald face got redder. He stood up. "I have to get out of here," he said. "Are you coming, Marcia?"

She scuttled out after him.

The reason for this story is that it ended up provoking Alger into **the** second and last time I saw him lose his temper.

———— ∞ ————

He and Isabel were coming to Totnes for Christmas that year. Another old friend of Dexter's was coming too, Harold Schonberg, who **was** music critic of the *Times* back then; he'd just lost his much beloved **wife,** and he didn't want to spend Christmas alone.

We had no room for anybody to stay in the house. We found **places** for the three of them in local bed and breakfasts.

Harold flew over first class. Alger and Isabel came the way **most** of us do, except that they came on separate flights. Alger wasn't just **a** convicted felon; his was a life full of legal tripwires: moral turpitude, adultery, whatever some cop or customs officer might dream up on **the** spot. Then there were the constant threats of violence from the public. The danger was just as great for Isabel if she traveled with him. **The** solution was two night flights, a day apart, Isabel first.

Alger admired the UK, thought the English the most civilized **people** on earth, the only other country he'd be prepared to live in. British customs officers took away his coat, jacket, shoes, tie, and kept him for **six** hours in a freezing room, nothing to eat, nothing to drink. They wouldn't let him telephone Isabel to tell her where he was; she waited with **no** idea of what was happening to him. Officers questioned him in rotating teams, left him alone, questioned him again. None of it was friendly. They brought in a separate trio of officers to perform a strip search.

They let him go with barely enough time to meet Isabel and Harold for the Christmas Eve train to Devon, afternoon, the last service before the holiday, packed, standing room only, a four-and-a-half hour journey in those days. Isabel often had ailments. Hypoglycaemia—too low a blood sugar content and usually something only diabetics have to worry about—was all the rage in New York. Everybody who was anybody had it. Isabel had it too. Halfway through the journey to Devon, she said she was going to faint unless she had something to eat. Harold told us later that Alger looked too exhausted to move, so he'd gone in search of food himself. He struggled to the buffet car, only to find it was no longer serving, then spotted a child with a sandwich only half eaten. So he stood and stared at her until she noticed him.

"Are you hungry, poor little man?" she said.

Harold licked his lips.

"Would you like half of my sandwich?"

The story amused Harold, but his irritation with Isabel soured the air. Soon after Christmas Eve supper, he left for his B&B. Dexter was tired. Toby was in bed. I had a Christmas dinner to make the next day. We knew nothing about Alger's ordeal with British customs or Isabel's long, painful, uncertain wait; but anybody could see that his consummate tact had deserted him. A decided lull in the conversation failed to push them out the door. I ended up telling my story about Marcia and Donald Davidson to fill the gap.

Alger was snappish at once. He said there was clearly such a thing as truth. What was the matter with me? How could I deny it?

I told him that my father had once posed the question for his students. "Well, I can't answer that," the student said, "but at least I know right from wrong."

"Then hurry home," my father said to him, "You've just solved the enigma that's plagued mankind since the beginning of history."

Alger wasn't amused. "Don't you think some things are right and some are wrong?"

I said I didn't know. Probably not.

"People *die* for truth." Alger was starting to tremble as he had at the restaurant with Niels.

I couldn't figure out what I was saying that upset him. "That doesn't mean it exists. What about Christ? What did he die *for*?"

"Perhaps because he knew he was right."

"About *what*?"

I've only once before blanked out completely, and I did again that night. It wasn't drink. It was Alger. He was shaking with anger by this time. God knows what he said next. I remember being aware only that I'd provoked something out of control and that he was bent on tearing me apart because of it.

Even the cat ran away and hid.

Maybe Donald had had to leave the room last time. This time it was me. The interior stairs to the upper floor in the Hermitage rose out of that large room Dexter and I had made; I got halfway up the flight before I even realized I'd bolted. I turned then, getting a belated glimpse of what this had been all about. "Alger, I really am talking about truth," I said. "You know, abstract truth. Like in books, like Feynman's 'dippy subject.' And here you are talking about your case."

He and Isabel left shortly after that.

———— ⣔⣔ ————

Dexter had great difficulty calming me. He made us a milk punch: brandy, rum, hot milk, nutmeg. Then he made another. Then another. I have no idea how many it took before I could sleep, but it had to have been close to four in the morning when I did.

An hour later, six-year-old Toby was poised at the top of the stairs, a manic grin on his face. "Christmas!" he screamed and dashed down the stairs.

That was only the beginning. I'd planned to serve two ducks and braised chestnuts for Christmas dinner. I'd plucked the ducks and shelled the chestnuts, a slow job since chestnuts have to stay whole for the dish to cook evenly. There was so much food with six people to feed over several days—shops stayed shut for the entire holiday back then— that our tiny English refrigerator was stuffed, crammed. Not a single thing extra could go into it, certainly not ducks and a flat casserole of shelled chestnuts. A disused, unheated stairwell separated our house from the back of a High Street shop; we'd turned it into a laundry room and store for garden and carpentry tools. I'd hung the ducks from the ceiling there and stored the chestnuts on top of the clothes drier, covered in aluminium foil.

On Christmas morning, I dragged myself out to bring the ducks inside so they would be at room temperature to cook.

Disaster. I'd forgotten to secure the door, and the cat had spent the entire night balancing on the chestnuts to leap at the ducks. He'd only caught them in a couple of places—a few claw tears here and there— but the chestnuts were partly spilled out on the floor. The rest were covered in cat hair.

Dexter and I held a consultation. I had to be alone. I really did. Most of all I had to make sure I didn't see Alger until I had myself—and my kitchen—under some control. Dexter said he'd take Alger, Isabel, Harold, and Toby off to Dartmoor while I rested and prepared some more chestnuts. The Riley was a pleasure to ride in. Harold agreed at once. Isabel did too. Toby jumped up and down with glee.

"Thank you, no," Alger said. "I'll stay here with Joanie."

There was an awkward pause.

Somebody once said that if Alger were standing at the bar with an ambassador and a message came in for the ambassador, the pageboy would hand it over to Alger without a second thought. The others left quietly. I was as hung over as I have ever been in my life; I sat, bleary with nausea, chestnuts on my lap, this most elegant of human beings opposite me. He talked about his son, his brother, his growing up, Harvard, his admiration for Justice Holmes. He told me that his sister had taught President Johnson's wife to play tennis. I hadn't known anything about a sister before that. He told me how Isabel planted summer vegetables in the garden of their Long Island cottage. Nothing about British customs or strip searches or the myriad humiliations that had become part of his daily life. No hint of the tormented beast with bandarillos stuck in its back. Not a single excuse.

But shortly before Dexter and the others returned, he smiled and summed up what he'd been saying. "You know, Joanie, I've led a happy life."

The citizen's apology to an equal he'd offended? That came later. The rooms Dexter and I had knocked together meant that the kitchen and the dining room were separated only part way by a waist-high counter. The cook was somewhat in the position of performer, and I was shaky as well as queasy by the time I was serving dinner.

Harold bragged that he could carve any beast on earth, and Dexter countered that he couldn't carve a single one.

I said, "*I* do the carving in this house." This brought on a mild discussion of male versus female carving that occupied the table while I went to get the ducks. I'd roasted them together on a platter, but the oven shelf was a typical British cock-up of a design. It slipped as I took them out. Splat! Splat! Two ducks on a stone floor, duck juice everywhere. I glanced up.

The only person who'd witnessed this disaster was Alger.

"Might I assist your carving out here?" he said, standing so that his body hid my scrambling around on the floor from the others. "The table's a bit crowded, don't you think?"

PART FIVE

Aftermath

46

1950 . . .

While Alger was getting ready to enter his cage at the West Street center in New York for his first day as a Federal prisoner, posters were going up all over California:

LET'S ELECT
Congressman
RICHARD NIXON
UNITED STATES SENATOR
The man who "Broke" the Hiss-Chambers
Espionage Case

Corrupt politicians and the Mafia go hand-in-hand. To this very day, wiseguys buy cops, FBI agents, judges, politicians. They control whole sections of cities and counties.

Mickey Cohen, Nixon's mentor, wrote in his memoir that the original orders to support Nixon had come from "the proper persons back east." These proper persons, he explained, were Meyer Lansky and Frank Costello, soon to consult Alger about his own conviction. A touching irony, but why would the Mafia choose Nixon? "If you were Meyer," explained Senate crime investigator Walter Sheridan, "who would you invest your money in? Some politician named Clams Linguini? Or a nice Protestant boy from Whittier, California?"[1]

In this senatorial race, our nice Protestant boy was facing Helen Gahagan Douglas, a beautiful woman pushing fifty, a Broadway star and opera singer, supporter of the New Deal and personal friend of Eleanor Roosevelt, Mr. Frank's favorite political figure. But then as everybody knows, for the Mafia business is business: nothing personal. And that was the fifties, the time of fluffy crinoline slips and dumb blondes, when women's colleges in America made it clear that bagging a husband was more important than working for the degree they awarded. Helen Douglas was the first woman Democrat ever to be elected to Congress, and by the time of her race against Nixon, she'd been in government much longer than he had. She was a person of heart too. William Miller, the House of Representatives doorman who'd seen Nixon gearing up for the drama of the pumpkin, said of her, "Had she been able to stay in Congress, who knows what good things she could have done for the poor?"[2] That was precisely the trouble. She was anti-big business, especially the oil companies. And the Mafia was heavily into oil.

Cohen reserved the Banquet Room in the Hollywood Knickerbocker Hotel. The guest list? "It was all gamblers from Vegas, all gambling money; there wasn't a legitimate person in the room." The aim was to raise $75,000, a considerable piece of money in those days. But while the crockery was being cleared away, Cohen's business manager whispered in his ear, "Mick, we didn't raise the quota. We're short $20,000." Cohen's solution was to bar the exits and make an announcement: "Lookit. Everybody enjoyed their dinner, everybody happy? Well, we're short of this quota, and nobody's going home till this quota's met."[3]

The quota was met. And then some.

The mob wasn't alone either. The whole of corporate America wanted this woman out of California. Oil money poured into the Nixon campaign from as far afield as Texas and Indiana. Not that oil was the extent of it. Money funnelled through crooked cracks in big business all over the country, lumber money, liquor money, bank money. Documents at the Nixon Library suggest campaign funds overall ran to $200,000. But billboards alone ran to $50,000. Television, well beyond the reach of most candidates back then, was crammed with ads for Nixon. One mere fortnight saw thirty-three Nixon spots on three San Francisco stations. Some estimates put the full figure at more than $4 million, a fabulous sum, something like ten times that amount in today's money. There was so much cash that the mob was handing out $100 bills at fund-raisers for other Republican candidates.

Nixon promised another "rocking, socking" campaign based on hard work, surprise, and keeping the opponent on the defensive. He gave instructions that audiences were to scream hysterically whenever he appeared. Skywriting planes wrote "NIXON" across the skies above beaches. A Nixon rally in central Los Angeles promised door prizes for everybody who attended. Blimps dropped leaflets that promised voters—as he had in his second Congressional campaign—that if they answered the telephone with the words, "Vote for Nixon," and if the call came from Nixon headquarters, they could win

PRIZES GALORE

Electric clocks, Silex coffee makers with heating units
General Electric automatic toasters
silver salt and pepper shakers, sugar and creamer sets,
candy and butter dishes, etc., etc.[4]

Four-page ads in newspapers showed Nixon as the "ardent American" and "the perfect example of the Uncommon Man." The *Los Angeles Examiner's* editorial cartoon took up a whole half page: Nixon with bulging biceps, a shotgun in one hand, a net labelled "Communist Control" in the other. Our hero was guarding a wall called "National Security." Behind it American farms and factories huddled. Running away in terror were rats labelled "Appeaser", "Propagandist", "Soviet Sympathizer." Its caption: "ROUGH ON RATS!"[5]

Nixon dubbed Helen Gahagan Douglas "The Pink Lady." He printed anti-Douglas fliers on pink paper; he said she was "pink right down to her underpants."[6] He advertised her as "Helen Gahagan Douglas, Alger Hiss's pet." An onslaught of anonymous phone calls: "Did you know that Helen Douglas is a Communist?"[7]

A Methodist minister who supported her had to take his phone off the hook; just supporting her invoked a barrage of "You're a Communist" accusations. A second telephone campaign ran alongside the first: "Did you know Helen Douglas is married to a man whose real name is Hesselberg?"[8] Her husband, a famous actor at the time, was a Jew. Newspapers printed pictures—many years old—of her with Paul Robeson, the "black Stalin."

It wasn't just a matter of words, pictures, and money either. Nixon's people seized Douglas's fliers and dumped them in the ocean. Nixon hecklers shouted her down at every stop on speaking tours, doused her in seltzer water right as she spoke, pelted her with red ink, tossed rocks at her car.

And Nixon the Lucky struck lucky yet again with war in Korea. In summer, the communist state of North Korea had invaded the very corrupt but democratic South. UN troops, heavily supported by the US Army and Navy, forced them back across the border, but on the very eve of the California election, Communist China intervened. Or so it seemed. The picture was murky. Information conflicted. When a newspaper editor asked the senatorial candidates if under the circumstances, they supported China's entry to the United Nations. Nixon shouted, "No!"

Douglas hesitated.

"This is the final straw," Nixon thundered. "Doesn't she care whether American lives are being snuffed out by a ruthless aggressor?"[9]

His win was landslide.

<hr />

Another winner who owed his career to Alger was America's Witch Finder General, Senator Joseph McCarthy of Wisconsin. He'd been as obscure as Nixon in the pre-Alger days, a boozing, foul-mouthed Nazi-lover voted "the worst US senator" currently in office by the Senate press corps. While Alger's conviction filled the headlines, a drunken McCarthy reeled onto a stage to give a Lincoln Day speech to the Republican Women's Club of Wheeling, West Virginia.

The Club had expected talk of housing, schools, roads. Instead they got a rant lifted straight from a speech of Nixon's: there was a "spy ring" at the heart of government" that "permits the enemy to guide and shape our policy." McCarthy held up a piece of paper. "I have here in my hand a list of two hundred and five: a list of names that were made known to the Secretary of State as being members of the Communist Party."[10]

The press went so crazy McCarthy didn't know how to handle it. "Listen, you bastards," he shouted at them, "I've got a pail full of shit and I'm going to use it where it does me most good."[11] In Salt Lake City, Utah, a few days later, he lowered the number to fifty-seven. A few days after that in a Senate speech, he raised it to eighty-one, said he could present a case-by-case analysis of them all.

McCarthy was Nixon on crack. Two hundred five Communists? Boot them out. Eighty-one loyalty risks? Name them, shame them. Fifty-seven spies? Toss them in prison. Precise numbers flew out of the Senator's mouth: 238 witnesses, 367, and more and more. Father Cronin, Nixon's informant on the subject, wrote of "mass espionage motivated . . .merely by fanatical devotion to the Soviet Union."[12] People were scared over their neighborhood fences. Are the Joneses secret Reds? Are the Smiths? "Twenty years of treason"—McCarthy's epithet for the Roosevelt and Truman administrations—had left the country diseased. J. Edgar Hoover, Director of the FBI, said American families were being "infiltrated, dominated, or saturated with the virus of communism."[13] That's when Nixon's right-hand man Stripling wrote that this virus brings Soviet Communists into "complete control over the human mind and body, asleep and awake, in sickness and in health, from birth to death."[14] Another HUAC Republican announced that "communism would make a slave of every American man, woman, and child."[15] Children as safely across borders as Canada started going to bed at night too frightened of Communists to turn out the lights.

McCarthy easily won back his Senate seat. All the Republicans he supported won. He became one of the most powerful men in the Senate. "We Americans live in a free world," he said in a television speech, "where we can freely speak our opinions on any subject, or on any man."[16]

Some thirty thousand un-American books were removed from library shelves. Several libraries went all the way with public pyres just like the Hitler Youth with their un-German books.[17] The government in *The Wizard of Oz* was Marxist. *The Adventures of Robin Hood* advocated the Communistic idea of distributing wealth.

Hundreds of teachers in New York alone lost their jobs for "disloyal" activities. Thousands of teachers across the country. Thousands of union members.[18] McCarthy's specially targeted victims made up a list of America's most gifted that was even longer than HUAC's; it included such luminaries as Albert Einstein, Thomas Mann, Leonard Bernstein, Charlie Chaplin, Sam Wanamaker, Aaron Copeland, Jules Dassin, Allen Ginsberg, Arthur Miller, J. Robert Oppenheimer, Linus Pauling, Paul Robeson, Louis Bunuel, Orson Welles. The government ordered an investigation into the loyalty of three million government workers, and terror in the State Department became a Washington joke: "A newspaperman walks up to a US diplomat and asks him what time it is. The diplomat looks over both shoulders and whispers, 'Sorry, no comment.'"[19]

President Truman, speaking at Detroit's 250th anniversary celebration, told his audience that on the Fourth of July in Madison, Wisconsin, "A hundred and twelve people were asked to sign a petition that contained nothing except quotations from the Declaration of Independence and the Bill of Rights. One hundred and eleven of these people refused to sign that paper—many of them because they were afraid that it was some kind of subversive document and that they would lose their jobs or be called Communists."[20]

I knew three people who got caught much as these feared they might be.

The first was Kate Way, the physicist who'd co-edited *One World or None* with Dexter. She was a feisty, independent-minded woman who'd once told me that the best love affair she'd had in her life—she'd had many—started just after her seventieth birthday. She was a physicist, an expert in atomic spin—the way atoms dance inside molecules—and she'd been one of the few women physicists to work on the Manhattan Project that manufactured the first atom bombs. She left government work after the war, co-edited that book with Dexter, and went on to help establish and produce two magazines—*Nuclear Data Sheets* and *Atomic Data and Nuclear Data Tables*—that I remember as nothing but rows of figures like tables of logarithms. One day she received a subpoena to appear in front of a grand jury in New York to answer charges: she'd attended a Communist meeting a decade before on a given date at a given place. Kate had no interest in politics. None. She'd never attended a political meeting, this one or any other.

"It's perfectly simple," she said to her lawyer. "I wasn't there."

"Where were you?" said the lawyer.

How could she possibly remember something like that?

"Then I'm afraid it's not so simple." He told her that the only way she could clear herself was to find somebody else who

- had attended that meeting;
- had been a Communist at the time;
- was no longer a Communist;
- remembered who was there and who was not;
- and most important, was willing to testify on her behalf.

Kate was a determined woman. Also she'd inherited money, a lot of it. She spared no expense. She hired teams of detectives. After an intensive search, they located a potato farmer in the Midwest who fitted all the requirements. There was just one snag. He had a crop to get in. He told the detectives to get lost.

Kate went herself. She walked across an acre of newly ploughed field, stood in front of his tractor until he'd agree. He flew to New York and testified. The charge against her was dropped—only to reappear a year later in exactly the same form. Again she cajoled the potato farmer into testifying. Again the charge was dropped.

It was brought a third time the following year.

My father's first wife, Dorothy Stahl, got caught too. She was a mathematician with the Department of Labor in Washington. Her transgression was her marriage to my father even though they'd been separated for quite some time when the FBI started questioning her about him.

She defended him; a couple of her statements survive in his file. The result? She lost her security clearance and with it her government job.

My father's own troubles began like Kate's. An unknown somebody said he'd been present at a meeting of the Communist Party in Los Angeles on a given day more than a decade before. He was lucky here. On that very day, he'd been delivering a well-publicised speech in San Francisco.

But he didn't stay lucky. Red-baiting brought more and more Republicans into Congress, and the Democratic administration couldn't hold out against the tide any longer. President Truman issued Executive Order 9835 prohibiting Federal employees from "sympathetic association" with Communists. The states followed quickly with HUAC-like panels that launched into teachers, cops, firemen, longshoremen, administrators, writers, artists. Americans with FBI files in local or national offices or both soon numbered in the hundreds of thousands.

The very first university to indulge in the new frenzy was the University of California—Nixon's home state—where my father taught economics. The Regents presented the staff with a Loyalty Oath. "Sign or get fired," they said. The vast majority of staff saw such oaths for what they were, a frightening step in the direction of Nazi thought control. Instil fear, division, compliance. Take away the right to independent thought, and people will stay under your thumb. Nothing could be further from the ideals of a university, and back then those ideals still had a little meaning.

The staff met. My father spoke. He had a strong, resonant voice with movement in it—something of those Biblical rhythms that make Obama such a powerful speaker—and there was nothing he felt more passionate about than the encroachment of fascism in America. He proposed a solution. Stick together. Refuse to sign as a group. His audience took a vote and agreed almost unanimously. A protest began.[21]

All of this is missing from his FBI file. There's not a single mention of the oath despite massive press coverage of it at the time. The only hints at its existence are those threats of deportation.

The Regents remained firm; the dissenters gained ground. The protest movement faltered, then collapsed. Faculty signed in droves. "I've thought of a motto to put over Berkeley's new faculty building," said my father's friend Max Radin, Professor of International Law. "Remember *The Wind in the Willows?* Mole spends a terrifying night in the forest pursued by beasts. The next day, the rabbits come out of their holes and admit that they knew all about it. 'So why didn't you help?' Otter asks. 'What, us?' said the rabbits. 'Do something? Us rabbits?' Now, that's what belongs over the new faculty building door:

"'What, us? Do something? Us *rabbits?*'"

While I was working on this book, I checked a website devoted to Berkeley's loyalty oath. Thirty-one faculty members held out against the Regents. I'd thought it was only my father and Max. What the hell, it was still very impressive. I asked my sister Judy if she'd realized the two of them weren't alone.

"Joanie, he signed."

"He did not."

"Of course he did, you dope. He kept his job."

There are matters of pride that hold a life together. This intransigence of my father's had been one for me. The only virtue in losing it was that I had an explanation for what had been inexplicable before.

One night, he swallowed close to twenty-five grams of Phenobarbital. It's a dose that could have killed ten men. The effect wasn't at all what he'd planned; the barbiturates stunned his gut. He couldn't absorb them. He survived—a miracle that made medical history—but they caused a massive stroke that paralyzed his body and destroyed his brain. He couldn't write or read or understand, not written words or spoken ones. The only phrase he could come out with—for pain or humiliation or gratitude or love—was "a cup of coffee."

When Alger first heard the verdict against him, he simply hadn't believed "such a blatant miscarriage of justice was possible." He swung into Don Quixote mode. "Nevertheless, I did not despair. My mind jumped immediately to the steps that would have to be taken to overturn this incredible verdict."

Half of his lawyers—friends and volunteers—wanted to expose the prosecution's illegal conduct; Kenneth Simon was just out of law school, and he was angry. "The process that convicted Alger had been tainted. He had not received a fair trial."[1] Simon argued for opening the brief with a "grabber" like a thriller. He wanted "to get up a soar, if only with indignation." After all, a judge is human. The other half of Alger's lawyers agreed with Alger's lawyerly strategy: a detailed tracking of those documents through the State Department to show he couldn't have given them to Chambers.

The resultant hybrid, as the despairing Simon put it, was dry and "abstruse."[2]

Appeal denied.

Alger filed a motion for a new trial.

The brief went to Judge Goddard, the judge who'd napped through his trial and sentenced him to prison.

Motion for a new trial denied.

Alger appealed.

The same three-judge panel who'd denied his first appeal denied this one too.

Alger appealed to the Supreme Court. The Court refused to hear the case.

As Chairman Thomas said, "Never mind the evidence." Richard Nixon was vice president by this time, and he'd seen proof of the greatest treason in American history inside a pumpkin. He'd seen handwritten notes, and a government expert had "declared conclusively and without qualification" that "the penmanship was that of Mr. Hiss." He'd examined microfilms making a pile three feet high: who could forget that? And in any case what court was going to impugn the word of a vice president?

It wasn't until the 1966 Freedom of Information Act that Alger got a chance to examine the evidence that had convicted him. He filed at once.

The lawyer in charge of his request for his files was Victor Rabinowitz; and from what he says, obstruction played a key role in the Act right from the beginning. There were "repeated requests" and "long delays."[3] He pursued the FBI for a decade. He learned that chunks of Alger's files had been "destroyed."[4] Unlike my father's, destruction wasn't tied to given days in given years; it came "at an unknown date." Further chunks were unavailable for reasons of "national security" and those "other sensitivities" that still hold back my mother's file.

But Alger's files were/are in a completely different league. They must have been truly Brobdingnagian once; the remains come to more than forty thousand to fifty thousand pages. Fifty thousand pages! A lowest estimate of forty thousand makes a pile more than fourteen feet high; it dwarfs Nixon's three-footer. This outpouring arrived over the course of ten years—those "repeated requests" and "long delays"—in batches of thousands of pages. About half were duplicates. The bulk of the remainder was "routine and uninformative." Of the remainder's remainder, whole pages were blacked out. When text was left behind, it made up only "tantalizing snippets" with "the important language" still blacked out.

Lawyers are better than the rest of us at getting government agencies to cough up, but Rabinowitz had just one argument: the blacked-out parts and the withheld parts weren't confidential. And how do you argue content when you don't know what it is? A judge had to read it and make the decision. Judges are supposed to be chosen by a random spinning of a wheel in the clerk's office; that word "random" is a lawyer's giggle, especially in high-profile cases.[5] Rabinowitz drew Judge Richard Owen, a Nixon appointee who "listened quietly and ruled against"[6] him on every point.

But back then—nearly half a century ago—the destroyers weren't as thorough as they'd become by 1998 when they went to work on my father. It was possible from the fragments in those forty thousand to fifty thousand pages to get more than just a glimpse of what had been going on in Alger's case.

In those days, a wiretap needed new permission every sixty days; agents had to cite information obtained in order to get it. Scraps from just such requests indicate how very much of the material is gone; a surviving sample chunk from a twenty-month period runs to twenty-nine tape series and many hundreds of pages of transcription. Other scraps indicate periodic twenty-four-hour surveillance with spot surveillance in between. People with suspected links to Alger and people who testified on his behalf ended up with wiretaps and mail interception too, houses searched without warrants, houses burglarized, documents photographed. Traces of these intrusions make it all too clear that the FBI provided a great mass of raw material to the prosecution: endless detail on friends, neighbors, children, servants, dinner guests, holidays, pets, purchases, commuting, furniture, and on and on. And it was with Bureau agents that Chambers spent many months of hard, daily grind trying to stuff what he could into his head in preparation for Alger's trials.[7]

I shudder to think how many laws all this activity breaks.

There were wiretaps on Alger's lawyers, both in their homes and at their offices. Not just wiretaps either. Letters to his lawyers ended up with Murphy, the prosecutor in both trials. Instructions followed: neither Murphy nor the FBI was to tell the Justice Department. At least one letter from Alger too went to Murphy—an informer in the Post Office passed it on—again with instructions to keep quiet.[8]

So much for attorney-client privilege.

Violating this privilege violates the defendant's rights under the Sixth Amendment to the Constitution. In the Judith Coplon case—the spy caught in the very act of passing information to a Russian atta-ché—wiretaps on her lawyers got her a new trial. "I'd like it explained to me," Chief Judge E. Barrett Prettyman said about the ruling, "how any appellant can have a fair trial if conversation between him and his counsel is intercepted."[9]

All the FBI's years of snooping produced not a single shred of evidence to support Chambers's accusations. Which is to say that, if anything, their investigations exonerated Alger. The prosecution didn't say a word about this to the defense. They didn't tell the defense about Chambers's sex confessions, and they just plain lied about his many confessions tying the end of his life as a Communist to the year 1937; they said no signed confessions existed. They said nothing at all about statements from Oxford University Press in early 1938 confirming that Chambers was working on a translation for them; he'd blabbed to his publisher that he was a fugitive from communism and that Russian agents were out to get him.[10]

Withholding evidence like this is obstruction of justice. It's a violation of the due process clause of the Fifth Amendment to the Constitution. Something similar—if on a far less extensive scale—happened in the Judith Coplon case too. In her new trial, she was convicted of both espionage and conspiracy; Justice Learned Hand overturned both verdicts because the prosecution had violated those very rights.

She went free.

In the Trial of the Century, on top of all the other legal transgressions, the prosecution kept a straight face while Chambers lied his head off on the stand.

Playing this fast and loose with the law has just got to be unprecedented in American courts.

The prosecution's wonderfully corrupt conduct made up only part of the secrets hidden in the fragments from those files. There were also revelations about the pretty typewriter that hung on Isabel's wall.

In the years after the trials—when the excitement died down—the defense hired their own experts; they disproved any connection between Priscilla and the typewriter in court. It couldn't even have belonged to the Hisses; it wasn't old enough. None of the boring documents had been typed on it.[11] There hadn't been just one alternate typewriter either. There'd been several. Several typists too.[12]

And the question of forgery? Nixon scoffed and went right on scoffing. "A typewriter is, as you know, almost the same as a fingerprint. It is impossible, according to experts in the field, to duplicate exactly the characteristics on one typewriter by manufacturing another."[13]

Alger's typewriter experts built one. Their forgery wasn't by any means a first either. A how-to explanation appeared well over a century ago during a court case in New Jersey. Typewriter forging as a trade began early in the First World War. Early in the Second, Sir William Stephenson headed a department called British Security Coordination; he and the FBI worked together in Canada near Lake Ontario at a place they called "Camp X." (How gloriously like the movies real spy-speak is.) "Camp X" included "Station M," and "Station M" specialized in false documents. This station, wrote Russell R. Bradford and Ralph B. Bradford, "could reproduce faultlessly the imprint of any typewriter on earth."[14]

A Michigan professor of economics, Stephen Salant, shows that US Army intelligence could do the same.[15]

The timing? When could any of these guys have got hold of the information they needed to start building? Alger had appeared at four HUAC hearings: a grand public show in the caucus room on August 5, a hard-won executive session on August 16, a hotel ambush on August 17, and a television extravaganza on August 25. On August 27, only two days after that final appearance, investigators subpoenaed the records of a real estate agent called Edward Case. There'd been typed correspondence in 1936 between him and Alger about a property in Westminster, Maryland.

Nearly three months to build a machine that matched Case's correspondence: that should be long enough.

Nixon? As his special counsel, John Dean, wrote, "The President was famous for reliving the Hiss case." He couldn't let it go, referred to it again and again throughout his life, revealed it bit by bit to his aides. Dean wrote that his boss told him that "the typewriters are always the key. We built one in the Hiss case."[16]

What seems odd is that they needed to build one. I'd have thought it would be easy to find an old one and repair it. Not so. The FBI had ninety agents scouring the country for a suitable candidate. They did find a man called Martin who remembered buying the Woodstock they wanted and a man called Grady who remembered selling it to him. Woodstocks carried serial numbers according to year of manufacture. Here's a memo addressed to Hoover in December 1948, about as Alger was being indicted: "The serial number of the typewriter sold to [Mr. Martin] would be less than 177, 000."[17] And yet the one that ended up in court was No. 230, 999, *way* too high; it could not have been manufactured until something like two years *after* Martin bought the machine. Hoover knew all about it. The FBI knew all about it. Freedom of Information reveals many FBI memos worried about it. Clearly there was something of a scramble to document this machine they knew was the wrong one; they couldn't find records of its being bought or sold, although they did locate numerous people who'd owned it. Not that any of this came out in court. Not even the obviously impossible serial number.

And yet this very typewriter became the heart of prosecutor Murphy's peroration; he pointed at the machine that he knew could not possibly have typed any of Chambers's documents and thundered, "Each of these documents, the typewritten documents, and the handwritten documents, each has the same message. And what is that message? 'Alger Hiss, you were the traitor.'"[18]

Over the years there have been many official denials of a typewriter manufactured for the purpose, but an Office of Strategic Services investigator called Harold Bretnall goes into the details that make a very different case:

Remember Schmahl? He's the man Alger hired to help in his quest for the broken-down Hiss machine, and he's the man who found it and turned it over to the FBI. Scraps from those forty thousand to fifty thousand pages show that he didn't limit himself to the typewriter; he was spilling everything he learned to the FBI. When it came to the trials, he spilled to the prosecution just as freely. What Freedom of Information doesn't reveal is that he was working undercover for Military Intelligence as well.

Schmahl is interesting: a multilingual German, graduate of the Military Intelligence Training Center in St Louis, a Special Agent in the Army's Counter Intelligence Corps.[19] The National Archives has the Army's file on the Hiss case, but the public isn't allowed to see much more than newspaper clippings, even though files on much less exciting figures than Alger contain—this is Prof Salant—"reams of Army-generated reports."[20] Why? I gather that I can't blame the archives themselves this time. Salant says the Army won't release the material.

The OSS investigator Bretnall worked with Schmahl. Many years after the trials were over, Bretnall told Alger's lawyers that Schmahl himself was involved in forging the typewriter that stood in front of the jury.[21] Bretnall was just a "consultant" on the job. He said his orders had come straight from "Wild Bill" Donovan, chief of the OSS.[22]

What really matters is that Bretnall had no doubts at all. "Hiss was framed," he said.[23]

❈

Freedom of Information's prize exhibit was the microfilm from the pumpkin.

The word "microfilm"—secret, exciting—is the word that appeared all over the media at the time and continues to appear in discussions of the case these many years later. But the rolls in the pumpkin turned out to be ordinary 35mm films from a hand-held camera, just exactly the kind for snapping the kids at the beach.

Three feet high? The entire cache, all of it together, came to well under a hundred and fifty pages, maybe a little over half an inch thick.

The Espionage Act of 1917—the law that describes spy material as information that might cause "injury of the United States" or "advantage of a foreign nation"—is the one that the US government used to execute the Rosenbergs, who passed technical plans to the USSR. It's what they'll use to prosecute Edward Snowden if they catch him. And the films from the pumpkin?

Experts developed them. One roll was completely blank. The other two were, well, mainly blobs and squiggles.

Technicians extracted what little information they could. There were no new handwritten pages. Not one, much less three of them. The blobs and squiggles dated from late 1937 and early 1938. They did indeed relate to the Navy. One frame reveals that carbon dioxide fire extinguishers, usually painted aluminium in color, would hereafter be painted red. Others revealed similar information about life rafts and parachutes. Every single page had come from the open shelves at the Bureau of Standards library.

All this "Top Secret" proof of treason had been available to any member of the public at any time.

After another twenty-five years, Nixon's grand jury testimony became public. There was no denying it anymore: he'd known all along that the greatest treason in American history was no more than pages from innocuous manuals.

There's more. On December 14, 1948, the Assistant Attorney General in charge of the investigation told Alger—in the presence of his lawyers—that he would probably be charged with perjury the next day. Perjury doesn't mean just lying under oath. It means lying about something crucial to the issue, something "material" to it. You are allowed to lie about your weight when you apply for your driver's license; but if you lie about having a license under another name, that's perjury because it's material to the application. No member of HUAC had been able to find anything in Alger's testimony to justify perjury; the Justice Department had dismissed any possibility of any charge on the basis of the dumb-waiter shaft papers—even the theft of the papers themselves—and so far the grand jury had seen nothing to counter that blanket dismissal. Which is to say that everybody present knew that all Alger had to do to stop this whole business right there and then was take the Fifth. But everybody present was also sure he wasn't going to do it. Naive as it sounds, he really did believe in truth and the rule of law; his reasoning was the same principled reasoning that put the Hollywood Ten behind bars: he had committed no crime and wasn't going to imply that he had. The next day the prosecutor asked him—certain that he would say no to both questions—if he had passed government documents to Chambers and if he had seen Chambers since 1937.

It was a second ambush, and Alger walked straight into it.[24]

The questions weren't material to the grand jury's investigations, and the prosecutor asked them for no other reason than to charge Alger with perjury. For no other reason at all. It's a form of entrapment, and this kind of entrapment is another violation of the Fifth Amendment, the very statute that Alger was refusing to invoke to defend himself. And there was yet another Fifth Amendment violation to come. The Special Assistant to the Attorney General in charge made it clear in his description of what went on that the jurors never even saw the three-page indictment they voted on. How could they? It wasn't drawn up until after they'd retired to deliberate and make that vote.

Alger's team went to work on a writ of error *coram nobis.*

It's an ancient legal procedure, sixteenth century, English Reformation. *Coram nobis:* in our presence, the presence being the king's. It's another type of appeal, but instead of going to a superior court, it goes to the court that rendered the original judgment. It can't rule on innocence or guilt. It's a fresh look at what might have gone wrong with the original trial. Even gutted, Alger's FBI file showed a wild abandon in the prosecution's efforts to take this man down any which way.

Richard M. Nixon was a disgraced ex-president by 1978, when Alger's *coram nobis* reached the District Court of the Southern District of

New York. Even so, the judge who took the case—selected by that giggle of a spun wheel—was again Nixon's own appointee, Judge Richard Owen, who'd sat silently through the plea for release of Alger's file. He sat just as silently through these proceedings.

Speed is important in such cases as this; normally judges rule right after oral arguments.[25] Judge Owen sat on Alger's *coram nobis* for four years. Four years! Then in twenty-five pages he found no fault with Chambers's testimony and decided that Alger had admitted the "most damaging" of the charges. "Nothing" presented to him placed the original verdict "under any cloud" or left him with any questions "whatsoever" about Alger's guilt.[26]

Alger appealed.

Appeal denied in a curt four lines.

The Supreme Court again refused to review the case. No comment.

How come this Judge Owen was picked twice in a row? How come the *coram nobis* sat for four years on his desk? How come there was denial after denial when the evidence is mind-bogglingly clear that the prosecution broke laws and violated Constitutional rights? That the FBI did too? That the "greatest treason conspiracy in this nation's history" was nothing but routine maintenance instructions from manuals in a public library? How come not even the Supreme Court would pay attention? This is one reason why it's so telling that William O. Douglas—longest-serving justice of the Supreme Court—wrote that "in my view no court at any time could possibly have sustained the conviction." And yet his very own court did just that.

And the money. Where did it all come from? Who authorized it? Forget junior congressmen choreographing hearings with rent-a-crowds, then flying whole committees to snazzy hotel suites to interview mystery witnesses who aren't a mystery. Forget press manipulation. It's the sheer manpower involved. Maybe Chambers is right for once when he says there wasn't an FBI field office in the country that was not in on the investigation. Alger's file certainly indicates droves of them. Then there's the Counter Intelligence Corps as well as the Office of Strategic Services. We're looking at hundreds of secret service agents—probably thousands of them—swarming together to fabricate a case against a single citizen. And I'd say we're looking at interference with the justice system that reaches all the way up to the Supreme Court.

There's got to be *some* way to explain such a thing, and I'm one of those people who has theories about everything.

In 1978, the same year that Alger filed for his writ of *coram nobis*, Alan Weinstein brought out a book called *Perjury*.[1] Nixon was right all along. Chambers spoke the literal truth. Fresh evidence from the Russian archives proved it.

A New Prosecution.

We need a review of our setting: the start of the Cold War. For more than a decade, according to Weinstein, the Soviets have been running the highest-placed agent they'd ever had in the US. He's perfect. He has no record of youthful Communist sympathies like the Hollywood Ten and the Cambridge Five. He does his work with no more than a single courier—his close friend—calling regularly at his house which can hardly help alerting the neighbors, the servants, the milkman, the paper boys. And yet he's so devious that many years of intensive FBI surveillance find no trace of him spying or even spending time with his friend the courier. And how amazing is that? The two of them together are a sight gag, as comic a pair as Laurel and Hardy: tall, elegant, perfectly groomed Alger with Chambers shuffling alongside him, a short, fat vagrant of a man, filthy hair flying everywhere, a dirty, rumpled suit, and a mouth that horrifies watchers every time he opens it. Even so, nobody's noticed, not the FBI, nor any of Alger's many friends and colleagues, not even the neighborhood kids. Nor has our spy ever given his government employers cause to doubt his loyalty. Then a committee of notoriously corrupt Congressmen—that he could easily ignore and that his friends urged him to ignore—issue a public statement saying somebody is accusing him of being a communist. Instead of ignoring it, he volunteers to testify in front of them.

The former British Secret Service Officer Vernon Hinchley just couldn't get his mind around it. The story was "impossible to understand."[2]

If he had been obeying Soviet instructions, he'd have kept a low profile. In the months that followed he disobeyed again and again. He didn't take the Fifth. He didn't run. He tangled with the agent provocateur Chambers. Maybe he had escape plans and never used them? The US Navy Intelligence expert Ladislas Farago says Soviet spies are trained to plan and rehearse their escape routes.[3] Svetlana says the famous spy Julius Rosenberg "had been arranging an escape ever since the Fuchs trial in London." There was "an FBI panic instruction, given just ten hours before the arrest, to place surveillance around the house's many exits 'even if he becomes aware of it.'"[4]

The prosecution in Alger's trials would have loved any hint of anything like this escape plan. If they found one, they never said so. If arrangements were made in Russia, nobody has found a trace of them.

Weinstein is not by any means the only writer to support Judge Owen's verdict on the basis of Russian archives. Book after book takes the same line, a dozen or so by now. All of them swallow Chambers whole, something not even Nixon could manage. All of them come to the same conclusion: guilty. All of them say the Soviet archives prove it.

These new books do differ from one another here and there. Some say Soviet records identify Alger as a spy called Lawyer or Jurist or Advokat or Doctor, although that turns out to be a Bessarabian Jew. Some say he's a spy called Master or Leonard or Mars or Ales. Ales is the one they tend to favor. It's a peculiar name to give an American agent; usually English-speaking people were given English-language code names. Ales could be a full-bodied beer, but it's more likely to be a Czech nickname for Alexander, pronounced A-lesh.

It's certainly unusual to have so many codenames. Mostly people have one or two.[5] Kim Philby was "Stanley." Guy Burgess was "Hicks."

Blunt was "Johnson." Not that having a codename makes a person a spy. Churchill was "Boar." Roosevelt was "Captain."

Whatever these recent books call Alger, they all conclude that he was guilty.

Part of the trouble may be that Weinstein and the others haven't actually visited the archives.[6] From what Svetlana says, it's awfully hard to get permission.[7] And anyway they don't speak Russian either, don't know anything about Soviet spy codes—and so little about the Soviet secret services that they confuse military branches with nonmilitary ones. Even so, they write that they "examined the records of the Comintern in the early 1990s" when "virtually all of its collections were open for research."[8] To be sure, one of their collaborators Dr. Felix Firsov—who certainly sounds like a real Russian who speaks Russian and knows cryptography—did analyze the collections back then. But not for their books. He was working on his own book, which he published in Russian. Alger has no role in it. Firsov's English-speaking co-authors explain that the reason for this is that Alger's "name never occurs" in the Comintern collections.[9] Which rather takes a reader aback coming from people who insist he's a spy on the basis of Russian archives.

Svetlana is a Russian citizen as well as a Russian speaker, a trained cryptographer and an expert in espionage; she holds a doctorate in history like Firsov, and her position gives her access to those Comintern files as well as the Moscow archives. Here's what she says:

> There is no mention of Alger and Donald Hiss in CP USA files either as open or as "undisclosed" ("*neglasny*") Communist Party members, or as members of any of the many Communist front organizations. I have not discovered a single instance of their names appearing on numerous support lists of various Communist Party causes and front campaigns. Neither do their names occur as participants in any Communist-related activities or associations. Similarly, their names do not appear among Soviet confidential contacts or as subjects of queries etc. in any publicly accessible Soviet party, diplomatic, or "cultural" files.

That makes two Russian-speaking, professional historians who have examined the Comintern files—as well as other archives—and found no trace of Alger Hiss. A third Russian-speaking investigator, a journalist called Alexander Vassiliev, visited the KGB's Press Office in Moscow and saw material relevant to the period. He wasn't able to visit the archives—that difficult-to-get permission kept him out—but he swore under oath in front of a full jury that he saw nothing to connect the State Department's Alger Hiss in any way with Soviet intelligence. He also testified that he'd told Weinstein exactly this.

What's truly weird is that he's the one on whom Weinstein et al rely most heavily.

Vassiliev's involvement came about because the KGB needed money for its pension fund. Russian Foreign Intelligence contacted Weinstein's publishers Random House and made a deal. An undisclosed sum changed hands. For this, the KGB was willing to provide "materials" that would allow Western writers to write books "on the basis of documents."[10] The Service's Press Officer, Major General Boris Labusov— the first of something like half a dozen Russian generals in this chapter and the one that follows—emphasised that the "materials" included "no official copies of documents," only "passages" and "citations" specially selected for Vassiliev. No photocopying allowed. Only notes. Major Gen. Labusov emphasized that "We, the Russian Intelligence Service, have no documents . . . proving that Alger Hiss cooperated with our service somewhere or anywhere."[11]

Here's the gist of what Vassiliev did find about Alger:

A woman called Hede Massing testified for the prosecution at Alger's second trial; she was a real Soviet agent with the cover name Redhead—only the one cover name, though—who'd been an actress in Vienna. She'd told her controller about a conversation she'd had at a party with the eminent Alger Hiss, the two of them having a flirtatious squabble over which of them was going to recruit their host for the cause.

Her controller didn't believe her. As Vasssiliev translated his comment, she "was unable to educate not only an agent, but [even] herself."

The FBI didn't believe her either.[12] She'd been confessing to them for a couple of years, and not a word about Alger until agents prompted her—and suggested a wrong answer might end in deportation. The party's hostess was certain the conversation never took place because she'd never invited Alger with the actress at the same time[13]; the party's host agreed. US State Department records show that both host and hostess were out of the country on all the possible party dates. They didn't testify for the defense in the trial for the very unpleasant reason that both were being tortured in Hungary as US spies. Which brings me to a second general in my tale. He's former KGB General Oleg Kalugin, chief of the Foreign Intelligence Department, and his comment was, "Some, not-too-honest KGB officers would gladly declare that 'Hiss is my agent.' In fact, he is not."[14] Kalugin wrote a book after the KGB accused him of being an American spy; he called it *Spymaster: My Thirty-Two Years in Intelligence and Espionage against the West.*[15] Alger Hiss is not even mentioned in the index.

Vassiliev also found two lists, now called Perlo's List and Gorsky's List, both of which show Alger's name "in clear", as Vassiliev puts it. But it's as obvious to any reader as it was to Vassiliev that references in them are to Alger in his official State Department role. Victor Perlo was a Marxist economist and the head of a Soviet spy ring. Alger's name appears on his list only for Perlo to explicitly deny any dealings with him. Anatoly Gorsky was the First Secretary of the Soviet Union in Washington's Soviet Embassy. With a job like that he had to know everybody and could hardly have avoided knowing Alger. He was also a spy who clearly knew the person with the favorite codename Ales; he sent a crucial cable concerning him (I'll get to it). In his list he does mention Alger but no hint of him as Ales. Which probably explains why Weinstein omits the Gorsky List altogether from both his books.[16]

John J. Lowenthal wasn't impressed by any of Vassiliev's research. Lowenthal was a professor of Law at City University of New York, a professional cellist, and a volunteer for the Hiss defense team; he noted mixups in dates, mixups in cover names, mixups in code names, mixups in the branches of Soviet secret services. He poo-pooed *all* of Vassiliev's KGB research in a specialist magazine called *Intelligence and National Security*; Amazon.com ran the article as a reader's comment. That made Vassiliev angry. He sued for libel. What seems odd at first glance is that he brought his suit in the UK. The journal had a bare 146 subscribers in the UK; Amazon.com is an American corporation, not all that often visited by the British, who have their own Amazon.co.uk, on which the reader's comment did not appear. But to this day British libel law makes it far easier to sue and win in London than anywhere else in the world; it's called "libel tourism," and it's a good moneymaker for an island dependent on financial services.

Vassiliev's suit turned into a full jury trial before Mr. Justice Eady of the High Court. Here was where he testified under oath that he'd never seen any document identifying Alger as Ales or any other spy. He actually swore to it. Speak of being taken aback. This was also where he testified that he'd told Weinstein so and had accused Weinstein of being "sloppy almost every time he quoted documents relating to Alger Hiss."[17]

Despite the virtual impossibility of losing, Vassiliev lost his case. He not only lost, he lost badly. A unanimous verdict against him—and £70,000 to pay in court costs.[18]

So what about the source references to archives in these books? There are pages and pages of them. And they look very mysterious, very daunting.[19] One of the sad things about us humans is that if anything looks like that, we tend to hurry past it, assuming it's important but definitely not for us. Take Weinstein's *The Haunted Wood: Soviet Espionage In America—The Stalin Era*, the book that provoked the lawsuit. We are told that sources come from "KGB Archives, Moscow." No mention of that press office or of mere "citations" selected by the Russians. For the chapter devoted to Alger, endnotes are started off with "File 17517, Vol. 3, pp. 70-72. This is followed by a string of 82 "ibid"s featuring a couple of different file numbers and lots of different page numbers.

They have to mean *something*, don't they?

They all come from Vassiliev's notes, and the only people who can check them out at source are a few select Russian scholars, none of whom can find any more evidence of Alger as a spy than Vassiliev himself could. Not to worry. The unidentified spy Ales *does* appear in those notes. Which takes us to the next step. All the authors have to do is substitute the name Alger Hiss whenever they run across the Czech nickname Ales.

This really took some effort to get into my head. Respectable academics simply substitute one name for another when it suits them? If you want to check for yourself, you can find all Vassiliev's notes in the Wilson Center digital archives.[20] You have to admit it's a pretty impressive sleight-of-hand: a famously loyal American morphs into a Soviet agent by the simple trick of sticking his name in place of a Soviet agent's wherever the agent appears.

Weinstein also interviewed witnesses, and they do sound damning. On the other hand, the witnesses started complaining right after publication. One of them said quotes attributed to him were "sheer poppycock. My son says I should consult a lawyer."[21] Another did call his lawyer. His name was Sam Krieger, and he sued both historian and publisher. Result? An out-of-court settlement for an undisclosed amount.[22]

But how extraordinary is that? Both Russians who researched for the prosecutors deny any connection between Alger and spying. Whenever the law gets involved—only twice so far—it supports Alger's innocence.

Never mind. Alger's guilty.

There are a number of spy handler confessions about, all of them by Russians who handled American spies. Where are the confessions of the lucky Soviet agent who handled this most important of all American betrayers? Are we talking about Chambers? No, no. Chambers insists he was only a courier. A spy for the Soviets had to have a handler in the Soviet secret services. Nobody claims the honor for Alger even though there'd be a lot of money in it. Glory too. Hollywood. A movie. And where are the confessions of co-conspirators? All the people Chambers named—every single one of them, in the Communist Party or out of it—denied any knowledge of Alger and espionage, even the ones who needed cash and could profit from it. They weren't at risk either. The statute of limitations protected them.

It's now more than eighty years since Nixon began his crusade. In all that time, nobody—not a single human being—Russian or American or any other nationality, has corroborated Chambers's tales of Alger as a spy. Nor has a single document shown up to support the idea.

⸻ ⠶⠶⠶ ⸻

In 1991 Richard Nixon himself went in search of bedrock for the mysterious-looking endnotes. John H. Taylor, director of his presidential library, wrote to another Russian general, Dimitri Volkogonov, making a formal request for the Soviet files on the Hiss case[24]. This general was head of the USSR Defense Ministry Military History, chairman of the parliamentary committee for the KGB and Communist Party Archives. An obvious person—probably *the* obvious person—for Nixon to approach. Nixon's representative Dimitri K. Simes delivered the letter personally.[23]

There is no record of what Volkogonov replied, although it does seem unlikely that Nixon would have kept quiet about it if the general had found proof of Alger as a Soviet agent.

The very next year Alger made the very same inquiry of the very same general.

Nobody claims that Volkogonov did the searching himself; he was Special Advisor to Prime Minister Boris Yeltsin and a busy man. He instructed Yevgeny Primakov, director of the Russian Intelligence Service, and his staff to locate all materials on the Hiss case.[24] This research brought up Alger in his official State Department capacity in the 1940s, including official diplomatic contacts with Soviet representatives. But the general stressed these were normal working relations in his professional capacity.

"Not a single document," he reported, "and a great deal of material has been studied, substantiates the allegation that Mr. A. Hiss collaborated with the intelligence services of the Soviet Union."[25]

As it turns out—a byproduct of that archival search—there's nothing to support Chambers as a spy either. Volkogonov reported that Chambers "had party contacts but not intelligence contacts . . . and not any kind of secret or spy information."[26]

A couple of writers of the accusing books asked if the general had examined everything that existed. The general admitted that he didn't have the clearance to examine *everything*. Not that any human being could in a single lifetime no matter how extensive the clearance. Many archives had been destroyed, hadn't they? The general admitted that this was true.

Aha! He's "retracted" his statement.

Now that's just plain naughty for people who haven't studied the Soviet material themselves, who haven't even been near the archives, who based their claims on research by somebody who hasn't been near them either and who know perfectly well that their own archives routinely destroy stuff. Nor do any of them mention Nixon's prior request—and the dead silence regarding it. Their only comment is that the general didn't take long enough to do a proper search after Alger's request. Did they expect him to repeat for a private citizen what he'd done at the official request of an American ex-president?

John Lowenthal, Professor of Law, asked the general, "In your opinion, if Alger Hiss had been a spy, would you have found some documents saying that?"

"Positively," said the general.

More than a decade later, in 2003, the very same year that Vassiliev lost his suit in front of Justice Eady of the London High Court, another Russian general vigorously seconded that "positively." This was Major General Julius Kobyakov of the SVR, who'd been Deputy Director of the KGB's American Division, another person who really would know.

He summarized his report with spelling mistakes that are charmingly his, not mine: "After carefull study of every reference to Mr. A.Hiss in the SVR"—that's the Russian Federal Security Service—"(KGB NKVD) archives, and querring sister services, I prepared an answer to Mr. J.Lowenthal that in essence stated that Mr. A.Hiss had never had any relationship with the SVR or its predecessors."

Then he added, "I am ready to eat my hat if someone proves the contrary."[27]

In 1996 the National Security Agency released the Venona Papers, coded Soviet cables monitored by the US during World War II. The originals are long gone. All that's left are decodings and partial translations—nobody knows how rough—and interpretation. Alger's new accusers seized on them. The two cables allegedly concerning Alger were numbered 1822 and 1579; Anatoly Gorsky, the diplomat of the Soviet Embassy and the Gorsky List, signed 1822. It's the one that mentions the agent Ales. A comment notes, "It would appear likely that this individual is Alger Hiss." "Likely"? The comment turns out to be no part of the original cable, nothing to do with the Soviets at all. Some unknown FBI decryptor added it. FBI Special Agent Robert Lamphere was in charge of the Venona project, and he's often credited with the speculation, but he told law Professor Lowenthal he'd never heard of it while he was with the FBI.[1] Nor did he mention it in his autobiography although he refers to Alger in non-Venona contexts and goes into detail about other Venona identifications, including spies Julius Rosenberg, Klaus Fuchs, Harry Gold, and Rudolph Abel.[2] The speculation isn't mentioned in his obituary either.[3]

The FBI tried to verify the speculation for twenty years. They failed. And abandoned the effort nearly half a century ago.

What with my family's records destroyed and palletized, the FBI as an archive facility could hardly impress me. As for their general accuracy in assessing the little they've kept of important files, a real treasure lurks in their newly released list of its files on famous dead people:

US Senator
b. 1908
McCARTHY JOSEPH   d. 1957   COMMUNIST

Isn't that glorious? The FBI condemns the arch anti-Communist as a Red? And this is an official record, not just some unidentified agent's stray comment.

The other Venona cable, 1579, actually mentions the name Hiss. It's a fragment sent from the Military Intelligence chief in New York to his director in Moscow and says a cable "has reported [gobbledygook] from the State Department by the name of HISS." "Gobbledygook" means that the Americans couldn't read the code. There's no mistaking the name Hiss though because it appeared in the Latin alphabet in the original cable. It's not as though the Soviet secret services were unfamiliar with Alger Hiss; as Gen Volkogonov noted, he appears frequently in his official capacity. The "[gobbledygook]" could just as well mean "an uncooperative diplomat" or "a well-dressed man" or "a famous patriot" as anything sinister. Here there's no first name—could be Alger, could be his brother, could be some other Hiss altogether. But referring to a spy without a cover-name? Spy-masters just don't do that.

That's the extent of the Venona papers on the case.

Another claim is that a Soviet ex-agent called Oleg Gordievsky named Alger as Ales *before* the Venona decrypts were made public.

This story begins in 1989 with an article in the *New York Review of Books* by intelligence expert Thomas Powers, who'd got a tipoff saying an unidentified agent called Ales was probably Alger Hiss.[4] The following year, Gordievsky and Cambridge historian Andrew Christopher repeated the Powers claim and—*very* important—credited him as their source.[5]

When the Venona decrypts were finally made public in 1995—six years later—this identification got dredged up as proof that Alger was indeed Ales. Prof Eric Alterman of the City University of New York was curious:

"When I called Powers to ask him where he heard the original story, he named a counterintelligence agent who had told him about it after seeing the very same Venona document. Powers said there was 'no question that the agent was referring to the same document that was just released.'"[6]

In short, the speculation noted on Venona 1822 proves the speculation noted on Venona 1822.

But now the claim expanded to include a new backup. Gordievsky wrote that he had heard an agent called Akhmerov say Alger was a spy in a lecture. Not that there's any mention of it in the Gordievsky autobiography, which came out the same year.[7]

This brings up yet another Russian general, Lieutenant General Vitaly Grigorievich Pavlov, head of the American section of the KGB's foreign intelligence department in 1940 and an agent for the department for a decade before that, during all of Nixon's "period in question." Akhmerov was dead by this time, but Pavlov had worked closely with him during World War II. He told Svetlana in 2002:

> "At the time when I first read in the press of the charges against State Department official Hiss I had an immediate question: could he really be involved? And I do remember exactly that on all lines, including operational, I was told clearly: he has nothing to do with foreign intelligence."[8]

He didn't believe a word of Gordievsky's story either:

> "I can say the following: No, in his lecture Akhmerov could not, as Godievsky writes, have said anything about Harry Hopkins or Alger Hiss, who were not agents of ours (and Akhmerov never encountered them). All of this is the pure fabrication."[9]

―――― ❦ ――――

But surely we can find *something* to damn Alger with, something to give this new prosecution substance. It's hard going, though, especially since nobody has found so much as a trace of cables and secret documents supplied by either Alger or Chambers. Not even Vassiliev. And then Ladislas Farago says all espionage encounters had to be arranged in Moscow. So does Vernon Hinchley. Nobody has found any evidence of plans for Alger or Chambers. Nor is there any evidence that the Soviets helped Alger financially. When he went on trial, the Soviets supplied no "money for the defense,"[10] something they'd most certainly have done if he'd been a real spy. Money for Judith Coplon, caught red-handed in the act of giving information to a Soviet agent. Money for Klaus Fuchs, a physicist who gave the Soviets the theoretical outline for a hydrogen bomb and spent fourteen years in England's Wakefield Prison. Money for Julius Rosenberg, executed as a spy at Sing Sing in 1953. Money for lots of others too. Nothing for Alger. What about when Alger was in prison? Any worries about him then? According to one of Alger's fellow prisoners, "All the top Commies in the country that were in jail at the time came through Lewisburg."[11] Svetlana found a report in Molotov's papers—he was Stalin's protégé—listing American Communists banged up in US jails "simultaneously with Hiss. In this Top Secret report for Molotov's eyes only, Hiss's name was not mentioned."[12]

What about the Russian public? Everybody loves spy stories. How does this hero fare in Russia? There's a lot on other famous turncoats. Klaus Fuchs: he's well covered. The Cambridge Five are all over the place. A book came out not long ago on Anthony Blunt.

But the Hiss case? There are *no* popular books about him in Russian. Not one. Nobody's heard of the man, not even the head of the foreign intelligence branch of the KGB and Chairman of the KGB. This is yet another general, Army General Vladimir Alexandrovich Kryuchkov. In 1996, he granted an interview to Pulitzer prize-winning author David Remnick, who "asked about spies and suspected spies . . .and was rebuffed with dutiful answers" until he reached the name Alger Hiss; "Kryuchkov looked utterly bewildered."

"'Alger who?

"'Hiss. Alger Hiss.

"'Who is that?'"[13]

All that exists in Russia are a few scholarly works that include references but don't even consider the possibility that Alger had anything to do with Soviet espionage. One such book dismisses the case out of hand as "a pretext to unfold in the country the persecution campaign of progressive public men."[14] Another sees only "obvious fabrication."[15]

Then it occurred to me, thinking of Dexter and his novel *The Accident*, that since nobody seems to be able to find solid evidence of guilt in Soviet documents, there might be proof of another kind to be found in the workings of the archives themselves.

Dexter told me that the project to build the atom bombs during World War II was an extraordinarily well-kept secret, even though a huge installation had to be built in a remote part of New Mexico. Thousands of tons of materials had to be transported there. Railway lines had to be diverted and their routes disguised to hide the destination. The army had been doing this for a number of months when a disabled newspaper reporter in Denver, confined to an apartment overlooking the railroads, noticed an increase in activity on lines heading out west. He plotted the activity, put together a pattern, discovered the secret.

Why not the same for Alger? If he really was a spy, surely the activity in the archives would greatly increase when he was under threat.

To get a sense of comparison, I asked Svetlana about other turncoats. She says there's an "obvious increase in entries" around such cases. "Take, for instance, the Fuchs case. In Molotov Papers we see Soviet secret TASS reports with Molotov's heavy pencil marks and notations—followed by instructions for publishing TASS official refutation. Same pattern around the arrest of Harry Gold in May 1950. Lots of activity around the arrest, investigation, and trial of Judy Coplon in 1949."

So what about Alger? What about his appearances in front of HUAC? His suit against his *agent provocateur*? His trials? What kind of activity went on in the Soviet archives during these crucial times?

What Svetlana says is:

"Total silence re Hiss."[16]

This is what started me thinking about why Gen Volkogonov was so positive that he'd have found *something* if Alger had been a spy, and why Gen Kobyakov found the whole idea such a joke that he'd eat his hat if anybody actually found anything. These days I listen to audible books at bedtime, and one of them was Ben Macintyre's life of Kim Philby[17]; I was half-asleep when I jolted awake on hearing Philby mention "the monstrous volume of paperwork [that is] an essential part of intelligence."

So that was it! I'd completely missed the most elementary reason for the general's certainty.

I had been thinking in terms of a file at the bottom of some unexamined cabinet saying the equivalent of "Alger Hiss was a spy," but first year sociology textbooks explain that all bureaucracies—without exception—create "mountains of paper." They say that "governmental bureaucracies are especially known for this," and the secret services of every country are vast governmental bureaucracies manned by literally thousands of bureaucrats.[18] The KGB, for example, employed over half a million people during the Cold War.[19]

Bureaucracies this big are Baroque, Byzantine operations with tasks broken into component parts and filtered down through chains of command to multitudinous levels of responsibility; somebody has to write a report for each component part, and various somebodies at each level have to collate and deal with what's gone on there. Just to complicate matters further, Alger once told me that such bureaucracies are put together—intentionally—so that one level doesn't know what another level is doing. I imagine this is especially true when the bureaucracy is dealing with state secrets.

Here's FBI agent Frederick Donner: "Much of an agent's time (and virtually all of the manager's day) is spent pushing paper . . . .If you examine the daily duties of FBI personnel, you would see that at least 75 percent of the time is spent on paperwork."[20]

Here's former CIA agent Lindsay Moran: "Anytime you do something operational or meet with an asset . . .there's a lot of paperwork involved . . .a tremendous amount of time spent writing . . . . For any operational meeting you might have—even if it lasts only fifteen minutes—you'll have hours of report-writing to do."[21]

The domestic arm of the British secret services explains: "Information and records management is a core business activity in MI5. It supports sustained, integrated research and analysis that underpins our work."[22]

Maybe the Soviet Union's bureaucracies were different? Here's a Cold War view: "The amount of paperwork originated by Soviet bureaucracy surpasses . . . what would be imaginable in any contemporary capitalist country . . . Bureaucrats are reluctant to take responsibility for any kind of decision without securing the approval of all channels involved."[23]

In the particular case of this supposedly prize asset who'd been in business for something like fifteen years, there'd certainly have to be documents Chambers transmitted, and after his four or five years on the job, there'd be many hundreds of them. There'd have to be as many years of reports from him about what Alger's doing—or not doing—assessments of the information he was supplying and directions for what he was to supply and back-and-fourth housekeeping details like meetings, arranging them, reporting on them. There'd have to be years of the same for Colonel Bykov. There'd have to be years of reports of information from a small army of the informants that are a crucial part of any secret service. Just think of the many informants from my father's unimportant file. But that's not all. Any agent has to be recruited, then put through a vetting process and then a training in spycraft; details of progress have to make their cumbersome way through bureaucratic channels in Moscow.

Then there's Chambers's defection in 1937 or 1938.

He opted out at a bad, bad time, right in the midst of the Great Purge and the Moscow show trials. We're talking about Joseph Stalin here, a paranoid megalomaniac at his most bloodthirsty. He had all of Russia in a state of terror, executing people right and left, somewhere around a million of them, sending droves more off to the Gulag. Nobody seems to know real numbers. From what Philby says, foreign agents were never fully trusted anyway, and when Chambers decided he was going to go to the FBI, Stalin would have had to assume that any-body who'd worked with him was likely to be—or quickly become—an informer or a double agent, and that FBI surveillance would intensify dramatically for all of them. Most important among these was the prize asset Alger. The idea that Alger could ever have overcome Stalin's sus-picions is pretty silly, but since Alger's accusers have the Soviets con-tinuing to use him, there'd have to have been a redoubling of watchers, informants, reports.

Alger would also have needed a new handler/courier and a new army of informants; these would have to cover the decade that included the entirety of World War II in which Alger played several important roles. Even if the numbers of documents transmitted from him didn't increase all that much, the decade of bureaucratic paperwork would have dwarfed whatever Chambers generated. One of Alger's significant roles was as part of the US delegation at Yalta, where Roosevelt and Stalin agreed on the Russian invasion of Japan. When the atomic bomb fell on Hiroshima on August 6, 1945, the day before that planned inva-sion, Roosevelt's betrayal of Stalin was absolute. The Americans had snatched the prize of Japan right out of his hands. If this didn't mean that Alger was a dead man at once, his position would be profoundly compromised. And for the second time.

Then there'd have to be an incredible flood of incoming documents when Alger volunteered to testify in front of HUAC, not just reports of it but a very great deal of very frightened discussion of what the hell to do about it. Stalin would be in a rage. Heads would roll in the Kremlin. A foreign agent under serious suspicion ever since Chambers's defection, doubly so since Hiroshima, and now he *volunteers* to talk to HUAC! This makes him as serious threat to the Soviet network as any agent in the world. It's almost impossible to imagine the damage he could do.

This is a man who has to be silenced.

Mountains and mountains of paper. And an assassination.

No wonder the generals were so certain. No wonder Alger as a spy sounds laughable to them. They *knew* Stalin. They *knew* what he'd do.

They also knew that if there were *any* evidence that Alger had spied for the Soviets, there would be way too much of it for anybody to miss.

But who trusts Russians? Or writers who aren't professional historians? Let's assume that despite all this Alger Hiss actually had been spying. Think what that says about the American and Soviet secret services. Here's a suspect who was the organizing Secretary General of the United Nations, the president of the Carnegie Endowment for International Peace, a man tipped as a possible Secretary of State, and the FBI finds no trace of subversive activity despite intensive surveillance over many, many years. And the enemy? The Russians? To whom this man was a great hero? So far as people with access to Soviet archives can tell, the Russians have no trace of subversive activity either.

That leaves us with the extraordinary idea that Alger Hiss as a spy means that two superpowers led up to World War II, conducted it, concluded it, and launched into the Cold War: all this with secret services that were deaf, dumb, and blind.

So why keep after this man with all these books? If the attraction is only finding a spy deep in the heart of government, there are far better candidates.

Soviet archives yield up an "informational file" for Secretary of State Dean Acheson and for Averell Harriman, presidential candidate, ambassador to the UK, governor of New York.[1] The FBI had extensive files on both of them too. Here's the entry for Harriman in that recently released list of files of famous dead people:

Ambassador
HARRIMAN WILLIAM AVERALL also spelled Averill
COMMUNIST[2]

Wonderful. Two spellings for Averell—and both of them wrong. Never mind. The FBI listed him as a Communist. *And* he has an "informational file" in the secret Soviet archives. He was at Yalta. He was ambassador to the USSR too. His Moscow office was bugged. Who's to say he didn't engineer that himself? As for Bullitt, the spy Ludwig Lore fingered him on record, and Svetlana found cables from him in Stalin's private archive, annotated in Stalin's own hand. Why isn't somebody going after him?

During a war people at a high diplomatic level have no choice but to make compromises the rest of us might consider dicey. Negotiations like the ones at Yalta are so tense precisely because crossings-of-the-line are obligatory. How does Roosevelt get Stalin to understand that he doesn't want Churchill to invade Japan while Churchill is sitting right there? How do Roosevelt and Churchill keep Stalin in the dark about an atom bomb when they're trying to agree on how to deploy it? A case could be made against any diplomat or politician of Alger's stature, and anybody could make a stronger case against many of them than the one against Alger.

There is HUAC, of course. If Alger wasn't a spy, the forty years of terror that the House Un-American Activities Committee imposed is completely unjustified. Maybe that's reason enough. McCarthy was an individual out of control. This committee was a government man-dated, government-funded arm of the House of Representatives, and it destroyed people on an epic scale with as little evidence as the judges in the Salem witch trials that Arthur Miller dramatized to expose the mass hysteria HUAC provoked and exploited. To this day it remains the greatest blot on American history since slavery.

———— ∞∞∞ ————

But I think there is more, and I have a theory.

The stumbling into Nazis is everywhere. Nazi cartels. Nazi military. Nazi contracts. FBI Agent Reynolds, quoting Confidential Informant T-27 about my father, writes that he was one of the few who didn't trust multinational corporations because of their connection to the "known activities of German fifth column agents."[3]

The phrase "fifth column" comes from the Spanish Civil War, when Franco claimed he would march on Madrid with four columns and be met by the fifth inside. Way back in 1943, the investigative journalist George Seldes wrote that "only the little seditionists and traitors have been rounded up by the FBI. The real Nazi Fifth Column in America remains immune."[4] There are a number of recent books that support the idea, including Stephen Kinzer's study of the Dulleses, *The Brothers*. Their sources include the Congressional Record, documents from the Justice Department's Economic Warfare Unit, reports of Treasury investigations, minutes of Embassy meetings, military intelligence memoranda and communications, corporate reports, letters in corporation files, investigative articles in magazines and newspapers.

Sources even include the Code of the Federal Regulations of the United States.

On December 13, 1941—two days after the United States declared war on Germany and the very day after Germany declared war on the United States—President Roosevelt himself signed into law an exception to the ban on Trading with the Enemy: it was alright to do so "provided it is authorized by the Secretary of the Treasury." The bill sped through Congress—the First War Powers Act—stamped and ready in five days.[5]

Given this, there's no way the government could have been unaware of at least some of what was going on, especially since so many of the moneymakers were in government themselves—or closely tied to it.

The Dulleses' patents for I. G. Farben were what created the rubber shortages in America. Their patents for I. G. Bosch stopped the Allies using direct fuel injection technology in diesel engine production, crucial in the manufacture of efficient trucks, tanks, ships, submarines, and planes.[6] The Rockefellers' Standard Oil of New Jersey shipped fuel to Nazi troops through Switzerland. The Bushes' Union Bank held millions of Hitler's funds. Ford built trucks for German occupation troops in France, where their business increased dramatically during the war. Alcoa shipped aluminum for airplanes to Germany and left the American military short.[7] The telephone conglomerate ITT helped improve German communication systems and build the V1 and V2 bombs that destroyed London. IBM had the contract for the punch cards that identified holocaust victims in Auschwitz.[8]

This industrial and financial cooperation laid the foundations for a new, international empire that had nothing to do with ideology. Nor was it limited to the United States. This was a new approach to the world's economy, banking, industry, and political power married as they were in what might be called "the German experiment." John Foster Dulles called that experiment an "economic and financial union"; he championed its spread over the globe as "a kind of supranational guild."[9]

When the war was over, the "supranational guild" moved into Germany to protect its assets and ensure its continued survival. One example of how this worked is I. G. Farben, makers of Zyklon-B, lethal gas for the Holocaust. It was a conglomerate to begin with. In 1945 the Allies split it back into its constituent parts. Bayer Healthcare is—and was—one of them. Another is—and was—BASF, right now the largest chemical company in the world.

Dulles's economic and financial union is now well-entrenched, even though most of us are unaware of its existence. It's the reason that bankers can bring about almost total collapses of global markets. Think of the Greenpeace leaks about TTIP, the planned Transatlantic Trade and Investment Partnership, which show multinationals consulted at every step of negotiations that give them the right to sue governments if laws to protect mere citizens get in the way of profits. It's just like the title of my father's book: *"Business As A System Of Power."* The economist's definition of Nazism.

But getting such a monumental structure to take hold in America without revealing its structure: that took some doing.

All those decades of a Republican dominated HUAC—close to *forty* years of it—all that money spent on it, all those lives ruined: the one and only justification for the pain, fear, waste, and destruction is Alger Hiss. HUAC went on doing its dirty work for twenty-five years after they'd put Alger in prison. They'd never caught anybody before him, and they never caught anybody after him. Not anybody else in all their forty years. Nobody. Not one spy.

The Red scare they whipped up, which concentrated anti-Communist paranoia around Alger Hiss, became for America what the Jews had been to Germany, a force to unify the people and deflect attention from an economic rearrangement that could not function freely without chipping away at their rights. The Democrats with their New Deal commitments were a barrier. A 1943 memorandum of a secret meeting of industrialists from several countries states that "the new Presidential elections must bring the United States on the side of the powers fighting for the reorganization of the world markets."[10] Republican election campaigns concentrated on the Red smear as their route to victory. J Parnell Thomas, chairman of HUAC, explained that the Republican National Committee had urged him "to set up spy hearings . . .in order to put the heat on Harry Truman."[11]

Chambers had no choice but to play the heroic role assigned to him; he had immunity from perjury, but that left him vulnerable to far more serious charges. Passport fraud. Credit fraud. Sodomy with its twenty-year sentence at hard labor. And just think what that FBI report indicating abuse of a young boy—true or not—could add to those horrors. Is it any wonder that the Bureau liked the story too much to question it?

But a scapegoat was missing. The public needed a human face to embody the red terror at home just as Stalin embodied it abroad; they needed an American focus for their nightmares.

It was the opening of the atomic age; for the first time in history, human beings could destroy themselves and their planet. All it took was the treachery of one spy stealing one secret—boom!—that was it. The idea is ridiculous—anybody with a little physics knows that—but the public believed it. HUAC needed that single face to convince them that a new kind of creature was slouching its way towards Bethlehem to be born: a fanatic who would betray his country for ideas, not money and whose ideas were inseparable from criminal acts. Such a person could demonstrate for one and all that New Dealers, liberals, progressives, nonconformists, radicals, subversives, spies, Communists and traitors were all a single inseparable breed. The hardcore Republicans had been right all along.

Svetlana thinks HUAC's original target was Lee Pressman. He was on Chambers's list before Alger was and also on all the lists that sprang up from it, and he'd have been a much easier victim. He was a Jew. He'd had a real, live Communist Party past. He'd have made a splash, a prominent lawyer, an ex-State Department official, a major force in the unions.

When Alger Hiss demanded the right to deny the charges against him before HUAC, he was walking straight into the role; there was no longer a need for Pressman or anybody else. Nowadays, the stream of books condemning Alger anew—with disproved evidence and mysterious-looking references to inaccessible Russian archives—cement his position as the scapegoat for America's role in the supranational guild.

But we're still missing an element.

"Were the Soviet Union to sink tomorrow under the waters of the ocean"—this is George Kennan, diplomat, historian, the "father of containment"—"the American military-industrial complex would have to remain substantially unchanged until some other adversary could be invented. Anything else would be an unacceptable shock to the American economy."[12]

He couldn't have known what form his prediction would take, but the war on terrorism that followed the collapse of the Soviet Union certainly fulfilled it. It's as much a fact as Communism. Osama Bin Laden was a real man. The Trade Center really was bombed. There really are jihadis and suicide bombers. The Islamic State is a living, breathing eruption of the Dark Ages right in our modern faces. Terrorism has advantages over Communism too; it's a worldwide movement, no boundaries or loyalties. Just like the guild itself.

But we common people need stories to make things come alive for us. We need a setting and a human history. Here's how I think this story goes. A world full of terror—from whatever source—has to be our setting. Chambers is the founding hero in our fight against it. Alger is the bogeyman. He's the one who made the threat real to us right back at the beginning. To this day he continues to serve as the embodiment of what happens when we let our guard down.

The Freedom of Information and Privacy Act became law in the US in 1966. The FBI had been destroying files before that—they'd already destroyed two chunks of my mother's—and went on trashing whatever it wanted to, whenever it wanted to, for nearly twenty years. Nobody has any idea what's been lost or how much or why.

In the 1980s came the Record Retention Plan with the stated aim of putting a little order into the destruction. The FBI is to retain files for twenty-five years, then hang on only to files that are historically important. The main criterion of importance is the "fat file theory": if there's lots of it, it's important.

And yet the National Archives told Alger's lawyer Victor Rabinowitz that unknown quantities of Alger's files had been "destroyed" while the mere leftovers amount to some forty thousand to fifty thousand pages.[1] My father's file says "Do not destroy" and "Historical Value" right on the cover, and most of it has been destroyed. As for thin files, where is the prophet who's going to say for certain that a little six-page file won't rock civilization a hundred years from now?

The Records Retention plan turns out to have little to do with retention. Under its provisions, the FBI is legally entitled to destroy *80 percent* of its archive[2]. What kind of library burns four out of every five books?

The only way to get at what's left is Freedom of Information, a difficult, difficult job, and not just for Alger and me. One blacklisted screenwriter—under FBI surveillance for twenty-six years, followed all over the globe, even aboard ship—finally managed to extract only a "haphazard" collection of 287 pages.[3] Economist John Kenneth Galbraith said of his own files: "an unparalleled mine of misinformation."[4] Even the National Security Archive at George Washington University says "an FOIA request should be a research tool of last resort."[5]

The situation is getting worse.

Jeremy Bigwood's work took him to Jay Lovestone, leader of the Communist Party of the USA, then a CIA informant, a major figure; in May of 1999, Pulitzer Prize winner Ted Morgan published a biography of him.[6] The Amazon blurb for the book reports an FBI file of some 5,700 pages as a major source. In June of 2012, Bigwood wrote to the National Archives to see that file for himself. The response: the FBI Records Management Division made a search and "determined that the file was destroyed on November 9, 2004."[7]

Sometime in the five-year period between Morgan's book and Jeremy's request, the file lost its historical value?

All these cases light up aspects of a modern phenomenon that Alger's case brings into sharp focus. When security agencies collect vast amounts of information on people, the truths that might come out are the least of it; what's really frightening is how easy it is to manhandle innocuous detail into evidence of a crime. Careful selection and careful destruction from within massive databases can frame any one of us for anything—and it's so much easier today than it was when Nixon and HUAC framed Alger. And it's not just about us individually. Nearly a century ago, my father warned of the Nazi dream to delete the old falsities—anything that reflected a less-than-glorious Germany—and so purify the record as well as the Aryan race. This extraordinary, state-mandated destruction of official archives certainly looks like today's spin on the dream. Bigwood put it even better than Brady did:

"Erasing history . . .so there can be a rewrite."[8]

The CIA suspects a Harvard-educated British subject of links to Al Qaeda. They abduct him, spirit him off to Guantanamo Bay, and torture him, never letting on what the charges are against him. After two years they release him abruptly, again without a word. He sues the US government for compensation.

The government's lawyer asks him, "Can you present any evidence that would prove you were *not* connected to Al Qaeda?"

The Englishman is taken aback. "Can I prove a negative? Are we being asked to do that now?"[1]

This scene is from a popular television series called *Boston Legal*, but the witty English philosopher Bertrand Russell made the same point:

Russell says to you, "There's a china teapot in an elliptical orbit between the sun and the earth."

You say indignantly, "No, there isn't."

He says, "Prove it."

Since he knows perfectly well you can't, does that mean there really *is* a china teapot in orbit out there?

It took me quite a time to realize that I couldn't disprove the existence of that china teapot with the new accusers. I point to the FBI's years of surveillance—and its total failure to find a shred of evidence of Alger's guilt. I point to the Russian scholars and archivists, to whom the idea is a joke. But that won't stop Alger's accusers. Ignore the mountains of paper too; you can always bypass something like that. They can keep on saying, "Well, maybe there's still something somewhere to prove him guilty." One of them actually claims that Alger's fifty years of fighting to clear his name is proof positive that he's guilty.

But *maybe*? Is that good enough? Our legal system embodies a cherished presumption of innocence. A person accused of a crime—spying or terrorism or shoplifting—doesn't have to prove anything about anything. Most assuredly not in American law. Not in British law either. Nor in Islamic law. Even China is coming around to the idea. It's the prosecution's job to prove suspects are what they're accused of being, not the suspects' to prove they are *not*.

In Alger's case, it's espionage we're talking about. That's serious, and there are standards of proof for it: two witnesses to the same overt act and documentation of intent to do damage to the state.

For the first phase of the drama, these people offer up only a single witness who can't even tell the truth about how many jobs he held or how many books he translated. His dumbwaiter-shaft batch of documentation—his proof of Alger's intent to do damage to the state—is so nonsecret that it was distributed to hundreds of State Department offices in a shopping cart. His pumpkin documentation—Nixon's proof of the greatest treason in American history—turned out to be instructions on how to paint fire extinguishers.

How can this happen in America? Why can't we listen to William O. Douglas, the longest-serving justice of the United States Supreme Court, when he writes: "No court at any time could possibly have sustained the conviction."[2]

As for the second phase of the drama, we're supposed to have a top-level Soviet agent who could bring down international spy networks, get God knows how many Soviet agents killed, and reveal God knows what-all Soviet secrets, and most of it on the paranoid Stalin's watch. Two witnesses? We don't have a single one. Nobody. Not in all the three-quarters of a century since the HUAC hearings began has a single witness come forth to testify to Alger as a spy. Documentation? A speculation from an unidentified FBI decryptor that the FBI gave up on half a century ago. That's it. Literally. The accusers' Russians can find no evidence. The Russian Russians—and more than a dozen experts have offered assessments of Soviet evidence—can find none.

Here's an alternative scenario. An American aristocrat believes himself to be a knight in shining armor and the bearer of a moral imperative. He looks the part, Hollywood handsome, Harvard brilliant, elegant, graceful. He has lived a charmed, happy life, achieved every goal he strove to achieve—and many that he hasn't—and is poised for the top. He *knows* there is a right way and a wrong way; he *knows* what these ways are and *knows* that he has a crucial role in correcting the global misunderstandings of them that caused two world wars and a terrible economic depression. But he has no street smarts at all; when the dirty fighter Nixon appears, Alger's unconscious snobbery and arrogance won't let him see this bumpkin as one of the smartest politicians in the country's history.

Alger didn't understand that he even *could* be destroyed until he was caged in the human zoo at the West Street center, a no-name convict en route to a stretch at Lewisburg. It's a Biblical downfall and a Greek tragedy: a story of boundless ambition in one man and classical hubris in another.

It's also a cover-up on an unprecedented scale. Alger really is America's Dreyfus. And it's about time the truth came out.

Alger was his confident, optimistic self when he filed for his writ of *coram nobis*.[1] He remained buoyant while the New Prosecution began its onslaught and while court arguments got delayed again and again. He wrote to Dexter that "a right wing organization is asking for permission to appear *amicus curiae* against my request! I regard this as (1) an honor + (2) an indication that the reactionaries think the FBI really needs help (and they do, their briefs so far have been lamentable)."[2] The intransigence of the National Archives to grant him his rights under Freedom of Information: that plainly grated. But the FBI only amused him; he assumed they were "playing actuarial roulette": wait until he's dead before they release any more material. He was certain the decision "will be such a conclusive victory for me that it will all be over next year."[3]

He never mastered a typewriter. All his letters were in longhand. It was a strong, confident script of the spiky variety, straight lines across the page, evenly spaced down it, getting tighter only if he was running out of space, always accurate, always dated. Then there's an abrupt change. "The British press may have carried the news—the bad news—of the denial of my *coram nobis* petition."[4] This is the first letter that isn't dated. The handwriting slopes markedly down to the right; the script is as shaky as he himself was when he was so furious with me that Christmas. "The opinion is a low blow," he wrote, "simply a vulgar, biased recital of the prosecution's loose + intemperate harangue." And then he goes straight on. "We are of course, appealing."

And so he did. Over the next year or so the handwriting regained most of its strength—if not all. Then came the denial of the appeal; the handwriting slanted right down again. The hand was shaking again. But the appeal was going to the Supreme Court; the script grew stronger, if not quite where it was before the denial of the appeal. Then the Supreme Court refused to hear the petition. There's a six-month gap in the correspondence. When it picks up, the handwriting is far worse, cramped now—tight, squeezed—as well as shaky and sloping.

In the next few years, Dexter and I saw him and Isabel as often as the ocean between us allowed. All hopes of overturning any of what Nixon had started were gone, but the maddening man slowly recovered his good spirits; he rarely mentioned his case, and his optimism remained half-infectious, half-annoying. On a late night walk through the ancient streets of Totnes, Dexter made some bleak comment; he was getting old and not liking it one bit.

"Look at that moon, Dexter," Alger said, taking his arm. "How can you be so gloomy when the moon shines like that?"

Then Alger began to go blind: macular degeneration. No more moons to shine at him. He couldn't read. His spirits remained undaunted; he'd loved being read to when he was a child, and now his many friends took turns reading out loud to him as he'd read out loud to Justice Holmes. He continued to write regularly even though he had to guide his right hand by feeling for the edges of the paper with his left, pen following from wrist to little finger as though the border of his hand were a ruler.

—∞—

Dexter came from a long-lived family, and the effects of old age on him were more or less in keeping with that. High blood pressure. Some osteoporosis. Because his balance wasn't so hot, we went to Plymouth for a brain scan; it showed some shrinkage, nothing too terrible really—the result of too many years of smoking—but still something you'd rather not have. We talked to our GP about it.

"If there's anything you really want to do," the GP said, "I'd plan it fairly soon. You know, while you're still feeling fit."

I'd always thought casting spells that made people die were one of the stupidest of ignorant superstitions. Not so. That morning, Dexter had been a man with a future, work to do, things to see. At noon came the GP appointment. By nightfall, he was a dying man, head sunk on his chest. Every day he went downhill. He shrank in height until he was no taller than I am. When he fell on the floor, he couldn't organize his arms and legs to get himself up. Within eighteen months, our GP was saying, "When he stops eating, you've lost him." I wasn't having that. Dexter's brother Tom was a doctor, an *American* doctor in Springfield, Illinois, where Dexter grew up; I'd take him home. Tom would succeed where the British were so clearly failing.

The trouble was, Tom was even older than Dexter; he'd always been jealous of his brilliant younger brother, and his brain was so doddery that he couldn't hide his delight at the mess his rival had become. His wife Mary Jane suffered a stroke not long after we arrived. Dexter's old childhood friends came to the hospital to visit. He was too tired to see them. They stopped coming. Old friends from New York telephoned. He was too tired to talk to them. They stopped calling. Toby came over from Cambridge, where he was working toward a doctorate in philosophy of science. He did his damnedest, but it was an ugly process to watch, and he was having troubles of his own that would have made being away from England extremely difficult at the best of times.

The one stalwart in all this was Alger. He wrote almost every day, an amazingly strong script for a blind man, although it did retain that downward slope. He never got an answer. Neither Toby nor I could face the idea of writing to anybody. The letters came anyway. He wrote about simple things: the pleasure that Thanksgiving hadn't been as commercialized as Christmas, the oddity of fads in children's names, had Dexter read a book about a dog named Tulip?

"A thought for the day," Toby said.

Toward the end, Dexter was too weary even to listen to me reading them out loud. "Oh no," he'd moan. After a while I no longer even opened the letters. But still they came. Right up to the very end.

"The old man's friend": that's what they call pneumonia. What can people be thinking of? Dexter drowned. It took him a week. I railed at my stupidity. Why had I thought one country would succeed where another failed? A dying man is a dying man. If I hadn't been so pigheaded, this one could at least have died in the comfort of his home. Toby blamed Tom. He blamed Mary Jane. He blamed me. Quite right too. There were bitter feelings. There were recriminations. When it was over with—corneas for science and funeral and wake—Toby left for England. I followed a month later.

Battles between parents and kids can get entrenched. I'd assumed the Springfield rift would heal with Tom and his wife no longer a daily reminder. I was wrong. Toby's first post-Dexter visit to Totnes worked only with a very great deal of booze and the good fortune that neither of us is a miserable drunk. The visits became rarer. He gave up work on his doctorate. He severed all connection with his aunt and uncle. Months stretched into years. I stayed in Totnes, made a life for myself. The rift with Toby only deepened, and it stayed that way for a decade.

Throughout all of this, Alger remained as much the stalwart as he had been through Dexter's death. Regular letters. Regular visits to London and regular invitations for me. He and Isabel always stayed at Durrants Hotel; I'd stay a night or so there. It's an elegant townhouse on the outside, but it was a crummy place inside in those days. Alger and Isabel liked it. It was so English, overstuffed chairs, rickety wardrobes, and lamps dressed in what my mother used to call "ladies' panties." And it was cheap, certainly within the budget of a retired salesman and his wife—and well within it if the wife has money of her own.

The last time I saw Alger, I was poor company, still scourging myself for taking Dexter to America. "What would you be thinking now if you hadn't done it?" Alger asked.

That hadn't occurred to me. "I'd probably hate myself."

"Just like now?"

"She's nodding," Isabel said.

He nodded too. "Sometimes there isn't a right thing to do." The three of us were sitting on the double bed in their hotel room because it was too small for chairs. We'd have been more comfortable in the lounge downstairs, but it was cheaper to have a drink upstairs. It's slightly awkward, three people on a bed. Isabel lay down in the middle of it. I sat on one side. Alger sat on the other with his neck twisted toward me even though he couldn't see anything at all anymore.

"Look at him," Isabel said irritably. "There he sits, an eager little puppy, a bright, good little puppy, trying to make you happy. He's happy. How can he be happy? What is he? A blind old man with nothing."

I was embarrassed, wasn't at all sure how to break the silence that followed.

There were ups and downs in the rift between Toby and me. It never really closed, and it was at one of its most painful periods—we hadn't seen each other in months—when I was sitting on that bed at Durrants. Since I'd finished flagellating myself, I covered my embarrassment by complaining about him. Why couldn't he come to terms with life after Dexter? Why couldn't he see that he still had a family? That Tom and his wife hadn't meant any harm? That they were just old? That they needed him? That *I* needed him?

Alger heard me out, thought a moment. "You can't change him, Joanie. You can only change the angle from which you view him."

It wasn't until I came to work on this book that I realized he'd been telling me not only the truth of what I should do but also the secret of how he'd coped with all those years of injustice. He couldn't change what had happened to him, so he'd managed to change the way he looked at it. He'd actually *done* it. And because of it, he'd managed to live, as he'd put it himself, "a happy life."

He died less than a year later.

Acknowledgments

Without four people this book would never have seen the light of day. My peerless agent George Lucas not only edited the rant out of the manuscript but stood by it through some really tough times; most authors can only pray for representation like his. Patricia Williams read the book in an early version, encouraged and encouraged, then read it in a later version and showed to Karl Sabbagh, editor extraordinaire, who had the guts to publish it. But perhaps most of all, I want to thank Evelyn Toynton, who advised on everything from the smallest detail to the most major theme and provided the support throughout that all writers crave and very few get.

One of the most surprising things about this project is that full documentation is right out there in the open for to anybody to see; there's no need for cryptic snippets from secret service archives inaccessible to ordinary citizens. Areas of expertise, though: they call for expert opinions. Politics, for example. Without Sylvia Sutherland—journalist, broadcaster, and five-term mayor of Peterboro, Ontario—I would not have been able to describe the terrifying times Alger lived in or the history that led to them. My cousin Eleanor, retired deputy district attorney, helped me with the complex legal issues involved. Svetlana Chervonnaya, historian, Moscow archivist, broadcaster, put my grasp of spies and spycraft on a far firmer foundation than TV and movies had left it. Jeremy Bigwood, researcher and investigative journalist, braved the National Archives and the FBI on my behalf. Jeff Kisseloff of the Nation Institute and world's expert on the Alger Hiss case did what he could to correct inaccuracies in manuscript. Tony Hiss, Alger's son, did the same. But I emphasize that any mistakes in in the book are entirely my responsibility.

Finally, I must once again thank the South Hams District Council for their Kafkaesque two-and-a-half-year pursuit of me through the courts; that's what fired in my interest in the injustice that had been done—and that continues to be done—to Alger Hiss and his family.

Bibliography

The Alger Hiss Story: Search For The Truth http://www.algerhiss.com/

Alger Hiss, Plaintiff, vs, Whittaker Chambers, Defendant, in the US District Court for the District of Maryland. Civil Case No 4176. Stenographic Typescript. November 1948.

Andrews, Bert & Peter Andrews. *A Tragedy of History: A Journalist's Confidential Role in the Hiss-Chambers Case.* Washington: Luce, 1962.

Archer, Jules. *The Plot to Seize the White House.* Delaware: Skyhorse Publishing, 2007.

Black, Conrad. *Nixon. Richard Milhous Nixon: The Invincible Quest.* London: Quercus, 2007.

Brady, Robert A. *The Spirit and Structure of German Fascism.* New York: The Viking Press, 1937.

Brownell, Will & Richard N. Billings. *So Close to Greatness: A Biography of William C. Bullitt.* New York: Macmillan, 1987.

Bullitt, Orville H., ed. *For the President: Personal & Secret.* Boston: Houghton Mifflin, 1972.

Bullitt, William C. *The Great Globe Itself: A Preface to World Affairs.* London: Macmillan, 1947.

Bullitt, William M. Letters from the Bullitt Family Papers, stored at The Filson Historical Society of Louisville, Kentucky.

Calomiris, Angela. *Red Masquerade: Undercover for the FBI.* Philadelphia: J. B. Lippencott, 1950.

Chambers, Whittaker. *Cold Friday.* New York: Random House, 1962.

Chambers, Whittaker. *Witness.* 50th Anniversary Edition. Washington: Regnery Publishing, Inc., 2001.

Chervonnaya, Svetlana. Documents talk.com: A non-definitive history: http://documentstalk.com/

Chervonnaya, Svetlana. Emails covering several years from August 2009 to January 2012.

Cohen, Mickey. *In My Own Words*. New Jersey: Prentice Hall, 1975.

Cook, Fred J. *The Unfinished Story of Alger Hiss*. New York: Morrow, 1957.

Cooke, Alistair. *A Generation on Trial; U.S.A. v. Alger Hiss*. London. Rupert Hart-Davis, 1950.

Dean, John W. *Blind Ambition: The White House Years*. New York: Simon & Schuster, 1976.

Dearborn, Mary V. *Queen of Bohemia: The Life of Louise Bryant*. New York: Houghtin Mifflin, 1996.

Farago, Ladislas. *War of Wits*. New York: Paperback Library, Inc. 1962.

Gabler, Neal. *An Empire of Their Own*. London: WH Allen, 1989.

Gardner, Virginia. *Friend and Lover: The Life of Louise Bryant*. New York: Horizon Press, 1982.

Gordon, Bernard. *The Gordon File: A Screenwriter Recalls Twenty Years of FBI Surveillance*. Austin, Texas: The University of Texas Press, 2004.

Haldeman, H. R. *The Haldeman Diaries: Inside the Nixon White House*. New York: G.P. Putnam, 1994.

Harbaugh, William H. *Lawyer's Lawyer: The Life of John W. Davis*. New York: Oxford University Press, 1973.

Hartshorn, Lewis. *Alger Hiss, Whitttaker Chambers and the Case That Ignited McCarthyism*. Jefferson, North Carolina: McFarland & Co, 2013.

Haynes, John Earl and Kyrill Anderson. *The Soviet World of American Communism*. New Haven, Connecticut: Yale University Press, 1998.

Hellman, Lillian. *Scoundrel Time*. Boston, Massachusetts: Little, Brown & Co., 1976.

Higham, Charles. *Trading with the Enemy: The Nazi-American Money Plot 1933-1949*. Nebraska: An Authors Guild BackinPrint.com Edition, 2007. Originally published by New York: Delacorte Press, 1983.

Hinchley, Col. Vernon. *Spy Mysteries Unveiled*. London: George G Harrap & Co Ltd., 1963.

Hinchley. Col. Vernon, *Spies Who Never Were*. London: Harrap, 1965.

Hiss, Alger. *In the Court of Public Opinion*. New York: Harper & Row, 1957.

Hiss, Alger. *Recollections of a Life*. London: Unwin Hyman Ltd., 1988.

Hiss, Alger. Letters to Dexter Masters and Joan Brady.

Hiss, Tony. Emails and telephone interviews on various dates.

Hiss, Tony. *Laughing Last: Alger Hiss*. Boston: Houghton Mifflin, 1977.

Hiss, Tony. *The View from Alger's Window: A Son's Memoir*. New York: Alfred A. Knopf, 1999.

Jacoby, Susan. *Alger Hiss and the Battle for History*. London: The Yale University Press, 2009.

Jowett, the Earl of. *The Strange Case of Alger Hiss*. New York: Doubleday & Co. 1953.

Kinzer, Stephen. *The Brothers: John Foster Dulles, Allen Dulles and Their Secret World War*. New York: Henry Holt and Company, 2013. Kindle edition.

Kisseloff, Jeff. The Alger Hiss story, algerhiss.com/

Kisseloff, Jeff. Series of interviews in August 2013.

Kulter, Stanley I. *Abuse of Power: The New Nixon Tapes*. London: The Free Press, 1997.

Lewis, Brad. *Hollywood's Celebrity Gangster: The Incredible Life and Times of Mickey Cohen*. BBL Books, 2007. Kindle edition.

Lisagor, Nancy & Frank Lipsius. *A Law Unto Itself: The Untold Story of the Law Firm Sullivan & Cromwell*. New York: William Morrow & Co., Inc., 1988.

Loftus, John and Mark Aarons. *The Secret War Against the Jews: How Western Espionage Betrayed the Jewish People*. New York: St Martin's Griffin, 1994.

Harvey Matuso, *False Witness*. New York: Cameron & Kahn, 1955.

Miller, William "Fishbait." *Fishbait: The Memoirs of the Congressional Doorkeeper*. New York: Warner Books, 1977.

Mitchell, Greg. *Tricky Dick and the Pink Lady: Richard Nixon vs, Helen Gahagan Douglas*. New York: Random House, 1998.

Mosley, Leonard: *Dulles: A biography of Eleanor, Allen, and John Foster Dulles and their Family Nework*, New York: the Dial Press, 1976.

Moynihan, Daniel Patrick. *Secrecy: The American Experience*. New Haven, Connecticut: Yale University Press, 1988.

Newspaper Archives. http://newspaperarchive.com Newspapers.com at Newspapers.com

New York Times Article Archives http://www.nytimes.com/ref

Nixon, Richard. *Six Crises*. New York: Doubleday & Co, 1962.

Pruessen, Ronald W. *John Foster Dulles*. New York, Macmillan, 1982.

Rabinowitz, Victor. *Unrepentant Leftist: A Lawyer's Memoir*. Urbana and Chicago: University of Illinois Press, 1996.

Reuben, William A. Alger Hiss (Untitled and unpublished manuscript dated Sept 11, 1997. Courtesy of the Tamiment library, New York).

Reuben, William A. Footnote on an Historic Case: In Re Alger Hiss, No. 78 Civ. 3433. New York: The Nation Institute, 1983.

Reuben, William A. The Dream of Whittaker Chambers (unpublished manuscript), Courtesy of the Tamiment library, New York.

Reuben, William A. The Honorable Mr. Nixon and the Alger Hiss Case. New York: Action Books, 1956.

Roberts, Martin. *Secret History*. Indiana: AuthorHouse, 2012. Kindle edition.

Rossinow, Douglas Charles. *Visions of progress: the left-liberal tradition in America*. Pennsylvania: Univ of Pennsylvania Press, 2007.

Ruddy, T. Michael. *The Alger Hiss Espionage Case*. Belmont, California: Thomas Wadsworth, 2005.

Salant, Stephen W. "Bringing Alger Hiss to Justice", *Successful Strategic Deception: A Case Study* (University of Michigan, MPublishing), quod.lib.umich.edu.

Seldes, George. *Facts and Fascism*. New York: In Fact, 2009.

Seth, Ronald. *The Sleeping Truth: the Hiss-Chambers affair: the case that split a nation*. London: Freewin, 1968.

Shevchenko, Arkady N. *Breaking with Moscow*. London: Grafton Books, 1985.

Simpson, Christopher, *Blowback: The First Full Acount of America's Recruitment of Nazis, and its Disastrous Effect on our Domestic and Foreign Policy*. New York: Weidenfeld & Nicholson, 1988.

Smith, John Chabot. *Alger Hiss: The True Story*. New York: Holt Rinehart and Winston, 1976.

Stripling, Robert and Bob Considine. *The Red Plot Against America*. Pennsylvania: Bell Publishing Company, 1949. (Reprint of the original by Kessinger Publishing.)

Summers, Anthony. *Official and Confidential, the official life of J Edgar Hoover*. London: Random House, 2011. Ebury Digital: Kindle edition.

Summers, Anthony. *The Arrogance of Power: The Secret World of Richard Nixon*. New York: Viking Penguin, 2000.

Tannenhaus, Sam. *Whittaker Chambers*. New York: Random House, 1997.

Theoharis, Athan. *Chasing Spies: How the FBI Failed in Counterintelligence but Promoted the Politics of McCarthyism in the Cold War Years*. Chicago: Irving R Dee, 2002.

Thomas, Samuel W. *Oxmoor: The Bullitt Family Estate Near Louisville, Kentucky Since 1987*. Louisville, Kentucky: Butler Book Publishing, 2003.

Tiger, Edith (Editor). *In Re Alger Hiss: Petition of Error Coram Nobis*. New York: Hill and Wang, 1979.

Toledano, Ralph de. *One Man Alone: Richard Nixon*. New York: Funk & Wagnalls, 1969.

U. S. Congress, House, Committee on Un-American Activities: Hearings Regarding Communist Espionage in the United States Government,

July-September 1948 (Government Printing Office, 1948). Text down-
loaded from archive.org/stream/hearingsregardin1948.

Weinstein, Allen. Perjury: *The Hiss-Chambers Case.* New York: Alfred A.
Knopf, 1978.

Wills, Garry. *Nixon Agonistes: The Crisis of the Self-Made Man.* New York:
Mariner Books, 2002.

Worth, E. J. *Whittaker Chambers: The Secret Confession.* London: Massard, 1993.

Yeadon, Glen & John Hawkes. *Nazi Hydra in America: Suppressed History of a
Century.* California: Progressive, 2008.

Zeligs, Mayer A. *Friendship and Fratricide.* New York: The Viking Press, 1967.

Endnotes

Introduction

1   How to recognize Communists during the Red Scare. "Recognizing a Communist: Armed Forces Information Film, No. 5" YouTube. "How to Spot a Communist Using Literary Criticism: A 1955 Manual from the U.S. Military", July 2nd, 2013. Openculture.com.

2   How to recognize terrorists in the UK today. "Terrorism and National Emergencies: Reporting suspected terrorism." Gov.uk. "Terrorism: Terrorism and national emergencies." Metropolitan Police. Content.met. police.uk.

Chapter 2

1   "Chambers had upped the charges . . ." See Chambers' testimony on the role of Communists in government before US House of Representative Committee on Un-American Activities in their "Hearings Regarding Communist Espionage in the United States Government". July-September 1948 (Government Printing Office, 1948) [hereafter HUAC Hearings], 3 August 1948. He specifically mentioned "The Alger Hiss cell . . ." on p 580 in that day's hearing.

2   "a matter of principle . . ." This is a comment Alger made over the crème brulee. See also William H. Harbaugh, *Lawyer's Lawyer: The Life of John W. Davis.* (New York: Oxford University Press, 1973), pp 446-447.

3   "think back" . . . "all kinds of people." Harbaugh, pp 446–447.

Chapter 3

1 "the destruction of life . . ." Robert Stripling and Bob Considine, *The Red Plot Against America*. (Pennsylvania: Bell Publishing Co., 1949), p 14.

2 "The aim and object of Communism are . . ." Stripling, p 14.

3 "you would be liquidated . . ." Stripling, p 266.

4 "the normal American cannot understand." Stripling, p 14.

5 "teachers, preachers, actors . . ." Stripling, p 272.

6 "foreign-born agitator . . ." David E. Rowe and Robert Schulmann, "What Were Einstein's Politics?", George Mason University's History News Network. Hnn.us.

7 Shirley Temple as Communist dupe. Shirley Temple Black. Child Star: An Autobiography. (New York: Warner Books, 1988). pp 252–253.

8 Mr Euripides and Christopher Marlowe: Benedict Nightingale, "Mr. Euripides goes to Washington", *New York Times*, Sept 18, 1988.

9 "Rules of evidence including cross-examination . . ." Annual Report of the Committee on Un-American Activities for the year 1953. p 130. Archive.org.

10 "greatest hotbed of subversives . . ." "Links Movie Chiefs to 'Big Plot on U.S.'" *New York Times*, July 1, 1945.

11 "destroying—as best and as subtly . . ." Stripling, p 71.

12 "disruptive . . ." "Testimony of Ronald Reagan", October 23, 1947. YouTube.

13 "from at I've heard . . ." "Gary Cooper HUAC Testimony Excerpt, 1947." YouTube.

14 "pink" Robert Taylor, "Robert Taylor HUAC Testimony Excerpt, 1947." YouTube.

15 "Fifth Amendment Communists" "The House Un-American Activities Committee" Published 13 August 2012, Civil Liberties. Uscivilliberties.org.

16 "Bertolt Brecht Speaks in the House Committee Un-American Activities." October 30, 1947. YouTube.

17 "On November 24, 1947, Nixon . . ." William A Reuben, unfinished Hiss Manuscript, Chapter 11, Tamiment Library, New York, See also The Tragedy of Albert Maltz: http://www.moderntimes.com/maltz/

Chapter 4

1 "show them promptly . . ." A. Hiss, Public Opinion, p 8.

Chapter 5

1 "Where everything is bent . . ." 1916 Advertisement for Powder Point Boys School King Caesar House Mass.

2 "Alger is the epitome of success." John Chabot Smith, *Alger Hiss: The True Story*. (New York: Holt Rinehart and Winston, 1976), p 50.
3 "most popular" T. Hiss, Laughing Last, p 39.
4 "a celestial time" T. Hiss, Laughing Last, p 55.
5 "You apply pressure . . ." T. Hiss, Laughing Last, p 61.
6 "could well be the Progress . . ." A. Hiss, Recollections, p 59.
7 "heady experience" A. Hiss, Recollections, p 68.
8 "RED 'UNDERGROUND'" *New York Times*, August 4, 1948 "communist cell." HUAC Hearings, 3 August 1948, pp 565, 566, 580.

Chapter 6
1 "Of course, he can get . . ." "Certainly there is no hope . . ." HUAC Hearings, August 3, 1948, p 579.
2 "shocking and utterly untrue . . ." HUAC Hearings, 3 Aug 1948, p 585.
3 "My attention has been called . . ." HUAC Hearings, 4 August 1948, pp 585, 586.

Chapter 7
1 Alger's response to the crowded Caucus room, A. Hiss, Public Opinion, p 8.
2 "drew perhaps the biggest turnout . . ." Stripling, p 11.
3 "under the leadership of men . . ." HUAC Hearings, 3 August 1948. p 579.
4 "who were plotting the overthrow . . ." HUAC Hearings, 6 August 1948, p 622.
5 Russian spies in the government in 1943: HUAC Hearings, 6 August 1948. p 624.
6 "a factory was flown entirely to Russia" HUAC Hearings, 6 August 1948, p 624.
7 Information about the development of the atom bomb. "Manhattan Project: Oak Ridge" Olivedrab.com.
8 "the widespread ramifications of this intense . . ." HUAC Hearings, 6 August 1948 p 64.
9 "Tom Tippett, E. J. Lever . . ." HUAC Hearings 6 August 1948, p 624.
10 "whether the applicant associates with Negroes . . ." HUAC Hearings, 5 Aug 1948, p 634.
11 "an organizer for the Communist Party . . ." HUAC Hearings, 5 Aug 1948, p 630.
12 "Whose wife has been a known Communist . . ." HUAC Hearings, 5 Aug 1948, p 632.

13   "went to fight in Spain . . ." HUAC Hearings, 5 Aug 1948, p 631.

14   "Truman does not want the truth . . . HUAC Hearings, 5 Aug 1948, p 630.

15   "could rightfully be termed the spawning ground . . ." HUAC Hearings, 5 Aug 1948, p 638.

16   "Mr Alger Hiss." HUAC Hearings, 5 Aug 1948, p 642.

Chapter 8

1   "New Deal" as the "Jew Deal": Gabler, Neal. An Empire of Their Own (London: WH Allen, 1989), p 365.

2   "Be seated." HUAC Hearings, 5 Aug 1948, p 642.

3   Stripling's annoyance, Stripling, p 111.

4   "I am not and never have been a member . . ." HUAC Hearings, 5 Aug 1948 p 643. Here and elsewhere in dealing with the hearings, I've pulled together chunks of testimony for the sake of coherence and cut repetitions, but no speeches are altered in any substantive way or taken out of context. Every word quoted appears in the transcripts.

5   "I do not know Mr Chambers . . ." HUAC Hearings, 5 Aug 1948, pp 585, 586.

6   " . . .have never laid eyes on him." HUAC Hearings, 5 Aug 1948, p 643.

7   "I was angered . . ." A. Hiss, Public Opinion, p 10.

8   "I did not." HUAC Hearings, 5 Aug 1948, p 646.

9   "As far as I know . . ." HUAC Hearings, 5 Aug 1948, p 646.

10   "I hoped he would be." HUAC Hearings, 5 Aug 1948, p 647.

11   "I wish I could've seen . . ." HUAC Hearings, 5 Aug 1948, p 646.

12   "The name means absolutely nothing . . ." HUAC Hearings, 5 Aug 1948, p 647.

13   "candid-camera angle from under the chin . . ." HUAC Hearings 25 Aug 1948, p 1140.

14   "I hope you're wrong in . . ." HUAC Hearings, 5 Aug 1948, p 647.

15   "is much heavier than he was . . ." HUAC Hearings, 5 Aug 1948, p 641.

16   "I do know he said that . . ." HUAC Hearings, 5 Aug 1948, p. 647. The misquoted passage: HUAC Hearings, 3 August 1948, p. 572.

17   "When you left the Communist Party . . ." HUAC Hearings, 5 Aug 1948, p 650.

18   "government officials." HUAC Hearings, 5 Aug 1948, 644.

19   "He was simply a pale nonentity . . ." A. Hiss. Recollections, p.203.

20   "the darkly handsome Nixon" Alistair Cooke, *A Generation on Trial; U.S.A. v. Alger Hiss* (London: Rupert Hart-Davis, 1950), p 85.

21   "sharp, incisive, even sarcastic" A. Hiss, Recollections p. 12.

22 Another witness to the proceedings said Nixon turned crimson. Sam Tanenhaus, *Whittaker Chambers* (New York: Random House, 1997), p 234.
23 "Regardless of whether . . ." HUAC Hearings, 5 Aug 1948, p 644.
24 "The Chair wishes to express the appreciation . . ." HUAC Hearings, 5 Aug 1948, p 659.
25 "Hiss won the day completely." Richard Nixon, *Six Crises* (New York: Doubleday & Co, 1962), p. 9.

Chapter 9

1 "There was no grass to be preserved . . ." A. Hiss, Recollections, p 188
2 "As I had done nothing to flee from . . ." A. Hiss, Recollections, p. 188
3 "No person of Jewish blood . . ." quoted in Robert Brady's *The Spirit and Structure of German Fascism* (New York: The Viking Press, 1937), p 53.

Chapter 10

1 "How is the Committee going . . . The committee stands convicted." Nixon, *Six Crises*, p 9.
2 "Strip, you fellows have really put your foot in . . ." Stripling, p 116.
3 "an elite group, an outstanding group" HUAC Hearings, 3 Aug 1948, p 577.
4 "There is no basis for the statements . . ." HUAC Hearings, 3 Aug 1948, p 578.
5 "I deny unqualifiedly . . ." HUAC Hearings, 5 Aug 1948, p 642.
6 "complete fabrications" HUAC Hearings, 5 Aug 1948, p 643.
7 "completely unfounded." HUAC Hearings, 5 Aug 1948, p 658.
8 "transmitting secrets . . ." HUAC Hearings, 5 Aug 1948, p 646.
9 "We're ruined!" Stripling, p 116.
10 "Hiss said, 'So help me . . .'" Stripling, p 111.
11 "You cannot be a Communist . . ." Stripling, p 169.
12 "Do you solemnly swear . . ." HUAC Hearings, 5 Aug 1948, p 642.
13 Nixon claims never to have heard of Alger Hiss before Chambers mentioned him: Nixon, Six Crises, p 6.
14 Nixon also claims that nobody at HUAC had met Chambers before the hearings: Richard Nixon, June 26, 1950, Speech to the House of Representatives, as quoted in William A. Reuben, *The Honorable Mr. Nixon and the Alger Hiss Case* (New York: Action Books, 1956), p 8.
15 "Dies . . . assumed Chambers was the chief KGB . . ." Whittaker Chambers FBI file, L. R. Pennington to D. M. Ladd, dated February 3, 1949.
16 Ruben Hiss manuscript chap 7, p. 8 Martin dies wrote that WC" had come to my office several times" during world War two and "for some time" prior to 1948.

17   "Chambers began to contact my very able chief investigator and secretary, Robert Stripling." Quoted from Martin Dies regular column in the May 1964 issue of *American Opinion.*

18   Nixon's August Interim Report, Reuben, *Dream* p 35

19   "tomorrow's witness on the subject of Russian . . ." William A. Ruben, The Dream Of Whittaker Chambers, p 34, footnote p 49. Unpublished manuscript from the Tamiment library in New York. HUAC hearings August 3 page 562.

20   Records on Alger: Anthony Summers, *The Arrogance of Power: The Secret World of Richard Nixon* (New York: Viking Penguin, 2000), p 65.

21   Investigation on the grounds that Alger might "become" disloyal, William A Reuben, Unpublished work entitled Hiss Manuscript, Chap, 21, p 5.

22   Several staff members were former FBI agents: Roberts, Loc 1928. "we should be able to establish . . ." Nixon, *Six Crises,* p 12.

23   "Often people are convicted of a related . . ." Email to the author, 02 Apr 12 "I do not know Mr Chambers . . ." HUAC Hearings 4 Aug 1948, pp 585-586.

24   "a red party book . . ." Whittaker Chambers, *Witness.* (Washington: Regnery Publishing, Inc., 2001) p 207.

25   Mandel working for HUAC since 1939: Mayer A. Zeligs, *Friendship and Fratricide.* (New York: The Viking Press, 1967) Note p 78.

26   Chambers using the name "Carl" during the time he knew Alger: Nixon, *Six Crises,* p 8.

27   "I carefully read the entire transcript . . ." HUAC Hearings, 5 Aug 1948, p 646.

Chapter 11

1   Nixon's mother's back ground: Summers, *Arrogance of Power,* p 5.

2   Scholarships to both Harvard and Yale: Summers, *Arrogance of Power,* p 15.

3   "Shifty eyed" Nancy Lisagor & Frank Lipsius, *A Law Unto Itself: The Untold Story of the Law Firm Sullivan & Cromwell* (New York: William Morrow & Co., Inc.) 1988, p 168.

4   Nixon as prosecuting attorney Flint in Ayn Rand's *Night of January 16th*: Scott Meredith. "Richard the Actor." *Ladies Home Journal,* Sept 1975, pp 52-54.

5   "A man who can't hold a hand in a first-class poker . . ." "Tricky Dicky" by Michael Kaplan, Poker Player, October 2005. Pokerplayer.co.uk.

6   "He became tops . . ." Bela Kornitzer, The Real Nixon. Pokerplayer.co.uk.

7   "I once watched him bluff . . ." Stephen Ambrose, The Education of a Politician. Pokerplayer.co.uk.

8   "mystery" The biographer quoted was David Wise, *The American Police State* (New York: Random House, 1976), p 130 fn, as cited in Summers, *Arrogance of Power*, p 62.

9   "aircraft firms such as Bell and Glen Martin" Ralph de Toledano, *One Man Alone: Richard Nixon* (New York: Funk & Wagnalls, 1969), p 40.

10 Kontinentale Ol A. G.: Loftus, John and Mark Aarons, *The Secret War Against the Jews: How Western Espionage Betrayed the Jewish People* (New York: St Martin's Griffin, 1994), p 221.

11 Profits for German and American investors: Lisagor, Chapter 8, "Nazi Clients", p119-142, and Chapter 9, "The Dulles War Machine", pp 143-159. See also Charles Higham, *Trading with the Enemy: The Nazi American Money Plot 1933-1949* (New York Delacorte Press, 1983).

12 Drew Pearson. "Merry-go-round: Dulles Linked With Nazis." Bell-McClure Syndicate. October 4, 1948.

13 Dulles vouched for Kontentale: Loftus, Secret War, p 221.

14 John Foster Dulles as Farben's lawyer: Lisagor, *A Law Unto Itself*, See Chapters 8 and 9. See also Higham, *Trading with the Enemy*.

15 Stephen Zinzer. *The Brothers: John Foster Dulles, Allen Dulles and Their Secret World War* (New York: Henry Holt & Co, 2013) (Kindle edition) Loc, 880.

16 "gave the Nazis a stranglehold . . ." Lisagor, *A Law Unto Itself*, p 148.

17 "most significant wartime activity . . ." Lisagor, *A Law Unto Itself*, p 146.

18 "to keep quiet about what he had seen . . ." Loftus, *Secret War*, p. 221, 557; Summers, Arrogance of Power p. 62, Note 3 p 488.

19 "WANTED-Congressman candidate . . ." Toledano, *One Man Alone*, p 45.

20 "Are you a Republican and are you available?" by Mae Brussell (from The Realist, August 1972) http://www.maebrussell.com/Mae%20Brussell%20Articles/How%20Nixon%20Actually%20Got%20Into%20Power.html

21 "A little fish house where politicians . . ." Summers, *Arrogance of Power*, p 54.

22 Mickey Cohen, *In My Own Words* (New Jersey: Prentice Hall, 1975), p 232.

23 "bad feeling" . . . "a three-card Monte dealer" Ibid, p 234.

24 "I jewed him down to $5,000," Ibid, p 233. Space for Nixon for Congress headquarters: Ibid, p. 378.

25 Assessment of Jerry Voorhis. Conrad Black, *Richard Milhous Nixon: The Invincible Quest* (London: Quercus, 2007), p 81.

26 Nixon's campaign expenses of $40,000: Black, Richard Milhous Nixon: p 87.

27 "not for ads but for planted news stories . . ." W. E. Smith. Letter to Drew Pearson, Oct 27, 1952. Drew Pearson Papers.

28 "six pro-Soviet votes" Richard M. Nixon: A Life in Full, Conrad Black page 83

29 "A vote for Nixon is a vote . . ." Kenworthy, E.W., "In the shadow of the President" *New York Times.* 5 August 1956.

30 "Did you know Jerry Voorhis had Communistic . . ." Drew Pearson, "Washington Merry-go-round", Bell-McClure Syndicate, Nov 1, 1968.

31 "I know Jerry Voorhis wasn't a Communist" Greg Mitchell, *Tricky Dick and the Pink Lady: Richard Nixon vs, Helen Gahagan Douglas* (New York: Random House, 1998), p 43.

32 "The important thing is to win." Lamar Waldron, *Watergate: The Hidden History: Nixon, the Mafia, and the CIA* (Berkeley, CA: Counterpoint, 2012), p 35.

33 "In a class by himself was young, handsome Alger Hiss . . ." May 28, 1945: Zeligs, p 338.

34 Life magazine's "Picture of the Week", July 16, 1945: Zeligs, p 338.

35 "a product of New World courtesy . . ." Cooke, p 108.

36 "Nixon had his hat set for Hiss . . ." Weinstein, Perjury (Author interview), p 17.

Chapter 12

1 My economist father's two relevant books are: Robert A. Brady *The Rationalization Movement in German Industry* (New York: Columbia University Press, 1933); and *The Spirit and Structure of German Fascism* (New York: The Viking Press, 1937).

2 Robert A. Brady: "The records which may be responsive . . ." Letter to Jeremy Bigwood from David M. Hardy, Section Chief, Record/Information Dissemination Section, Records Management Division, Federal Bureau of Investigation, Washington, D.C, 20535, 9 Nov, 2010. FOIPA Request no.: 1155796-000.

3 Mildred Edie Brady:"The records which may be responsive . . ." Letter to Bigwood from David M. Hardy, Section Chief, Record/Information Dissemination Section, Records Management Division, Federal Bureau of

Investigation, Washington, D.C, 20535., 27 Nov 2010, FOIPA Request No.;1157018-000.

4 "be inserted in our Simple Case processing . . ." National Archives to Bigwood.

Chapter 13

1 December 15, 2010 Alger as a bad case of a "name" person: A. Hiss, *Public Opinion*, p 9.

2 "I discussed it by telephone with my lawyer . . ." Zeligs, p 10.

3 "Dulles was strongly opposed . . ." Zeligs, p 10.

4 "Unknown to Hiss, Nixon . . ." Harbaugh, p 447.

5 The Dulles brothers' collaboration with the Nazis is detailed in many books. See Kinzer, *The Brothers;* Yeadon, Glen & John Hawkes, *Nazi Hydra in America: Suppressed History of a Century.* (California: Progressive, 2008); Higham, Charles, *Trading with the Enemy,* Seldes, George, *Facts and Fascism* (New York: In Fact, 2009).

6 "convict the sonofabitch . . ." Kulter, Stanley I., *Abuse of Power: The New Nixon Tapes* (London: The Free Press, 1997) p 10.

7 "I had to leak stuff . . ." Kulter, *Abuse of Power* p 7.

8 "the whole spy case." William Reuben, *The Honorable Mr Nixon and the Alger Hiss Case* (New York: Action Books, 1957), p 17.

9 "a Committee spokesman" Reuben, *The Honorable Mr Nixon,* p 17.

10 "mystery witness" to corroborate Chambers: "Mystery Witness May Crack Soviet Spy Case: Reds Claimed Sent Uranium", AP report, Aug 6, 1948.

11 "a special committee . . ." Reuben, *The Honorable Mr Nixon,* p17.

Chapter 14

1 Letters about traffic with the devil: Roberts, *Secret History* Loc 559, Also Zeligs, *Friendship and Fratricide,* pp 55-60.

2 Mark Van Doren pronounces the play "brilliant": Zeligs, 69.

3 'daily life' of a young Communist . . ." "Whittaker chambers in the CP USA files 1927-1932", DocumentsTalk.com.

4 "I suddenly awoke in the midst of having . . ." Zeligs, p 216.

5 "expected the worst" Zeligs, Friendship and Fratricide, p 118

6 "always reminding everyone . . ." Zeligs, p 61, Zeligs interview with Trilling.

7 "literally dozens of people in Greenwich Village . . ." E. J. Worth, *Whittaker Chambers: The Secret Confession* (London: Mazzard, 1993) Letter to the author, p 38.

8   "a desperate sort of secret agent . . ." Zeligs, p 127.

9   Chambers uses a dead baby's identity to get a passport: Zeligs, p 264-265.

10 Chambers steals identity of Jay Lea Chambers: Edith Tiger, (Editor). *In Re Alger Hiss: Petition of Error Coram Nobis* (New York: Hill and Wang, 1979) Exhibit 5, p 138-140.

11 Chambers remaining listed in the Baltimore telephone directory: Hartshorn, Lewis, *Alger Hiss, Whitttaker Chambers and the Case That Ignited McCarthyism* (McFarland & Co.: 2013), p 146.

12 "furloughed", awaiting a position for which he was "deemed qualified": Zeligs p. 296 letter to Mr. Jay V. David Chambers, 2124 Mount Royal Ter., Baltimore, MD, from Janet L. Wile, Senior Administrative Secretary, for the Director.

13 Details of Jay Lea Chambers's dossier disappearing from the State Department files. Zeligs, footnote 23 page 252. "Private investigator's report" from the Hiss defense files, November 1, 1948.

14 Visit to Mark van Doren: Van Doren, *Autobiography of Mark van Doren* (New York: Harcourt Brace and code, 1958), pp 218-19.

15 English publisher worried that his "violently anti-Communist views" *In Re Alger Hiss,* p 59.

16 "hiding from the Russian Secret Service" Tiger, Edith (Editor). In Re Alger Hiss, 1979, p 59.

17 Chambers inspired by Krivitsky, seeks out Levine, Hartshorn, pp 252-254.

18 "the tranquil years" Title of Chapter 10, Witness Whittaker Chambers

19 US Attorney General Thomas Donegan, head of the FBI's "Comintern Apparatus Squad" "Baltimore Documents, A Legal Issue" Documentstalk.com "loose memory".

20 "FBI Silvermaster File/Thomas J Donegan 1945-1950", Vol. 147, Serials 3691-2730 Documentstalk.com.

Chapter 15

1 "undisclosed destination." AP Report, 5 Aug 1948.

2 "revelations were so startling . . ." INS News Report, Aug 7, 1948.

3 "Mr. Hiss in his testimony was asked . . ." HUAC Hearings, 7 Aug 1948, p 661.

4 "My relationship with Alger Hiss quickly . . ." HUAC Hearings, 7 Aug 1948, p 670.

5 "kind of informal headquarters." HUAC Hearings, 7 Aug 1948, p 665.

6 "The only thing I recall was a small leather . . ." HUAC Hearings, 7 Aug 1948, p 667.

7 Chambers can remember no other details of the Hisses' house: HUAC Hearings, 7 Aug 1948, p 665.

8 "They cared nothing . . ." HUAC Hearings, 7 Aug 1948, p 666.

9 "He was forbidden to go . . ." HUAC Hearings, 7 Aug 1948, p 669.

10 "a man of great simplicity . . ." HUAC Hearings, 7 Aug 1948, p 666.

11 "puny" . . .

12 "he had rather long, delicate . . ." HUAC Hearings, 7 Aug p 669.

13 "his walk, if you watch him from . . ." HUAC Hearings, 7 Aug 1948, p 668.

14 "his hand cupped . . ." HUAC Hearings, 7 Aug 1948, p 668.

15 "I was told by Mr Peters." HUAC Hearings, 7 Aug 1948, p 662.

16 "individually" HUAC Hearings, 7 Aug 1948, p 663.

17 "rather pious about paying . . ." HUAC Hearings, 7 Aug 1948, p 663.

18 "No, I did not." HUAC Hearings, 3 Aug 1948, p 569.

19 Collins as dues-collector who gave Chambers a bagful of money: HUAC Hearings, 3 Aug 1948, p 571.

20 "came to 10 percent . . ." HUAC Hearings, 3 Aug 1948, p 571.

21 "made an affidavit concerning . . ." HUAC Hearings, 7 Aug 1948, p 671.

22 "MR NIXON: At what period did you know . . ." HUAC Hearings, 7 Aug 1948, p, 662.

23 Length of hearing: 10:30AM on p 660 to 1:10PM on p 672. HUAC Hearings, 7 Aug 1948.

24 "For a year I lived in hiding . . ." HUAC Hearings, 3 Aug 1948, p 566.

Chapter 16

1 Andrews known as a man who'd do anything for a story: Smith, *Alger Hiss,* p 190.

2 "to be kept between these . . ." HUAC Hearings, Aug 16, 1948 p 936.

3 Nixon shows testimony to Rogers and Kersten: Smith, *Alger Hiss,* p 191.

4 "In view of the facts Chambers has . . ." Nixon, *Six Crises,* p 21. See also earlier reference, Summers, *Arrogance of Power,* p 62 note 3, p 488.

5 "digging into all phases . . ." Reuben, *Honorable Mr Nixon,* p 22.

6 "unable to find a flaw . . ." AP report, Aug 14, 1948

7 "Mystery Witness Talks . . ." UP Report, 7 Aug 1948.

8 "Key Witness Heard . . ." William R. Conklin, *New York Times,* Aug 8, 1948.

9 "visited Chambers at his farm . . ." See Reuben, *Honorable Mr Nixon,* p23.

10 "lying on the critical issues . . ." See Reuben, *The Honorable Mr Nixon,* p22.

11   "the spy case." See Reuben, *The Honorable Mr Nixon,* p 22.

12   "A stranger had unaccountably said . . ." A Hiss, *Public Opinion,* p 13.

13   "Chambers in his secret testimony . . ." A Hiss, *Public Opinion,* p 12.

14   "A dramatic face-to-face . . ." Datelined Washington, 15 Aug 1948.

15   Hoover warns of connection between Rockefellers' Standard Oil of New Jersey and the Reichsbank: Higham, *Trading with the Enemy,* p 21.

16   The Bush family and the Union Bank: Ben Aris and Duncan Campbell, "How Bush's grandfather helped Hitler's rise to power", *The Guardian,* 25 September 2004.

Chapter 17

1   "photographers scrambled, crouched for angle shots . . ." Chambers, *Witness,* p 538.

2   "no more than five feet tall . . ." Lester Cole, *Hollywood Red: The Autobiography of Lester Cole* (California: Ramparts Press, 1981), p 273.

3   "As at the first hearing . . ." A Hiss, *Public Opinion,* p. 20.

4   "Do you recall having known . . ." HUAC Hearings, 16 Aug 1948, p 938.

5   "Your testimony is then . . ." HUAC Hearings, 16 Aug 1948, p 938.

6   Nixon repeats the timeframe nine times: HUAC Hearings, 16 Aug 1948, pp 398 (3 times), 492, 944, 953, 954, 960, 962.

7   Alger again refuses to identify from photographs: HUAC Hearings, 16 Aug 1948, p, 940, 947.

8   "I honestly have the feeling . . ." HUAC Hearings, 16 Aug 1948, p 946.

9   "You can be very sure when . . ." HUAC Hearings, 16 Aug 1948, p 946.

10   "I have written a name on this pad . . ." HUAC Hearings, 16 Aug 1948, p 948.

11   "Never mind feelings . . ." HUAC Hearings, 16 Aug1948, p 949.

12   "Either you or Mr Chambers is lying." HUAC Hearings, 16 Aug 1948, p 951.

13   "Has no bearing on his credibility?" HUAC Hearings 16 Aug 1948, p 952.

14   "You show me a good police force . . ." HUAC Hearings 16 Aug 1948, p 952.

15   "You have made your position clear . . ." HUAC Hearings, 16 Aug 1948, p 952.

16   "I met him when I was working . . ." HUAC Hearings, 16 Aug 1948, p 955.

17   "I can't remember when it was I finally . . ." HUAC Hearings, 16 Aug 1948, p 957.

18   "Yes, in the sense that I said . . ." HUAC Hearings, 16 Aug 1948, p 969.

19   "That is why I say I can't believe . . ." HUAC Hearings, 16 Aug 1948, p 970.

20   "Very bad teeth," HUAC Hearings, 16 Aug 1948, p 956.

21   "were decayed and one of them was split . . ." A Hiss, *Public Opinion*, pp 12-13.

22   "a devastation of empty sockets . . ." Smith, *Alger Hiss*, p 217.

23   "Do you think those are relevant questions . . ." HUAC Hearings 16, Aug 48, p 971.

24   "Mr. Hiss, the Committee has unanimously . . ." HUAC Hearings 16, Aug 48, 972.

Chapter 18

1   "Here I was intent on revisiting . . ." A. Hiss, *Recollections*, p. 188.

2   "I could not hope to better my lot . . ." A. Hiss, *Recollections*, p 190.

3   "self-confidence remained boundless . . ." A. Hiss, *Recollections*, p. 190.

4   "she's always known, as I did . . ." T. Hiss, *Laughing Last*, p 186.

5   "deeply embedded altruism . . ." Zeligs, p.173.

6   "Isabel has, I'm sure, covered . . ." Personal letter: Alger Hiss to Joan Brady and Dexter Masters 14 December 1968.

7   "All the odds clearly favour . . ." Personal letter: Alger Hiss to Dexter Masters, 28 Sept 1968.

8   "was a time of intellectual aberration . . ." Personal letter: Alger Hiss to Dexter Masters, 28 Sept 1968.

9   "I am coming in May or June . . ." Personal letter: Alger Hiss to Dexter Masters, 28 Sept 1968.

10   "Isabel brought back a glowing account . . ." Personal letter: Alger Hiss to Dexter Masters, 20 Sept 1969.

11   "My great moral dread . . ." T. Hiss, *Laughing Last*, p 51.

12   "despite an alpha double plus intellect . . ." Tony Hiss, *The View from Alger's Window: A Son's Memoir* (New York: Alfred A. Knopf, 1999), p 227.

13   "I just couldn't believe . . ." T. Hiss, *Laughing Last*, p 131.

14   "I remember he told me . . ." HUAC Hearings, 16 Aug 1948, p 958.

15   Story about the homeless man: Jeff Kisseloff, telephone conversation with the author, 22 Aug 2013.

16   "dissonance in the system . . ." Joe Kloc, "Too Close for Comfort", New Scientist 12 Jan 2013, pp 35-37.

17   "Indeed you can usually tell when . . ." *Reflections of a Siamese Twin: Canada at the End of the Twentieth Century* (Penguin Books Australia: September 24, 1998).

Chapter 19

1   "I again had the sense of . . ." A. Hiss, *Public Opinion*, p 37.

2   "public grilling" A. Hiss, *Public Opinion*, p 80.

3   "You are the guests of the Committee . . ." HUAC Hearings, 13 Aug 1948, p 904.

4   "Just a minute, right there. .." HUAC Hearings, 13 Aug 1948, p 881.

5   "I would say you had an athlete's heart . . ." HUAC Hearings, 13 Aug 1948, p 882

6   "as they jump out of windows." Drew Pearson's "Washington-Merry-Go- Round." Bell-McClure Syndicate, Dec 27, 1948.

7   "HISS ADMITS ACQUAINTANCE . . ." AP Report, 17 Aug 1948.

8   "LIE DETECTOR TEST FOR . . ." *Herald Tribune*, 17 August 1948.

9   "The Committee had been unable to reach a decision..." UP and AP Reports, 16 Aug 1948, very widely published; also INS Report, Aug 17, 1948.

10 "Alger Hiss, who first denied knowing . . ." Rose McKee, Reuben, *Honorable Mr Nixon*, p 37.

11 "an improvised hearing room." A. Hiss, *Public Opinion*, p 81.

12 "The record will show . . ." HUAC Hearings, 17 Aug 1948, p 274.

13 "In that connection, Mr. Hiss . . ." HUAC Hearings, 17 Aug 1948, p 977.

14 "Short, plump, perspiring . . ." A. Hiss, *Public Opinion*, p 85.

15 "Mr. Hiss, the man standing here is Mr . . ." HUAC Hearings, 17 Aug 1948, p 977.

16 "May I ask him to speak?" HUAC Hearings, 17 Aug 1948, p 977.

17 "Mr. Chambers, will you . . ." HUAC Hearings, 17 Aug 1948, p 978.

18 "tight", "high-pitched", "strangled" A. Hiss, *Public Opinion*, p 85.

19 "with a low and rather dramatic roundness . . ." HUAC Hearings, 16 Aug 1948, p 960.

20 Chambers's voice: "Whittaker Chambers Teaser Trailer" YouTube.

21 "Could you open your mouth wider?" HUAC Hearings, 17 Aug 1948, p 978.

22 Chambers admitted to name George Crosley long after hearing: Reuben, *Honorable Mr Nixon*, p 31.

23 "I feel very strongly that he is Crosley . . ." HUAC Hearings, 17 Aug 1948, pp 978, 979.

24 "Do I have Mr. Nixon's permission?" HUAC Hearings, 17 Aug 1948, p 985.

25 "Not to my knowledge..." "That is the answer." *HUAC Hearings*, 17 August 1948, pp 986-987.

26 "a vast sense of relief" A. Hiss, *Public Opinion*, p 90.

27 "To come here and discover . . . do it damned quickly." HUAC Hearings, 17 August 1948, p 988.

28 "recoiled as if he had been pricked . . ." Nixon, *Six Crises*, p 36.

29 "Mr. Hiss maintains . . ." HUAC Hearings, 17 August 1948 p 992.

30 "You are fully aware . . ." HUAC Hearings, 17 August 1948 pp 990, 989, 993.

31 "Alger Hiss not only knew . . ." INS Report, Aug 18, 1948.

32 "'The impression given to the public,' Nixon said . . ." AP release dated Wash, DC, August 17, 1948.

Chapter 20

1 For a current discussion of Nixon's leaks to the South Vietnamese, see Michael A. Cohen, "Nixon: Not Just Criminal, But Treasonous", *The Guardian*, 11 Jan 2013.

Chapter 21

1 Classification of Mildred Edie Brady's files confirmed by the National Archives: June 21, 2011 and April 27, 2011.

2 The files . . .include information on how . . .": "Records of the Federal Bureau of Investigation (Record Group 65); FBI Records Declassified Under the War Crimes Disclosure Act." Archives.gov.

3 Alger role Nye Committee investigations into United Aircraft deals with Germany for use: Smith, *Alger Hiss*, p 8.

4 "nearly all armed with American guns . . ." The Mail Archive, "Report of Nye Committee Hearings Sept 1934" Mail-archive.com.

5 Bush Union Bank and I. G. Farben: Ben Aris and Duncan Campbell. "How Bush's grandfather helped Hitler's rise to power." *The Guardian*, 25 September 2004.

Chapter 22

1 "unimportant" A. Hiss, *Public Opinion*, p 104.

2 Hoover leaking Nixon: Summers, *Arrogance of Power*, p 65.

3 "Let's put it this way. He had . . ." Anthony Summers, *Official and Confidential, the Official Life of J Edgar Hoover* (Random House. Kindle edition), Loc 3577, p 196.

4 Involvement of US Army's Counter Intelligence Corps in the Hiss case: Stephen W. Salant, "Bringing Alger Hiss to Justice", Successful Strategic Deception: A Case Study (University of Michigan, MPublishing), quod. Lib.umich.edu.

5   The information "was handed to" Nixon: Walter Trohan, letter to Lou Nichols, Jan 10, 1974, quoted in Summers, *Arrogance of Power,* p. 78.

6   "Nixon was playing with a stacked deck . . ." Summers, *Arrogance of Power,* p 66.

7   "I deny them categorically." Donald Hiss, HUAC Hearings, Aug 13 1948, p 929.

8   "I should go to jail." HUAC Hearings, Aug 13 1948, p 933.

9   Chambers had described "furniture, paintings on the walls . . ." HUAC Hearings, Aug 18, 1948; Reuben, *Honorable Mr Nixon,* p 34.

10 "Richard M Nixon predicted that . . ." Reuben, *The Honorable Mr Nixon,* p 33.

11 "Representative Nixon, Republican of California, said . . ." Reuben, *The Honorable Mr Nixon,* p 36.

12 "Alger Hiss was linked . . ." Reuben, *Honorable Mr Nixon,* p 38.

Chapter 23

1   "Ballyhooed into a circus" HUAC Hearings, 16 Aug 1948, p 972.

2   The day was "infernal": Cooke, p 85

3   "Sweltering", "blistering" *The News,* Frederick, Maryland 26 August 1948, p 1.

4   "sun rays like hammer blows" *Logansport Press,* Logansport, Indiana, August 26 1948, p 1.

5   "the operation within the Government . . ." HUAC Hearings, 25 Aug 1948, p. 1075.

6   "Mr. Alger Hiss was a member . . ." HUAC Hearings, 25 Aug 1948, p 1075.

7   "As a result of this hearing . . ." HUAC Hearings, 25 Aug 1948, p 1076.

8   "Mr. Stripling, the first witness." HUAC Hearings, 25 Aug 1948, p 1076.

9   "Not at this point," HUAC Hearings, 25 Aug 1948, p 1078.

10 International Soundphoto, Aug 27, 1948. See "Alger Hiss Spying" YouTube.

11 "I don't recall a man . . ." HUAC Hearings, 25 Aug 1948, p 1148.

12 Nixon quotes them all quoting Nixon: HUAC Hearings, 25 Aug 1948, p 1148-1149.

13 "The impression is that you categorically . . ." HUAC Hearings, 25 Aug 1948, p 1127.

14 "Never mind the evidence . . ." HUAC Hearings, 25 Aug 1948, p 1123.

15 "to innumerable people. Without hesitancy . . ." HUAC Hearings, 25 Aug 1948, p 1140.

16   "I would just like to register a protest . . ." HUAC Hearings, 25 Aug 1948, p 1081.

17   "Just checking through the record . . ." HUAC Hearings, 25 Aug 1948, p 1095.

18   "Well, now, just a moment on that point . . ." HUAC Hearings, 25 Aug 1948, p 1097.

19   "I wish you would make a statement . . ." HUAC Hearings, 25 Aug 1948, p 1097.

20   "Never mind. You keep quiet . . ." HUAC Hearings, 25 Aug 1948, p 1143.

21   "No, no. You be quiet . . ." HUAC Hearings, 25 Aug 1948, p 1144.

22   "On every point on which we have been . . ." HUAC Hearings, 25 Aug 1948, p 1160.

23   "to the best of my recollection" HUAC Hearings, 25 Aug 1948, p 1106.

24   "suavity" HUAC Hearings, 25 Aug 1948, p 1141.

25   "it is very hard to know very much . . ." HUAC Hearings, 25 Aug 1948, p 1098.

26   "a very agile young man" HUAC Hearings, 25 Aug 1948, p 1117.

27   "a very clever young man." HUAC Hearings, 25 Aug 1948, p 1139.

28   "Either you or Mr Chambers is the damnedest . . ." HUAC Hearings, 25 Aug 1948, p 1141.

29   "I have had some occasion to check . . ." HUAC Hearings, 25 Aug 1948, p 1175.

30   "to make the statements about me . . ." HUAC Hearings, 25 Aug 1948, p 1166.

31   "risks" "assassination" "ambush"? HUAC Hearings 27 Aug 1948, p 1109.

32   "You admitted frankly that you . . ." HUAC Hearings, 25 Aug 1948, p 1200.

33   "We are caught in a tragedy . . ." HUAC Hearings, 25 Aug 1948, p 1191.

34   "At that last meeting in 1938 . . ." HUAC Hearings, 25 Aug 1948, p 1178.

35   "Well, now, will you describe . . ." HUAC Hearings, 25 Aug 1948, p 1190.

36   "come before this committee, as they so frequently . . ." HUAC Hearings, 25 Aug 1948, pp 1206-1206.

Chapter 24

1   "Spy Probers Hunt 1929 . . ." AP Report, 26 1948

2   "Committee Fails to Trap Hiss . . ." UP Report, Aug 26, 1948.

3   "Hiss vs Chambers", *Washington Post,* August 27, 1948.

4   "Death Toll Climbs to Five" *Zanesville Signal,* Zanesville, Ohio, 29 Aug 1948.

5   "200 Deaths Blamed on Heat" *Middletown Times Herald,* Middletown, New York, 30 Aug 1948.

6   " . . .certainly wasn't doing anything directly for the Russians." William A. Reuben, "Libel." The Alger Hiss Story.

7   "badly shaken": "Hiss and Chambers: Strange Story of Two Men", by Robert Whalen, *New York Times,* December 12, 1948.

8   "a definite, provable link . . ." Reuben, *Honorable Mr Nixon,* p 45.

9   "There is no longer any doubt in my mind . . ." Smith, *Alger Hiss,* pp 233, 234.

10 "personal knowledge . . ." Stephen J. Whitfield, *Culture of the Cold War,* (Johns Hopkins University Press, 1996) p 30.

11 "Roosevelt administration . . .criminally 'soft' . . ." Cooke, p 37.

12 "a waking plot initiated long ago . . ." Cooke, p 37.

13 "A cornerstone of the Republican campaign . . ." Fred Cook, "Typewriters Are Always the Key", *New York Times,* 14 Oct 1977.

14 "SENSATIONAL SPY DISCLOSURE . . ." INS Report, 31 Aug, 1948.

15 "INQUIRY TO EXPOSE THIRD . . ." *New York Times,* Sep 3, 1948.

16 "Well, Alger, where's that suit?" Lloyd Chaisson, *The Press on Trial,* (Praeger, 1997) p 137.

17 "Deeply emotional people . . ." Chambers, p 719.

18 "the spirit of a man on the rack . . ." Chambers, p 721.

19 "to remove me as the one dangerous . . ." Chambers, p 721.

20 little Chamberses calling Nixon "Nixie": Chambers, footnote p 173.

21 "HISS BRINGS SUIT AGAINST . . ." *New York Times,* Sept 28, 1948.

22 "I welcome Alger Hiss's daring suit." Chambers, Witness, p 722.

23 "Communists in High Places." *The Independent,* Long Beach Cal, 3 Oct 1948.

24 "HEAR THE TRUTH" *Reno Evening Gazette,* Reno, Nevada, Oct 4, 6, 7 1948, pages 13, 2, 13 respectively.

25 "are afraid of the political . . ." Reuben, *Honorable Mr Nixon,* p 49.

26 "one eye on publicity . . ." Reuben, *Honorable Mr Nixon,* p 47.

27 "Could you give one name of anybody . . ." Reuben, *Honorable Mr Nixon,* p 50.

28 Reports re Communist spy rings in the State Department: AP Report, *Oakland Tribune,* 14 October, 1948, p 1.

29 "one of the undergrounds . . ." UPI report, 14 October 1948.

30   "DEWEY DEFEATS TRUMAN" 4 November 1948, UPI photograph.

Chapter 26

1   "You must cut yourself off . . ." *Red Spy Queen: A Biography of Elizabeth Bentley,* p 97, attachment to email from Svetlana Chervonnaya, 12 October 2009.

2   "to assist the bankers . . ." Heynes & Klehr, *The Soviet World of American Communism* (New Haven, Connecticut: Yale University Press,1998) p 281-282.

3   "Our abandonment of Europe . . ." Alger Hiss, "Basic Questions in the Great Debate. Here are the five most often asked questions about the Marshall Plan—and an attempt to answer them." *New York Times Magazine,* 16 Nov 1947.

4   "for the purpose of determining the extent . . ." FBI Memo for the attorney general re Alger Hiss, Nov 30 1945, Daniel Patrick Moynihan, *Secrecy: The American Experience* (New Haven, Connecticut: Yale University Press) 1988, p 68

5   "may have been a member . . ." Moynihan, Secrecy, p 68.

6   "Hiss had closely read the Smyth . . ." Ibid.

7   "The best genius in espionage . . ." Ladislas Farago, *War of Wits* (New York: Paperback Library, Inc., 1962), p 153.

8   "You keep as low as possible . . ." Email from Chervonnaya, 26 July 2009.

9   "It is impossible to understand . . ." Hinchley, Col Vernon, *Spies Who Never Were* (London: George G Harrap & Co Ltd., 1965), p 210.

10   "Chambers was an agent provocateur . . ." Email from Chervonnaya, 26 July 2009.

11   "do everything possible . . ." Farago, *War of Wits,* p 134.

12   The Russians seemed to have ignored Alger's entanglement with HUAC etc.: Email from Chervonnaya, 26 Jul 2009.

Chapter 27

1   "The library was a large room . . ." Chambers, p 730-731.

2   "felt incredibly alone . . ." Chambers, p 733-734.

3   "Mr. Chambers, will you state . . ." Stenographic Typescript in the case of Alger Hiss, Plaintiff, vs, Whittaker Chambers, Defendant, in the US District Court for the District of Maryland. Civil Case No 4176. P1.

4   "the international apparatus" Alger Hiss, ibid., p 182.

5   "You can be shot by them . . ." Ibid., p 181.

6   "very soft brown eyes and hair . . ." Ibid., p 175.

7 "weekly" meetings with Bedacht: Zeligs, p 121.

8 "in fifteen minutes" Zeligs, p 117.

9 "The first thing to note . . ." William a Reuben, The Dream of Whittaker Chambers (unpublished manuscript), page p 555 William A Reuben papers, Tamiment library.

10 "incredible" William Reuben, "Libel" The Alger Hiss Story.

11 "about a year and a half" Alger Hiss, Stenographic Typescript, p 33.

12 "perhaps six months" ibid., p 39.

13 "My locker was forced open . . ." Ibid., p 40.

14 Esther worked for the Soviet Trading Company Amtorg: Roberts, Loc 525.

15 $10,000 inheritance: Reuben, "Libel".

16 "We were married . . ." Stenographic Typescript in the case of Alger Hiss, Plaintiff, vs, Whittaker Chambers, Defendant, in the US District Court for the District of Maryland. Civil Case No 4176.

17 " . . .is not beyond possibility." Reuben, "Libel".

18 A quiet study group blossoms into a Communist cell: E. J. Worth, *Whittaker Chambers: The Secret Confession* (London: Massard, 1993).

19 "not particularly interesting": Smith, *Alger Hiss* p 239. Alger Hiss, Plaintiff vs. Whittaker Chambers, pp 313-318.

20 "small severe figure . . ." Cooke, p 151.

21 Details and quotes re Ester Chambers's testimony come from Reuben, "Baltimore Documents".

22 "We would go to Ypsilanti . . ." Zeligs, p 237, quoted from Trial Transcript p 1063.

23 "In response to your request . . ." William A. Reuben "The Baltimore Documents" An Excerpt From The Crimes of Alger Hiss, algerhiss.com. http://algerhiss.com/media/books/texts-and-excerpts/william-reuben-2002-ii/

Chapter 28

1 "so constituted that in every question . . ." Chambers, p 777.

2 "little sling" Chambers, *Witness*, p 741.

3 "big, plump and densely covered . . ." Chambers, *Witness*, p 763.

4 Inaccuracy of Chambers's description of the envelope: "The Experts: Daniel Norman", The Alger Hiss Story.

5 Marbury shocked to see documents: Smith, Alger Hiss, p 247.

6 "Colonel Bykov raised the question . . ." Reuben, "The Baltimore Documents".

7 "Original documents, not copies . . ." Hinchley, *Spies Who Never Were*, p 200

8   "The spy's hardest task . . ." Hinchley, Col Vernon. *Spy Mysteries Unveiled*, (London: George G Harrap & Co Ltd., 1963), p 167.

9   "Stalin didn't trust anyone, up to paranoia . . ." Email from Chervonnaya, 10 October 2009.

10   "important papers would be . . ." Hartshorn, p 198.

11   "absolutely counter to accepted . . ." Ronald Seth, *The Sleeping Truth*, (London: Leslie Freewin, 1968), p 162.

12   "Chambers's story is wildly . . ." Hinchley, *Spies Who Never Were*, pp 199-200.

13   "When procuring information . . ." Farago War of Wits, p 153.

14   "set pattern or routine . . ." Arkady N. Shevchenko, *Breaking with Moscow* (London, Grafton Books, 1985), p 49.

15   "it is a strict rule of Soviet espionage . . ." Farago, *War of Wits*, pp 161-162.

16   "If the meetings were to be regular . . ." Email from Chervonnaya, 11 Dec 2012.

17   "Usually, as a recognition signal . . ." Email from Chervonnaya, 7 December 2012.

18   "There would be a password . . ." Email from Chervonnaya, 11 Dec 2012.

19   "There occasionally came . . ." Allen Weinstein, *Perjury*, p 176.

20   "must have been genuinely mad . . ." Seth, *The Sleeping Truth*, p 185.

Chapter 30

1   "bombshell" Stripling, p142.

2   "a startling development . . ." Smith, *Alger Hiss*, pp 253, 254.

3   "in a frenzy" Stripling, p 143.

4   "A hunch" Nixon, p 47.

5   "I'm so goddamned sick and . . ." Summers, *Arrogance of Power*, p 69.

6   Amphibious plane standby: Summers, *Arrogance of Power*, p 71.

7   "he was so delighted with something . . ." Miller, William 'Fishbait'.

8   *Fishbait: The Memoirs of the Congressional Doorkeeper* (New York: Warner Books, 1977), p 63.

9   Squashes in the shape of in an arrow pointing to this pumpkin Drew Pearson, "The Washington Merry-Go-Round: Midnight Ride to Maryland", Dec 10, 1948. The Bell Syndicate, Inc.

10   "Hiss-Chambers has produced . . ." Nixon, *Six Crises*, p 48.

11   "Case clinched. Information . . ." Nixon, p 48.

12   "Hiss's handwriting identified . . ." Nixon, p 48.

13   "Before I was out of bed . . ." Chambers, p 754.

14   "so Communists wouldn't . . ." AP Report, *La Crosse Tribune*, 5 Dec 1948 (NewspaperArchive.com).

15 "microfilmed copies of documents . . ." AP Report, *Logansport Press*, 4 Dec 1948 (NewspaperArchive.com).

16 Chambers's claims. William A. Reuben, "The Baltimore Documents", An Excerpt From The Crimes of Alger Hiss. AlgerHiss.com

17 "Will reopen hearings if . . ." Reuben, *Honorable Mr Nixon*, p 54.

18 "is no longer one man's word . . ." Reuben, *Honorable Mr Nixon*, p 57.

19 "conclusive proof of the greatest treason . . ." Summers, *Arrogance of Power*, p 69.

20 "SPY NETWORK IN STATE . . ." AP Report, byline Douglas B. Cornell with the subheadline "Grand to consider new shocking evidence", *Dixon Evening Telegraph*, 6 Dec 1946, p 1 (NewspaperArchive.com).

21 "Chambers Claims He Hid . . ." UP report, 8 December 1948.

22 "SAYS HISS LET OUT WAR . . ." AP report 7 Dec 1948.

23 "The audience received no hint . . ." Reuben, *Honorable Mr Nixon*, p 59

24 "any and all information and . . ." Reuben, *Honorable Mr Nixon*, p 60.

25 "declared conclusively and without qualification . . ." Reuben, *Honorable Mr Nixon*, p 58.

26 "Recent disclosures before the House Committee on Un-American . . ." *Honorable Mr Nixon*, Reuben, p 63.

27 "Plot to Seize . . ." AP report, 5 Dec 1948.

28 "800 Moscow-trained American Communists . . ." AP Report, 6 Dec 1948.

Chapter 31

1 "a messenger for the House" Benjamin Weiser, "Nixon Lobbied Grand Jury to indict Hiss on Espionage Case" *New York Times*, 12 Oct 1999.

2 "worth nothing whatever" "Excerpts from Grand Jury Hearings Relating to the Alger Hiss Case, December 1948": Law2.umkc.edu.

3 "As most of you are aware . . ." "Excerpts from Grand Jury Hearings"

4 "Without question, there will be an all-out attempt . . ." This Press Interview appears many places. I found it in *The Landmark*, p 1, a North Carolina paper, (NewspaperArchive.com).

5 "Their crime, in effect, is treason." Reuben, *Honorable Mr Nixon*, p 62.

6 "TOP SECRETS" "Spies got away" AP Report, December 15, 1948, See The Post-Standard, Syracuse, New York, Page 1.

Chapter 32

1 "I have seen it suggested in the papers . . ." "Sayre Testifies before the grand jury", December 22, 1948, *Alger Hiss Story*.

2 "the greatest treason conspiracy" Summers, *Arrogance of Power*, p 69.

3   "We won the Hiss case in the papers," Nixon tapes. Kutler, Stanley I.
    Abuse of Power, p7.
4   "I had him convicted before . . ." Kutler, *Abuse of Power*, p 9.

Chapter 33

1   I wrote an early draft of the scenes in Louisville something like thirty
    years ago on the basis of notes both Dexter and I took at the time.
2   Nora Iasigi Bullit, Three Weeks in Russia, "Privately Printed, 1936".
3   "The young Communist is a fine animal . . ." N. Bullitt, p 47.
4   "zigzagged down through vineyards and forests . . ." N. Bullitt, p 62.
5   The original of the Nixon letter was last known to be in the possession of
    Lowry Watkins, Nora Bullitt's grandson.

Chapter 34

1   "unavailable . . .the records are palletized" David Hardy, Section Chief,
    Record/Information Dissemination Section, Records Management
    Division, Department of Justice to Bigwood, Feb 14, 2001: re FOIPA
    Request No.: 1160518: Subject: MASTERS, DEXTER.
2   Access to Dexter's file as the FBI's responsibility: April 6, 2011, to Big-
    wood from Martha Wagner Murphy, Chief, Special Access FOIPA,
    National Archives re Case NW 35470.
3   "Wherever I dig, I stumble upon . . ." Email from Chervonnaya, 4 August
    2009.
4   "It is Big Ben on steroids." Email from Bigwood, 14 Nov 2010.
5   "A secret history of the United States government's . . ." Eric Lictblau,
    "Nazis were given 'Safe Haven' in US, Report says", *New York Times*. 13
    Nov 2010. (Nytimes.com).
6   "There is another aspect to safe-haven . . ." Email from Chervonnaya, 16
    Nov 2010.

Chapter 35

1   History of the Woodstock typewriter: Smith, *Alger Hiss*, p 282.
2   Condition of the Woodstock typewriter: Smith, *Alger Hiss*, pp 282, 283.
3   Puzzlement over brand of typewriter: Smith, *Alger Hiss*, pp 282, 283.
4   Number of agents at as high as 250: Denise Noe. "The Promising Mr
    Hiss", The Alger Hiss Case. Trutv.com/library.
5   Every FBI field office in America involved: Chambers, Witness, p 787.
6   "with the assistance of the FBI . . ." "Hiss and the Evidence", Humanities
    and Social Sciences Online, H-net.msu.

7   Hisses' ex-OSS agent Schmahl looking for a Woodstock: "Sleuth 'Hired by Hiss' Touched off hunt for Typewriter here." Quod.lib.umich.edu.

8   John McDowell confirmed date: Smith, *Alger Hiss*, p 363.

9   "On December 13, 1948, FBI agents . . ." John Lowenthal, "What the FBI knew and hid." *The Nation*, 26 Jun 1976.

10 FBI records re Horace Schmahl finding typewriter: Salant, "Bringing Alger"; Cook, Ghost.

11 "To the best of my knowledge the FBI . . ." Stephan Salant, Athan Theoharis & David Levin. "Alger Hiss: An Exchange." *New York Review of Books*, April 1, 1976.

12 "I guess you know what I want to talk . . ." Fred J. Cook, "The Ghost of A Typewriter", *The Nation*, 12 May 1962.

13 Pleasure at finding the typewriter: Cook, "The Ghost of A Typewriter".

Chapter 36

1   "COMMUNIST CONSPIRACY . . ." AP Report, Feb 2, 1949.

2   "The spy story of the century" AP Report, Feb 2, 1949, Feb 15, 1949.

3   "SPYING AIM OF REDS DECLARED . . ." *New York Times*, Jan 28, 1949.

4   "An international conspiracy" UP Report, March 4, 1949

5   "COMMUNIST CURBS FORECAST" *New York Times*, 20 Apr 1949.

6   Layout of the court: Cooke, p 104.

7   "pink, genial rabbit of a man . . ." Cooke, p 102.

8   "If you don't believe Chambers . . ." Smith, *Alger Hiss*, p 300.

9   "low-down, nefarious, filthy" Cooke, p 118 & Smith, *Alger Hiss*, pp 281, 303, 396.

10 "the best in America, the most trustworthy . . ." Smith, *Alger Hiss*, p 281.

11 "Is this the conduct of a guilty man?" Smith, *Alger Hiss*, p 303.

12 "turned Washington upside down" Smith, *Alger Hiss*, p 275.

13 "I welcomed the chance to go to court . . ." T. Hiss, *Laughing Last*, p 132.

14 "I simply don't believe that . . ." Smith, *Alger Hiss*, p 274.

15 "Dick has a heck of a lot at stake in . . ." Tiger, ed, *In Re Alger Hiss: Exhibit 1*, page 121.

16 "be kept under cross . . ." Edith Tiger, editor, In Re Alger Hiss: Petition of Error Coram Nobis (Hill and Wang, New York, 1979). Letter from Victor Lasky to Murphy, June 1949, conveying Nixon's instructions. See Exhibit 1, page 121.

17 "He had a fine articulation of chin . . ." Cooke, p 108.

18 "sense of powerlessness" A. Hiss, *Recollections*, 153-155.

19 "rules for a game of chance." A. Hiss, *Recollections*, 134.

20 "You took that oath did you not?" Smith, *Alger Hiss,* p 305.

21 Description of Whittaker Chambers and Esther Chambers on the stand: Smith, *Alger Hiss,* p 326.

22 "at a red light in Norristown we . . ." Smith, *Alger Hiss,* pp 275-278.

23 "remained something of a mystery." Cook. Unfinished Story, p 51.

24 The book by Earl Jowett: *The Strange Case of Alger Hiss* (London: Hodder & Stoughton, 1953).

25 "the most extraordinary feature . . ." Jowett, p 178.

26 Angela Calomiris as CPUSA Finance Secretary. Mahoney, M.H. (1993). *Women in Espionage: A Biographical Dictionary* (Santa Barbara, California: ABC- CLIO), p 39.

27 Description of William Marshall Bullitt: Harbaugh, p 450.

28 "Mr Hiss' testimony . . .has been constantly . . ." William Marshall Bullitt. A Factual Review of the Whittaker Chambers—Alger Hiss Controversy.[A Trustee of the Carnegie Endowment for International Peace] (written in Nassau, Bahamas, November 27—December 4, 1948) while convalescing from pneumonia], p 29.

29 "another Benedict Arnold and another . . ." Plain Talk, August 1949. From A. Hiss, Public Opinion, p 299

30 "The only thing remaining . . ." Fred Cook "Hiss: New Perspectives on the Strangest Case of Our Time," The Nation, September 21, 1957. Algerhiss.com

31 Announcement of the hung jury: Cooke, 274.

32 "sat rigid, with a keen dizzy look . . ." Cooke, pp 275, 276.

Chapter 37

1 "I am confident that . . ." "The Woodstock Typewriter: Family Typewriter Plays Vital Role in Hiss Case" The Alger Hiss Story.

Chapter 38

1 "KAUFMAN ACCUSED OF HISS . . ." *New York Times,* 10 Jul 1949.

2 "Capitol Hill Demands Probe . . ." INS Report, 9 July 1949.

3 " . . .a full investigation should immediately . . ." INS Report, 9 Jul 1949.

4 "full facts of this trial are laid . . ." AP report, 9 Jul 1949.

5 " . . . the entire Truman administration . . ." AP Report, 10 Jul 1949.

6 " . . .bias bordering on judicial misconduct." *New York Times,* 10 Jul 1949

7 "minute examination . . ." *New York Times,* 19 Jul 1949.

8 "The matter should be turned over to the Judiciary . . ." *New York Herald Tribune,* 10 Jul 1948.

9 "degrading precedent" *New York Times,* 18 Jul 1948.

10 "dragged down the high position of the Supreme . . ." A. Hiss, *Public Opinion,* p 295.

11 "For acquittal—Louis Hill, a business secretary . . ." UP Report, 9 July 1949.

12 "had a conversation with a woman . . ." INS Report, 9 Jul 1949.

13 Nixon wanted the jury foreman the jury's foreman prosecuted: Summers, *Arrogance of Power* p 79.

14 Nixon pressed to have the four dissenting jurors subpoenaed before HUAC: Lowenthal, "What the FBI knew and hid".

15 "saleable merchandise" Mitchell, p 42.

16 "When your star is up . . ." Mitchell, p 45.

17 "3-Way G. O. P. Senate Race . . ." *New York Times,* 4 Nov 1949.

18 ". . . had been delivered into Soviet slavery." Bonnie K. Goodman. "Overviews and chronologies 1948", Presidential Campaigns and Elections Reference. Presidentialcampaignselectionsreference.wordpress.com.

19 "one per every 1,814 persons . . ." Sterling, p 15.

20 Hoover says 6,977 communists California, many in the movies: Mitchell, p 74.

21 "the American boys who were killed . . ." "The Cast: John Rankin" The Alger Hiss Story. See also Smith, *Alger Hiss,* p 332.

22 Alger disliked Stryker's "florid" style: T. Hiss, *View from Alger's Window,* p 87.

23 "solid background in corporate cases . . ." Smith, *Alger Hiss,* p 400.

Chapter 39

1 "being prepared for automation . . ." Letter from Janice Galli McLeod, Associate Director, US Department of Justice, in re FOIPA Request No.: 1171976- 00011 Jan 2012.

2 "unavailable for searches." Letter from David Hardy, Section Chief, Record/Information Dissemination Section, Record Managements Division, US Department of Justice, 30 Aug 2011.

3 "neither confirm nor deny the existence or nonexistence . . ." Letter from David Hardy 30 August 2011; letter from Fritz Mulhauser, Senior Staff Attorney, ALCU, 1 Oct 2011; letter from Michelle Meeks, Executive Secretary, Agency Release Panel, 23 May 2012.

4 "Apparently some of your mother's records . . ." Email from Bigwood 14 Dec 2010.

5   "Access Restricted" . . . "colored servant" Main file No. 100-3368. Subject: Robert A Brady. Reynolds Report, p 30.

6   Special Agent Galen W. Willis's introduction to the Brady interview, 14 Apr 1942. Reynolds Report, p 27.

7   "'flop house' run by a Jap." Brady FBI file, Reynolds report, 4 May 1942, p 12.

8   "violently anti-Nazi" Brady FBI file, Agent Schemerhorn, March 3, 1942 p 4.

9   "Nazi Germany is a capitalist's paradise." Brady FBI file. *Saturday Review of Literature*, 17 Jul 1937.

10 "a capitalist country would eventually . . ." Brady FBI file, Reynolds report, 4 May 1942, p 22

11 "Some of the American purges of the late 1940s . . ." Email from Bigwood, 14 Nov 2010

12 "the purge of the stringent antifascists . . ." Yeadon, p 276.

Chapter 40

1   "a magnificent old American bald eagle . . ." Cooke, p 282.

2   Description of Alice Roosevelt Longworth, her sister-in-law, and her daughter-in-law: T. Hiss, *Laughing Last*, p 134.

3   "equivocation" . . . "ineluctability." Donald H.J. Hermann, "Deception and Betrayal: The Tragedy of Alger Hiss: A Paper Delivered to the Chicago Literary Club", Chicago, Illinois, 13 Nov 2005.

4   "In the 60 years since the case . . ." Chervonnaya, 4 Oct 2009.

5   "I will just read off the first and . . ." Chambers, p 739.

Chapter 41

1   "relationship to our ambassador . . ." N. Bullitt, opening page.

2   "Chambers's 1939 statements to the Government . . ." William Marshall Bullitt, A Factual Review, p 16.

3   "a romantic idealist of conspiratorial temper . . ." Dearborn, Mary V., *Queen of Bohemia: The Life of Louise Bryant* (New York: Houghtin Mifflin, 1996), p 203.

4   Bill Bullitt's book making fun of Wilson: *Thomas Woodrow Wilson: A Psychological Study* (Boston: Houghton Mifflin republished in 1967).

5   Bullitt's book about the Soviet Union, *The Bullitt Mission to Russia* (New York: Huebsch, 1919).

6   Bullitt's novel, *It's Not Done* (New York: Harcourt Brace, 1926).

7 Gossip about Bullitt's sexual tastes: Will Brownell & Richard N. Billings, *So Close to Greatness: A Biography of William C. Bullitt* (New York: Macmillan, 1987), p 297.

8 "I love you." Brownell, p 229.

9 "was raving after Bullitt left his office . . ." Margaret Suckley, cited in Geoffrey C. Ward, ed., *Closest Companion: The Unknown Story of the Intimate Friendship between Franklin Roosevelt and Margaret Suckley* (New York: Simon & Schuster, 2009), pp 243, 244.

10 "savage about Roosevelt." Virginia Gardner, *Friend and Lover: The Life of Louise Bryant* (New York: Horizon Press, 1982), p 275.

11 William C. Bullitt, *The Great Globe Itself* (New York: Scribner's, 1946).

12 "forces of evil" Bullitt, Great Globe, p 180.

13 "overwhelming attacking forces . . ." Ibid., p 180.

14 "A repetitious and bitter . . .": "Sees Threat in Soviet Dictatorship Thinks Roosevelt Gamble Failied", Books of the Times, 15 Jul 1946.

15 Bill's article in *Life* magazine appeared in the August 30 issue, pp 83-92.

16 "did not recall either the name Hiss . . ." "Daladier Fails to Recall Hiss Warning" AP report, 9 Apr 1952.

Chapter 42

1 "proof of the greatest treason conspiracy in American history" Summers, Arrogance p 69.

2 "immutable witnesses"? Sidney Zion, "The Hiss Case: Mystery Ignored", New York, April 4,1978; Weinstein, Perjury, p 569"; Fred Cook, "Typewriters are always the Key"The New Times, Oct 14, 1977, p 30, accessed via The University of Michigan quod.lib.umich.edu

3 "odd assortment" Chabot Smith, p 335

4 Much of the material had appeared in *New York Times:* Roberts, Chap 8 and loc 2764.

5 Some of the material reported in conversations with Russians concerned information that the Russians already had: Chervonnaya 14 Oct 2009.

6 "vague reports about Japanese troop movements . . ." Smith, *Alger Hiss,* pp 339-340.

7 "The contrast is striking . . ." Email from Chervonnaya 28 Oct 2010.

8 "tedious, frustrating, at times ludicrous . . ." Smith, *Alger Hiss,* p 335.

9 "action copy", "code . . ." Smith, *Alger Hiss,* p 335.

10 Jay Lea Chambers personal dossier missing: Hiss Defense Files private investigator's report, 1 Nov 1948.

11 "pieces of identity" Zeligs, p 127.

12   "For you see, after six years . . ." William F. Buckley, Jr., ed. *Odyssey of a Friend: Whittaker Chambers's Letters to William F. Buckley, Jr., 1954-1961* (New York: Putnam, 1969), p. 87.

13   "a deeply tortured man who loathed . . ." Personal letter from Clare Booth Luce to William a Reuben, dated 18 September 1969, William A Reuben Papers, courtesy of Tamiment Library, New York.

14   "homosexualism . . . more than 30" "Chambers's Personal Crisis", *The Alger Hiss Story.*

15   "was termed a sissy" Hiss investigator, September 1948, quoted in William A. Reuben, *The Dream of Whittaker Chambers* (unpublished manuscript), Courtesy of the Tamiment Library, New York

16   "None of the boys had much use for him . . ." Oliver Pilat, "Report on Whittaker Chambers", "Home News" *New York Post*, 14 Jun 1949, p 3.

17   "a little girl named Vermilia." Alger Hiss investigator, quoted in Reuben, *The Dream*, p 207.

18   questioning classmates about Chambers's "effeminacy", ibid., p 240.

19   "he had a touch of lavender in him." Ibid., p 234.

20   Chambers's nickname as "Girlie" ibid., *The Dream*, p 228.

21   Chambers's "homosexual relationship" with Bub, Tanenhaus, pp 39-41.

22   The FBI, questioning Henry Bang years later, assumed the homosexual relationship with Bub. William A. Reuben papers, Tamiment Library, Box 4 Folder 24.

23   "The leaves so pensile, so tremulously hung . . ." "Lathrop, Montana," The Nation (June 30, 1926).

24   "As your sap drains out into me in excess . . ." "Tandaradei" Two Worlds (June 30, 1926).

25   Chambers's eight-page confession in longhand, 16 Feb 1949. For excerpts see "Chambers' Personal Crisis", The Alger Hiss Story.

26   "a revelation" "set off a chain reaction" Whittaker Chambers; statement to the Baltimore FBI, 17 February 1949, Tanenhaus, p. 344, See also "Chambers's Crisis" Algerhiss.com.

27   "in a strictly confidential manner" John Lowenthal, "Venona and Alger Hiss", Intelligence and National Security, Vol. 15, No. 3 (Autumn 2000), Algerhiss.com

28   "Is he a man of sanity?" HUAC Hearings, 25 Aug 1948, p 1164.

29   "A typical Communist smear" . . . HUAC Hearings, 25 Aug 1948, p 1166.

30   Treatment of homosexuals in 1950: Randolph W. Baxter, " 'Homo-Hunting' in the Early Cold War: Senator Kenneth Wherry and the

Homophobic Side of McCarthyism", Nebraska History 84 (2003): 119-132. Nebraskahistory.org.

31   Ernie Lazar's find: "Sometime in 1936 or later . . ." Freedom of Information and Privacy Acts. Subject: Hiss Chambers. File number: 65-14920. Section: vol. 26 serials 3192-3312.

32   "I was there and chambers was not." A Talk by Dr. Timothy Hobson (two parts) at the 5 Apr 2007 conference on Alger Hiss and History at NYU. See the Alger Hiss site.

33   "under their thumb." "Interview with Alger Hiss—Hiss on Coram Nobis." The Advocate, Suffolk Law School Fall 1978. Interview conducted 2 Nov 1978 with Joseph P. Ippolito, Herbert Travers, & Prof. Charles P Kindregan.

34   Hoover's coercion of witnesses well known. Roberts, Loc 2290.

35   Condition of pages from the dumbwaiter shaft: "The Experts: Daniel Norman", The Alger Hiss Story.

36   "The point about the pumpkin . . ." Chambers, p 755.

37   "BULLITT MESSAGE SHOWN . . ." William R. Conklin, *New York Times,* 2 Dec 1949, Front page.

38   "if France should begin serious negotiations" Bullitt to Hull Jan 25 1938; AP Report December 2, 1949. See previous endnote; this is from the same NYT story.

39   "his dear old friend comrade Bullitt . . ." "Guenther Reinhardt Dossier", Documentstalk.com.

40   "microfilm copies from photocopies of documents for Moscow . . ." Email from Chervonnaya 11 Mar 2009.

41   "Bill might be selected" Personal letter from WM Bullitt to Orville Bullitt, 31 Aug 1948.

42   Chambers knew Marshall Bullitt: Chambers, p 511.

43   "Richard Nixon landing there in a helicopter . . ." Msnsxtra.com/local 13 Jun 2009.

44   "An ambassador's reports . . ." Nixon, Six Crises, p 54.

Chapter 43

1   "I knew that we had demonstrated the failure . . ." A. Hiss, *Recollections,* pp 156.

2   "Each of these documents . . ." A. Hiss, *Recollections,* pp 156-159.

3   "That's a hanging charge." A. Hiss, *Recollections,* pp 152, 153, 156-157.

4   "acquittal in fifteen minutes" Alger Hiss, Recollections, p 156.

5   "The dumb sons of bitches . . ." A. Hiss, *Recollections,* pp 156, 157.

6   "quiet and restrained" A. Hiss, *Recollections*, p 157.
7   "They had to be." A. Hiss, *Recollections*, p157.
8   Description of the guilty verdict as it was delivered: Cooke, p 335.

Chapter 44

1   "Three years at Lewisburg . . ." T. Hiss, *View from Alger's Window*, p 65, also *Laughing Last*, p 3.
2   "No one can be prepared for the dehumanizing . . ." Yahoo Answers.
3   "cage" . . ."zoo" A. Hiss, *Recollections*, p 161.
4   "speaking tube." A. Hiss, *Recollections*, p 165, 166.
5   "wise" . . .tolerant." Stephen D. Cox, *The Big House: Image and Reality of the American Prison* (New Haven, Connecticut: Yale University Press: 2009), p 23, 24.
6   "I got to say for Hiss . . ." Kutler, *Abuse of Power*, p 18.
7   "He seems to be taking his incarceration . . ." T. Hiss, *View from Alger's Window*, p 229.
8   "the law, as I'd been taught it . . ." A. Hiss, *Recollections*, p 175.
9   "regarded her as President Roosevelt's conscience." Alger Hiss, Recollections, p 175.
10 "surprised to learn . . ." Ibid.
11 "The modern Benedict Arnold." T. Hiss, *View from Window*, p 229.
12 " . . .continue on." A Hiss, *Recollections*, p 181.
13 "He undoubtedly should be able . . ." T. Hiss, *View from Window*, p 229.
14 A second education for Alger: T. Hiss, *View from Alger's Window*, p 130.
15 What Alger learned from prison: T. Hiss, *View from Alger's Window*, p 226.
16 "Jail is where Alger became a human being." T. Hiss, *View from Alger's Window*, p 222.
17 "Never! Don't ever send anybody . . ." Smith, *Alger Hiss*, pp 432, 433.
18 "In my sleep I always dreamed of freedom . . ." A Hiss, *Recollections*, 167.

Chapter 46

1   "If you were Meyer . . ." Brad Lewis, *Hollywood's Celebrity Gangster: The Incredible Life and Times of Mickey Cohen* (BBL Books, 2007. Kindle edition) Loc 7525.
2   "Had she been able to stay in Congress . . ." Miller, Fishbait, p 103.
3   "It was all gamblers from Vegas . . ." Cohen, *In My Own Words*, p 235. Also Lewis, *Celebrity Gangster*, Loc 3907 Mitchell, p 232.
4   "PRIZES GALORE Electric clocks . . ." Mitchell, p 231.

5 The Los Angeles Examiner's editorial cartoon: Mitchell, p 232.

6 "pink right down to her underpants." Mitchell, p 230.

7 Anonymous phone calls: Mitchell, p 230.

8 "Did you know Helen Douglas is married . . ." Mitchell, p 230.

9 "This is the final straw . . ." Mitchell, p 237.

10 " 'spy ring'" at the heart of government . . ." "Joseph McCarthy, 'Speech at Wheeling, West Virginia'(9 February 1950)." Advances in the History of Rhetoric. University of Maryland Advances.umd.edu.

11 "Listen you bastards . . ." "The McCarthy Trials & The Hollywood Ten", Mt Holyoke College website Mtholyoke.edu (4 Jun 2013).

12 "mass espionage motivated" Father John Francis Cronin, The Problem of American Communism in 1945: Facts and Recommendations. A Confidential Study for Private Circulation. mdhistory.net

13 "infiltrated, dominated or saturated . . ." J. Edgar Hoover HUAC Testimony" Cal Poly College of Liberal Arts Cla.calpoly.edu.

14 "complete control over the human mind . . ." Stripling, p 169.

15 "Communism would make a slave . . ." HUAC Hearings, 3 Aug 1948 p 574.

16 "We Americans live in a free world . . ." "Senator Joseph R. McCarthy's Reply to Edward R. Murrow", See It Now (CBS-TV, 6 Apr 1954) Media Resources Center, Moffitt Library, UC California 510.642.8197 Lib. berkeley.edu (17 February 2014).

17 Libraries burning books like the Hitler Youth: Jon Henley, "Book-burning: fanning the flames of hatred". The Guardian, 10 September 2012.

18 Jobs lost as a result of McCarthy accusations: Victor Rabinowitz, Unrepentant Lefitst. Chicago (The University of Illinois Press, 1996) pp 100-101.

19 "A newspaperman walks up to a US diplomat . . ." Drew Pearson "Washington-Merry-Go-Round", Bell-McClure Syndicate, 21 Apr 1950.

20 "A hundred and twelve people" Truman, Address in Detroit at the celebration of the City's 250th Anniversary, July 28, 1951. Trumanlibrary.org

21 Response to Robert Brady's speech: Email from Doug Dowd, 15 Sept 2010.

Chapter 47

1 "The process that convicted Alger . . ." Kenneth Simon. "One of Hiss's Lawyers Recalls the Man and the Case".

2 Alger Hiss Story "abstruse", Simon.

3   "repeated requests" . . . "long delays." Rabinowitz, p 14.

4   Alger's filed "destroyed" Rabinowitz, p 145.

5   "random" choice of a judge in high-profile cases: Rabinowitz, p 144.

6   "listened quietly" Rabinowitz, Unrepentant Leftist, p. 144.

7   FBI spent many months with Chambers in preparation for Alger's trials: Fred J. Cook, "A Whole New Ballgame", *The Nation*, 11 Oct 1980.

8   Extent and illegality of surveillance of Alger: ibid.

9   "I'd like it explained to me . . ." Ibid.

10 OUP confirmed that Chambers translating and "hysterical and suffering from persecution mania" "Paul Willert's Account", Alger Hiss Story.

11 None of papers in court typed on typewriter in court: "The Experts: Evelyn Erlich", Alger Hiss Story.

12 Several typists at work, not just one: Tiger ed, *In Re Alger Hiss,* pp 65-100.

13 "A typewriter is, as you know . . ." Summers, *Arrogance of Power,* p 71.

14 "could reproduce faultlessly the imprint of any typewriter . . ." Russell R. Bradford and Ralph B. Bradford, *An Introduction to Handwriting Examination and Identification* (Chicago: Nelson-Hall Publishers, 1992), quoted in "A History of Forgery by Typewriter" Alger Hiss Story.

15 US Army intelligence could also reproduce faultlessly the imprint of any typewriter: Salant, "Bringing Alger" "The President was famous for reliving . . ." John W. Dean, *Blind Ambition: The White House Years* (New York: Simon & Schuster, 1976), p 186.

16 "The typewriters are always the key . . ." Dean, p 57 Schmahl spilling what he knew to the FBI.

17 "The serial number of the typewriters sold . . ." "What the FBI Knew And Hid," by John Lowenthal (*The Nation,* 26 Jun 1976 Algerhiss.com.

18 "Each of these documents" The Pumpkin Papers: Key Evidence in the Alger Hiss Trials Trials, UKMC School of Law website

19 Tiger, *In Re Alger Hiss,* pp 20-32. Schmahl working undercover for Military Intelligence: Salant, "Bringing Alger".

20 "reams of Army-generated reports." "A Conversation with Stephen Salant, Creator of 'Successful Strategic Deception: A Case Study'", interview by Rebecca Welzenbach on 14 Jul 2010: Publishing.umich.edu.

21 Schmahl involved in forging the typewriter: Salant, "Q &A: Did Army Spooks Build the Woodstock?" The Alger Hiss Story Schmahl working undercover for Military Intelligence: Salant, "Q & A", Alger Hiss Story.

22 Bretnall's orders from Donovan, chief of the OSS: Roberts, Loc 137.

23   "Hiss was framed." Summers, *Arrogance of Power,* p 73.

24   Crime created for Alger and the grand jury: Robert L. Weinberg. "Not Guilty As Charged: A Revised Verdict for Alger Hiss", The Champion, May/June 2008, p 18. National Association of Criminal Defense Lawyers. Nacdl.org.

25   Judges normally rule right after oral arguments: Email from Eleanor Barrett, 21 Jan 2013.

26   "Nothing" presented placed the original verdict "under any cloud": William A. Reuben, *Footnote on an Historic Case: In Re Alger Hiss,* No. 78 Civ. 3433 (New York: The Nation Institute, 1983), p 2.

Chapter 49

1   Allen Weinstein, *Perjury: The Hiss-Chambers Case* (New York: Alfred A. Knopf, 1978).

2   "impossible to understand." Vernon Hinchley, *Spies,* pp. 200, 210.

3   Soviet spies trained to plan and rehearse their escape routes: Farago, *War of Wits,* p 153.

4   "had been arranging an escape ever since the Fuchs trial . . ." Email from Chervonnaya, 28 Jul 2009.

5   Prevalence of code names: " 'Spies': Fact or Fiction", a review of *Spies: The Rise and Fall of the KGB in America* (Yale University Press, New Haven: 2009), by Jeff Kisseloff, Alger Hiss Story.

6   The new accusers not visiting the Russian archives themselves: Amy Knight, "The Selling of the KGB", The Wilson Quarterly, Winter 2000. Reproduced at The Alger Hiss Story.

7   Hard to get permission to visit Russian archives: Email from Chervonnaya, 28 July 2009.

8   "collections were open for research." Harvey Klehr, John Earl Haynes, and Kyrill M. Anderson, "The Soviet World of American Communism" (New Haven, CT, and London: Yale UP, 1998), pp. xv-xvi (CP USA records through 1944).

9   "indeed, his name never occurs" *The Secret World Of American Communism,* Klehr, Haynes, and Firsov (Yale University press, New Haven and London, 1995) p. 321.

10   The lucrative book deal: Amy Knight, "The Selling of the KGB", *The Wilson Quarterly,* Winter, 2000.

11   "We, the Russian Intelligence service . . ." John Earl Haynes and Alexander Vassiliev, Spies: The Rise and Fall of the KGB in America (Yale University Press, 26 May 2009), p xlviii.

12 FBI not believing Massing: Kisseloff, review of *Spies*.

13 Alger and Massing never invited to the Fields' at the same time: Herta Field's letter to Dr. Staeheim of the defense, quoted in Kisseloff, review of *Spies*. Fields out of the country on all the possible party dates: "Dinner Party at the Fields III, Skeletons in the Closet (1990-2009)" DocumentsTalk.com. Fields being tortured in Hungary as US spies: Letter from Noel Field to Alger Hiss, July 21, 1957. Harvard Law School Library Special Collections.

14 "Some, not-too-honest KGB officers": Lowenthal, "Venona and Alger Hiss".

15 Oleg Kalugin's book, Spymaster, New York: Basic Books Revised Edition, 2009. Kindle Edition.

16 The "Perlo List" Introducing a Document Missing From The Haunted Wood By Dr. Svetlana Chervonnaya http://algerhiss.com/history/new-evidence-surfaces-1990s/interpreting-russian-files/alexander-vassiliev/the-vassiliev-notebooks/the-story-behind-the-perlo-list/ Gorsky's list: "Gorsky's List" (II) By Dr. Svetlana A. Chervonnayahttp://algerhiss.com/history/new-evidence-surfaces-1990s/interpreting-russian-files/alexander-vassiliev/the-vassiliev-notebooks/gorskys-list-analyzed/

17 "sloppy almost every time he quoted documents relating to Alger Hiss." David Lowenthal, "Did Allen Weinstein Get the Alger Hiss Story Wrong?" History News Network.

18 Unanimous verdict against Vassiliev: Alexander Vassiliev v. Frank Cass & Co, London, Case Reference [2003] EWHC 1428 (QB), [2003] EMLR 761. Court Queen's Bench Division; Judge David Eady presiding. Date of Judgment 13 Jun 2003.

19 the mysterious reference numbers: the haunted Wood—Soviet espionage in America the Stalinist era. Random House, Inc., 1999. Modern library paperback edition, 2000, pp 347-349.

20 Wilson Digital Archive, International History Declassified Vassiliev Notebooks http://digitalarchive.wilsoncenter.org.

21 "sheer poppycock . . ." Maxim Lieber, quoted by Victor Navasky, editorial in *The Nation*, 8 Apr 1978.

22 Out-of-court settlement for an undisclosed amount: Victor S. Navasky, *A Matter of Opinion* (Picador, 2006), pp 239-242. "Letters to the Editor", *The Nation*, 17 Jun 1978. Other Weinstein witnesses: David Lowenthal, "Did Allen Weinstein Get the Alger Hiss Story Wrong?" George Mason University History News Network Monday, 2 May 2005 - 02:20 Hnn. us/articles.

23 Nixon Volkogonov correspondence: Lowenthal 2000, footnote 68. "Letters from Nixon and John H. Taylor, director of the Nixon presidential library, to Volkogonov in 1991, delivered personally to Volkogonov by Nixon's representative Dimitri K. Simes: tel. confs. Kai Bird with Simes, March 25, 1993, the author with Taylor, April 14, 1994; letter from Hiss to Volkogonov, Aug. 3, 1992 (note 72)." Confirmed by Kai Bird to Joan Brady in an email dated 30 March 2016.

24 Gen Volkogonov's search of the archives: Amy Knight, "The Selling of the KGB", *The Wilson Quarterly*, Winter, 2000 http://algerhiss.com/media/books/reviews/amy-knight/.

25 Dimitri Volkogonov, quoted in Wikipedia: Dimitri Volkogonov.

26 Chambers "had . . . not any kind of secret or spy information." Lowenthal 2000; Interview, 15 Oct 1992 (note 72).

27 "After carefull study of every reference . . ." Email from Julius Kobyakov to Lowenthal, Fri, 10 Oct 2003. Humanities and Social Sciences Online. Michigan State University. H-net.msu.

Chapter 50

1 Lamphere tells Lowenthal that he never saw Venona 1822 or the Ales speculation: Venona conference in 1996 ; Lowenthal, "Venona and Alger Hiss" (n 62).

2 Lamphere's autobiography: *FBI-KGB War: A Special Agent's Story* W.H. Allen / Virgin Books; 1st ed. (3 Dec 1987).

3 Lamphere's obituary: Douglas Martin, "Robert J. Lamphere, 83, Spy Chaser for the F.B.I., Dies", *New York Times*, 11 Feb 2002.

4 Powers confirms that Gordievsky's reference is to his tipoff: Venona 1822: Eric Alterman "I Spy With One Little Eye" (*The Nation*, 29 Apr 1996).

5 Gordievsky and Cambridge historian Andrew Christopher repeat the Powers and credit him as their source in their book *The Agony of Deceit: KGB; The Inside Story* (HarperPerennial; 1st HarperPerennial Ed edition, Oct. 1991).

6 "no question that the agent was referring to the same document . . ." Eric Alterman "I Spy With One Little Eye" (*The Nation*, 29 Apr 1996).

7 Gordievsky's autobiography: Oleg Gordievsky, *Next Stop Execution*, (Endeavour Press, 14 Apr 2015).

8 Svetlana's interview with Pavlov: Quoted by Matthew Stevenson, *Remembering the Twentieth Century Limited*, (New Hampshire: Odysseus books, 2009) p 114.

9 Pavlov confirms that Gordievsky's claim is "pure fabrication": Vitaly G. Pavlov, Chapter One: "I Discover America", *Operation "Snow": Half a Century in KGB Foreign Intelligence*, (Geya Publishers, Moscow, [Translated from the original Russian]) p 39.

10 "money for the defense" Chervonnaya, 27 Jul 2009.

11 "All the top Commies in the country . . ." Email to JB 27 Jul 2009."

12 "Simultaneously with Hiss" Zeligs, Friendship and Fratricide, p. 394.

13 "Kryuchkov looked utterly bewildered.": *Resurrection: The Struggle for a New Russia* (New York: Random House, 1997; London: Picador/Macmillan, 1998), p. 320.

14 "a pretext to unfold in the country the persecution . . ." G. Usachev, *John Foster Dulles* (Moscow: Mysl, 1990), pp. 167-8.

15 "obvious fabrication" . . . "pure fabrication." Lowenthal, "Venona and Alger Hiss", Intelligence and National Security, Vol. 15, No. 3 (Autumn 2000).

16 "Total silence re Hiss." Email from Chervonnaya, 26 Jul 2009.

17 *A Spy among Friends, Kim Philby and the Great Betrayal* by Ben McIntyre, audible edition.

18 Structure of bureaucracies: Cliffnotes Study Guides Cliffsnotes.com.

19 The KGB employed over half a million . . . Spy Secrets: the Russian KGB: Topspysecrets.com.

20 FBI agent Frederick Donner: *A Broken Badge Healed? The FBI, A Special Agent In The Cancer Within Both* by Frederick Donner, Google Books, p 13.

21 CIA agent Lindsay Moran: "Q&A: Lindsay Moran—A Former CIA Agent Reflects on Old School Tradecraft in a High-Tech World," *Pursuit Magazine*, Topspysecrets.com.

22 "Information and records management is a core activity of MI5": https://www.mi5.gov.uk.

23 "The amount of paperwork originated by Soviet bureaucracy": *Soviet Society Today*, Michael Rywkin, Google Books, p 32.

Chapter 51

1 Informational files on Secretary of State Dean Acheson and Averell Harriman: Email from Svetlana, 26 July 2009 and 24 Jan 2013.

2 Harriman as a Communist in FBI files of famous dead people. See Governmentattic.org the Dead List posted 09 Jan 2012.

3 "known activities of German fifth column agents." FBI report on Robert A. Brady. Report made by S W Reynolds, May 4, 1942, p 26, concerning "Robert Alexander Brady, Head Social Economist, Office of Price Administration, Office of Emergency Management".

4   "only the little seditionists and traitors . . ." Seldes, *Facts and Fascism* (New York: In Fact, 1943).

5   The First War Powers Act: General License Under Section 3(a) of the Trading with the Enemy Act. December 13, 1941. The Code of Federal Regulations of the United States, 1941 Supplement. Washington: United States Government Printing Office, 1942, p 359.

6   Dulles agreements with Farben: Lisagor, A Law unto Itself, p 146, 148.

7   Alcoa agreement with German cartel: Seldes, *Facts and Fascism,* p 68.

8   IBM had the contract for the punch . . .See Edwin Black, *IBM and the Holocaust: the strategic alliance between Nazi Germany and America's most powerful corporation* (New York: Crown, 2001).

9   "economic and financial union . . . a kind of supranational guild" Kinzer, The Brothers, Loc 1343.

10 "the new Presidential elections must bring . . ." Seldes, *Facts and Fascism,* p 71.

11 "to set up spy hearings . . ." Harbaugh, p 447.

12 "Were the Soviet Union to sink tomorrow . . ." quoted by Norman Cousins, *At a Century's Ending: Reflections 1982-1995* (Norton, 1997, Part II: "Cold War in Full Bloom", p. 118.

Chapter 52

1   Unknown quantities of Alger's file "destroyed": Rabinowitz, *Unrepentant Leftist,* p145

2   The FBI legally entitled to destroy 80 percent of its archive: "The Department of Forgetting: How an obscure FBI rule is ensuring the destruction of irreplaceable historical records." Alex Heard, *Slate,* 24 Jun 2008. Slate. com.

3   The blacklisted screen writer's file: Gordon, Bernard. Note to the Reader: The Gordon File: A Screenwriter Recalls Twenty Years of FBI Surveillance (Austin, The University of Texas Press, 2004).

4   John Kenneth Galbraith's comment on his own FBI files: Gordon, *Gordon File,* p 189.

5   "an FOIA request should be a research tool of last resort." National Security Archive at George Washington University: Gwu.edu.

6   Ted Morgan's biography of Lovestone: *A Covert Life: Jay Lovestone: Communist, Anti-Communist and Spymaster* (New York: Random House, 1999).

7   "determined that the file was destroyed . . ." Letter dated 7 Jun 2012 to Bigwood from Martha Wagner Murphy, Chief Special Access and FOIA Staff, National Archives.

8   "Erasing history . . .so there can be a rewrite." Email 13 Nov 2010 from
    Bigwood.

Chapter 53

1   "Can you present any evidence" David E Kelly, Boston Legal, Series 2
    episode 10.
2   "No court at any time" William O Douglas, Go East, Young Man, (Ran-
    dom House: New York 1974), p 379.

Chapter 54

1   Alger files for his writ of *coram nobis:* Personal Letter A. Hiss to D. Mas-
    ters, 27 Jul 1978.
2   "a right wing organization is asking for permission . . ." Personal Letter
    A. Hiss to D. Masters, 14 Apr 1980.
3   "will be such a conclusive victory for me . . ." Personal Letter A. Hiss to
    D. Masters, 28 Jul 1981.
4   "The British press" "The opinion is a low blow" Undated letter from Alger
    to Dexter after the denial of his appeal by Owen, July, 1982.

Index